Personal Diplomacy in the EU

At a time when the economic troubles and bailouts of Greece and other European economies are casting significant doubt on the future viability of the Eurozone and the EU, it is crucial to examine the origins of the political will and leadership that is necessary to move the integration process forward. This book makes a significant conceptual and empirical contribution by elucidating the extent to which the integration process hinges not on institutions and norms, but on the relations among leaders. Vogt conducts a comparative diplomatic history of three critical junctures in the process of European integration: the creation of the Common Market (1955–1957), British accession (1969–1973), and the introduction of the Euro (1989–1993). He illustrates how personal diplomacy, leadership constellations, and the dynamics among leaders enable breakthroughs or inhibit accords. He also reveals how the EU's system of top-level decision-making that privileges institutionalised summitry has operated in the past and suggests – in a separate chapter – why it has come to atrophy and prove more dysfunctional of late.

Roland Vogt is Assistant Professor of European Studies at the University of Hong Kong.

Routledge Advances in European Politics

For a full list of titles in this series, please visit www.routledge.com

120 **Policy Making at the Second Tier of Local Government in Europe**
What is happening in Provinces, Counties, Départements and Landkreise in the on-going re-scaling of statehood?
Edited by Xavier Bertrana, Björn Egner and Hubert Heinelt

121 **The Politics of Trauma and Peace-Building**
Lessons from Northern Ireland
Cillian McGrattan

122 **Eurozone Politics**
Perception and reality in Italy, the UK, and Germany
Philip Giurlando

123 **Politics of Identity in Post-Conflict States**
The Bosnian and Irish experience
Edited by Éamonn Ó Ciardha and Gabriela Vojvoda

124 **Unequal Europe**
Social divisions and social cohesion in an old continent
James Wickham

125 **Clientelism and Economic Policy**
Greece and the Crisis
Aris Trantidis

126 **Challenges to Democracies in East-Central Europe**
Edited by Jan Holzer and Miroslav Mareš

127 **Iceland's Financial Crisis**
The Politics of Blame, Protest, and Reconstruction
Edited by Valur Ingimundarson, Philippe Urfalino and Irma Erlingsdóttir

128 **Personal Diplomacy in the EU**
Political leadership and critical junctures of European integration
Roland Vogt

Personal Diplomacy in the EU

Political leadership and critical junctures of European integration

Roland Vogt

LONDON AND NEW YORK

First published 2017
by Routledge
2 Park Square, Milton Park, Abingdon, Oxon OX14 4RN

and by Routledge
711 Third Avenue, New York, NY 10017

First issued in paperback 2018

Routledge is an imprint of the Taylor & Francis Group, an informa business

© 2017 Roland Vogt

The right of the Roland Vogt to be identified as author of this work has been asserted by him in accordance with sections 77 and 78 of the Copyright, Designs and Patents Act 1988.

All rights reserved. No part of this book may be reprinted or reproduced or utilised in any form or by any electronic, mechanical, or other means, now known or hereafter invented, including photocopying and recording, or in any information storage or retrieval system, without permission in writing from the publishers.

Trademark notice: Product or corporate names may be trademarks or registered trademarks, and are used only for identification and explanation without intent to infringe.

British Library Cataloguing in Publication Data
A catalogue record for this book is available from the British Library

Library of Congress Cataloging-in-Publication Data
Names: Vogt, Roland (C. Roland) author.
Title: Personal diplomacy in the EU : political leadership and critical junctures of European integration / by Roland Vogt.
Other titles: Personal diplomacy in the European Union
Description: New York, NY : Routledge, 2016. | Series: Routledge advances in European politics ; 128 | Includes bibliographical references and index.
Identifiers: LCCN 2016020627 | ISBN 9781138651715 (hardback) | ISBN 9781315624648 (ebook)
Subjects: LCSH: European federation—History. | European Union—History. | Europe—Economic integration—Political aspects. | European Union countries—Foreign relations. | Political leadership—European Union countries.
Classification: LCC JN15 .V627 2016 | DDC 341.242/2—dc23
LC record available at https://lccn.loc.gov/2016020627

ISBN 13: 978-1-138-60469-8 (pbk)
ISBN 13: 978-1-138-65171-5 (hbk)

Typeset in Galliard
by Apex CoVantage, LLC

To Marina, Andrew, and James

Contents

Preface viii

Introduction 1

PART I
Leadership as a conceptual framework 17

1 Making sense of critical junctures in European integration 19

2 The influence of leadership: personal diplomacy and risk-taking 37

PART II
Leadership and critical junctures of European integration 51

3 Personal diplomacy and trust, 1955–1957 53

4 Changes in leadership constellations, 1969–1973 94

5 Problem-solving leadership, 1990–1993 136

6 What's next? From leadership to crisis management 178

Conclusion 191

Glossary and abbreviations 199
Bibliography 201
Index 225

Preface

Since the end of World War II, Europe has made a remarkable transition. Out of the ruins of war, barbarism, and division has emerged a wealthy, peaceful, democratic, and resourceful continent. Yet today the sentiments of many Europeans are not those of joy about the accomplishments of the past but those of anxiety about an uncertain and increasingly insecure future. Europe's elected representatives are perceived as no longer being able to decisively confront the challenges the continent is facing. From unemployment to the Eurozone debt crisis, from problems with immigration to the threats of Jihadi terrorism, from the rise of nationalist and anti-Islamic populist parties to the public's apathy to unresponsive and self-serving bureaucracies, there is a sense that politics merely muddles through rather than tackling the problems at hand.

As a diplomatic historian, I have for a long time been interested in the way ideas, identities, norms, and people shape the conduct of foreign policy. Unfortunately, much of the study of foreign policy has gradually come to privilege conceptual parsimony over nuance and rich historical detail. I am somewhat sceptical of catch-all theoretical explanations of why countries behave the way they do. The world is too complex, eclectic, and diverse to fit into the neatness of theories of international relations.

This book is an endeavour to illustrate that European integration – a key transformative process in today's Europe – is not just a product of geopolitics or functional institutionalisation. As I was conducting the archival research for this book, I was struck by the sheer volume of information politicians and officials at the highest level of government receive on a daily basis. Everybody in the machinery of government looks to them – the presidents, prime ministers, and chancellors – for guidance, cues, and signals of how to conduct affairs with other countries. Internally, cabinets, parties, and governing coalitions have diverging factions and often opposing foreign policy preferences. Our heads of government are surrounded by advisors and officials, but their advice is frequently tentative and contradictory. What our elected leaders tend to fall back on to make sense of this onslaught of information are their own political instincts, personal experiences, historical analogies that come to mind, and consultations with their foreign counterparts. This is what an analysis of personal diplomacy is getting at.

When reading about foreign policy in Europe today, we hear a lot about what the UK, France, or Germany are doing, but we hear much less about the persons who are actually in charge of this process. We assume that the conduct of foreign policy is something larger than the individuals in office. But the state papers in archives are full of documents in which officials ask ministers for permissions and ministers ask prime ministers for decisions. Officials prepare for all kinds of options and eventualities, but the decisive impetus for foreign policy decisions always comes from the top.

The overall argument of this book might not be new to some or find favour with everyone. I am not saying that leaders can decide it all, but merely that little is gained for our understanding of how foreign policy works if we ignore who they are, what they think and do, and how they interact. Without understanding the obstacles our decision-makers face and the pressures they are under, it will be difficult to make sense of the growing disarray that is threatening the very fabric of the project of European unity.

This book is the product of one individual researcher doing a lot of archival and documentary research. Yet it benefited enormously from myriad discussions, debates, arguments, and consultations with multiple friends, colleagues, and fellow researchers. They provided valuable criticism, feedback, advice, and support. They have challenged my viewpoints and inspired me to think in new and unforeseen ways, opening my eyes to seeing our world in a different light. My most special thanks goes to those mentors and professors who have left an indelible imprint on my own thinking about international affairs: Wayne Cristaudo, James K. Oliver, Mark J. Miller, and José Ramón Montero Gibert. Much gratitude also goes to Sebastian Kaempf, Santiago Andrés Engelhardt, Martin Chung Chi Kei, and many others with whom I have talked at length about this book and many other global issues. I would like to thank Andrew Linklater, William Bain, Graeme Davies, Tim Dunne, Michael Foley, Roland Bleiker, Roger Scully, and Sander Gilman for their comments and suggestions. At the University of Hong Kong, where the book was completed, I am heavily indebted to my wonderful colleagues, who have been supportive of my research efforts and have been helpful in so many ways: Stefan Auer, Andreas Leutzsch, James Fichter, Bert Becker, Paul Urbanski, Li Chong, Wong Heung-Wah, Christopher Hutton, John Carroll, John Wong, and Louise Edwards. I remain especially grateful to Kendall A. Johnson, who as head of school provided constant personal and academic support, encouragement, and mentorship. At Routledge, I would like to thank Simon Bates, Brenda Foo, and their teams for their professionalism, support, and efficient handling of the review, editing, and publication process.

My interest in history and politics is in large part due to my parents, Martin and Heilwig Vogt. Yet my greatest individual and most heartfelt debt goes to my wife, Marina Ma Vogt, and my sons, Andrew and James. With their love, compassion, and affection they show and remind me every day what really matters in life. They are the bedrock of my life.

Hong Kong
January 2016

Introduction

> I often hear the word 'Europe' from the mouths of those politicians, who wanted from other powers something they did not dare to demand in their own name.
> – Otto von Bismarck

This book deals with the influence, possibilities, and limitations of political will and leadership in the complex negotiations and summit diplomacy that have characterised postwar European integration. In this book, I set out to cast doubt on the narrative that European integration is either a dynamic political and economic process on auto-pilot or the product of federalist visionary idealism. Despite the fact that European integration is closely linked to the creation of common institutions, norms, regulations, and law, as well as integrated economies and lofty ideals, these factors have proven to be thin glue in times of crisis. Time and again, national decision-makers have altered, superseded, or ignored the common institutions and norms – and rarely in a spirit of federalist idealism – whenever doing so was politically expedient. The institutions and norms that are designed to hold the European project together are much more fragile and open to contestation than is ordinarily assumed. Recurrent treaty revisions and institutional redesigns illustrate the extent to which major constitutive rules in the European Union (EU) are still far from being consolidated. In short, much of the gains achieved in terms of European integration have depended not on norms and institutions, but on political will and the ebb and flow of what I call the personal diplomacy among leaders.

Europe's inability to sort out its migration crisis and ongoing economic problems – which have plunged the continent into deep political and social turmoil – is yet again testament to the fact that in the absence of determined leadership the European project stalls and that significant political will in the major European capitals is required for integration to move ahead. What has propelled the project of European integration along throughout the last six decades is the emergence of unforeseen – and unpredictable – constellations of leaders (often at moments of crisis) to push new, and often controversial, initiatives forward and bury others. This book suggests that this mode of decision-making, in which summit diplomacy, personal rapport, and mutual trust among national heads of government play a central role, is now reaching a saturation point. The EU has become too big, too diverse, too complex, too politicised, and too unwieldy for a handful of politicians to be able to give clear guidance and purpose to the integration process. Increasingly, the small-circle decision-making mode – personal diplomacy – that worked so effectively until the early 1990s has given way to institutional inertia, public disenchantment, and uneasiness about the EU's future.[1]

Currently, the EU stands again at a critical juncture. Uncertainty in the Eurozone and the EU at large has begun to erode public confidence in the project of ever-closer integration in Europe.[2] It has also cast doubt over the very legitimacy of the EU itself.[3] Austerity, economic stagnation, and high levels of immigration are gradually nurturing apathy and dissatisfaction with the way Europe's governments and the EU are handling the political, economic, and social challenges ahead.[4] Nowadays, media commentators point to a crisis of leadership in Europe, with no one being in charge or able to solve the continent's ills. Following the landmark referendum in June 2016, the British electorate has voted to withdraw from the EU altogether. France, Spain, and Italy are too economically weak, and Germany too hesitant – given its history and its fears of permanent monetary transfers – to mobilise the necessary political energies and financial means to decisively overcome the crisis.

But the notion of a crisis of leadership is nothing new or recent. In fact, it is a recurring feature of the integration process itself and has characterised the way new integrationist proposals were initiated, negotiated, and implemented. Almost all the major breakthroughs in the history of European integration – the Common Market, the Euro, and numerous rounds of enlargement – were born out of moments of uncertainty and upheaval, not just out of rational cost-benefit calculations of national interests or bouts of visionary idealism. The ability of leaders to build trust among themselves, to shut out opponents, sideline critics, and assuage the public's discontent, to dominate the political discourse, and to take risks in terms of their own personal prestige and political capital have been key facilitators of the milestones in the integration process that are now taken for granted.

The purpose of this book is to draw attention to how important elements of personal diplomacy – the personal 'chemistry' and trust among leaders, their interactions, and their own ideas and gestures – were and continue to remain crucial for the integration process and its future evolution. What becomes apparent is that political leadership sits at the heart of many – if not most – institutional, legal, and regulatory innovations in international settings. The outcomes of major international negotiations are rarely predetermined by abstract notions of national interests, and the behaviour of states is deeply affected by changes in leadership. The quest of this book is thus to posit personal diplomacy, along with leadership and its associated risks, at the heart of the analysis of European integration and to explore how doing so can sharpen a nuanced understanding of the realistic possibilities and limitations of European integration in the future.

* * *

In a 19 January 1956 directive to his cabinet – which came to be known as the *Integrationsbefehl* (order to integrate) – West German Chancellor Konrad Adenauer wrote:

> The contemporary international situation contains extraordinary dangers. In order to deflect them and in order to introduce a more favourable development, decisive measures are necessary. These include a clear, positive German attitude to European integration. The key statesmen of the West see in this European integration the hinge of development . . .
>
> From this results, as a guideline of our policy, that we should implement the conclusion of Messina decisively and without diluting it.
>
> The political character of this decision, which should not only lead to technical cooperation due to specialised considerations but also to a community . . . , must be observed even more strongly than was the case so far. All other specialised considerations have to be put to the service of this political target . . .
>
> I request that the considerations presented above be understood as guidelines of policy . . . and be acted upon accordingly.[5]

In this document, Adenauer both affirmed his authority and instructed his cabinet to implement his European policy preferences: integration into the Western alliance,[6] a positive attitude to European integration, and support for the proposal to set up a Common Market. In hindsight, it is easy to forget the extent to which these policy principles encountered criticism, opposition, and outright rejection in the Federal Republic.[7] Adenauer faced stiff parliamentary opposition, as well as internal discord, over his European objectives and policies.[8] Against the advice of some senior members of his government, Adenauer determined to support the Common Market proposal reached at Messina in June 1955.[9] Thereby he practically rejected alternative plans for a free trade area which would have included Britain, tying Germany instead to the politically and economically unstable French Fourth Republic, which was struggling with a colonial uprising in Algeria. Whether this decision best reflected West Germany's economic and security interests was then a matter of intense debate. The Minister of Economic Affairs, Ludwig Erhard, clearly expressed his criticism and displeasure in his 11 April 1956 letter to Adenauer:

> This monomaniac attitude, which approves of everything that can possibly be sugar-coated as 'European', will not lead to a lasting European solution or pacification. I have therefore lamented your so-called 'order to integrate', which approves of any form and method of cooperation, including also those partial solutions that will in effect not result in a true integration,

but in a dismemberment and disjuncture of the national economies. Those who want to combat and destroy the functions of a European economy in the spirit of a common market will have to support such partial solutions, and we are again on the best way of succumbing to this error. Economic mistakes and economic sins will not be healed by proclaiming them to be European.[10]

As this episode illustrates, the history of key developments in European integration is inextricably linked to the choices political leaders make. The European policies pursued by governments across Europe are not undisputed, universally accepted, or consistently backed by public opinion. Neither are they predetermined by external economic conditions, geopolitical imperatives, or the demands of domestic politics. Political decision-makers have to interpret their social environments, exercise their judgement, countenance conflicting advice, and take risks.

National leaders occupy a central role in framing the objectives of European policies, building public support, and negotiating the terms and mechanisms of integration. Their collective willingness to invest political capital and personal prestige has been a necessary condition to ensure the success of many a European initiative. This does not mean that leaders can single-handedly determine events and outcomes (as the failed plebiscites in France, the Netherlands, and Ireland in the mid-2000s have shown) or that they are wholly detached from political pressures or unaffected by external events.

Yet European integration and its surrounding diplomatic activity bear the mark of the leadership of a surprisingly small number of individuals and their conceptions of Europe. A number of critical junctures in the integration process – the so-called *relance* leading to the Treaties of Rome (1955–1957), British accession to the Common Market (1969–1973), the negotiations on economic and monetary union (EMU) (1990–1993), and the more recent Eurozone crisis management – illustrate the mutually constitutive manner in which leadership opportunities and constellations and moments of crisis have come to shape the political project of ever-closer unity in Europe.

Understanding these critical junctures, which will be analysed in more historical detail throughout this book, matters because they are illustrative of the constitutive influence of personal diplomacy and political leadership in the integration process. Very little, if anything, in the history of the EU has ever been inevitable or irreversible. The ongoing discussions on how to fix the Eurozone (which required emergency bailouts for Greece, Ireland, Portugal, Spain, and Cyprus) has clearly revealed the extent to which political momentum hinges on individual leaders – notably Angela Merkel, but also ECB President Mario Draghi. Few things move in Brussels when national leaders – in particular those of Germany and France – do not agree.

In the past, national leaders had an extraordinary degree of autonomy in formulating their countries' European policies. This is now slowly receding.[11] Leaders' ability to get along, to share common understandings of what Europe is and what the purpose of integration should be, has often facilitated breakthroughs in negotiations and decision-making. Their perceptions of and aspirations for Europe matter insofar as they influence and frame how their bargaining positions and strategies on the European diplomatic scene are understood and enacted, thereby making some policies and forms of integration more likely than others. The argument is not that national interests are unimportant, but rather that leaders play a significant role in defining, identifying, and constructing them in the first place.

This book is not an exhaustive chronological account of the history of European integration. It neither develops a general theory of leadership nor makes the case for a 'great men' narrative,[12] in which heroic and visionary leaders 'endowed with superior qualities'[13] solely determine the course of European politics. Instead, the book captures the diplomatic history of key moments in European integration, positing a nexus between leadership and moments of crisis as an important explanatory factor for understanding why postwar Europe moved in the direction it did, and illustrating a pattern of decision-making that is gradually losing viability. Drawing on extensive documentary sources from numerous archives, the European conceptions, ideas, policies, and motives of British, French, and German leaders that have made a major imprint in the political landscape of postwar European integration, and continue to do so until today, are elucidated.

European integration: between moments of leadership and crisis

The global financial crisis that started with the collapse of the investment bank Lehman Brothers in September 2008 has pushed Europe into a period of protracted and significant economic and political disarray. In the face of economic stagnation and financial uncertainty, the institutional, legal, and regulatory mechanisms that were supposed to hold the project of European unity together have turned out to be weak and inadequate to fully stem the financial markets' loss of confidence in the edifice of economic and monetary union.[14] Since the introduction of the Euro, the economies of Europe have converged less than expected and the common rules and treaties have now been bent, often in legally controversial ways, to enable emergency rescue operations to save Greece and others from bankruptcy and the Eurozone from breakup. All attention has now turned to the leaders of Europe's main economies – in particular, Germany – to rescue both the Eurozone and the EU from gradual atrophy and decay. Brexit and the fear of a major migration crisis in Europe have added to this predicament. If ever there was doubt about the crucial role national leaders play in European integration, the current economic, financial, and migration crises are visible proof that they exert a peculiar influence – particularly at moments of upheaval and uncertainty. But are these high hopes in the leaders of Europe realistic? Can these leaders accomplish this hope, even if they wanted to? What is their room for manoeuvre on the European stage and what kind of constraints and opportunities do they face? How can and do they exert influence and how has this changed over time?

These are some of the central questions this books addresses. In a nutshell, the main line of argumentation is as follows: Leadership and political will have been a much more decisive factor in the process of European integration than is frequently assumed. Moments of crisis have often produced leadership opportunities and incentives to take risks on European affairs in order to move European politics in a preferred direction. Leaders were able to shape developments on European politics not only because of the public's so-called permissive consensus, but also because the context of intergovernmental bargaining that characterises European politics is amenable to giving leaders significant control and autonomy to come to decisions amongst themselves. This autonomy is now eroding, as European integration moves away from the spheres of technocratic 'low politics' on the one hand and foreign policy on the other and begins to impinge directly on Europeans' lives. The austerity measures imposed as part of the financial rescue packages for Greece, Ireland, Portugal, and others amplified this trend further and have doused much of public enthusiasm for Brussels and everything related to the EU. The results of the 2014 elections of the European Parliament (EP), which saw a sharp increase in so-called populist and Eurosceptic parties, is illustrative of these long-term shifts in voter preference and attitudes towards the EU as a whole.

The forms of European crisis management and summitry intended to stem the Eurozone and migration crises have so far been insufficient to proactively reverse the potentially existential erosion of market trust, public legitimacy, and political support that has spread all across the continent. In politics, the media, and the business world, people decry a leadership crisis in Europe. But the perceived absence of leadership is hardly new, as the contributors to Jack Hayward's 2008 edited volume, *Leaderless Europe*, illustrated.[15] A decade ago, after the French and the Dutch had voted against the European constitutional treaty, *The Economist* asked:

> Where are today's equivalents of other figures in the Europhile hall of fame: Monnet, Adenauer, Kohl, Mitterrand? Europe's crisis, it is said in the corridors of Brussels, is above all a crisis of leadership.[16]

Yet despite the fact that major developments in European integration are so closely identified with the names of a few leaders, much of the analysis of European politics focuses on impersonal variables – functional dynamics, conflicts of interests, economic necessities, and geopolitical structures. Structural and institutionalist explanations – especially in their functional variety – tend to dominate scholarship.[17] Both narratives suggest that the process of voluntary and institutionalised cooperation, which has characterised European politics since 1945, emerged as a reaction to political and economic necessities. In the beginning, the argument goes, West European nation-states needed economic integration for their prosperity and wanted to contain Germany and the Soviet

Union for their security. The European project then developed further either because it was in the national interest of states to do so, or because institutional path-dependencies altered state preferences and narrowed their choices, making it hard to leave or alter the common institutions once established. The integration process is seen to have resulted from intergovernmental bargains on national interests. Integration was necessary because West European states *had to* cooperate. States defended their national interests as best they could, and European outcomes reflected a bargain with which everybody could live.

In this narrative, material structures, as well as institutions and law, come to exert overwhelming influence over the behaviour of national leaders. It is assumed that decision-makers know what their interests are. It is also assumed that national interests and preferences 'can be readily deduced from objective conditions and material characteristics of a state.'[18] From this point of view, individuals have few choices and ultimately play a minor role in the major scheme of things. It does not matter who is in office, because decision-makers have to submit eventually to the demands of economic necessities and Realpolitik.

This common explanation is, however, partial and incomplete. It is partial because the national interest is treated as a determinant of governmental preferences and policies, as well as of leaders' behaviour. This is not something which is reflected in the overwhelming body of empirical documentary evidence at archives, but is rather an assumption that derives from theories of intergovernmental bargaining. Furthermore, it is incomplete because the ability of leaders to shape and define the national interest in the first place is bracketed and their pivotal role in negotiations remains underestimated. The late Stanley Hoffmann claimed that 'leaders matter' because 'choices were made – openly or implicitly – that could have been very different.'[19]

The consequences of making theoretically derived assumptions about the behaviour of leaders – and thereby underestimating their role, contributions, and choices – become clear once European integration is analysed in concrete historical contexts.[20] As Christian Reus-Smit claims,

> the universal rational actor is a myth. Historically and culturally constructed contingent beliefs define how actors understand themselves, and who they think they are not only affects their interests but also the means they entertain to realise those interests.[21]

Finnemore suggests that 'interests are not just out there waiting to be discovered; they are constructed through social interaction.'[22]

What this means in practice can be illustrated by the following examples: What exactly is the national interest of Germany, France, or Britain? Is it really in Germany's interest to mutualise European sovereign debt and to guarantee the solvency and liquidity of banks in Europe's troubled southern periphery? Does deeper integration – through Eurobonds, a fiscal and banking union, and a common European treasury – render Germany better off than a less-integrated European free trade area, which would allow it to build on its global success as an export-driven economy? Is it really in France's long-term interest to advocate deeper integration when it is fearful of German influence and economic power in the EU and when French politicians are reluctant to embark on structural changes to the French economy? Is it, as the leading advocates of Brexit have successfully advocated, in Britain's interest to withdraw from the EU altogether, at a time when China and other emerging economies are becoming the new growth engines of the global economy?

National leaders not only formulate policies, but are also central to the definition of what kind of goals and policies their governments pursue. In regards to European policies, it *does* matter who holds office. Yet why is this (rather commonsensical) insight not reflected more concretely in the scholarship on the history of European integration? Why does so much of the literature privilege abstract material structures as explanatory factors over people, ideas, and identities? Why do the statesmen whose actions were so important for the integration process attract relatively little academic interest? Can conventional explanations not be complemented by a more detailed and historically nuanced analysis of how the interventions of European leaders shaped the integration process?

In order to achieve this analysis, it is imperative not to take for granted that European integration is automatic, irreversible, and ultimately predetermined by economic conditions, security imperatives, or other political necessities. Claims that the outcomes of European negotiations reflect long-term national preferences and interests are *ex post facto* explanations of events. Will Turkey one day be a member of the EU? Will more member states follow Britain's example and withdraw from the EU? Will the Eurozone stay together? Will the Schengen agreement of open internal borders survive? At this time, nobody knows and few dare to predict what will happen. When concrete contexts of European negotiations are analysed, it becomes clear that divergent interpretations of national interests, European objectives, and policy options abound. Different leaders have different ideas about what they want to do in Europe and how they want to achieve it. They understand, judge, and interpret their political and social environments differently and foresee divergent political options.[23]

Some politicians are more successful than others in advocating, nurturing, and implementing their European preferences and goals. Some leaders find themselves in an environment which is favourable to their ideas, while others are constrained by events. Some leaders have to react to external developments, while others succeed in setting the agenda themselves. In any case, leadership, the definition of national interests and goals, and policy-making are social phenomena, which change, fluctuate, and adapt to diverse circumstances.

Given this complexity, it is imperative *not* to assume that national interests are given and immutable, that leaders cannot adapt, or that ever-deeper integration has to occur somehow. Instead, it is important to understand how leaders come to make their choices, how they deal with ambiguous advice, why they follow one set of policies over another or discard potential alternative paths of action.

With their privileged control of resources, their position in the institutional framework of the state, their access and exposure to the media, and their political leverage, leaders have the capability to exercise substantial autonomy for finding agreements amongst themselves.[24] In the politics of European integration, summitry has become a way of life,[25] as the cases of the peculiar partnerships of Konrad Adenauer-Guy Mollet, Georges Pompidou-Edward Heath, Helmut Kohl-François Mitterrand, and Angela Merkel-Nicolas Sarkozy attest. This is what I call personal diplomacy – a form of diplomatic encounters and interactions among individual leaders in which persuasion, personal 'chemistry,' mutual trust, gestures, and convictions often play an important role.[26] Yet despite the prominence of individual politicians in European decision-making, most of the literature is focused not on the effects of agency but those of structures. A more detailed exploration of leadership in the context of European integration is therefore necessary.

Why leadership?

Leadership is a word that is frequently used but badly understood. Throughout this book, I wish to instil some clarity into the concept and how it helps to explain the role of personal diplomacy in the history of the EU. As defined in James MacGregor Burns' Pulitzer Prize-winning tome on the topic, 'leadership over human beings is exercised when persons with certain motives and purposes mobilise, in competition or conflict with others, institutional, political, psychological, and other resources so as to arouse, engage, and satisfy the motives of followers.'[27] In this sense, leadership is understood neither as a characteristic of an individual's personality traits nor as an outcome of an individual's position in the governmental hierarchy. I do not argue that the persons under consideration were born as leaders or became so because of unique features of their character and personality. Not every person elected to the highest political office of a state automatically becomes a leader. In fact, most politicians are not *leaders* but *managers*, i.e. mere administrators of the state's institutional and parliamentary energies. Only few muster the courage to invest their political capital, popularity, and re-election chances into prominent political initiatives – especially on a secondary issue such as Europe.

Instead, one has to understand leadership as a relationship in which political decision-makers engage in a 'consequential exercise of mutual persuasion, exchange, elevation, and transformation.'[28] Individual decision-makers *can* exercise leadership in certain aspects of policy-making, but this does not mean that they necessarily do so in other realms as well.[29] For instance, as will be seen in Chapter 4, the interventions of Edward Heath were imperative to get Britain into the Common Market.[30] However, he is widely regarded as failed prime minister because of his inability to get a handle on pressing domestic issues – strikes, power shortages, and the escalating violence in Northern Ireland – throughout his time in office.[31] Leadership is thus context- and issue-specific. In some circumstances, especially in times of crisis and upheaval, decision-makers encounter enabling opportunity structures (favourable public opinion, parliamentary majorities, financial resources, external support, etc.) in order to advance particular items on the political agenda. In other circumstances, decision-makers are constrained by unfavourable conditions, which they are unable or unwilling to alter.

Leadership thus is a social relationship which develops and changes over time. In consequence, the study of leadership is inherently contextual, political, and biographical.[32] It is contextual because actors are embedded in specific historical contexts, cultural terrains, and political, economic, and social circumstances, which influence and shape their personalities and behaviour. As human beings, we cannot escape the legacies of the past, the shadows of our upbringing, and the dynamics and trends of our times.

The study of leadership is political in the sense that leaders advocate policies, and subscribe to values, beliefs, ideologies, and identities, which are highly subjective and hence often strongly contested.[33] Leaders have to make choices – political choices – regarding the reasons, strategies, and aims of the activity of a state in a competitive political environment.[34]

Lastly, the study of leadership is biographical, given that individual leaders interpret the world around them in unique and personal ways.[35] Leaders are 'situation-interpreting individuals,'[36] but what matters is their interactions with others. Leadership, as Raymond Cohen puts it, is a form of 'theatre of power' in which rituals, gestures, and the art of diplomatic signalling play an important role.[37] Leaders are simultaneously representatives of their respective states – and thus bound to a specific aesthetic in public performances – and individuals with unique ambitions, thoughts, and backgrounds.[38] In consequence, an examination of leaders' attitudes to, and decisions on, European integration has to take account of how they – as a group – understand the environment in which they act, and what kind of possibilities, constraints, and obstacles for specific policies they can envisage. For some, such as Adenauer, Europe was framed in civilisational terms, being closely related to Catholic social theory, anti-Communism, and the fear of a resurgent German nationalism.[39] He famously got along well with Charles de Gaulle after their first meeting at Colombey-les-Deux-Églises in 1958, despite his well-documented initial scepticism about de Gaulle.[40] For others, such as Willy Brandt, Europe was a pragmatic political notion, designed to facilitate closer cooperation between European states as well as the palpable diffusion of the East-West tensions dividing the continent.[41] For Angela Merkel, in turn, Europe and European integration is seen much more through the prism of German domestic political calculations than was the case with her predecessors.[42]

The ideas which leaders hold about Europe emanate from personal experiences and backgrounds, ideological and religious convictions, historical insights, and political considerations, among other influences. Sometimes, these ideas do not resonate profoundly with popular ideas and understandings of Europe. A case in point is François Mitterrand's and Helmut Kohl's support and advocacy for the introduction of the Euro in the early 1990s. While Mitterrand and Kohl believed economic and monetary union to be crucially important for the development of Europe, much of public opinion failed to be persuaded by the technical arguments or the political enthusiasm for introducing the Euro.[43] The unintended consequences of this 'rush' towards the single currency were the many so-called birth defects of the Euro, which are now testing the cohesion and solidity of the Eurozone.[44]

The practices of European integration depend on continued reproduction over time. In general terms, the history of European integration reveals that nothing is set in stone. Institutions, policy-making procedures, and the scope and realms of political activity can be – and have been – changed. Understanding the role of political leaders in this relationship is crucial to understanding why the EU has struggled to come to terms with the challenges it faces.

This book reveals two things. On the one hand, it demonstrates that important constitutive relationships exist between the leadership of individual decision-makers, their conceptions of Europe, and the definition and pursuit of national interests in European diplomacy. By bridging the stark divide between structurally deterministic and 'great men' explanations of political processes and events, the emphasis shifts to individual leaders' perceptions of their political contexts, as well as their autonomy in combining national and European objectives and in influencing the course of European initiatives. While the forms and material constraints of leadership have altered from context to context, political leadership nonetheless remains a key factor for changing the parameters of integration.

On the other hand, the book explores a dimension of the integration process which much of the literature has overlooked or neglected. Dealing as it does with broad structural trends and path-dependent institutional dynamics of European integration, the literature says little about the small coterie of top-level decision-makers who headed national governments and who were personally involved in European negotiations. The research reveals that many leaders had little knowledge of or interest in the details of European integration. Yet they had clear ideas about what they thought was best for their country, what they wanted Europe to stand for, what they wanted integration to achieve, and how they sought to further national objectives by European means.

In some cases, such as Konrad Adenauer's, their European inclinations have already attracted significant academic interest.[45] In others, such as Guy Mollet's or Willy Brandt's, their understanding of – and attitude to – European integration is less well-known. Many of the leaders analysed throughout this book are often not even recognised as being major figures in the history of European integration. Georges Pompidou, for instance, is rarely identified as an influential 'father' of Europe.

Although biographical material exists about some of the leaders under consideration, often little is known about their conceptions of Europe. To give an example: there is a substantial amount of literature on Anthony Eden,[46] but the few studies on Eden's European policies pale in comparison with the works on the Suez crisis during his time as Prime Minister.

Plan of the book

The first part of the book examines structural and institutional explanations of European integration and shows that these say little about how leaders think about Europe, how they frame their European objectives, what purposes they envision for the integration process, and by what mechanisms they want to achieve it. There is analytical purchase in using leadership as a key explanatory factor. A conceptual framework – informed by social constructivism – is designed to examine the role of personal diplomacy and leadership in the context of European integration. By understanding leadership as a social relationship, it is possible to explore how agency, ideas, and identities have come to influence the path of European integration and diplomacy.

The second part of the book applies this conceptual framework to three different periods of postwar European diplomacy. The critical junctures of 1955–1957, 1969–1973, and 1990–1993 were moments at which the direction, purposes, and mechanisms of European integration were significantly and deliberately transformed. The concluding chapter addresses the current problems for decision-making in Europe. It illustrates the extent to which personal diplomacy is increasingly less effective in addressing the urgent – some would argue existential – challenges to the viability of the EU: the dysfunctionality of the Eurozone; the difficulties the EU and its member states have in formulating a common defence posture vis-à-vis Russia and the security threats emanating from the Middle East; the loss of public support for integration; the decay of the Schengen free movement agreement; and the prospect of more plebiscites on EU membership following the UK's Brexit referendum.

This book's comparative historical analysis highlights an important personal dimension of the study of European integration. Much can be gained by not assuming that fixed national interests or abstract institutional dynamics determined leaders' behaviour.[47] Perceptions of national interests, interpretations of the global political and economic environment, and ideas and proposals for European cooperation are contingent and socially constructed phenomena. Leaders can – but not always do – play a substantial role in these processes of social construction. The book brings these agent-structure interactions together: it shows how leaders responded to the political and economic conditions they encountered; how their personal and political inclinations led them to favour a particular approach to European integration; how their interventions and contributions made some outcomes more likely than others; and how scholarship can help to make sense of these interactions. This line of argumentation is not the only valid one, and it neither denies the importance of structures and institutions nor argues that leadership should be the only or mono-causal explanatory factor. Yet the book can and does demonstrate the utility of taking leadership seriously by pointing 'to a pattern of consistent failure of conventional approaches in explaining certain phenomena and offer[ing] an alternative explanation consistent with the evidence.'[48]

Notes

1. *Frankfurter Allgemeine Zeitung*: 'Baustelle ohne Gerüst: Die Europäische Union erscheint vielen als komplexes und abstraktes Konstrukt' (2 December 2014).
2. L.B. Smaghi, *Morire di Austerità. Democrazie europee con le spalle al muro* (Bologna: Il Mulino, 2013).
3. See C. Parsons and M. Matthijs, 'European Integration Past, Present and Future: Moving Forward through Crisis' and M. Matthijs and M. Blyth, 'Conclusion: The Future of the Euro: Possible Futures, Risks, and Uncertainties,' in *The Future of the Euro*, M. Matthijs and M. Blyth eds. (Oxford: Oxford University Press, 2015), pp. 210–232; pp. 249–269.
4. F. Scharpf, 'Monetary Union, Fiscal Crisis and the Disabling of Democratic Accountability,' in *Politics in the Age of Austerity*, A. Schäfer and W. Streeck eds. (Cambridge: Polity, 2013), pp. 108–147. See also: *Financial Times*, 'Europe Will Stumble before It Learns to Stand Tall' (7 December 2015).
5. Auswärtiges Amt, *Die Auswärtige Politik der Bundesrepublik Deutschland* (Cologne: Verlag Wissenschaft und Politik, 1972), pp. 317–318.
6. R.G. Hughes, *Britain, Germany, and the Cold War: The Search for a European Détente 1949–1967* (Abingdon: Routledge, 2007), p. 38.
7. M. Segers, 'Der Streit um die deutsche Europapolitik in den 1950er Jahren,' in *Deutsche Europapolitik Christlicher Demokraten. Von Konrad Adenauer bis Angela Merkel (1945–2013)*, H.J. Küsters ed. (Düsseldorf: Droste, 2014), pp. 295–330.
8. M. Gehler and H. Meyer, 'Konrad Adenauer, Europa und die Westintegration der Bundesrepublik Deutschland im Kontext von privaten und politischen Netzwerken,' in *Deutsche Europapolitik Christlicher Demokraten. Von Konrad Adenauer bis Angela Merkel (1945–2013)*, H.J. Küsters ed. (Düsseldorf: Droste, 2014), pp. 145–147.
9. U. Lappenküper, *Die Aussenpolitik der Bundesrepublik Deutschland 1949 bis 1990*, Enzyklopädie Deutscher Geschichte, Vol. 83 (Munich: Oldenbourg, 2008), p. 13.
10. K. Adenauer, *Briefe 1955–1957. Rhöndorfer Ausgabe*, R. Morsey and H.-P. Schwarz eds. (Berlin: Siedler, 1998), doc. 142 fn 284.
11. For a broader exploration of the erosion of political control, see M. Naím, *The End of Power: From Boardroom to Battlefields and Churches to States, Why Being in Charge Isn't What It Used to Be* (New York: Basic Books, 2013).
12. See P. Pomper, 'Historians and Individual Agency' *History and Theory* 35 (3) (1996): 281–308.
13. R.M. Stogdill, *Handbook of Leadership: A Survey of Theory and Research* (New York: Free Press, 1974), p. 17.
14. *Financial Times*, 'The Biggest Danger for the Euro Is the Lack of Trust' (11 July 2014).
15. J. Hayward ed., *Leaderless Europe* (Oxford: Oxford University Press, 2008).
16. *The Economist*, 'Charlemagne: Europe's Lost Leaders' (9 July 2005).
17. See C.J. Bickerton, D. Hodson, and U. Puetter eds., *The New Intergovernmentalism: States and Supranational Actors in the Post-Maastricht Era* (Oxford: Oxford University Press, 2015).
18. M. Finnemore, *National Interests in International Society* (Ithaca: Cornell University Press, 1996), p. 8.
19. S. Hoffmann, 'The Case for Leadership,' *Foreign Policy* 81 (1990–91): 20–38.
20. C. Hay and D. Wincott, 'Structure, Agency and Historical Institutionalism,' *Political Studies* 47 (1998): 954.

14 *Introduction*

21 C. Reus-Smit, 'The Idea of History and History with Ideas,' in *Historical Sociology of International Relations*, S. Hobden and J.M. Hobson eds. (Cambridge: Cambridge University Press, 2002), p. 132.
22 Finnemore, *National Interests*, p. 2. See T. Christiansen, K.E. Jørgensen, and A. Wiener eds., *The Social Construction of Europe* (London: Sage, 2001).
23 C. Parsons, *A Certain Idea of Europe* (Ithaca: Cornell University Press, 2003).
24 See L. Helms, *Presidents, Prime Ministers, and Chancellors: Executive Leadership in Western Democracies* (Basingstoke: Palgrave Macmillan, 2005); D.H. Dunn ed., *Diplomacy at the Highest Level: The Evolution of International Summitry* (Basingstoke: Macmillan, 1996); K. Hamilton and R. Langhorne, *The Practice of Diplomacy: Its Evolution, Theory and Administration* (London: Routledge, 1996).
25 D. Reynolds, *Summits: Six Meetings That Shaped the Twentieth Century* (Philadelphia: Perseus, 2007), pp. 401–403.
26 On the concept of personal diplomacy, see K. Larres, *Churchill's Cold War: The Politics of Personal Diplomacy* (New Haven, CT: Yale University Press, 2002).
27 J.M. Burns, *Leadership* (New York, NY: Harper and Row, 1978), p. 18.
28 *Ibid.*, p. 11.
29 M. Foley, *Political Leadership: Themes, Contexts and Critiques* (Oxford: Oxford University Press, 2013).
30 C. Lord, *British Entry to the European Community under the Heath Government of 1970–74* (Aldershot: Dartmouth, 1993).
31 P. Ziegler, *Edward Heath: The Authorised Biography* (London: Harper Press, 2010); J. Campbell, *Edward Heath: A Biography* (London: Jonathan Cape, 1993).
32 J.S. Nye, *The Powers to Lead* (Oxford: Oxford University Press, 2008).
33 See C.W. Freeman, *Arts of Power: Statecraft and Diplomacy* (Washington, DC: United States Institute of Peace Press, 1997).
34 N.O. Keohane, *Thinking about Leadership* (Princeton: Princeton University Press, 2010).
35 B. Shamir, H. Dayan-Horesh, and D. Adler, 'Leading by Biography: Towards a Life-Story Approach to the Study of Leadership,' *Leadership* 1 (1) (2005): 13–30.
36 E.C. Hargrove and J.E. Owens, 'Introduction: Political Leadership in Context,' in *Leadership in Context*, E.C. Hargrove and J.E. Owens eds. (Lanham, MD: Rowman and Littlefield, 2003), p. 6.
37 R. Cohen, *Theatre of Power: The Art of Diplomatic Signalling* (Harlow: Longman, 1987).
38 *Ibid.*
39 W. Weidenfeld, *Konrad Adenauer und Europa: Die geistigen Grundlagen der westeuropäischen Integrationspolitik des ersten Bonner Bundeskanzlers* (Bonn: Europa Union, 1976).
40 M. Sutton, *France and the Construction of Europe, 1944–2007: The Geopolitical Imperative* (Oxford: Berghahn, 2007), pp. 86–87; W. Loth, 'Politische Integration nach 1945. Motive und Antriebskräfte bei Konrad Adenauer und Charles de Gaulle,' in *Europäische Einigung im 19. und 20. Jahrhundert. Akteure und Antriebskräfte*, U. Lappenküper and G. Thiemeyer eds. (Paderborn: Schöningh, 2013), pp. 142–143.
41 G. Schöllgen, *Willy Brandt: Die Biographie* (Munich: Ullstein, 2003). See also M. Herkendell, *Deutschland Zivil- oder Friedensmacht? Außen- und sicherheitspolitische Orientierung der SPD im Wandel (1982–2007)* (Bonn: Dietz, 2012), pp. 58–68; W. Brandt, *Ein Volk der guten Nachbarn: Außen- und Deutschlandpolitik 1966–1974*, Frank Fischer ed., *Berliner Ausgabe*, Vol. 6 (Bonn: Dietz, 2005).

42 G. Packer, 'The Quiet German: The Astonishing Rise of Angela Merkel, the Most Powerful Woman in the World,' *The New Yorker* (1 December 2014); G. Langguth, 'Die Europapolitik Angela Merkels,' in *Deutsche Europapolitik Christlicher Demokraten. Von Konrad Adenauer bis Angela Merkel (1945–2013)*, H.J. Küsters ed. (Düsseldorf: Droste, 2014), pp. 271–293.
43 J. Anderson, *German Unification and the Union of Europe: The Domestic Politics of Integration Policy* (Cambridge: Cambridge University Press, 1999).
44 See J. van Overtveldt, *The End of the Euro: The Uneasy Future of the European Union* (Chicago: B2 Books, 2011).
45 See Weidenfeld, *Konrad Adenauer und Europa*; and H.-P. Schwarz, 'Adenauer und Europa,' *Vierteljahrshefte für Zeitgeschichte* 27 (4) (1979): 471–523.
46 See D.R. Thorpe, *Eden: The Life and Times of Anthony Eden First Earl of Avon, 1897–1977* (London: Pimlico, 2004); D. Dutton, *Anthony Eden: A Life and Reputation* (London: Arnold, 1997); V. Rothwell, *Anthony Eden: A Political Biography 1931–57* (Manchester: Manchester University Press, 1992); R. Rhodes James, *Anthony Eden* (London: Weidenfeld and Nicholson, 1986); A. Carlton, *Anthony Eden: A Biography* (London: Allen Lane, 1981); S. Aster, *Anthony Eden* (London: Weidenfeld and Nicholson, 1976).
47 See S. Rosato, *Europe United: Power Politics and the Making of the European Community* (Ithaca: Cornell University Press, 2011); S. Rosato, 'Europe's Troubles: Power Politics and the State of the European Project,' *International Security* 35 (4) (2011): 45–86; D. Beach, *The Dynamics of European Integration: Why and When EU Institutions Matter* (Basingstoke: Palgrave Macmillan, 2005); W. Mattli, *The Logic of Regional Integration: Europe and Beyond* (Cambridge: Cambridge University Press, 1999).
48 Finnemore, *National Interests*, p. 5.

Part I
Leadership as a conceptual framework

1 Making sense of critical junctures in European integration

After 1945, the case for some form of cooperation among West European states was strengthened by two developments: the Cold War and increasing economic interdependence among the major industrialised economies of the West. With the benefit of hindsight it is easier (albeit not necessarily more accurate) to see European integration as a response to these circumstances. Yet to the decision-makers at the time it remained unclear how European cooperation could be achieved, what institutional shape it would take, and what objectives it should serve. The political, strategic, and economic environment did not provide leaders with clear choices or guidance. Martin Hillenbrand points to the 'peculiar mixture of idealism and economic hardheadedness' that characterised the early supporters of European unity, as well as their 'realistic adaptability in the face of reverses.'[1] Throughout the six-decade quest for ever-closer union, national decision-makers have responded to their environment but also attempted to change it – often times unsuccessfully – according to their preferences. The task for the scholar and analyst is thus to 'reconstruct the structure of choices and dilemmas actors faced,'[2] in order to elucidate how the major milestones in European integration came about.

To give an example: throughout the 1960s, the integration process was heavily influenced by the persona of Charles de Gaulle. The French president not only sought to limit the degree of supranationalism in the European Commission, but also twice blocked British membership in the Common Market. He claimed to have done so in France's national interest, wanting to share neither French sovereignty with a supranational institution nor France's privileged position with another powerful European state.[3] In contrast, his successor Georges Pompidou (who shared de Gaulle's distrust of supranationalism as well as many of his ideological inclinations) nonetheless proposed to safeguard, enlarge, and strengthen the Common Market. His interventions were indeed instrumental in arranging British membership in the Common Market, as will be seen in Chapter 4. Pompidou not only accepted its institutional make-up, but also came to regard it as an extension of (rather than a threat to) French influence.[4] It was Pompidou who – together with West German Chancellor Willy Brandt – put British membership in the Common Market on the European political agenda in December 1969.[5] Pompidou also claimed to act in France's best interest, yet his actions and strategies were almost diametrically opposed to de Gaulle's.

The example of de Gaulle and Pompidou underlines the idea that 'states do not always know what they want.'[6] Both de Gaulle and Pompidou occupied the highest office of state, had similar access to and command of resources and power, and faced similar strategic, economic, and political conditions; yet they contributed very differently to European integration. How can this difference be understood if it is assumed that the behaviour of leaders derives from exogenous national interests, economic necessities, and the characteristics of an anarchic international system?

By concentrating on the leaders themselves and by illustrating the contexts of their decision-making, a fuller picture can be gained of the complexities of European politics. How did leaders think about Europe? How did they understand their role, interests, and objectives? When did they perceive opportunities for exercising leadership and what kind of pressures were they under? The assumption that leaders' interests are given, rationally defined, and effectively pursued needs to be challenged.

Beyond structuralism and institutionalism

The extensive and diverse scholarship on the evolution of the EU is characterised by an important dichotomy when it comes to making sense of major changes in the integration process. On the one hand of the debate on European integration are what I would call *structural* accounts of integration, which are inspired by – certain variations notwithstanding – a deterministic understanding of the international system and the global economy. From this point of view, European integration is by and large a geopolitical project which is driven by states, reflects their core national interests, and advances their projection of power.[7] Integration is seen to result from 'responses to impulses from beyond Europe, or "exogenous shocks."'[8] This scholarship highlights the effects of external systemic trends on integration, as well as states' reactions to them. It casts doubt on the notion – often alluded to in the EU's political rhetoric – that the root of the integration process is an idea or vision of a united Europe. Instead, as John Mearsheimer has continuously argued since the early 1990s, European integration primarily continues to serve and advance core and self-centred state interests.[9] Its momentum stems neither from idealism nor popular rejection of the nation-state, but from the pursuit of state interests through cooperative means, as Alan Milward has suggested:

> [I]ntegration was not the supersession of the nation-state by another form of governance as the nation-state became incapable, but was the creation of the European nation-states themselves for their own purposes, an act of national will.[10]

This approach to the study of European integration is clearly manifested in the following paragraph from Andrew Moravcsik's acclaimed book *The Choice for Europe*:

> European integration resulted from a series of rational choices made by national leaders who consistently pursued economic interests . . . that evolved slowly in response to structural incentives in the global economy . . . The primary motivation of those who chose to integrate was not to prevent another Franco-German war, bolster global prestige and power, or balance against the superpowers. Nor – as numerous historians, political scientists, and members of the European movement continue to maintain – does integration represent a victory over nationalistic opposition by proponents of a widely shared, idealistic vision of a united Europe . . . To be sure, technocratic imperatives, geopolitical concerns, and European idealism each played a role at the margin, but none has consistently been the decisive force behind major decisions . . . Governments cooperated when induced or constrained to do so by economic self-interest, relative power, and strategically imposed commitments . . . The dominant motivations for governments . . . reflected not geopolitical threats or ideals but pressures to coordinate policy responses to rising opportunities for profitable economic exchange.[11]

While this narrative about the evolution of the EU does not preclude the view that leadership could have mattered in some circumstances, it nonetheless assumes that the necessities of national security and political economy ultimately shape what heads of government do. The behaviour and preferences of state leaders is subservient to 'trade flows, competitiveness, inflation rates, and other basic data [which] predict what the economic preferences of societal actors – and therefore governments – should be.'[12]

Some observers note that strategic security imperatives, rather than economic factors, set up the framework for economic integration.[13] Others suggest that integration came about as a response to the strategic security threats posed by the Soviet bloc as well as fear of a revival in German power. From this point of view, 'economic integration was the means, peace was the end' of the integration process.[14] European outcomes not only reflect state interests, but also the relative power of Europe's most influential states. By default, this means that the influence of other actors (supranational entrepreneurs, institutions) is expected to 'exert little or no causal influence.'[15]

Moreover, assumptions about both the nature and the content of leaders' interests are derived from theory rather than empirical observation and documentary evidence. Broadly speaking, the claim is that leaders and governments seek to protect and advance the national interest. Leadership becomes equivalent to statecraft. From this vantage point, it does not matter whether the national interest is framed in terms of prosperity, security, or power, and little is said about how leaders perceive, judge, frame, and pursue diverging interests.[16]

Accounts of European integration, such as Mearsheimer's, that are informed by neorealism and related theoretical schools regard the interests of European states to be determined by security concerns emanating from the international strategic context. As such, leaders' objectives derive from the demands of power politics and the relative power resources at their disposal. The proposition is that the integration process reflects 'high politics': state interests such as security and geopolitical and strategic gains.[17]

Alternative, more liberal-intergovernmentalist, accounts of integration, such as Moravcsik's, deviate from neorealism in two ways. On the one hand, national preferences are assumed 'to be domestically generated and not derived from a state's security concerns' and, on the other, the bargaining power of a given state is seen to be 'determined by the relative intensity of preferences and not by military or other material power capabilities.'[18] Liberal-intergovernmentalism holds that it is 'low politics' state interests such as trade, commercial advantage, and prosperity that guide European negotiations.[19] A 'sequential model of preference formation,'[20] in which the interests of domestic constituencies are wedded to the demands of intergovernmental bargaining processes, is marshalled to explain the interests and behaviour of governments in EU negotiations.

Yet as Stanley Hoffmann, John Gillingham and others have indicated, both neorealist and liberal-intergovernmentalist explanations need to be questioned for their 'most obvious' neglect of 'the role of leadership' in the complex web of diplomatic interactions that is so characteristic of the EU.[21] Thus I maintain that it is necessary to explore leadership and personal diplomacy in more empirical and historical detail.

Institutionalism

On the other hand of the scholarship on European integration is large body of scholarship that is primarily interested in the emergence of common supranational institutions, and in analysing the impact of this on European politics.[22] Institutions are seen to exert a significant influence on the conduct of international relations, enabling states to solve cooperation problems and realise goals that autonomy and self-help could not otherwise provide.[23] Rather than solely understanding integration as a response to external economic, strategic, or political necessities, institutionalism suggests that integration followed from both external demands and internal logic.

Institutionalism tends to draw on functionalism and game theory, as well as the related assumption of the rationalism of actors. From this vantage point, common institutions serve as a mechanism to fill functional collective action gaps in those realms of governance which nation-states are no longer able to cover effectively. Processes of institutional development, 'spillover,' path-dependence, and bureaucratisation are seen to profoundly shape the practices of European integration, permeating even the actions of member states. Institutionalism seeks to explain how and why integration has continued to evolve and develop, even in the absence of a common threat such as the Soviet Union. It departs from structural accounts by arguing that European outcomes do not always reflect the preferences of member states. In consequence, institutionalism posits that the European institutions, apart from playing a pivotal entrepreneurial role in EU negotiations, have a generative influence over state interests and policy choices.

The institutionalist literature is predisposed to explaining international cooperation, the creation of international organisations and regimes, and the emergence in Europe, and indeed elsewhere, of governance structures beyond the nation-state. It challenges the 'pessimistic conclusions about cooperation' of structural approaches and argues that 'the behaviour of states may not be fully explicable without understanding the institutional context of action.'[24] The process of voluntary cooperation and integration among the states of Europe, within its dense institutional and governance network, is therefore of great interest. Institutionalism holds that

> despite the lack of common government in international politics, sustained cooperation is possible under some fairly well defined conditions. These conditions include the existence of mutual interests that make joint (Pareto-improving) gains from cooperation possible; long-term relationships among relatively small number of actors; and the practice of reciprocity according to agreed-upon standards of appropriate behaviour. Such cooperation is not the antithesis of conflict but constitutes a process for the management of conflict.[25]

European integration thus emerged because the problems and challenges facing Europe's states could only be addressed through common and cooperative means. The claim is that international institutions are rational and efficient mechanisms for dealing with collective action problems shared by all European countries. While they 'do not expect cooperation always to prevail,' institutionalists argue that 'interdependence creates interests in cooperation.'[26] The reason for the emergence of international institutions – such as in Europe – is thus functional and instrumental. States create international institutions and regimes to deal with problems which no one state can effectively manage alone. Incentives to form international regimes 'depend most fundamentally on the existence of shared interests.'[27]

> [W]ithout consciously designed institutions . . . problems [of uncertainty and transaction costs] will thwart attempts to cooperate in world politics even when actors' interests are complementary. From the deficiency of the 'self-help system' (even from the perspective of purely self-interested national actors) we derive a need for international regimes.[28]

Alec Stone Sweet and Wayne Sandholtz mirror this understanding and apply to it the context of European integration. In their opinion,

> the causal mechanism [of integration] is quite simple: increasing levels of cross-border transactions and communications by societal actors will increase the perceived need for European-level rules, coordination, and regulation.

In fact, the absence of European rules will come to be seen as an obstacle for the generation of wealth and the achievement of other collective gains.[29]

The common European institutions perform collective policy tasks which states (due to globalisation or economic interdependence) can no longer execute effectively on their own. The emergence of supranational institutions is, in consequence, a necessary step for ensuring continuity and growth in intra-European economic exchanges.[30] As economic interdependence increases over time, so does the logic of institutionalised cooperation.

From this vantage point, the setting up of common institutions is rational because every state gains (in absolute terms) from mutual cooperation, and because institutions can provide technical expertise for the management of specific issues.[31] Institutions are also efficient because they embed state commitments and stipulate common rules which all member states subscribe to. This facilitates compliance, reduces transaction costs and uncertainty about state interests, and alleviates cheating and free-riding.[32] Furthermore, it is claimed that the detachment of international institutions from the pressures of domestic politics enhances their effectiveness and impartiality.

This line of institutional argumentation is at odds with structural views, such as Mearsheimer's, that international institutions reflect the interests of powerful states and are ultimately incapable of altering the competitive dynamic (or even rivalry) among them.[33] From the institutionalist perspective, states and leaders are interested in cooperation and institutionalisation because a rational cost-benefit analysis of their preferences reveals that cooperation leads to more optimal outcomes. Unlike structural accounts, which note that states are reluctant to pool sovereignty and authority unless they make significant gains, institutionalists argue that states do so because cooperation is in their best interest.

Yet institutionalism also takes into consideration that, once established, institutions develop unintended consequences, path-dependencies, and interests of their own, which affect subsequent political negotiations and outcomes.[34] For Stone Sweet and Sandholtz it is clear that '[o]nce supranational institutions are born, a new dynamic emerges,' which influences European outcomes.[35] George Tsebelis and Geoffrey Garrett went further in asserting that '[s]ince institutions determine the sequence of moves, the choices of actors, and the information they control, different institutional structures affect the strategies of actors and hence the outcomes of their interactions.'[36]

There are two points institutionalism makes about leaders and interests. First, it claims that functional necessities, as well as pressures from domestic groups (lobbies, political parties, civil society groups), determine leaders' interests. Second, it is assumed that leaders can rationally judge how best to pursue interests through an effective cost-benefit analysis of divergent policy options. Both assumptions underestimate the capacity of leaders to define, frame, and pursue interests in ways which are not necessarily rational or predictable.

To give an example: it is doubtful whether Helmut Kohl's advocacy and support for the introduction of the Euro throughout the 1990s was pressed on him by business leaders or by public opinion. It is also doubtful whether the introduction of the Euro was necessarily in Germany's best economic, fiscal, or political interest, nor did previous commitments to institutional development and increasing economic interdependence result in an unstoppable dynamic for EMU. Karl Kaltenthaler reveals in his examination of the run-up to the Euro that the Bundesbank and the Finance Ministry, but also powerful banks and corporations, feared that EMU would 'import inflation' into Germany.[37] Much of the German public was concerned about losing the mark as a national symbol, a sentiment that the current Eurozone debt and financial crisis has again exacerbated.

These assumptions about leaders' interests underestimate the degree of differences and severity of debates about what a state should pursue in Europe and how it should do so. Stathis Kalyvas notes that 'functional approaches ignore choices, alternative possibilities, conflicts, and their consequences; they hence overlook actors and their preferences and strategies.'[38] In consequence, institutionalist accounts of European integration 'are generally *post hoc* in nature. [They] observe institutions and then rationalize their existence.'[39] This approach glosses over the extent to which alternative courses of action were possible and potentially risky choices had to be made by leaders.

The institutionalist literature on European integration has long grappled with this issue of determinism. For instance, the early neofunctionalism of Karl Deutsch, Ernst Haas, and Leon Lindberg provided a theory of European integration,[40] but has been challenged by its empirical record. They argued that institutions addressed functional gaps, and policy areas were best managed if entrusted to experts and technical specialists. Yet they believed in an 'automaticity' of the integration process, 'leading to an ever-growing field of responsibilities being entrusted to international agencies.'[41]

According to this line of reasoning, institutions are created by relevant actors to improve the coordination of tasks and the provision of services. In a second instance, however, these relevant actors are influenced and transformed by the same institutions they set up; integration is thus a 'two-way process.'[42] New forms of governance would arise when actors adapted to the new institutional environment by making it either the central locus of political activity or by developing loyalties to it. Haas suggested that

> . . . group pressure will spill over into the federal sphere and thereby add to the integrative impulse. Only industries convinced that they have nothing to gain from integration will hold out against such pressures . . . More commonly still, groups are likely to turn to the federal authority for help in the solution of purely national problems if the local government proves uncooperative . . . [M]ajor interest groups as well as politicians determine their support of, or opposition to, new central institutions and policies on the basis of advantage. The 'good Europeans' are not the main creators of regional community that is growing up; the process of community formation is dominated by nationally constituted interest groups with specific

interests and aims, willing and able to adjust their aspirations by turning to supranational means when this course appears profitable.[43]

The determinism implicit in the concept of 'spillover' has been called into question;[44] it was heavily criticised throughout the 1960s and 1970s, and again after the failed plebiscites on the EU Constitutional Treaty in 2005. European integration has been stalling or regressing ever since. As Mette Eilstrup-Sangiovanni and Daniel Verdier have argued, general accounts based on assessing 'levels of economic interdependence' are generally a 'poor predictor of integration.'[45]

More recent institutionalist scholarship has taken this criticism into account.[46] Instead of assuming automaticity in the integration process, the unintended consequences of the EU's institutionalisation are stressed, as well as the fact that integration has changed the interests and behaviour of member states themselves. Particular attention is paid to the influence of the European Court of Justice (ECJ) on integration,[47] the emergence of institutional path-dependencies,[48] and the increasing bureaucratisation of European governance. It is revealed that the integration process has often not matched state preferences, and that it acquired a dynamic of its own. In doing so, close attention is paid to the dynamics of institutionalisation and its effects on actors' preferences and behaviour. Common institutions lead to a so-called loop of institutionalisation, whereby European institutions shape the 'context for subsequent interactions: how actors define their interests, what avenues are available to pursue them, how disputes are resolved.'[49]

Studying the effects of institutions on actors made this literature more interested in the concepts of socialisation, social learning, and path-dependency.[50] As Lindberg stated, if 'political integration . . . is going on, then we would expect to find a change in the behaviour of the participants.'[51] The interests of one actor adapt and change throughout negotiations and bargains with other actors. Institutionalists treat the formation of state interests as endogenous to bargaining processes[52] and claim that European institutions wield some influence on the formation of state interests. Derek Urwin reckons that

> [t]he penetration of the European fabric by the EC [European Community] has been sufficiently deep for the member governments and national groups increasingly to define their own interests and to plot their actions upon supposition of the EC's permanency and the importance of the EC level of decision-making.[53]

Herein lays the *problematique* of institutionalism. On the one hand, it asserts that the interests of political actors are not exogenously given notions, determined by the demands of the state. Yet, on the other hand, it reaffirms the assumption that not only are institutions functionally necessary, but also that negotiations and bargains among different actors lead to efficient and rational outcomes. This line of argumentation glosses over the fact that actors' interests are shaped by numerous influences, which cannot only be pinned down to the bargaining processes in European negotiations. Leaders make choices, which are highly relevant to European negotiations, but which are not necessarily efficient or rational.

To come back to the earlier example, Kohl's support and advocacy for EMU after 1990 might have been necessary in order to achieve French support for Germany's unification, but it is disputable whether this was economically sound and unavoidable. Making a functional argument, which suggests that the introduction of the Euro was not only an economic and financial necessity, but also an efficient and rational decision, underestimates the cross-linkages actors make between issues and policy areas. In short, it underestimates the agency of individual national leaders because it treats international negotiations and bargaining processes, rather than the actors themselves, as reference points for the definition of interests.

This does not mean that institutional accounts of European integration fail to provide important insights into the EU's bureaucracy and its policies. Yet their explanations of critical junctures in the integration process remain partial and deterministic. When accounting for important turning points in the history of European integration, institutional accounts rely on functional and *post hoc* explanations. The role of national political leaders does not figure prominently.[54] Instead, leadership is confined either to the role of institutions in bringing about European innovations[55] or to the transactional role of supranational entrepreneurs who facilitate success in negotiations.[56] Institutional accounts suggest an impersonal narrative of integration in which abstract functional imperatives and institutional dynamics trump the influence of individual leaders.[57]

Exploring personal diplomacy and leadership

I consider it imperative not to make assumptions about the behaviour and choices of leaders without analysing whether these assumptions held true in historical practice. Therefore, my intention is to fill this gap about the role of personal diplomacy and leadership in the construction of the EU. Some of the choices European leaders made cannot be fully explained by either structural or institutional theories. These theories remain partial so long as the contributions of individual decision-makers are largely ignored. Decision-makers have the ability to interpret, frame, implement, and prioritise interests and policies.

John Peterson and Elizabeth Bomberg claim that the 'conceptual distinction' structuralists and institutionalists draw between governments and supranational institutions is ultimately 'unsustainable.'[58] National and European politics are often too interrelated to withstand clear analytical separation. Politicians frequently blame Brussels for unpopular decisions and policies at home, but use European integration to advance national objectives, thereby often strengthening – sometimes inadvertently – the EU's structures. Desmond Dinan sheds light on this close interlinkage of the demands on leaders and the innovative possibilities of their agency:

> Although political pragmatism may explain the scope and shape of the European Communities, a felicitous combination of idealism and national self-interest characterised the early years of European integration. The architects of the new Europe appreciated the popular appeal as well as the necessity of pooling national sovereignty. But European integration could not have flourished and Euro-idealism would have foundered if the undertaking had not worked to the ultimate advantage of the countries concerned.[59]

Leadership is a relational and contingent notion in which decision-makers respond to the demands of their constituents while simultaneously altering the latter's perceptions and preferences.[60] Economic necessities and security imperatives, institutional dynamics and bureaucratic politics, play a role in this process. Yet so do identities, as well as ideas about how to perceive interests and how to pursue them.[61] In Keohane and Nye's assessment,

> [s]tate choices reflect elites' perceptions of interests, which may change in several ways. The most obvious is political change. An election, coup, or generational evolution can lead to a replacement of leaders and thus bring in quite different viewpoints about national interests. The change in 'national interests' may not reflect new affective or cognitive views in the society at large. Rather the leadership change may reflect domestic issues or other factors unrelated to foreign policy.[62]

As far as European integration is concerned, different leaders have framed their interests differently, sometimes even in opposing ways. Changes in the perception, definition, and pursuit of national interests can be stark or subtle. Even when leaders are concerned with the same political issue, they perceive divergent ways of addressing and dealing with it. This explains why certain features of European integration, which have a lot to do with perceptions, ideas, and identities, have endured:

> the logic of economic integration; French fear of falling behind; general concern about Germany's predominance; the potential for Franco-German leadership; British scepticism; and the small country syndrome (small member states' fear of hegemony).[63]

Especially given the elitist nature of European decision-making, it is germane to examine leadership and leadership dynamics.[64] In his 2003 book *The Struggle for Europe*, William Hitchcock notes that

> integration was a process conceived and driven by elites, who never subjected their ideas to the voting public. The European Union has come into being as the product of international bargaining by government leaders: the public never asked for it, and when called on to ratify European treaties – albeit

rarely – European voters often show significant scepticism toward the erosion of national sovereignty.[65]

Similarly, Dinan argues that

> national leaders decided to share sovereignty in supranational organisations primarily because they perceived that it was in their countries' (and therefore their own) interests to do so. Ideas, intellectual fashion, opportunity, conviction, calculation, personal predilection, and ambition all played a part.[66]

Due to the fact that 'history-making decisions' in European integration[67] are mostly taken at the highest political level, the role, views, and objectives of top-level decision-makers deserve closer scrutiny.

In structural and institutional accounts of European integration it makes little difference, for instance, whether Charles de Gaulle, Georges Pompidou, or François Hollande is in charge of France. It is assumed that they ultimately pursued the same French national interests. Yet this assumption leaves little scope for accounting for the differences in perception, interpretation, and judgement of these interests, as well as for the often sharply varying European choices of individual leaders.

For example, in early 1955, the idea for a *relance* emerged, intending to put efforts for European integration back on track, something that was achieved with the Treaties of Rome in 1957. The treaties are widely regarded as the institutional precursor of the contemporary EU. But how did this important innovation in European affairs come about? Why did national decision-makers support these proposals? Conventionally, the relevant literature answers these questions either by looking at state interests or the functional need for economic regulation and the creation of economies of scale.

Structural accounts focus on states and reveal how this innovation in European politics reflected the intergovernmental bargains and interests of Europe's nation-states. From this point of view, states only acquiesced to the Common Market because it was in their interest to do so, responding to the need for economic growth by founding a common market and customs union. Alan Milward explains national negotiation positions by looking at postwar economic reform, concerns with industrial modernisation, and the need for improved market access.[68] Andrew Moravcsik suggests that narrower commercial interests and export promotion were central to British, French, and German preferences.[69] Both emphasise the intergovernmental nature of the bargaining process, and implicitly suggest that leaders followed these objective national interests. National positions depended not on who was in charge of government, but on structural economic necessities dictated by external trends.

Milward claims that European nation-states had 'the will . . . to survive as an organisational entity.'[70] Achieving national prosperity was therefore necessary to sustain domestic post-war political compromises everywhere. The importance of foreign trade to that prosperity was great and was magnified in the political and economic thought of the time.[71]

The Common Market was

> a commitment to guarantees of future commercial policy without precedent in European history. And the solemnity of that guarantee was emphasised by the promise to reach an 'ever-closer union.'[72]

This notion of an 'ever-closer union' is therefore by this definition not an idealistic, federalist-inspired concept, but a commitment of nation-states to 'an entirely different model' of political economy.[73] This casts doubt on the view that the Common Market is an outcome of the actions of a 'small band of leading statesmen with a shared vision.'[74]

This line of inquiry leaves little conceptual room for any form of personal diplomacy or leadership interventions. If the negotiations for the Common Market are understood to be the outcome of economic necessities and states are assumed to have stable interests, the dynamics of leadership matter only marginally and reactively. Entrepreneurial leadership – as was ascribed by contemporaries to Paul-Henri Spaak and Jean Monnet – is seen to have had almost no impact on the outcomes of the negotiations. Illustrative of this approach is Moravcsik's *Choice for Europe*. He casts doubt on the relevance of Guy Mollet's 'pro-European ideology'[75] as an influential factor for reaching agreements in 1955–1957. Only in the case of Konrad Adenauer could a 'geopolitical objective' have mattered apart from the pursuit of economic and commercial interests.[76] Moravcsik even accepts that the decision about whether or not to pursue the Common Market was placed 'in Adenauer's hands,' but does not inquire into Adenauer's role further.[77] Instead, he suggests that 'leading European statesmen in each country understood that trade liberalisation was in one form or another inevitable' and that the 'relative competitiveness [of their economies] determined much of their thinking about [the] preferred geographical scope and substantive domain' of integration efforts.[78]

This view of the history of European integration is disputed by institutionalists. Rather than understanding the Common Market as a mechanism to advance narrowly defined national interest, institutionalists claim that its creation was necessary to counter national inefficiencies in economic management, regulation, and planning in times of increasing economic interdependence. For Linda Cornett and James Caporaso, the 'formation of the [Common Market] combined a pragmatic emphasis on solving concrete problems with dramatic ideas about how to tame or transcend the nation-state.'[79] The main problem facing the states of Western Europe was how to sustain the high economic and productivity growth rates. In the gradual postwar shift from 'wartime state' to 'welfare state,'[80] growth was necessary in order to support a new consensus around the welfare state as a key hinge of the legitimacy of government. Given that economic growth was fuelled by exports, Western Europe needed to overcome its economic separation into exclusive national markets and regulatory regimes, which hindered the creation of high-productivity economies of scale.

From the functional point of view, 'central institutions are required in order to *represent* the common interests which have brought the Member States together, and in order to *accommodate* such conflicts of interest as will inevitably arise.'[81] The root of these potential conflicts of interests was the growing strength of the West German economy, which became 'both the cause and effect of the formation of the new customs union.'[82] The institutional explanation thus emphasises the global political and economic conditions of the 1950s, which made cooperation necessary and institutionalisation an effective mechanism to tackle common problems:

> Economic development, political change and technological advance have combined to make Western Europe both smaller and more dependent upon both internal cooperation and external factors. It was reduced status and interdependence which persuaded some people that more intense and formal cooperation would be both valuable and necessary.[83]

Wolfgang Wessels expands on this line of argumentation, suggesting that

> [w]hen they established the European Community in 1957, the member states sought to ensure more effective policymaking. The converse of these ambitions, however, was the loss of national autonomy that increased integration and cooperation entailed. As time passed, the basic dilemma has increased: The higher the interdependence among European countries, the stronger the propensity to move to Community rather than national policy; but this propensity reacts adversely on national autonomy. As interdependence rises, whether the result of market forces or government policy, the propensity to move to Community activity increases, as common or coordination actions become more effective.[84]

This suggests a need and dynamic for economic integration, to which decision-makers had to react:

> The dilemma of West European governments is that successful economic performance is a major prerequisite for the stability of these welfare and service states. Governments in power see their electoral fate as being directly linked with the state of their economy and a sufficient performance of state services. To achieve this goal, West European economies have to be open to an international and European division of labor. With economic interpenetration, however, interdependencies increase and the (at least de facto) autonomy of national systems decrease.[85]

Institutional explanations understand the Common Market not only as a necessary mechanism for economic management, but also as the start of a process of further and ever-deeper integration and institutionalisation.

While structural and institutional explanations work as *ex post facto* accounts, they implicitly assume that leaders had little option but to engage in a process of gradual economic integration and institutionalisation. But were the supposed benefits of the Common Market proposals really that obvious to the decision-makers at the time? A closer look at the historical context reveals that this was not the case. The *rélance* was controversial both in individual countries and in intergovernmental negotiations. In Germany and France, significant political divisions existed around the question of whether to support the Common Market proposal. As Gillingham quotes,

> [f]ear . . . had seized French business and especially government officialdom at the idea that the wall of protection . . . built up during the prewar, war, and postwar years might one day come down and that French industry would then have to face foreign competition without customs duties, quotas, or state subsidies.[86]

Similarly, Craig Parsons notes that the 'Common Market had almost no support in France. Most French businessmen in 1955 favoured "as little change as possible."'[87] Even French farmers only started to support the Common Market proposal in early 1956, after top French officials began 'systematic lobbying of interest groups, especially farmers.'[88]

In Germany, the government was split between those like Adenauer who supported the Common Market, and those who – like Ludwig Erhard – 'vigorously championed' a British plan for an OEEC free-trade area without supranational institutions and without a common external tariff.[89] The latter feared that 'Paris sought to create a protectionist European bloc that would cut Germany off from its wider markets.'[90] Many German business organisations and trade unions had significant doubts about the repercussions the establishment of a common market would have in France. Even the Dutch, who first tabled the proposals in 1955, had doubts about its merit. Fearing protectionism, they had to be dissuaded (as late as February 1957) from 'abandoning the common market venture and joining the British in their efforts to create a free trade zone.'[91]

In all the participating countries, no clear consensus of what was in their best national interest existed. It was highly disputed whether participating in the negotiations and eventually joining the Common Market was beneficial. Neither business groups, trade unions, nor the public clamoured for the establishment of the Common Market. The public was, in fact, overwhelmingly wary of the concept of supranationality.

It is in this kind of concrete historical contexts that personal diplomacy and leadership have meaningful analytical purchase and explanatory relevance. The implication is that the *rélance* of 1955–1957 succeeded not only because decision-makers invested their political capital and prestige to support it, but also because they managed to work out their differences and gain mutual respect and trust. As will be seen in Chapter 3, this was especially the case with Guy Mollet and Konrad Adenauer. The challenge is now to go beyond the structural and institutionalist approaches and devise a conceptual framework for the study of leadership in European integration.

Notes

1. M.J. Hillenbrand, 'An Assessment of the EC Future,' *Annals of the American Academy of Political and Social Science* 531 (1994): 169.
2. S.N. Kalyvas, *The Rise of Christian Democracy in Europe* (Ithaca: Cornell University Press, 1996), p. 13.
3. D.J. Mahoney, *De Gaulle: Statesmanship, Grandeur, and Modern Democracy* (New Brunswick: Transaction, 2000).
4. T. Diallo, *La Politique Étrangère de Georges Pompidou* (Paris: Librairie Général de Droit et de Jurisprudence, 1992).
5. C. Hiepel, *Willy Brandt und Georges Pompidou. Deutsch-französische Europapolitik zwischen Aufbruch und Krise* (Munich: Oldenbourg, 2012).
6. Finnemore, *National Interests in International Society* (Ithaca: Cornell University Press, 1996), p. 128.
7. J.M. Grieco, 'State Interests and Institutional Rule Trajectories: A Neorealist Interpretation of the Maastricht Treaty and European Economic and Monetary Union,' *Security Studies* 5 (3) (1996): 277–307; J.M. Grieco, 'The Maastricht Treaty, Economic and Monetary Union and the Neo-Realist Research Programme,' *Review of International Studies* 21 (1995): 21–40.
8. See J. Peterson and E. Bomberg, *Decision-Making in the European Union* (Basingstoke: Palgrave, 1999), p. 253.
9. J. Mearsheimer, 'Back to the Future: Instability in Europe after the Cold War,' *International Security* 15 (1) (1990): 5–56; see also S. Rosato, *Europe United: Power Politics and the Making of the European Community* (Ithaca: Cornell University Press, 2011).
10. A.S. Milward, *The European Rescue of the Nation-State*, second edition (London: Routledge, 2000), p. 18.
11. A. Moravcsik, *The Choice for Europe: Social Purpose and State Power from Messina to Maastricht* (London: Routledge, 1998), pp. 3–6.
12. A. Moravcsik, 'The Future of European Integration Studies: Social Science or Social Theory,' *Millennium* 28 (2) (1999): 377. On the economic dynamics for integration, see B. Balassa, *The Theory of Economic Integration* (London: Allen and Unwin, 1961).
13. See M. Shaw, *Theory of the Global State: Globality as an Unfinished Revolution* (Cambridge: Cambridge University Press, 2000), p. 247.
14. K.E. Smith, *European Union Foreign Policy in a Changing World* (Cambridge: Polity, 2003), p. 28.
15. M.A. Pollack, 'International Relations Theory and European Integration,' *Journal of Common Market Studies* 39 (2) (2001): 225.
16. See K.N. Waltz, 'Political Structures,' in *Neorealism and Its Critics*, R.O. Keohane ed. (New York: Columbia University Press, 1985), pp. 70–97.
17. J.J. Mearsheimer, *The Tragedy of Great Power Politics* (New York: W.W. Norton, 2001); J.J. Mearsheimer, 'The False Promise of International Institutions,' *International Security* 19 (3) (1994–5): 5–49.
18. Pollack, 'International Relations Theory,' p. 225.

19 See L. Tsoukalis, *The Politics and Economics of European Monetary Integration* (London: George Allen and Unwin, 1977), pp. 28–29.
20 Pollack, 'International Relations Theory,' p. 225.
21 S. Hoffmann, 'The Case for Leadership,' *Foreign Policy* 81 (1990–91): 21; J. Gillingham, *European Integration 1950–2003: Superstate or New Market Economy?* (Cambridge: Cambridge University Press, 2003), p. 34.
22 A.-M. Burley and W. Mattli, 'Europe before the Court: A Political Theory of Legal Integration,' *International Organization* 47 (1) (1993): 41–76; E.B. Haas, *The Uniting of Europe: Political, Social, and Economic Forces, 1950–1957* (Palo Alto: Stanford University Press, 1958); J. Jupille and J.A. Caporaso, 'Institutionalism and the European Union: Beyond International Relations and Comparative Politics,' *Annual Review of Political Science* 2 (1999): 409–425; L.N. Lindberg, *The Political Dynamics of European Economic Integration* (Palo Alto: Stanford University Press, 1963); W. Mattli, *The Logic of Regional Integration: Europe and Beyond* (Cambridge: Cambridge University Press, 1999); P. Pierson, 'The Path to European Integration: A Historical Institutionalist Analysis,' *Comparative Political Studies* 29 (2) (1996): 123–163; F. Scharpf, *Governing in Europe: Effective and Democratic?* (Oxford: Oxford University Press, 1999); G. Schneider and M. Aspinwall eds., *The Rules of Integration: The Institutionalist Approach to European Studies* (Manchester: Manchester University Press, 2001); A. Stone Sweet and T.L. Brunell, 'Constructing a Supranational Constitution: Dispute Resolution and Governance in the European Community,' *The American Political Science Review* 92 (1) (1998): 63–81; W. Sandholtz and A. Stone Sweet eds., *European Integration and Supranational Governance* (Oxford: Oxford University Press, 1998); J. Tallberg, 'The Power of the Presidency: Brokerage, Efficiency and Distribution in EU Negotiations,' *Journal of Common Market Studies* 42 (5) (2004): 999–1022.
23 R. Axelrod and R.O. Keohane, 'Achieving Cooperation under Anarchy: Strategies and Institutions,' *World Politics* 38 (1) (1985): 226–254.
24 R.O. Keohane, *After Hegemony: Cooperation and Discord in the World Political Economy* (Princeton: Princeton University Press, 1984), pp. 13–14.
25 R.O. Keohane and J.S. Nye, 'Introduction: The End of the Cold War in Europe,' in *After the Cold War: International Institutions and State Strategies in Europe, 1989–1991*, R.O. Keohane, J. Nye, and S. Hoffmann eds. (Cambridge: Harvard University Press, 1993), pp. 4–5.
26 Keohane, *After Hegemony*, p. 8.
27 Ibid., p. 79.
28 Ibid., pp. 87–88.
29 A. Stone Sweet and W. Sandholtz, 'Integration, Supranational Governance, and the Institutionalization of the European Polity,' in *European Integration and Supranational Governance*, W. Sandholtz and A. Stone Sweet eds. (Oxford: Oxford University Press, 1998), p. 11.
30 N. Fligstein and A. Stone Sweet, 'Constructing Polities and Markets: An Institutionalist Account of European Integration,' *American Journal of Sociology* 107 (5) (2002): 1213.
31 A. Hasenclever, P. Mayer, and V. Rittberger, *Theories of International Regimes* (Cambridge: Cambridge University Press, 1997); L. Martin, 'The Rational Choice of Multilateralism,' in *Multilateralism Matters: The Theory and Praxis of an Institutional Form*, J.G. Ruggie ed. (New York: Columbia University Press, 1993), pp. 91–124.
32 Keohane, *After Hegemony*, p. 97.
33 See Mearsheimer, *Tragedy*.
34 See Hasenclever et al., *Theories*.
35 Stone Sweet and Sandholtz, 'Integration,' p. 5.

36 G. Tsebelis and G. Garrett, 'The Institutional Foundations of Intergovernmentalism and Supranationalism in the European Union,' *International Organization* 55 (2) (2001): 384.
37 K. Kaltenthaler, 'German Interests in European Monetary Integration,' *Journal of Common Market Studies* 40 (1) (2002): 75.
38 Kalyvas, *Christian Democracy*, p. 8.
39 Keohane, *After Hegemony*, p. 80.
40 See K. Deutsch, *Political Community and the North Atlantic Area* (Princeton: Princeton University Press, 1957); Haas, *Uniting of Europe*; Lindberg, *Political Dynamics*.
41 Tsoukalis, *Politics and Economics*, p. 23.
42 Haas, *Uniting of Europe*, p. 19.
43 *Ibid.*, p. xxxiv.
44 See B.F. Nelsen and Alexander C-G. Stubb eds., *The European Union: Readings on the Theory and Practice of European Integration*, second edition (Basingstoke: Macmillan, 1998), pp. 145–146, 242.
45 M. Eilstrup-Sangiovanni and D. Verner, 'European Integration as a Solution to War,' *European Journal of International Relations* 11 (1) (2005): 101.
46 On the 'inadequacy of functional theories,' see R.O. Keohane, 'Governance in a Partially Globalized World: Presidential Address, American Political Science Association, 2000,' *American Political Science Review* 95 (1) (2000): 4.
47 A. Stone Sweet and J.A. Caporaso, 'From Free Trade to Supranational Polity: The European Court and European Integration,' in *European Integration and Supranational Governance*, W. Sandholtz and A. Stone Sweet eds. (Oxford: Oxford University Press, 1998), pp. 92–133; Burley and Mattli, 'Europe before the Court'.
48 Pierson, 'Path to European Integration'.
49 Stone Sweet and Sandholtz, 'Integration,' p. 17.
50 J. Checkel, 'International Institutions and Socialization in Europe: Introduction and Framework,' *International Organization* 59 (2005): 801–826; J. Checkel, 'Why Comply? Social Learning and European Identity Change,' *International Organization* 55 (3) (2001): 553–588.
51 Lindberg, *Political Dynamics*, p. 9.
52 See O.R. Young, *Governance in World Affairs* (Ithaca: Cornell University Press, 1999); Hasenclever et al, *Theories*.
53 D.W. Urwin, *A Political History of Western Europe since 1945*, fifth edition (London: Longman, 1997), p. 324.
54 See J. Hayward ed., *Leaderless Europe* (Oxford: Oxford University Press, 2008).
55 See J. Tallberg, *Leadership and Negotiation in the European Union* (Cambridge: Cambridge University Press, 2006); D. Beach, *The Dynamics of European Integration: Why and When EU Institutions Matter* (Basingstoke: Palgrave Macmillan, 2005).
56 See S. Bunse, *Small States and EU Governance: Leadership through the Council Presidency* (Basingstoke: Palgrave, 2009); M.A. Pollack, *The Engines of European Integration: Delegation, Agency and Agenda Setting in the EU* (Oxford: Oxford University Press, 2003); L. Hooghe, *The European Commission and the Integration of Europe: Images of Governance* (Cambridge: Cambridge University Press, 2002); W. Sandholtz and A. Stone Sweet eds., *European Integration and Supranational Governance* (Oxford: Oxford University Press, 1998).
57 See R.H. Ginsberg, *Demistifying the European Union: The Enduring Logic of Regional Integration*, second edition (Lanham: Rowman and Littlfield, 2010).
58 J. Peterson and E. Bomberg, *Decision-Making in the European Union* (Basingstoke: Palgrave, 1999), p. 254.

36 *Leadership as a conceptual framework*

59 D. Dinan, *Europe Recast: A History of European Union* (Boulder: Lynne Rienner, 2004), p. 11.
60 See J.M. Burns, *Leadership* (New York, NY: Harper and Row, 1978).
61 Peterson and Bomberg, *Decision-Making*, p. 254.
62 R.O. Keohane and J.S. Nye, *Power and Interdependence*, third edition (New York: Longman, 2001), p. 284.
63 Dinan, *Europe Recast*, p. 8.
64 The elitist nature of European decision-making was formally extended by the creation of the European Council in 1974. The framework for high-level decision-making was deliberately made to emphasise 'informality' and 'political leadership': P. Ludlow, *The Making of the European Monetary System: A Case Study of the Politics of the European Community* (London: Butterworth Scientific, 1982), p. 14.
65 W. Hitchcock, *The Struggle for Europe: The History of the Continent since 1945* (London: Profile Books, 2003), p. 6.
66 Dinan, *Europe Recast*, p. 1.
67 Peterson and Bomberg, *Decision-Making*.
68 Milward, *European Rescue*.
69 Moravcsik, *Choice*.
70 Milward, *European Rescue*, p. 223.
71 *Ibid*.
72 *Ibid.*, p. 222.
73 *Ibid.*, p. 223.
74 *Ibid.*, pp. 318–319.
75 Moravcsik, *Choice*, pp. 120–121.
76 *Ibid.*, pp. 93–94.
77 *Ibid.*, p. 137.
78 *Ibid.*, p. 136.
79 L. Cornett and J.A. Caporaso, '"And Still It Moves!" State Interests and Social Forces in the European Community,' in *Governance without Government: Order and Change in World Politics*, J.N. Rosenau and E.-O. Czempiel eds. (Cambridge: Cambridge University Press, 1992), p. 220.
80 Gillingham, *European Integration*, p. 4.
81 Lindberg, *Political Dynamics*, p. 8 (emphasis in the original).
82 Gillingham, *European Integration*, p. 4.
83 D.W. Urwin, *A Political History of Western Europe since 1945*, fifth edition (London: Longman, 1997), p. 323.
84 W. Wessels, 'The EC Council: The Community's Decisionmaking Center,' in *The New European Community: Decisionmaking and Institutional Change*, R.O. Keohane and S. Hoffmann eds. (Boulder: Westview, 1991), pp. 134–135.
85 *Ibid.*, p. 135.
86 Gillingham, *European Integration*, pp. 44–45.
87 Parsons, *Certain Idea*, p. 103.
88 *Ibid.*, p. 108.
89 Gillingham, *European Integration*, p. 48. On the differences between Adenauer and Erhard, which permeated cabinet discussions on European policies, see the minutes of the 171st cabinet meeting of 13 February 1957: Bundesarchiv *KP* online.
90 J.G. Giauque, 'Bilateral Summit Diplomacy in Western European and Transatlantic Relations, 1956–63,' *European History Quarterly* 31 (3) (1996): 430.
91 P.-H. Laurent, 'The Diplomacy of the Rome Treaty, 1956–57,' *Journal of Contemporary History* 7 (3/4) (1972): 215.

2 The influence of leadership
Personal diplomacy and risk-taking

> Leadership is the art of getting someone else to do something you want done because he wants to do it.
> – Dwight D. Eisenhower

> The true statesman is the one who is willing to take risks.
> – Charles de Gaulle

European integration needs to be thought of as a *process* shaped by the interaction of structural and ideational factors, leaders' divergent interpretations of their interests and preferences, and diverging legacies, as well as and ideas and conceptions about Europe and a country's place in it. From the point of view of the diplomatic historian, as Thomas Otte explains,

> every political action, be it in actual deed or in the shape of a policy recommendation, is based on a set of premises, preconceived values and axioms . . . Decision-makers are mostly guided by 'their own instinctive reactions, traditions and modes of behaviour.' They are the products of their age, their national traditions and social environments; they are influenced by the prevailing modes of thought of their time . . . The key to a more thorough understanding of the past lies in these broad assumptions, the 'thought-world' and intellectual coordinates of policy-makers and their advisers.[1]

The intention of this book is to reveal those sets of contexts and relationships which facilitated the emergence of particular milestones of European integration, which can only be fruitfully undertaken if decision-makers are placed at the heart of these contexts and relationships. After all, they are the ones who frame, represent, and negotiate their respective national positions, and they are the ones who ultimately choose one set of policies over another. Naturally, the 'socio-political environment limits considerably the individual's freedom to choose political roles and actions.'[2] But this does not mean that leaders did not have to make choices or take risks. Gillian Peele reminds us that it is central to the task of the political scientist not only to depend on 'explanatory power' that derives from the 'analysis of structures' but also to 'inevitably address . . . the issue of agency and explore the difference made by key actors.'[3] Furthermore, it is imperative not to overlook and under-research the personal relationship between leaders.[4]

Little is gained by merely producing an actor-centric narrative of European integration, in which leaders play a uniquely heroic role.[5] The frequent distinction between 'villains and heroes'[6] is not useful, as leadership is not an innately moral or normative category. Leaders – even supposedly good ones – break the rules, deceive, misinform, and lie, and there are plenty of historical anecdotes to back this up.[7] The intention should not be to determine whether someone was a good or bad European leader, but to examine why and how someone chose a particular European policy initiative, invested significant political capital and risk into it, disregarded potential viable alternatives, or decided against another path of action.

The contexts of leadership: personal characteristics, resources, followership

Any exploration of leadership and its impact on political processes and decision-making needs to deal with the difficult task of defining and delineating the concept.[8] The definition can touch upon the character of leaders, their followers, their organisational context, the agenda of political problems at hand, leadership techniques, and the effects of leadership. In Lewis Edinger's general definition, leadership is

> related to a disproportionate measure of direct or indirect control over public offices and policies . . . Generally, political leadership is seen as focusing directly on governmental control over public policy decisions at the intra- and interstate level, and indirectly control over the sources and consequences of such decisions.[9]

Yet some political scientists recognise that 'too great a focus on the context robs the notion of leadership of its core which must allow for some notion of personal style and individual creativity.'[10] Specifying what leadership is, and how it plays out in particular historical contexts, touches upon the debate about agency and structure. Erwin Hargrove and John Owens point out that 'agency does not act in a vacuum,' but is bound by 'structure in historical context.'[11] In this sense, the 'boundaries of possible action are set by context, but there is flexibility within the boundaries.'[12] Analysing leadership thus needs to be balanced between structurally deterministic and exclusively agent-centred – 'great man' – accounts of politics.[13] Robert Tucker, for instance, calls for a kind of 'situationism' in studying leadership, meaning that 'qualities making for leadership success in one set of circumstances, might militate against in another.'[14] From this point of view, 'different leadership skills and traits are required in different situations.'[15]

Most analyses of leadership have grappled with the question of the characteristics of leadership, the conditions for it, and the concrete contexts which facilitate it. In general, leadership is seen to originate from three distinct foundations and roles. First, personal characteristics and traits, charisma, and the biography of an individual can be regarded as crucial conditions for the emergence of leadership.[16] Second, leadership can emerge out of an individual's command of specific institutional, economic, and political resources – as well as power.[17] Third, leadership can be understood as a phenomenon that grows out of complex leader-follower interactions in concrete historical circumstances.[18] Leadership can thus be 'positionally' or 'behaviourally' defined, depending on whether the leader affects other people as a result of his institutional position or because of his own behaviour.[19]

Writing in 1950, Lester Seligman warned that the 'preoccupation with the "essence" of leadership has long beset the conception of leadership.'[20] He proposed to go beyond the 'long search for leadership traits' and instead sketch a 'more organic view' of leadership, which should 'permit a convergence of points of view.'[21] In his 'synthetic' and 'relational' understanding, leadership is dependent upon 'acceptance within particular contexts.'[22] For Seligman, leadership is not about status or traits but rather a 'working relationship among members of a group' in which the leader demonstrates – more than other group members – the skill and capacity to carry out 'cooperative tasks.'[23]

The major analytical task consists of uncovering empirically the extent to which individual leaders chose to pursue particular forms and mechanisms of European integration, thereby moulding the historical contexts they found themselves in. In this sense, it is important to conceptualise agency in general – and leadership in particular – as a social and fluid relationship of interactions between individuals and their social and physical environments. The social-theoretical underpinning for the mutual constitution of agents and structures is a hallmark of numerous constructivist analyses in International Relations and International History.[24] Constructivists stress the relational and intersubjective character of agents and structures. This emphasis is particularly useful for studying and assessing the impact of leadership on the process of European integration.

As James Burns suggests, 'we must see power – and leadership – as not things but as relationships. We must analyse power in a context of human motives and physical constraints.'[25] The conceptualisation of leadership as a relationship, as well as a form of power,[26] is highly illustrative for the purposes of this book. By stressing the relational nature of leadership, it becomes possible to elucidate and assess the actions and choices of individual decision-makers in relation to other politicians and the public, as well as to the larger political, economic, strategic, and social conditions of a particular historical period. After all, leadership plays out differently in different political and institutional settings, and often politicians exercise leadership on one issue but not others. Leadership is therefore contingent upon specific interactions in particular contexts.

On this point, Burns argues that the 'essence of the leader-follower relation' is the 'interaction of persons with different levels of motivation and of power potential, including skill, in pursuit of a common or at least joint purpose.'[27] Leadership implies 'some congruence between the objectives of the leader and the led.'[28] It becomes legitimate only when the power exercised by the leader is justified by 'appeal to something over and above his own personal motives.'[29] It is due to the contingency of these interactions that a relational conceptualisation of leadership is particularly well-placed for assessing the role and impact of leadership on political processes. The broader relational understanding of leadership also makes it easier to highlight to what extent individual leaders managed to achieve some autonomy of action for following specific policy choices.

In the case of European integration, the historical evidence reveals two things: First, national leaders are often drawn by what Michael Foley calls the 'allure of the foreign' – i.e. the opportunity and ambition to develop their leadership ambitions in the fields of foreign policy. Second, major transformations in the integration process often came about at moments of uncertainty or crisis, when leaders enjoyed a significant amount of autonomy on European affairs.[30] Autonomy was not a sufficient condition for altering the practices of European integration, but it was a necessary one: '[W]hen governments have strongly held irreconcilable positions, no zone of possible agreements exists.'[31] This applies both domestically and internationally, and means that leaders' autonomy for influencing the integration process had also to be carved out both domestically and internationally.

Often leaders' autonomy on European integration did not extend to public support or support from their bureaucracies for their policies.[32] In some cases, leaders' autonomy came about as a result of public disinterest in European affairs. In other cases, leaders had to use the power and influence of their office, as well as their connections, to sideline opponents and bureaucrats or to brush aside the misgivings of the public. Yet, regardless of the fact of how leaders' autonomy was achieved, it functioned as an enabling condition for exercising effective leadership. Hargrove and Owens observe that leadership is 'most likely to emerge in situations that are unstable, changing, and ill-defined.'[33] It is therefore especially in periods of strong political contestation, uncertainty, or crisis that the 'exogenous interventions of imaginative individuals'[34] can trigger 'dynamic processes of innovation' geared towards political change.[35] It is especially in 'highly complex situations, where there is also a strong pressure for an agreement' that opportunities emerge for translating 'leadership resources into influence over outcomes.'[36]

It is in this sense that not only the skills of leaders, but also the nature of their power, needs to be illustrated. The emphasis on power is crucially important for the study and analysis of leadership. Leadership is seen as 'a special form of power':

> Leaders are a particular kind of power holder. Like power, leadership is relational, collective, and purposeful. Leadership shares with power the central function of achieving purpose.[37]

Yet leadership is also 'unlike naked power-wielding,' coercion, and domination, and is thus 'inseparable from followers' needs and goals.'[38] In this sense, all leaders are 'actual or potential power holders, but not all power holders are leaders.'[39] Seen from this vantage point, leadership can be defined as

> leaders inducing followers to act for certain goals that represent the values and the motivations – the wants and needs, the aspirations and expectation – *of both leaders and followers.*[40]

By highlighting the importance of followers it becomes clear that leadership is fundamentally different from coercive forms of exercising power. Instead, effective leaders gain their influence through persuasion, manipulation of their followers' preferences, and effective coalition-building. Rather than forcing people to do something they would not otherwise do, political leaders exercise their influence by setting the agenda of political debate, framing political issues, negotiating agreements between conflicting parties, and selling compromises to the electorate or public. Leadership has numerous constraints, which arise out of the social context. The very embeddedness of the leader within a social system constrains his or her behaviour. The role of a leader is influenced by the expectations of others – in terms of role performance and adherence to appropriate forms of behaviour – but is also conditioned by the efforts of others to change and modify the leader's own behaviour and preferences.[41] Pfeffer claims that the 'pressures to conform to the expectations of peers, subordinates, and superiors are all relevant in determining actual behaviour.' The behaviour of leaders can therefore not be divorced from the social contexts in which it occurs.[42]

Leadership shares with power the 'central function of achieving purpose.'[43] Yet while dictators impose political objectives through coercion and single-handedly define the purpose of political activity themselves, political leaders in today's liberal democracies have to take the interests, preferences, and attitudes of their followers and negotiating partners into consideration. In consequence, leaders need to work consciously to gain autonomy and tread carefully to gain the trust of their followers.

Typologies of leadership

As far as the purpose of leadership is concerned, three types of leadership are generally identified: transactional leadership, transformational leadership, and moral leadership.[44] These derive from the roles leaders play, the institutional position they hold, and the objectives they follow.[45] In Karl Kuhnert and Philip Lewis' definition, transactional leaders

> give followers what they want in exchange for something the leaders want . . . Transactional leadership represents those exchanges in which both superior and the subordinate influence one another reciprocally so that each derives something of value.[46]

In the context of intergovernmental European negotiations – in which all participants are at least *de jure* equal and in which they hold a blocking veto – transactional leadership often takes the form of negotiation skills. Transactional leaders are those who strive for successful compromises among the Community member states, in which all negotiating sides feel they have a stake and therefore do not make use of their veto. In institutional contexts it is often attributed to the concept of 'entrepreneurship.'[47]

Transformational leadership aims at changing the goals and beliefs of followers. It is a 'creative'[48] or 'inspirational'[49] form of leadership, seeking 'novel lines of political action which "inspire" those following [the leader] into imitating his action, associating themselves with him.'[50] Often this is referred to as charismatic or visionary leadership. Transformational leaders aim at altering the parameters of what is politically possible or viable, either in order to secure their place in history or to come closer to their political objectives.[51]

In the context of European integration, decision-makers face fewer institutional constraints on exercising transformational leadership because of the fluidity of the institutional arrangements and the personal and informal nature of the decision-making arrangements of the European Council. Given that integration is an ongoing political process, leaders can – in certain circumstances – find and create opportunities to change it according to their preferences.

While transactional leadership encompasses exchanges (i.e. trading of votes among legislators), negotiations, and compromises, transformational leadership occurs when 'one or more persons *engage* with others in such a way that leaders and followers raise one another to higher levels of motivation and morality.'[52] Ultimately, Burns argues, transformational leadership 'becomes *moral* in that it raises the level of human conduct and ethical aspiration of both leader and led, and thus . . . has a transforming effect on both.'[53]

The purpose of such a typology is to reveal and characterise ideal-types of leadership. It can be expected that, to some extent, most leaders have characteristics of all three leadership forms. Yet different leaders focus more on some issues than others, some are better at persuasion than others, and some are better negotiators than others. What emerges, then, is a detailed – yet broad – overview of diverging forms of exercising leadership.

Developing such an overview is helpful for purposes of this book. A number of diverging leadership forms and styles are clearly identifiable in the history of European integration. To give an example, Jean Monnet and Charles de Gaulle exercised a transformational form of leadership, seeking to fundamentally alter the structures constraining political actions and opportunities.[54] But whereas Monnet generated *indirect* behind-the-scenes leadership by establishing and managing elite networks,[55] Charles de Gaulle's leadership style was *direct*, oriented towards the public, and highly focused on the stature of his personality and reputation.[56] A form of transactional leadership was, for instance, that of Paul-Henri Spaak, which stemmed from his ability and skills in negotiations.[57] Moral leadership is often attributed to the moral advocacy and political activism of figures like Mahatma Gandhi, Mother Teresa, Martin Luther King, or Nelson

Mandela.[58] Postwar European integration did not produce moral leaders of this sort, and the only ones who could come close to being identified with a moral form of leadership might be Winston Churchill and Václav Havel.

The risks of leadership

The ubiquity of the word 'leadership' is such that it is assumed that everybody has the potential to learn how to become a leader. Leadership workshops are now part and parcel of management training programmes in companies, as well as business and public administration curricula in universities. This assumption that everybody can learn to become a leader is flawed, because one intrinsic element of the exercise of leadership is risk-taking. Yet in the abstract and removed environment of a leadership workshop, the pressures and temptations for risk-taking cannot be realistically recreated. What is taught is not leadership, but improved forms of organisational management, as there is a major distinction between management – which is tantamount to the administration of organisational dynamics – and leadership. The manager-politician may be adept at reducing unemployment or improving public services, but the leader-politician ends up altering the political and ideational landscape altogether.

Especially in politics, taking risks – especially uncalculated ones – is not something that is intrinsic to human nature. On the contrary, it is arguably impossible to predict under what kind of circumstances politicians are willing to take risks. Usually, it is at unforeseen moments of great uncertainty, upheaval, and crisis that leaders emerge, and they are often those who were not obvious candidates destined for leadership.[59] Crisis and uncertainty create new incentive structures, open opportunities for those who wish to alter existing practices and forms of behaviour, and enable new voices to be heard.

Politicians – especially in western democracies – have a material incentive to get re-elected, need the support of others to get their projects ahead, and are frequently dependent on external financial sources.[60] All of this acts as a constraint to exercising leadership, because doing so may well upset a politician's chances for re-election, diminish his popularity and support, and be opposed to the interests of those who fund campaigns and the political machinery. Politicians couch themselves in the rhetoric of leadership, change, and transformation, but do in fact face circumstances that mitigate against change. Politicians are routinely confronted with events, problems, challenges, and crisis which they need to react to. Solving and addressing these issues becomes easier when the responsibility for any action is spread among many governmental and parliamentary actors. Sheltering from ultimate responsibility becomes an endemic interest of political actors, because it helps to prolong the tenancy of office and power.

All forms of political leadership make it necessary to upset the people by winning new allies and dropping old ones, departing from existing policy-making practices, and advocating novel ways of understanding a society and its purpose.

44 Leadership as a conceptual framework

Leadership involves the 'tricky art of balancing pragmatism and principle.'[61] Sometimes it is expedient for decision-makers to show flexibility and willingness for accommodation, while at other times it is necessary to show steadfastness and principled resolve. Getting this balancing act wrong can have major consequences for politicians. In 1938–1939, Neville Chamberlain's now-infamous appeasement policy vis-à-vis Hitler's Germany enjoyed significant public and elite support, while Churchill's obsession with principles was seen to be dangerous and misguided. Once the war broke out in 1939, Churchill's position was vindicated, whereas Chamberlain's political career was finished.

The willingness to take risk – both personally and in political terms – is central to the exercise of leadership because without it, decision-makers remain administrators or managers of state activity, not of leaders of it. Leadership involves significant costs, and therefore most politicians tend to shy away from it. The exercise of leadership involves upsetting established patterns of doing things and usually runs counter to the interests of those who have benefitted from these established practices.

Risk-taking comes in numerous forms and levels of intensity. Some leaders act against their advisors or stop listening to them. Others take electoral gambles by calling for an election at a time when their support is unsure. Some leaders stand fast on a controversial issue despite overwhelming public disapproval, while others mobilise support and become the public persona of an initiative. The power, authority, and legitimacy leaders in western democracies have to make decisions do not automatically reduce or augment their willingness to take these risks. Both leadership and risk-taking are contingent on singular circumstances and contexts. It is therefore not surprising that even those who are regarded as great leaders get the balance between accommodation and principle, and continuity and risk-taking, wrong. Winston Churchill proved a gifted leader during World War II, but his failure to accommodate to a changed set of public aspirations and expectations cost him the general election in July 1945. Many leaders lead on one issue, but fail on another. Nelson Mandela's historic presidency is praised for his leadership in reconciling the deeply divided and resentful racial groups in post-Apartheid South Africa, but his record on economic development, corruption, and foreign affairs is more contested. Politicians are not leaders *all the time* and they do not take risks *all the time*.

Leadership and purpose

The study and analysis of leadership is not only concerned with the mechanisms, instruments, and conditions of leadership, but also inquires about its purpose. When leaders take risks, they need to persuasively articulate why they do so and what they think they will achieve in order to overcome opposition to their preferred course of action. In this sense, leadership is connected to a range of discourses, norms, and ideas, which give meaning to political action and which leaders use to rally and advocate their policy preferences. Leaders' choices cannot be solely explained by structural or institutional factors. As Parsons notes, the

> structural circumstances rarely dictate a specific course of action, and even institutional constraints may admit of multiple interpretations. The cognitive lenses through which actors interpret their surroundings shape how they respond to structural or institutional pressures.[62]

In the history of European integration, these 'cognitive lenses' were specific ideas and conceptions of the idea of Europe. An assessment of the impact of leadership on European integration will not only unearth the unique ways in which individuals succeeded in gaining autonomy on European affairs, but will also elucidate to what end leadership was used. This emphasis on the purpose of leadership is strongly underlined in the relevant literature.[63] In the context of this research project, it is helpful to place significant analytical interest on the issue of purpose. After all, when the purpose of leaders' attitudes and policies regarding Europe is taken into account, it becomes clear that competing elite-conceptions of Europe existed – and continue to exist. The major controversies about European integration were often not about technical and procedural matters, but about distinct – and sometimes irreconcilable – understandings of what Europe is and what it should accomplish. In this sense, leaders' interests and preferences regarding Europe were framed and shaped by specific understandings of the concept of Europe. Significant analytical purchase can be gained from elucidating the ideational background of European integration, as well as the way specific leaders linked ideas about Europe to practical policies in specific historical contexts.

In the context of European integration it is illustrative not only to study the leadership of individual decision-makers, but also to ask about the purpose they had in mind when embarking on a specific policy. Over the last six decades, European integration has largely been an elitist project which has often failed to gain strong public support. Due to the nature of cooperation among European nation-states, elite agreements and compromises have been central to the course of the integration process. Major transformations and changes in rules, procedures, institutions, and membership have overwhelmingly occurred when elite conceptions of European integration converged. When leaders' conceptions clashed – as was the case, for instance, between the Gaullist and the technocratic functional-supranational approach during the 'Empty Chair crisis' in 1965–1966 – the result was stagnation and immobility on European affairs.

Given that leadership is contextual, political, and biographical, it is imperative to analyse both the form and the style of leadership, as well as its content. The content and objective of decision-making is important because it sets the parameters for the kind of story, argument, or message a leader develops. Leaders and followers are constantly and inextricably linked in a dense system of interactions, through which a confluence or transformation of their respective interests, preferences, values, and ideas can occur. Constructivists have expanded the list of variables that need to be taken into consideration by including identities, ideas, beliefs, values, norms, language, and symbols as important analytical factors.

The study of elite-conceptions entails to some extent a belief that 'individuals matter, and that a few individuals matter a great deal.'[64] Yet it is necessary to underline once again that the intention is not to develop a 'great man' account of European integration, but to explore what leaders thought about Europe and how that influenced their actions and decisions. As Burns points out,

> 'elite theorists' commit the gross error of equating power and leadership with the assumed power bases of preconceived leaders and power holders, without considering the crucial role of the motivations of leaders and followers.[65]

The examination of diverging elite-conceptions of Europe does not assume a straightforward causal linkage between ideas, interests, and behaviour. Rather, the analysis of elite-conceptions is geared towards revealing those ideas which framed leaders' thinking on Europe, and which permeated the conceptualisation of the national interest vis-à-vis Europe. In this sense, constitutive and generative relationships do not exist in one direction (ideas > interests > behaviour) only. Instead, it is more likely that numerous constitutive mechanisms and feedback mechanisms operate simultaneously and in various directions.[66] Elite-conceptions therefore are not the only influence on leaders' decisions on Europe; the broader historical, economic, and political context also influences their conceptions of it.

From this starting point, the work of 'empirical analysis, then, should involve delineating the resources available and tracing the ways that they are deployed in practice, while sticking close enough to the data that statements about available resources have more of an empirical than a conceptual character.'[67] The task, therefore, is to examine how elite-conceptions of Europe informed leaders' thinking and decisions regarding European integration. This entails looking carefully at historical evidence from the specific contexts in which these interactions occurred, and then tracing the linkages leaders made between ideas, the development of policies, and ultimate decisions and agreements.

At the root of leaders' preferences for European integration rests a particular understanding and interpretation of the idea of Europe, along with national aspirations, historical memories, and institutional legacies. It made a significant difference whether a leader regarded Europe as a cultural community with strong civilisational ties and a powerful cultural-historical heritage and legacy, or as an economically expedient customs union and free trade area through which domestic prosperity could be enhanced. While these differences may not have necessarily led to diverging institutional outcomes, they mattered nonetheless for the way Europe as a political reference point was approached, dealt with, and sold to the public.

The argument made throughout this book is not that some leaders were more European than others. Rather, what the empirical analysis reveals are the different ways leaders thought about Europe. Some leaders wanted to institutionalise European cooperation on a supranational level, while others wanted to leave nation-states in control of European affairs. Some leaders sought to make of Europe a political community, whereas others saw no need for going beyond a customs union and a free trade agreement. Some leaders aimed at overcoming Europe's nationalisms, while others defended its diverse national identities, cultures, and customs. When assessing the impact of leadership on the process of European integration it is therefore imperative to explore the kind of Europe individual leaders sought to construct.

A close relationship exists between leadership on the one hand and the idea of Europe on the other. Leadership had to be exercised by individual decision-makers in order to shape and transform the practices of European integration. In this sense, leadership was necessary in order to advance a particular idea of Europe. Yet it is also leaders' interpretation of the idea of Europe which guides their strategies and policies. The analysis of the impact of leadership and elite-conceptions of Europe on the process of European integration will focus closely on this mutually constitutive relationship.

***

Leadership (on Europe or anything else) is not a static concept. Rather, it is a relational, fluid, and intersubjective notion. Leadership is a dynamic social relationship which can develop and falter over time. Leadership does not mean that a single decision-maker can single-handedly determine a political outcome. The concept does suggest, however, that the behaviour of individual statesmen is not completely predetermined and constrained by social structures either. Leaders willing to take risks can alter constraints on policies, transform the objectives of policy-making, and influence their implementation. The next three chapters examine how they did so at three different moments in European integration.

What is derived from this historical analysis is not testable hypotheses for a general theory of leadership but pieces of evidence which support the view that leadership is a contingent social relationship. Light is shed on how personal contacts among leaders, trust, shared worldviews, historical memory, and perceptions influenced European integration. Leaders who enjoyed autonomy for formulating European policies were also more successful in lending their support to a particular European initiative. Guy Mollet, in 1956, achieved this autonomy by linking his European policies to the fate of his government on an unrelated issue (the conflict in Algeria). Other leaders, such as John Major in the early 1990s, never managed to achieve this autonomy, facing a politicised domestic constituency on European affairs. In analysing three key developments in European integration, it can be shown that the integration process and the EU's institutions are more dependent on elite political backing, goodwill, and supportive leadership than is widely assumed.

Notes

1 T.G. Otte, 'Eyre Crowe and British Foreign Policy: A Cognitive Map,' in *Personalities, War, and Diplomacy: Essays in International History*, T.G. Otte and C.A. Pagedas eds. (London: Frank Cass, 1997), p. 15.
2 L.J. Edinger, 'Political Science and Political Biography,' in *Political Leadership: Readings for an Emerging Field*, G.D. Paige ed. (New York: Free Press, 1972), p. 226.
3 G. Peele, 'Leadership and Politics: A Case for a Closer Relationship?' *Leadership* 1 (2) (2005): 188.
4 See M. Foley, *Political Leadership: Themes, Contexts and Critiques* (Oxford: Oxford University Press, 2013); M. Foley, *John Major, Tony Blair and a Conflict of Leadership: Collision Course* (Manchester: Manchester University Press, 2002); N.O. Keohane, *Thinking about Leadership* (Princeton: Princeton University Press, 2010); J.S. Nye, *The Powers to Lead* (Oxford: Oxford University Press, 2008).
5 P. Pomper, 'Historians and Individual Agency,' *History and Theory* 35 (3) (1996): 281–308.
6 T.L. Price, *Leadership Ethics: An Introduction* (Cambridge: Cambridge University Press, 2008).
7 See W. Isaacson ed., *Profiles in Leadership: Historians on the Elusive Quality of Greatness* (New York: Norton, 2010).
8 A comprehensive overview of different definitions of leadership can be found in R.M. Stogdill, *Handbook of Leadership: A Survey of Theory and Research* (New York: Free Press, 1974) and G. Paige, *Political Leadership: Readings for an Emerging Field* (New York: Free Press, 1972).
9 L.J. Edinger, 'The Comparative Analysis of Political Leadership,' *Comparative Politics* 7 (2) (1975): 257.
10 Peele, 'Leadership,' p. 192. The notion of innovative leaders is discussed and analysed in G. Sheffer ed., *Innovative Leaders in International Politics* (Albany: State University of New York Press, 1993).
11 E.C. Hargrove and J.E. Owens, 'Introduction: Political Leadership in Context,' in *Leadership in Context*, E.C. Hargrove and J.E. Owens eds. (Lanham, MD: Rowman and Littlefield, 2003), p. 4.
12 *Ibid.*, pp. 1–2.
13 Pomper, 'Historians'.
14 R.C. Tucker, 'Personality and Political Leadership,' *Political Science Quarterly* 92 (3) (1977): 383–393.
15 *Ibid.*, p. 384.
16 See J.M. Post, *Leaders and Their Followers in a Dangerous World: The Psychology of Political Behavior* (Ithaca: Cornell University Press, 2004).
17 J.C. Rost, *Leadership for the Twenty-First Century* (Westport: Praeger, 1993).
18 See J.M. Burns, *Leadership* (New York, NY: Harper and Row, 1978).
19 Edinger, 'Comparative Analysis,' pp. 255–256.
20 L.G. Seligman, 'The Study of Leadership,' *The American Political Science Review* 44 (4) (1950): 912.
21 *Ibid.*, 912–914.
22 *Ibid.*
23 Seligman, 'Study,' p. 912.
24 Indicative of the constructivist literature in International Relations are Finnemore, *National Interest*; T. Hopf, *Social Construction of International Politics: Identities and Foreign Policies, Moscow, 1955 & 1999* (Ithaca: Cornell University Press, 2002); P. Katzenstein, *The Culture of National Security: Norms and Identity in World Politics* (New York: Columbia University Press, 1996); M.E. Keck and K. Sikkink, *Activists beyond Borders: Advocacy Networks in International Politics*

(Ithaca: Cornell University Press, 1998); A. Klotz, 'Norms Reconstituting Interests: Global Racial Equality and U.S. Sanctions against South Africa,' *International Organization* 49 (3) (1995): 451–478; C. Reus-Smit, *The Moral Purpose of the State: Culture, Social Identity, and Institutional Rationality in International Relations* (Princeton: Princeton University Press, 1999); A. Wendt, *Social Theory of International Politics* (Cambridge: Cambridge University Press, 1999) among others.
25 Burns, *Leadership*, p. 11.
26 See C.J. Friedrich, 'Political Leadership and the Problem of the Charismatic Power,' *The Journal of Politics* 23 (1) (1961): 3–24.
27 Burns, *Leadership*, p. 19.
28 J. Pfeffer, 'The Ambiguity of Leadership,' *The Academy of Management Review* 2 (1) (1977): 10. This congruence is especially salient for leaders of democracies: see R.C. Tucker, *Politics as Leadership* (Columbia: University of Missouri Press, 1981).
29 O.F. Kirkeby, *The Virtue of Leadership* (Copenhagen: Copenhagen Business School Press, 2008), p. 17.
30 Foley, *Political Leadership*, p. 255.
31 D. Beach, *The Dynamics of European Integration: Why and When EU Institutions Matter* (Basingstoke: Palgrave Macmillan, 2005), p. 31.
32 L. Helms, *Presidents, Prime Ministers, and Chancellors: Executive Leadership in Western Democracies* (Basingstoke: Palgrave Macmillan, 2005).
33 Hargrove and Owens, 'Introduction,' p. 6.
34 *Ibid.*
35 *Ibid.*, p. 4.
36 Beach, *Dynamics*, p. 29.
37 Burns, *Leadership*, p. 18.
38 *Ibid.*, p. 19.
39 *Ibid.*, p. 18.
40 *Ibid.*, p. 19 (emphasis in the original).
41 Pfeffer, 'Ambiguity,' p. 107.
42 *Ibid.*
43 Burns, *Leadership*, p. 18.
44 J.M. Burns, *Transforming Leadership: A New Pursuit of Happiness* (New York: Grove, 2004).
45 M.G. Hermann, 'Leaders, Leadership, and Flexibility: Influences on Heads of Government as Negotiators and Mediators,' *Annals of the American Academy of Political and Social Science* 542 (1995), Flexibility in International Negotiation and Mediation: 148–167.
46 K.W. Kuhnert and P. Lewis, 'Transactional and Transformational Leadership: A Constructive/Developmental Analysis,' *The Academy of Management Review* 12 (4) (1987): 649.
47 See O.R. Young, 'The Politics of International Regime Formation: Managing Natural Resources and the Environment,' *International Organization* 43 (3) (1989): 355.
48 Tucker, 'Personality,' p. 385.
49 Friedrich, 'Political Leadership,' p. 15.
50 *Ibid.*, p. 21.
51 Burns, *Transforming Leadership*.
52 Burns, *Leadership*, p. 20.
53 *Ibid.*
54 H. Gardner, *Leading Minds: An Anatomy of Leadership* (New York: Basic Books, 1995).

55 M. Bromberger and S. Bromberger, *Jean Monnet and the United States of Europe* (New York: Coward-McCann, 1969); D. Brinkley and C.B. Hackett eds., *Jean Monnet: The Path to European Unity* (London: Macmillan, 1991); F. Duchêne, *Jean Monnet: The First Statesman of Interdependence* (London: W.W. Norton, 1994); F.J. Fransen, *The Supranational Politics of Jean Monnet: Ideas and Origins of the European Community* (Westport: Greenwood, 2001); M. Holland, 'Jean Monnet and the Federal Functionalist Approach to European Union,' in *Visions of European Unity*, P. Murray and P. Rich eds. (Boulder: Westview, 1996), pp. 93–108; R. Mayne, 'The Role of Jean Monnet,' *Government and Opposition* 2 (1966): 350–360; E. Roussel, *Jean Monnet, 1888–1979* (Paris: Arthème Fayard, 1996); W. Yondorf, 'Monnet and the Action Committee: The Formative Period of the European Communities,' *International Organization* 19 (4) (1965): 885–912.
56 P.G. Cerny, *The Politics of Grandeur: Ideological Aspects of de Gaulle's Foreign Policy* (Cambridge: Cambridge University Press, 1980); E. Jouve, *Le Général de Gaulle et la Construction de l'Europe*, Vol. 1 (Paris: Librairie Générale de Droit et de Jurisprudence, 1967); R. Massip, *De Gaulle et l'Europe* (Paris: Garimard, 1963); L. Pattison de Ménil, *Who Speaks for Europe? The Vision of Charles de Gaulle* (London: Weidenfeld and Nicolson, 1977).
57 M. Dumoulin, *Spaak* (Brussels: Editions Racine, 1999).
58 See Gardner, *Leading Minds*; Hermann, 'Leaders'.
59 Foley, *Political Leadership*; Nye, *Powers to Lead*.
60 Helms, *Presidents*.
61 Isaacson, *Profiles*, p. 11.
62 C. Parsons, *A Certain Idea of Europe* (Ithaca: Cornell University Press, 2003), p. 5.
63 See P. Murray and P. Rich eds., *Visions of European Unity* (Boulder: Westview, 1996).
64 Gardner, *Leading Minds*, p. 295.
65 Burns, *Leadership*, pp. 22–23.
66 T. Risse, '"Let's Argue!:" Communicative Action in World Politics,' *International Organization* 54 (1) (2000): 1–39; J. Checkel, 'The Constructivist Turn in International Relations Theory,' *World Politics* 50 (2) (1998): 324–348; H. Müller, 'Arguing, Bargaining and All That: Communicative Action, Rationalist Theory and the Logic of Appropriateness in International Relations,' *European Journal of International Relations* 10 (3) (2004): 395–435.
67 P.T. Jackson, 'Making Sense of Making Sense: Configurational Analysis and the Double Hermeneutic,' in *Interpretation and Method: Empirical Research Methods and the Interpretive Turn*, second edition, D. Yanow and P. Schwartz-Shea eds. (Armonk: M.E. Sharpe, 2014), pp. 267–283.

Part II
Leadership and critical junctures of European integration

Part II

3 Personal diplomacy and trust, 1955–1957

The Treaty of Paris – which was to establish a European Defence Community (EDC) – was rejected in the French National Assembly on 30 August 1954. The five other signatory states had already ratified the treaty, and it was incumbent on the French parliament to pass it. The proposal under consideration – which French Prime Minster René Pleven had tabled in 1950 – contained measures to rearm West Germany while embedding it in a European institutional framework and army. Although the proposal had been initiated by France and counted on US support,[1] it laid bare a 'new cleavage on Europe,' especially in France.[2] Political elites and the French public were deeply divided about the idea of creating a common European army with German participation only nine years after the end of World War II.[3] Communists and Gaullists were adamant in their absolute opposition to the EDC, while other mainstream parties were internally divided on the issue.[4] Nationalist sentiments eventually combined with 'anti-federalist opinion,'[5] as well as the painful memories of the German occupation of France, preventing the ratification of the EDC by a substantial parliamentary majority.[6]

The French parliamentary rejection of the Treaty of Paris was a shock and setback for the early supporters of European integration.[7] While the issue of West German rearmament was settled soon after by incorporating the newly created *Bundeswehr* into NATO and the WEU,[8] the early hopes for and optimism about the prospects for European cooperation and unity had taken a major hit.[9] Moreover, the episode illustrated the extent to which many politicians across Europe remained wary of Germany and its rearmament, and sought further mechanisms to contain it.[10]

Despite this setback, an idea for a new approach to integration came about as soon as the heated French debate about the EDC had subsided. Since September 1954, the United States had repeatedly tried to commit European governments to not giving up on the path of integration.[11] In early 1955, Dutch and Belgian policy-makers circulated first plans for a new effort at European integration, focusing this time on the economy. In the eyes of the Dutch and Belgians, the EDC plan had failed because it had been over-ambitious. Their remedy was a more cautious approach. Future efforts at political integration would have to be achieved by less politically contentious means, through long-term gradual economic integration.[12] The failure of the EDC made 'more oblique' economic forms of integration necessary.[13] Political unification of Europe was now to be accommodated in non-supranational arrangements for economic integration, with nation-states wielding heavy influence over future decision-making processes.[14] In a 4 April 1955 memo from Dutch Foreign Minister Johan Beyen to his Belgian counterpart, Paul-Henri Spaak, the first sketches of a new initiative aiming at the creation of a European Common Market were drawn up.[15]

Also in reaction to the EDC debacle, Jean Monnet, the president of the European Coal and Steel Community (ECSC) High Authority and a driving force of integration in his own right, resigned in February 1955. Monnet wanted to establish an informal elite lobby group so as to exercise indirect influence over a network of key players in regards to pro-integrationist European policies.[16] One of his main successes was to get the support of the West German Social Democratic Party (SPD) for his pet project, Euratom. Needing a replacement for Monnet, the foreign ministers of the six ECSC countries met in the Sicilian resort of Messina from 1–3 June 1955 to discuss Monnet's successor and the Dutch-Belgian proposals.[17]

The core aim of this initiative was a process of gradual horizontal – and not sectoral – economic integration.[18] This entailed abolishing intra-European tariffs and quotas, creating a customs union, establishing a common external tariff, and harmonising economic policies. The intention was to stay clear of sensitive military and political issues as well as the more narrow, industry-specific approach of previous integration efforts (such as in coal and steel). Due to the EDC fiasco, a viable new alternative for integration was sought.[19]

In spite of its economic nature, the Common Market proposal contained an important political dimension. It was expected that economic integration would produce 'closer relations' between member states, thereby gradually heightening the interdependence among them to such an extent that war would become unthinkable.[20] The promoters were 'highly conscious' of these aims and their political implications.[21] This new technical pattern for integration proposed starting with a customs union and ECSC integration, through which closer political cooperation would gradually emerge.[22] Messina was thus regarded as the beginning of a new attempt at integrating Western Europe through economic means. The conference posited practical and immediate objectives for incremental economic integration,[23] yet ultimately aimed at 'selling' political integration through economic means, thus achieving political 'integration through stealth.'[24] Spaak in particular sought to 'masquerade' the proposals' political essence.[25]

Horizontal economic integration was not a popular move, since it would mean stronger economic competition, further liberalisation, and an end to protectionism and *dirigisme*.[26] Especially in Fourth Republic France, which was by then perceived as the 'sick man of Europe,'[27] there were numerous reservations in economic circles, which were steeped in a tradition of state intervention and protectionism.[28] In addition, the public mood in France for European integration had been soured by the EDC controversies, its political system was highly unstable, and it was embroiled in colonial uprisings in Indochina and a worsening conflict in Algeria.[29] If this had not been enough, Britain's ambivalent attitude and reluctance to participate in European initiatives,[30] as well as the strong growth in West German economic power and public confidence, which troubled many of its neighbours, did not augur well for the prospects of the Messina proposals.[31] To make any new integrationist initiative succeed, substantial political will would have to be marshalled.

This became the task of intergovernmental negotiations held in Brussels following the Messina conference.[32] Throughout the negotiations, the severity of the numerous obstacles and widespread opposition to the proposals became ever more apparent.[33] The Common Market plan tabled at Messina was based on only vague public and political support. Most importantly, the French mood for integration and supranational institutions was subdued, and French business elites remained wary of trade liberalisation.[34] In West Germany, senior government figures such as Ludwig Erhard and Franz-Josef Strauss questioned both the economic rationale of the Common Market and the wisdom of pooling atomic energy policy in a common agency.[35] Last but not least, Britain did not take part in the negotiations until November 1955, sending a relatively junior observer – Under-Secretary at the Board of Trade, Russell Bretherton – as representative.[36] All major West European governments, business leaders, and publics were either largely uninterested in the Messina proposals or – at least partially – opposed to them.[37]

The conventional explanations of how the Treaties of Rome ultimately came about either claim that it 'was a response to the expansion of foreign trade'[38] or that 'narrower commercial concerns – above all, export promotion' determined national preferences and policies.[39] These explanations tend to overlook the extent to which these proposals on European integration were controversial in political terms at the time. Deactivating these political sensitivities and opposition required a great deal of political will and accommodation by national leaders, without whose personal interventions the Common Market proposal might not have prevailed.

The Brussels negotiations began with an important personal intervention. At Messina, French Foreign Minister Antoine Pinay had disregarded his instructions and agreed for further negotiations on the Common Market to be taken up under the guidance of a 'political personality.'[40] Spaak was chosen to chair the Brussels talks, which commenced on 9 July 1955. Pinay's oversight – deliberate or not – set in motion a prolonged process of intergovernmental bargaining, which lasted from July 1955 until the spring of 1956.[41] In this time, the Spaak and the other representatives turned 'Pinay's small step into a major community project.'[42]

By late 1955, when Spaak was supposed to deliver a first report on the work of the committee, little progress had been made. The negotiations had become entangled and stalled on numerous technical issues relating to the scope of economic integration, the mandatory nature of tariff reductions, the fate of agriculture, the status of France's overseas territories and colonies, and differences over Community ownership of nuclear fissile material. A ministerial gathering at Noordwijk in September 1955 proceeded without a draft report; the report was only published in April 1956 and discussed at yet another conference, this time in Venice, in May 1956. The so-called Spaak Report,[43] written by his closest advisers, later became the basis for the Treaties of Rome, which established Euratom and the Common Market. What Spaak had done throughout these prolonged negotiations was to succeed in linking both proposals and pursuing them as a take-it-or-leave-it 'package deal' that could not be easily unpicked.[44] While France was originally more interested in a common nuclear energy agency than the Common Market,[45] the opposite was true for West Germany.[46] The United States supported both proposals.[47]

Moreover, viable alternatives to the Common Market plan continued to be discussed and pursued. French elites – encouraged by former Prime Minister Pierre Mendès-France – were either susceptible to the idea of forging closer intergovernmental cooperation on European affairs under Franco-British direction or thought that traditional bilateral agreements with Britain and West Germany were most realistic.[48] The fact that the French government altered its position on the Common Market proposal had less to do with economic and geopolitical factors – which weighed heavily on the Fourth Republic – than with a change of political leadership that took place in January 1956.[49]

Parliamentary elections in France in January 1956 significantly altered the prospects of the *rélance*, as this period in the history of European integration came to be known. The elections produced a 'razor-thin legislative victory' for a left-centre coalition campaigning on a 'social-policy platform,'[50] and produced a fragile 'parliamentary situation where the only possible majority was one made of pro-integration parties.'[51] Guy Mollet was unexpectedly chosen as Premier over Pierre Mendès-France, mainly because he opposed Algerian independence and partly because he shared 'pro-community sympathies' with President René Coty.[52] The resulting change of government in Paris brought new impetus to Franco-German relations, as well as a more conciliatory French stance in the Brussels negotiations.

Mollet formed a cabinet in which pro-European politicians (such as Foreign Minister Christian Pineau and Secretary of State for Foreign Affairs Maurice Faure) took decisive control over European policy.[53] Mollet was firmly committed to Euratom and was less reserved about the Common Market proposal than either of his predecessors, Mendès-France or Edgar Faure.[54] Faced with the burdens of a deteriorating economy and increasing balance-of-payments problems, as well as the Algerian conflict, the new government decided that the Common Market could indeed be a solution to, rather than a catalyst of, France's malaise.[55] This new attitude towards European integration was reflected in Mollet's inaugural speech of 31 January 1956, as well as in the assessment of foreign governments.[56]

Yet Mollet had to fight his own doubts, as well as an uphill battle against public disinterest, bureaucratic opposition, and the major concerns of industrialists, farmers, and trade unions alike.[57] In April 1956, the Spaak Report received a 'glacial' reception in French bureaucratic circles, and neither agricultural nor business associations were enthusiastic about creating a Common Market.[58] Subsequent French efforts to proceed with Euratom first and delay the Common Market faltered in the face of resistance from the other countries.[59] Faced with these difficulties and with an increasing feeling of 'desperation,'[60] Mollet decided to pursue numerous alternatives to the Common Market and Euratom *junktim*. One of these was the secret and undiscussed plan for an Anglo-French economic union which Mollet proposed – in September 1956 – to British Prime Minister Anthony Eden. This 'daring solo diplomatic foray' by Mollet was 'rebuffed' by Eden,[61] because Britain questioned its economic viability and political repercussions in the days leading up to the joint British, French, and Israeli invasion of Suez.

Faced with Eden's non-committal European stance, Mollet somewhat reluctantly decided in September 1956 to push for the package deal and secure its ratification.[62] Once his mind was made up, he and the other pro-integrationist members of his cabinet became more proactive in taking on the critics of the *relance* directly. Throughout the summer of 1956, the key figures in the French government – including Mollet himself – had already lobbied interests groups in support of the Common Market and Euratom. While Euratom was widely welcomed in French political and economic circles,[63] opposition to the Common Market was solid. Promising numerous safeguards and transition clauses, the Mollet government succeeded first in winning over those trade unions which were not directly linked to or controlled by the French Communist Party.[64] Yet French industrialist and farmer associations proved more resistant to Mollet's pro-European charm offensive, being especially wary of supranational institutions.[65] Their full support was only secured much later, after Mollet had gained a series of German concessions on the Common Market, particularly with regards to the inclusion of France's overseas territories.[66]

The French change of attitude towards European policy in general, and the Common Market in particular, reflected well upon the Brussels negotiations. Once France had accepted the Spaak report and Mollet had succeeded in getting unexpectedly strong parliamentary support for Euratom in July 1956,[67] the technical negotiations under Spaak began to make substantial progress. Yet the final outcome of the Brussels negotiations was still uncertain, due to unresolved bilateral issues between France and Germany. Having decided in September 1956 to make a push for the Common Market and Euratom, Mollet also decided to settle these bilateral obstacles with Adenauer.[68]

The Adenauer-Mollet agreements of 1956–1957

Directly affecting the fate of the Brussels negotiations were a number of unresolved Franco-German differences, many of which have now been almost forgotten. For instance, a major problem was the status of the Saar, which had been under French administration since 1945. Moreover, the Brussels negotiations themselves produced differences between the two countries, which needed to be addressed in order to make the Common Market plan work. Examples of these were the French desire for harmonisation in social legislation and its demand for inclusion of its overseas territories into the Common Market framework. Given that France and Germany were the key to a successful outcome of the *relance*, the resolution of their bilateral differences was of great European importance.[69]

With the benefit of hindsight it can be said that Mollet's victory in the elections of January 1956 effectively increased the pace and closeness of Franco-German relations. He ended up facilitating bilateral negotiations over the Saar and reaffirming Adenauer's opinion that a Common Market with France was both viable and beneficial.[70] Yet at the time, Mollet's commitment to European integration had been tainted by ambiguous statements and contradictory policies in other policy areas,[71] and Adenauer had residual suspicions of Mollet's socialist policies and ideological inclinations. It was not until mid-1956 that Mollet and Adenauer managed to establish closer personal relations.[72] Adenauer in particular came to trust and appreciate Mollet, but retained some doubts about other members of the French government (notably Foreign Minister Pineau), as well as the Socialist Party (SFIO) (Jules Moch being a case in point).[73]

Meeting in Luxembourg in June 1956 and again in Bonn in September 1956, Adenauer and Mollet first proceeded to negotiate an agreement regarding the Saar.[74] Franco-German relations had suffered from the unexpected outcome of the Saar referendum of October 1955, when a clear majority of the Saar's inhabitants rejected a plan for Europeanising the territory, something which Adenauer had personally supported and publicly advocated.[75] In consequence, it came as a great relief when a treaty regulating the territory's return to German political and economic jurisdiction (after a three year transition period) was signed on 27 October 1956. Important for the Brussels negotiations were not the details of the Saar compromise, but the de-blocking of an increasingly stagnant Franco-German bilateral agenda.[76] The solution to the Saar issue established a pattern of Franco-German cooperation, which has greatly impacted European integration ever since.[77]

The increasing closeness of Adenauer and Mollet reflected positively on the Brussels negotiations.[78] German negotiators had often been frustrated with French tactics, a situation which undermined Adenauer's pro-integrationist position and resolve.[79] It was only through personal meetings with Mollet that Adenauer became convinced of the sincerity of Mollet's European objectives and leadership. Mollet, whose fear of French isolation had dramatically increased after September 1956, realised that French obstructionism could have the paradoxical effect of turning Adenauer away from France to support either an Atlanticist or more independent foreign policy, to the detriment of France. He therefore decided to use Adenauer's 'will to succeed'[80] to build a Franco-German entente which would strengthen French influence over Germany. Adenauer, in turn, came to realise the grave vulnerability of Mollet's government and the French Fourth Republic, and decided to defend Mollet's position and tactics against criticism at home.[81] In two major instances of summit diplomacy, the personal intervention and leadership of Adenauer and Mollet can be clearly illustrated.

The first of these moments of personal diplomacy came about on 6 November 1956, when Adenauer visited Mollet in Paris at the height of the Suez crisis. The French government interpreted Adenauer's visit as an important gesture and 'an act of solidarity' with France.[82] Half of the French Council of Ministers turned up at the Gare de l'Est to greet a much-surprised Adenauer.[83] In what became an emotional and symbolic meeting, Adenauer reaffirmed his commitment to build Europe together with France.[84] This significantly enhanced Mollet's trust of Adenauer.[85] *The Times* reported that the summit had noticeably reduced French doubts about West German policy and motives.[86] It also reassured Mollet to stay the course on his pro-integrationist European policies, which were so controversial at home.

The meeting had been scheduled in advance and was supposed to deal with the Saar agreement. However, the uprising and subsequent Soviet intervention in Hungary, as well as the abandonment of the military operations in Suez, completely changed its nature and significance.[87] Adenauer was with Mollet in Paris when Eden informed him of his unilateral decision to abandon military operations in Suez due to American pressure.[88] Adenauer's visit thus occurred in a context of great confusion, urgency, and crisis. He later claimed that it would have been 'catastrophically wrong' to postpone or re-schedule his visit, as some members of his government and the opposition had advised him to do.[89] As French Foreign Minister Christian Pineau reckoned, at the summit Mollet and Adenauer became personally committed to seeing the Common Market proposals succeed – under Franco-German partnership. Both Adenauer and Mollet, in their own way, drew the conclusion that Suez was a turning point that somehow made closer European integration more necessary, realistic, and desirable.[90] The crucial outcome of Adenauer's visit to Paris was that both leaders began to mobilise their personal political capital to secure a deal on the Common Market. Their goodwill towards each other was now clearer than ever before, and Adenauer and Mollet began to lose their residual hesitations to become personally involved in and identified with the fate of the Common Market. In his biography of Adenauer, Charles Williams calls the rapport that emerged between the two leaders 'almost idyllic.'[91] Their mutual sense of the merits, purposes, and mechanisms of European integration began to overlap more tightly. Spending little time on technical details, their much-improved personal rapport helped to break the stalemate on outstanding Franco-German differences in the Brussels negotiations.[92] Both leaders came to an agreement so quickly that they scarcely read through the text of what they had agreed to, and that from that moment onwards, 'the negotiations proceeded at speed to a completed treaty text.'[93]

The second crucial instance of personal diplomacy by Adenauer and Mollet occurred in Paris on 19–20 February 1957. At this meeting, they resolved the controversial inclusion of the French overseas territories into the Common Market. Knowing that trade between metropolitan France and its overseas territories was greater in value than trade between France and its ECSC partners, Mollet had decided to insist on the inclusion of French territories into the Common Market in October 1956.[94] He wanted an agreement that would 'bind their European partners to a permanent responsibility' for the territories' welfare.[95] Hammering out this compromise demanded substantial concessions from both sides, which were significantly disputed in Paris and Bonn. Mollet insisted that he would only be able to sign and secure ratification for the Common Market if it could be seen as a European solution to the challenges facing the French Union. Germany was asked to make substantial financial contributions to the French overseas territories through a common investment fund.[96] This also meant giving preferential trade access to products from these territories – a move that was highly controversial in free trade-oriented Germany.

Surprisingly, Adenauer readily agreed to these concessions, since he was convinced that Mollet was running out of time to deliver French parliamentary agreement for the Common Market.[97] Between 15 and 22 January 1957, Mollet initiated a pre-ratification debate in the National Assembly to test support for the European Economic Community (EEC) and Euratom treaties.[98] Adenauer chose to follow the Common Market plan, even when this entailed weighty financial contributions to the French colonial cause, for which there was almost no support in Germany.[99] Moreover, upon his return from Paris, Adenauer defended his controversial financial concessions, making the unconvincing claim that this would open up new markets for German exports and prevent Soviet encroachment in Africa and the Middle East.[100] Until the Treaties of Rome were signed, he also attempted to conceal the internal quarrels about his European policies, even delaying a parliamentary debate on the matter.[101]

It is in this specific context that the impact of the personal relationship between Adenauer and Mollet mattered. Adenauer in particular decided that financial aid and diverging economic interests should not get in the way of a Franco-German rapprochement.[102] For Adenauer, reconciliation with France was both a pressing foreign policy goal and a personal objective. Had Adenauer's and Mollet's behaviour been solely determined by commercial interests, it is doubtful that the compromises reached would have been agreed to.[103]

Both leaders were willing to make painful concessions and exercise leadership because they already trusted each other and because their European objectives began to overlap. Their leadership did not just consist of managing the timing and scope of the Common Market proposal, since economic currents had 'made the trend toward trade liberalisation inevitable.'[104] What both leaders had in common was not a similarity of national interests, but a personal meeting of minds and a mutual commitment to an integrated Europe under Franco-German leadership. Both were willing to stake their personal political capital and prestige on the Common Market proposal, something that was neither popular nor necessarily politically expedient.

Personal diplomacy and the rélance

The negotiations leading to the Treaties of Rome were characterised by numerous instances of direct personal interventions and leadership, but three prominent examples stand out.

First, on several occasions the viability of the Brussels negotiations hinged upon Spaak's negotiation skills, ability to persuade, and personal engagement. Participants in the negotiations repeatedly credited Spaak for his management of the Brussels negotiations, claiming that it was essential for their eventual success.[105]

Second, as seen above, the interventions of Adenauer and Mollet were crucial. As representatives of two of the most significant political and economic powers, their choices and behaviour were of utmost importance. Adenauer had long been a recognised pro-integrationist, who had supported previous efforts at integration – including the EDC.[106] Given his advanced age, growing domestic opposition to his foreign and European policies, and challenges to his authority, other European leaders became convinced that the Common Market was only feasible so long as Adenauer was in power.[107] The fallout of the Algerian conflict and the Suez crisis for Mollet's pro-integrationist government further exacerbated this sense of urgency. Observers of the Brussels negotiations claimed that any deal on the Common Market had to be reached before Adenauer and Mollet lost office. This urgency was recognised and used for political pressure.[108] The willingness to make unpopular concessions, tackle domestic opposition, and openly sell a controversial European initiative to a disinterested public were the hallmarks of the Adenauer-Mollet leadership constellation.

Third involved the ambiguous British stance towards the Common Market. Spaak, Adenauer, and Mollet wanted British participation and were willing to make significant concessions to accommodate the UK. Alas, Eden declined to get involved, expecting that without the UK the Brussels negotiations would simply collapse.[109] Eden could have chosen to exercise significant leadership on Europe, as he had done in late 1954 when he engineered the NATO/WEU deal.[110] As Prime Minister, he had resources at his disposal, governed Western Europe's most powerful state, and commanded personal prestige and influence among Western leaders. Also, after 1945 it seemed that 'Britain's reputation, built up by its survival of the Nazi onslaught and participation in Europe's liberation, stood high enough for it to take the leadership of the continental nations.'[111] Yet Eden's choice cannot be solely explained in structural terms of defending national interests. Rather, he was unwilling to invest political capital into an initiative which he thought would fail.

Due to Eden's marginal interest, innovations in European integration were left by default to Spaak, Adenauer, and Mollet. Their choice for the Common Market was influenced by external events, but also shaped by their own ideas about European integration. They shared pro-integrationist convictions, albeit not always overlapping ones. They used the renewed momentum on European integration to address specific national priorities: Spaak intended a strong institutional European framework to embed Germany, Adenauer wanted to regain international influence, and Mollet sought to modernise the French economy and develop a new relationship with its overseas territories.[112] While using the rhetoric of European unity in public, their objectives were less visionary and more limited. The Common Market was not chosen on the basis of an idealistic vision of a united Europe, but neither did national interests determine the behaviour of leaders.

Paul-Henri Spaak: the skilled negotiator

Paul-Henri Spaak – a former Socialist Prime Minister of Belgium and its Foreign Minister throughout the *relance* – was widely credited for the eventual success of the Common Market.[113] His leadership is a classic example of transactional leadership, i.e. the wherewithal to broker deals. Like most other members of the Parti Socialiste Belge (PSB), Spaak was generally supportive of initiatives on European integration.[114] As the representative of a small country with limited power and resources, he could not force compromises on Britain, France, or West Germany, but could only induce them to find agreements among themselves.[115] He therefore attempted to become a 'chief architect'[116] of interstate bargains among the major players.

In contrast to Mollet and Adenauer, Spaak had to make significant adjustments to his preferences on European integration. His key objectives were the containment of Germany through common institutions, British participation in European integration, and the acceptance of the principle of supranationality. Only on the first of these objectives did Spaak achieve what he thought was necessary. In a letter to Eden, Spaak reaffirmed that his core European goal was to find a de facto solution to the 'German question,' so long as Adenauer was still in power:[117]

> European integration gives Germany a framework which limits its expansion and establishes a community of interest which guarantees it and which guarantees us against certain [German] temptations and adventures.[118]

Similarly, in a February 1956 meeting with Harold Macmillan, then still Chancellor of the Exchequer, Spaak suggested that 'he had never been interested in EDC or any other of the European groupings except from the point of view of containing Germany. He thought this [the Common Market plan] was the last opportunity.'[119] Believing that a European settlement of the German question would only happen while Adenauer was still in office, Spaak was convinced he was acting against time. His 'urgent desire for speed' in the negotiations, which worried British decision-makers, was nonetheless also an important catalyst for the Common Market deal.[120] Spaak's behaviour fostered the so-called rush to Rome[121] of late 1956, when it became clear that only Adenauer and Mollet could viably deliver on the Common Market. Whereas Adenauer faced elections in September 1957, Mollet's governing coalition was under severe strain due to Algeria and the fallout from the Suez crisis.

Spaak intended to contain German power by means of economic integration and through a supranational institutional framework. While economic integration would be a practical mechanism to prevent German aggression while embedding it closely in the Western alliance, a supranational institutional framework would enable his native Belgium to keep a voice in the decision-making process.[122] Yet supranationality was the first of his objectives that he had to alter his stance on when the lack of French elite support for supranational institutions became obvious in the wake of the EDC failure in 1954.

It was harder for Spaak to perform a pragmatic adjustment on the political circumstances and historical sentiments around the issue of British participation in European integration. His affinity to Britain was well-established, having spent over four years in England during World War II.[123] He 'regarded Europe without the leadership of Britain as having no future.'[124] He was even prepared to find a '*système particulier*' for Britain, in order to ensure its participation in European integration.[125] He insisted that the negotiations should provide for an essential British role in Europe.[126] However, despite his flexibility in trying to accommodate the British, Spaak was not an Atlanticist willing to fundamentally alter – or even abandon – his objective of German enmeshment in a European order in order to secure British approval. Britain's hostile attitude towards all forms of supranational integration disappointed him.[127] He drew a painful lesson from his experiences with British policies towards Europe:

> . . . I had consistently advocated Britain's participation in the building of Europe and had even urged that she should be Europe's leader. However, after Churchill's return to power I came to realise that we must do without Britain's support if we were to make any headway. This was a severe disappointment. I decided to support Jean Monnet's view: 'Create a United Europe and Britain will join. It is by succeeding that you will convince her.'[128]

Having resigned himself to the fact that Britain would take part in neither Euratom nor the Common Market, Spaak nonetheless longed for a Franco-German compromise on European integration. Given the numerous obstacles, British opposition, and a general lack of enthusiasm for the initiative across Europe, it became Spaak's challenge to keep the negotiations going. He argued that '[w]here there is a political will, there are no insurmountable technical problems. Where there is no such will, each technical problem becomes a pretext for the failure of negotiations.'[129] In consequence, the quest was to prevent technical considerations from wrecking the outcome of the negotiations. This is where Spaak's contribution and transactional leadership mattered. By preventing a French withdrawal, Spaak sustained the necessary momentum for the Common Market initiative to survive.

In his handling of the Brussels negotiations, Spaak was aided by Pierre Uri and Hans von der Groeben, two trusted advisers he had chosen as his assistants. While Uri and von der Groeben wrote the Spaak report of April 1956 (which became the basis for the Treaties of Rome), Spaak aimed to structure the negotiations. His negotiation style and techniques were widely accepted to have facilitated the compromise that was finally reached in March 1957. Among the features of his 'closed diplomacy' approach[130] was Spaak's accommodation of French sensitivities. He treated their demands with special care, dispelling the protectionist instincts of the French political and economic elite, and held most negotiations in French as a concession to national pride. He also overcame French resistance to the Common Market not by pointing to the 'disorder, inflation, and hopeless colonial wars' usually attributed with the Fourth Republic, but by emphasising 'the real seeds of economic revolution that were begun by the Fourth Republic,' for which the Common Market could provide further modernisation and growth.[131] His sense of optimism and his will to succeed invigorated the negotiation process.

Spaak created small groups of experts and specialists to discuss technical details and then report back to the politicians assembled in the committee he chaired. The expert groups were secluded at Val-Duchesse chateau, working out draft texts before presenting them to the foreign ministers at periodic meetings. His 'closed diplomacy' approach to the negotiations also meant that 'little publicity [was] given to the stumbling blocks or the accomplishments' of the groups of experts.[132] Rather, he encouraged free and relaxed dialogue by holding frequent lunches and dinners, at which the experts could express their views directly. In order to create a productive atmosphere, Spaak 'never allowed the national delegates to feel they were at the mercy of a time-table, but he often pushed long sessions into the night and early morning hours if some delegation appeared weakened and ready to concede.'[133] Spaak himself was proud of the 'effects of his oratory and more especially his acts of conciliation had in actually achieving practical results in the cause of European unity.'[134] He was also adamant about toning down the federalist rhetoric that had accompanied previous attempts at integration, including the failed EDC. For the Common Market, Spaak wanted a supranational institution that could act independently of national governments, but he realised that the current of opinion would not allow such a radical innovation.[135] The presentation of the negotiation's results therefore 'required clever camouflaging and prudently worded arguments'[136] in order not to provoke hostile reactions from governments or the public. He overcame opposition to the incremental supranationalism of the Common Market's institutional architecture by embedding national governments in the decision-making framework through the Council of Ministers. In this way, he could argue that governments were in control, while forcing them into a framework of cooperation. Crucially, Spaak combined the proposals for Euratom and the Common Market into a single package deal, which Paris had to take or leave.[137] This linkage of both proposals greatly facilitated Franco-German negotiations, as it forced France to engage with the Common Market while preventing West German scepticism of

Euratom from acting as an excuse for not seeking compromises with France on the Common Market.

Spaak's successful transactional form of leadership became an example to follow. Yet his main contribution to the *rélance* was his determined will not to let technical details and discrepancies to get in the way of a Franco-German agreement on European integration. Unlike other national leaders, Spaak became an expert of the dossiers and subjects under negotiation. Immutable Belgian national interests or its economic condition did not determine the extent of his personal involvement to rescue the *rélance* from suffering the same fate as the EDC in 1954. Rather, his intense interest and personal engagement in the negotiations was predicated on two considerations. First, he realised that some form of bilateral rapprochement between France and West Germany was necessary to make the Common Market work. He could not force this deal, but merely facilitate it. Second, he was convinced that time was running out for the Common Market. Mollet was under increasing pressure over Algeria and an ageing Adenauer would soon face re-election, and Spaak believed that neither of their successors were as willing to deliver on the Common Market. Consequently, his leadership consisted of preventing opponents of the proposals in France and Germany from derailing the negotiations as a whole.

Adenauer and Mollet: to trust or not to trust?

Throughout the negotiations, the viability of the Common Market initiative was highly dependent on continuing political will. Significantly, Adenauer and Mollet 'encouraged initiative rather than caution' and managed to overcome domestic opposition to the proposals under consideration.[138] Both leaders used their authority, personal prestige, and institutional influence to overcome and deflect criticism of their pro-integrationist policies, albeit at different times and in different circumstances.[139] Adenauer, for example, used his executive privilege (*Richtlinienkompetenz*) to order his ministers to follow him on European integration, as the famous 'order to integrate' of 19 January 1956 attests. Adenauer also intervened personally in internal matters of the *Auswärtiges Amt* and the Ministry of Economic Affairs in order to secure the promotion of pro-integrationist officials to key positions.[140] In addition, he consistently raised the issues of German participation in the Atlantic alliance, European integration, Franco-German reconciliation, and anti-Communism in his speeches at a time when these were strongly challenged by the SPD and other political forces.[141] Even before the Federal Republic was created in 1949, Adenauer had already advocated that a customs union and gradual economic integration would be the safest bet for establishing good neighbourly relations among the states of Western Europe.[142]

Mollet also intervened personally, actively lobbying farmers organisations, employers' associations, and trade unions in support of the unpopular Common Market, and did not shy away from testing parliamentary support for his pro-integrationist policies. He wanted to prevent a repetition of the EDC debacle, and therefore was keenly aware of the necessity to assuage parliamentary concerns about the Common Market and integration with Germany.[143]

Although coming from very different political and ideological backgrounds – Adenauer was a Roman Catholic Christian Democrat with a sound (though slowly eroding) parliamentary and public support base, while was Mollet a Socialist heading an unstable governmental coalition – both leaders were keen on European unification. Knowing that the Brussels negotiations could only succeed with combined French and West German support, they used summit meetings to overcome outstanding obstacles.[144] Yet the Adenauer-Mollet understanding was not a natural configuration of similar personalities and shared interests.[145] Rather, the closeness between both decision-makers developed over the latter part of 1956, when their attitudes on the Common Market converged. Facilitating their willingness to exercise leadership on European integration were issue-linkages with other pressing concerns of their times.

For Adenauer, European integration aimed at overcoming the limitations that were imposed on Germany after World War II. He was able to do so by accommodating his policies and behaviour to the international context, while holding on to a number of key foreign policy principles.[146] These were linked to broader debates on the policy of *Westintegration*, as well as the issue of Germany's eventual unification.[147] His goals were not only to regain equality of rights and security for West Germany, but also to tie it 'irrevocably' to the Western democracies.[148] The fact that his policy of embedding West Germany firmly in the Western alliance eventually became a 'new line of tradition' of the Federal Republic[149] should not deflect from the fact that Adenauer's pro-Western and pro-integrationist choices were highly controversial at the time.[150] Yet Adenauer wanted these choices to be lasting legacies of his chancellorship and was prepared to invest political capital and personal prestige in order to see them succeed. The international context of the late 1950s facilitated a 'fortunate congruence'[151] between these foreign policy goals, thereby aiding Adenauer's efforts.

Heinrich von Brentano (who became Foreign Minister in June 1955) said in 1953 that the 'aim of Germany's policy must be . . . to lead the country from its position of dependence into that of a co-operating nation with equal rights in the community of free peoples.'[152] Acting as a representative of a country which was 'highly dependent' on Britain, France, and the United States, this objective was imperative to every foreign policy decision taken by Adenauer.[153] This was also the case on matters of European integration, a subject to which the chancellor attributed great personal and emotional importance. He wanted to commit postwar West Germany to European supranational integration, believing that it would provide 'an effective framework for German political rehabilitation as well as for economic regeneration and growth.'[154]

In consequence, Adenauer conceded – often reluctantly – to Mollet's demands and strongly encouraged all forms of integration that would 'heal the wounds' of World War II.[155] It had taken Adenauer a long time to reduce mistrust in Germany and to diminish the limitations imposed by the occupying powers. His proven record of tying the Federal Republic firmly into the Western alliance gradually gained him the support and trust of other foreign leaders, who were otherwise still wary of West Germany's role, influence, and intentions.[156] Adenauer capitalised on this trust by linking progress on European integration to the progressive dismantlement of Allied control over West Germany. This policy led to a series of foreign policy successes, which further confirmed Adenauer's conviction that *Westintegration* was right. Among these successes were the restoration of de facto West German sovereignty in May 1955, the creation of the *Bundeswehr*, the solution of the Saar problem in September 1956, and the creation of the Common Market in March 1957.

> The foundation of the EEC . . . was assured, and, as became clear much later, with it the most important project of Adenauer's policies in Europe, which would endure way beyond his death. Seen from this viewpoint, the crucial months of 1956 and the beginning of 1957, in which it was uncertain whether the EEC would ever come into being, were, in the long term, the most successful of his fourteen-year chancellorship.[157]

Throughout late 1956 and early 1957, Adenauer became more assertive in his advocacy and support of the Common Market. Animated by growing concerns over the reliability of the American commitment to Western Europe and Germany, Adenauer sought to get the Common Market signed as quickly as possible. Facing federal elections in September 1957, he believed that ratification had to be achieved before the electoral campaign started in earnest. His input in the decision-making processes regarding European integration was high throughout this period. European policy remained a domain of the Federal Chancellery and not the foreign or economic affairs ministries.

For Mollet, European integration was first and foremost a mechanism to control West Germany by embedding it in international institutions. Yet Mollet also linked his pro-integrationist European policies to key domestic concerns. On the one hand, his popular handling of the Algerian conflict provided him some immunity against attacks on his European policies. On the other hand, the Common Market plan in particular became an instrument for forcing internal economic reforms, as well as for safeguarding France's special relations with its overseas territories. Mollet was a key force supporting the concept of *Eurafrique*, which sought to link Western Europe to its former colonial possessions through close economic, political, and cultural ties.[158]

Another component of their convergence on the Common Market proposal was the United States and the Suez crisis. Adenauer's pro-American attitudes and policies received a significant blow in July 1956, when a plan by Admiral Arthur Radford, chairman of the US Joint Chiefs of Staff, which sought to diminish the number of American troops stationed in Europe, became public.[159] Adenauer was deeply worried about this development, and it lastingly undermined his trust in American intentions regarding Europe.[160]

Mollet, for his part, was also sympathetic to the United States and the Atlantic alliance. Yet the Suez crisis – which ended with a unilateral British withdrawal from military operations under American pressure – illustrated France's limited options in international affairs. In the wake of Suez, the French government became 'infected with a distrust of the United States and disappointment with the British,' perceptions which drew Mollet closer to European integration.[161] The Suez debacle convinced him that a strengthening of Europe's political role needed to be achieved, especially so as to protect French interests in relation to the two superpowers.[162] A more decisive step towards rapprochement with Germany was therefore deemed politically desirable.[163] Moreover, Mollet (who had doubts about the economic repercussions of the Common Market) felt that the Messina proposals remained the only economic and political alternative available to France. France's deteriorating financial, economic, and political conditions fostered Mollet's conviction that the Common Market would contribute to solving these ills. Euratom was also perceived as the only viable alternative on defence and security matters.

Rather than sharing similar interests, German and French European policies overlapped because Adenauer and Mollet interpreted the structural circumstances they encountered (i.e. the geopolitical, economic, and parliamentary conditions) in a way compatible with integration. This closeness in the interpretation and perception of their countries' possibilities and limitations facilitated their leadership in support of the Common Market. It was due to their shared conviction that integration was the only viable way forward that both Adenauer and Mollet became active protagonists in the diplomatic process to secure agreement on the Common Market. Their leadership is a key explanatory component, which structural and institutionalist explanations of the *relance* overlook.

Adenauer sought to achieve his Western-oriented foreign policy goals through an 'imaginative, and indeed courageous, process of political and economic integration, and by soft power mechanisms.'[164] This outlook reflected not only the chancellor's limitations in foreign policy (due to Germany's special status), but also his personal political inclinations and experiences.[165]

Five central components of Adenauer's European policy can be identified: anti-Communism,[166] gaining allied trust and avoiding isolation, achieving sovereign equality for West Germany, preventing the resurgence of German nationalism and militarism, and fostering economic progress.[167] All of these elements were couched in a civilisational rhetoric.[168] His Europe was a 'Catholic Western Europe,' centred on a Franco-German éntente and partnership with the US.[169] For Adenauer, Europe was 'the strongroom in which the Christian-occidental tradition is safely preserved, a well of spiritual strength and a place for peaceful work [which] will defend itself against anyone threatening its peace and its liberty, but it will be the enemy of no one.'[170] His conception of Europe was based on a cultural understanding of the continent, stressing especially its Christian (Roman Catholic) roots and heritage. Adenauer emphasised that Europeans shared a common history and similar traditions (i.e. Christianity), but repudiated the assumption that this entailed the existence of an organic feeling of community among the peoples of Europe.[171] Rather, he thought that feelings of solidarity and mutual trust could develop on the basis of these shared historical experiences and traditions. He regarded Europe as being distinct from the Soviet Union in both political and cultural essence. Adenauer often stressed his 'unwavering hostility' towards the Soviet Union, while he identified closely with the United States and its policies.[172] From his point of view, the 'Communist atheism' propagated by the Soviet Union symbolised its political, cultural, and ideological antagonism towards the free and Christian Europe. He believed that his 'policies of strength' vis-à-vis the Soviet Union would ultimately entrench the West's superiority, prevent Soviet expansionism, and lead to more conciliatory attitudes in Moscow.[173]

Adenauer and Mollet feared Soviet communism. Their interest in European integration was in no small part based on the perceived need to secure a privileged relationship with the United States for fundamental political, economic, and strategic reasons.[174] Adenauer subsumed European integration under the transatlantic alliance, believing that the relationship with the United States was beneficial in the short term, while European integration was necessary in the long run. Both leaders objected to plans for Third Force Europe[175] or a European Europe situated independently between the United States and the USSR.[176] This transatlantic and anti-Communist stance served as an element of distinction from many European federalists and Gaullists, who advocated an independent Europe subservient to neither superpower.[177] Yet fearing a US-Soviet arrangement without European consultation, and contemplating the possibility of an American retreat from Europe, both leaders were adamant about building a European fall-back position (*Rückfallposition*).[178] The construction of a European safety net under Franco-German leadership appealed to Adenauer in particular, because he worried not only about the American commitment to Europe but also about the sincerity and ability of Britain to secure Western Europe.[179]

Adenauer's and Mollet's pro-American and pro-integrationist policies were also designed to overcome divisive European nationalisms, which had often impeded progress on European affairs. Mollet sought to calm the rising tide of nationalism, inflamed throughout the EDC debates, because it hampered his European policies. It was Mollet's intention to confront and placate the Eurosceptic and anti-German Gaullist, Poujadist, and Communist forces in the National Assembly.

But nationalism presented Adenauer especially with the most serious obstacle to the achievement of meaningful and lasting European integration. He realised that a re-ignition of German nationalism would automatically undo his progress on foreign policy and shatter the trust of his Western allies, which he had slowly gained.[180] He rejected nationalism not only because he had personally suffered under the terror of the Nazis' racist and ultranationalist dictatorship, but also because he feared that a resurgent German nationalism prevented the normalisation of relations with its neighbours. Adenauer wanted (West) Germany to cease to be a security concern for its neighbours, especially France. Thereby he sought to gradually overcome the occupation status, gain international respectability, and expand his political manoeuvrability. In consequence, he consistently rejected all (mainly Soviet) offers for German unification under the condition of neutrality, and he confronted those critics who advocated neutrality. Also, he was convinced that only the secure embedding of West Germany in the Western alliance would make this potential resurgence of German nationalism and militarism improbable.[181] Integration with the West would both be a 'prophylaxis'[182] against a resurgent German nationalism and a 'protection of Germany from itself.'[183] It is in this sense that Adenauer's interest in European integration was embedded in personal experiences and severe doubts about his countrymen's nationalist instincts. He consistently reminded fellow Western leaders that he was the only German chancellor who preferred European unity to the unity of his country.[184]

The Common Market proposal in particular presented Adenauer with the opportunity to combine his objective of reconciliation with a viable economic and political project. In his opinion, the Common Market would contribute to secure West Germany's and Western Europe's strength against the Soviet Union. After the EDC debacle, he knew that the success of his objectives depended on Mollet's success in France. Therefore, Adenauer was willing to overcome strong domestic opposition – notably from Ludwig Erhard – to his approach to European integration and make important 'concrete concessions' to Mollet.[185] Adenauer became convinced that only by making an 'unmistakable German option for the West' and by gaining 'France's intangible trust and goodwill' could he realise his vision of Europe.[186] Adenauer thought that economic cooperation through the Common Market would not only lead to closer Franco-German collaboration and reconciliation, but would also 'change the way that Europeans thought about each other.'[187] Transcending the nationalist rivalries between France and Germany remained Adenauer's pre-eminent political reason for integration. Yet he realised the severity of France's problems and became convinced that Mollet was an 'honest European'[188] with whom he could build the Common Market and achieve Franco-German rapprochement. These considerations made Adenauer more amenable to concede to Mollet's demands.

France's military engagement in Algeria and Suez had the effect of exacerbating deep divisions among the French political elite. Mollet's pro-European parliamentary support base was weakened not only by its small majority, but also by the sheer severity of the issues facing France. Mollet's 'European cabinet was holding on to power by a thread, menaced by the colonial problem, domestic inflation, the French-right and the ultra-nationalists.'[189] These divisions contributed significantly to the instability of the Fourth Republic. Seen from this angle, policy-making on European integration 'offered a potential escape' from the *immobilisme* and structural weakness of the Fourth Republic.[190] Mollet used European policy-making in general, and the Brussels negotiations in particular, in order to gain 'German side-payments in investments and aid for the French Union' and to reform the 'nationalist trading system,' which he deemed 'anachronistic.'[191]

Due to the internal split of Mollet's Socialist party (SFIO) over the question of Europe and its 'broadly hostile' attitude to economic liberalisation, Mollet assembled support for his European policy from outside the party. Together with the conservative industrialist Antoine Pinay, and the rural centrist Maurice Faure, whose support was crucial for the success of the Common Market, Mollet 'shared little besides a model of a desirable Europe.'[192] This external support was essential in order to pursue Mollet's policies on Europe.

It was Mollet's priority and ambition to use his position to further the creation of an integrated Europe. His vision of Europe was not only 'pro-British' – believing that a European community without Britain would be 'unthinkable'[193] – but also centred on the premise that safeguards to 'limit the transfer of national sovereignty' were necessary.[194] In this sense he shared Spaak's cautious approach to the *relance*, given that he was aware of the unpopular reception any federalist-inspired proposal would receive in France. He also shared with Spaak a conviction that an integrated and viable Europe would strengthen the Atlantic alliance with the United States. He supported this belief – even during the 'darkest moments'[195] of the Suez crisis – hoping that Eden could be converted to the idea of a unified Europe constructed around an Anglo-French axis. But while the Suez crisis triggered a turn to Europe in France, Britain sought a quick reestablishment of its 'special relationship' with the United States. These divergent reactions led Mollet closer to Adenauer, with whom he overcame the remaining stumbling blocks for creating the Common Market. For instance, their crucial cooperation on the Saar question, which had continued to strain the fast-improving Franco-German relations, paved the way for important compromises on European integration.[196] Its resolution greatly enhanced the expectations that the creation of the Common Market would be politically feasible and achievable. In consequence, the 'Brussels discussions then went into high gear.'[197]

Mollet chose to pursue the controversial and unpopular proposals of the Spaak report over other alternatives because these pro-community leaders were able to assert their views amid a 'deeply cross-cutting battle of ideas.'[198] It is questionable, however, whether it was the 'supremacy of pro-community ideas' among Mollet's coalition or the pursuit of French economic interests which explained the French government's choice for the Common Market.[199] The conciliatory attitude of the five and the victories of France in securing its national economic interests during the Brussels negotiations are often over-emphasised. This emphasis 'unduly disregards the overriding theme of reciprocal compromise and concessions,' as well as the 'give and take atmosphere' that developed as a result of Mollet's and Adenauer's cooperation on the Brussels negotiations.[200]

Eden's reluctance: the myth of a 'missed opportunity' for leadership?

If leadership is solely a matter of a decision-maker's institutional position, power, access to resources, and ability to persuade, Anthony Eden would in all likelihood have played a crucial role in the negotiations for the Common Market. He was – until late 1956 – a fairly popular prime minister, who was extraordinarily well-versed in foreign affairs, and whose ability to persuade and strike intergovernmental bargains was widely recognised. Moreover, Spaak, Adenauer, and Mollet actively sought British engagement and leadership on European integration. Yet throughout the *rélance*, Eden and his government played only a subdued role, with Eden taking 'no interest in the issue at all.'[201] His government hoped that the whole idea would be 'still-born,'[202] seeing it as another sign of the 'endemic' enthusiasm in Western Europe for integration following the end of World War II.[203] Being neither supportive of the Common Market and Euratom proposals nor opposed to them, Eden's position was ambiguous and frustrated Spaak in particular.[204] Some in his government wanted to whole thing to 'die of its own accord.'[205] In consequence, Eden was subsequently accused of 'lack of foresight'[206] on European affairs, his uninterested behaviour amounting to a 'missed opportunity' to lead Europe:

> How are we to explain Britain's neglecting to take a lead in Western European affairs when it was open to her in the late 1940s and in the 1950s? In retrospect, this seems to be the fundamental and most costly mistake in postwar policies; moreover, it cannot be attributed to the uncontrollable nature of the changes in Europe; its causes must be sought in the faulty perceptions, anticipations and priorities of the successive British governments.[207]

Eden had the power, resources, and ability at his disposal to exercise substantial leadership on European integration, but chose not to do so. It is in this context that the motives and reasons for Eden's leadership – or lack thereof – are significant.[208]

Eden had taken over as Prime Minister upon Churchill's resignation on 6 April 1955. His short-lived government lasted until the fallout from the Suez crisis forced his resignation on 9 January 1957. His time in office nearly covers the entire period of the *rélance*, during which he was preoccupied – especially during the Suez crisis – with policies towards the Middle East and a deteriorating transatlantic relationship, and consequently engaged only marginally in the negotiation processes following the Messina conference.[209]

Eden was 'bored' by the whole undertaking, and for him and his advisors the idea of Europe had become 'a damnable nuisance.'[210] Eden, who was famous for his 'restless meddling in other ministers' business,'[211] as well as being 'content to tackle finite, immediate concerns while postponing consideration of broader issues,'[212] was conspicuously absent from this phase of European policy-making. To some extent this resulted from the low priority that senior civil servants in Whitehall and Eden's advisors in Downing Street attributed to the *rélance*. There was an 'overriding impression' of a 'lack of controversy in Britain' over the Messina proposals.[213] The issue of whether to join the Common Market or reject it was 'left for decision by the Foreign Office, which rejected membership as incompatible with Britain's perceived world role.'[214] Furthermore, Eden was given 'only intermittent and confusing advice . . . presumably because it seemed technical and unpressing.'[215] Macmillan, first Foreign Secretary and later

Chancellor of the Exchequer, was equally 'sceptical, like nearly all British politicians, about the preparations for "relaunching" Europe.'[216] Macmillan 'was no driving force on Europe.'[217] Macmillan's own ambiguity reinforced Eden's attitude, and Eden became more concerned about the French position and 'cheating' in negotiations within the OEEC, arguing that no 'special leniency' should be offered to France.[218]

Already in a speech delivered at Columbia University on 11 January 1952, Eden – then still Foreign Secretary in Churchill's government – said:

> You will realise that I am speaking of the frequent suggestions that the United Kingdom should join a federation on the continent of Europe. This is something which we know, in our bones, we cannot do.
>
> We know that if we were to attempt it, we should relax the springs of our action in the Western democratic cause and in the Atlantic association which is the expression of that cause. For Britain's story and her interests lie far beyond the continent of Europe. Our thoughts move across the seas to the many communities in which our people play their part, in every corner of the world. These are our family ties. That is our life: without it we should be no more than some millions of people living on an island off the coast of Europe, in which nobody wants to take any particular interest.[219]

In Eden's eyes, Britain's traditional political and cultural bonds, as well as foreign policy interests, concerned the Commonwealth and the transatlantic alliance with the United States.[220] Britain's relations with Western Europe came in a distant third. Already as Foreign Secretary he had subscribed to the 'overriding dictum for Britain in the post-1945 world: "Never be separated from the Americans."'[221] In consequence, 'any project [of integration] must be Atlanticist as well as European, keeping the Americans in Europe – which was a universal British obsession.'[222] The emphasis on safeguarding the transatlantic alliance, even when he had his own personal doubts about the United States,[223] can be attributed to the fact that 'Eden grasped the fundamentally reduced nature of Britain's postwar economic and military power.'[224] He feared that a politically, economically, and militarily viable Europe would ultimately relieve the United States of its strategic military engagement on the continent, and anticipated that the UK would not be able to shoulder its global interests and responsibilities alone.

On the issue of postwar European integration, he pursued an ambivalent strategy. He had welcomed the creation of the ECSC in 1950, and was instrumental in the 1954 re-armament of West Germany in the context of NATO/WEU, after the EDC proposal had collapsed.[225] Yet he declined British participation in the Common Market on political grounds, basing his arguments on the importance of the Commonwealth and his suspicion of supranational institutions. He remained sceptical and aloof throughout the Brussels negotiations.[226] The fact that Britain's trade was still overwhelmingly with Commonwealth countries,[227] and that the Commonwealth was regarded as a 'hinterland' for

Britain's great power ambitions, merely strengthened Eden's reluctance to get involved in European economic integration.[228]

Eden's political depiction of a 'desired Europe' entailed a 'Europe of sovereign states, which would act together as a loyal ally of the United States.'[229] Any form of transfer of national sovereignty to supranational institutions was seen as a threat to core British interests and identity. On the economic front, Eden envisaged a 'Europe that would constitute a free-trade area without interventionist central policies, and open to commerce with the rest of the world.'[230] This was the tenet of his government's plans for an OEEC free trade area, also known as 'Plan G.'[231] In this sense, his conception of Europe differed significantly from that of Spaak, Adenauer, or Mollet.[232] This is exemplified by a letter from the British ambassador in Paris, Gladwyn Jebb, to Foreign Secretary Selwyn Lloyd:

> Whereas in the United Kingdom, which as well all know, is in Europe but not of Europe, we rather tend to regard our own association with the Common Market chiefly, if not entirely, as an economic proposition which can be decided on simple grounds of commercial self-interest, this is very far from the idea of the continentals. Most of them . . . are concerned to 'make Europe' in a physical sense. To that extent, when they meet us, they are often talking in a different language.[233]

The period between 1955 and 1957 was thus marked by substantial differences over European policies between the UK on the one side and the so-called Six on the other. This rift extended well beyond the disagreements over economic policy, tariffs, and the institutional nature of European integration.[234] An attitude to European integration that could not be easily reconciled with the integrationist moves behind the *relance* was prevalent in Britain.[235]

For the Six, the *relance* served – in spite of all their own disagreements – to regain the lost momentum over the integration process, allowing them to press ahead with gradual economic integration and thereby edge closer to goal of political unification. In contrast, for Britain, 'the whole question of where Britain stands in the world today and in what context she envisages her international future' was at stake.[236] The main premises of economic integration and supranational institutions were shared by neither British elites nor the public. Eden himself fostered the conviction that Britain's role and interests went far beyond Europe. He was reluctant to participate in the Brussels negotiations, fearing that the establishment of the Common Market would fundamentally alter the UK's predominant economic and trade patterns, political position, and cultural self-understanding. He also rejected the establishment of supranational institutions on the grounds that Britain ought not to be 'locked' into a relationship with Western Europe that would harm its Commonwealth and transatlantic interests.[237] Macmillan shared this view, advocating a fine balance between the UK's 'triple duties.'[238] This understanding also reflected majority opinion in Parliament in both the Conservative and Labour parties.[239] Eden received advice that if the UK and the Commonwealth could not join the Common Market, the Common Market should in turn join the Commonwealth.[240]

Instead of making the case for Britain's role in Europe, Eden stressed the political, economic, and cultural divide between continental Europe and Britain. Europe was seen as only one among many realms of British policy overseas. Strong economic, political, and cultural bonds existed with the Commonwealth and the United States, meaning that these realms were often attributed priority over European affairs. In contrast, continental Western Europe, despite its geographical proximity, appeared to be foreign in political and cultural terms. Continental European countries were often deemed 'unstable and hostile.'[241]

The 'postwar concept of Britain located inside three interlocking circles' continued to dominate opinion.[242] From this point of view – articulated first by Churchill – Britain's role and interests were understood to lie at the intersection of three circles of interests, influence, and responsibilities: the Commonwealth, the Atlantic alliance with the United States, and 'ranking as a poor third – Europe.'[243] This self-understanding of Britain is strongly linked to the perception of its status as a world power and empire, with a global (rather than European) geo-strategic and economic outlook.

Crucial to Eden's behaviour was this worldview, common among the British establishment. American support had been vital for British defence and security in the two world wars, and its economy was highly dependent on American finance. An understanding of cultural similarities and shared interests, of '"Anglo-Saxon" liberty . . . and interests,'[244] was seen to bind the United States and Britain together. Even disagreements over the United States' wariness to support Britain's imperial and colonial ambitions throughout the Commonwealth, as well as over European policy-making, could not dispel the strong feeling of commonality across the Atlantic. The significance of the transatlantic alliance continued, despite the fact that 'Britain's ties with the United States were loosening, and awareness of the growing strength of continental Europe was growing.'[245] It also survived the strains of the Suez crisis, during which France and Britain had lost vital American support. In the wake of the Suez debacle, Eden set out to repair his relationship with Eisenhower, and asserted the UK's imperial and Commonwealth links – albeit unsuccessfully.[246] In France, Mollet drew the opposite conclusion. There, Europe was now seen 'more as a boost than a threat to French influence' and Mollet moved decisively in direction of the Common Market.[247] The differences in impulse behind British and French reactions to the Suez crisis led both countries to follow different political priorities regarding European integration.

Eden's conviction that the UK's interests laid beyond Europe strongly shaped the European policy-making options that were perceived to be available. In defending his perception of the national interests, Eden drew on rhetorical and cultural resources which revealed a deep cognitive gap between continental Europe and Britain. This was characterised by three main elements.

First, in a cultural sense, the UK was seen to be '*with* Europe but not *of* it';[248] Britain was still struggling 'to make up her mind whether she is really part of Europe.'²⁴⁹ Spaak recalled that throughout the Brussels negotiations he had the feeling that

> the British were not yet ready to take part in our European venture. The overwhelming majority of them believed that it was more important for them to strengthen their Commonwealth ties than to bring Britain closer to the Continent. They considered supra-national tendencies which were emerging among the Six unacceptable and thought European unity a good subject for wistful speeches rather than realistic proposition.²⁵⁰

The Common Market was expected to 'cause economic and political friction, ultimately undermining the cohesion of the Western alliance.'²⁵¹ The spectre of damaged Commonwealth and transatlantic relationships served as a powerful incentive to resist the Brussels negotiations from succeeding in the first place.²⁵² This was attempted by trying to 'sabotage' the negotiations through an alternative plan for a free trade area in the context of the OEEC,²⁵³ which later led to the creation of the European Free Trade Association (EFTA) rivalling the Common Market.²⁵⁴

The significance Eden attached to the Commonwealth and the transatlantic alliance depended not on political and strategic considerations alone. It also was consistently asserted that strong cultural 'bonds of amity' existed across the Atlantic, 'precisely because [Americans] were believed to be kinsmen.'²⁵⁵ In contrast, an attitude of distinctiveness prevailed towards continental Europe, which had been re-ignited by the traumatic experiences of World War II. Eden was neither indifferent nor antagonistic to 'continental federalist aspirations,' but believed that such aspirations 'were not for Britain.'²⁵⁶ A 'triumphalist reading of British nationalism'²⁵⁷ reaffirmed these Commonwealth and transatlantic bonds – fostered during the course of two world wars – to the detriment of cultural affinities with continental Europe.

Second, the common self-understanding in Britain as a world power dominated political rhetoric and permeated the public's imagination. Britain sought to 'preserve the heritage of a nation which was historically and by priority a world power before being a European power.'²⁵⁸ Eden's conceptualisation of British national interests 'depended on a continuing belief in Britain's world role, on a confidence in the talents of British diplomacy and on a pride in the Westminster model of parliamentary democracy.'²⁵⁹

Starting from the conviction of the solidity and superiority of British institutions, it appeared to be unwise to sacrifice the Commonwealth and Empire 'in the cause of binding ties with Western European states which looked fragile, were prone to support statist economic policies – and in some cases had dubious institutional and historical legitimacy.'²⁶⁰ Hence, a 'brief for British aloofness from continental projects' surfaced, with few seeing the need for severing Britain's powerful links to the United States and the Commonwealth for 'an experiment in European constitutionalism.'²⁶¹

Reflecting this widespread attitude, Eden deemed the chances of success of the Common Market proposal to be 'negligible at best, not least because British participation had been ruled out at an early stage.'[262] Severe misjudgements about the nature, scope, and purpose of the functional supranational project of European integration followed from the overestimation of Britain's capacity to influence policy and state behaviour on the continent.

Third, while having promoted European political and economic integration for the continental countries of Western Europe in the immediate postwar period, the British political elite remained unconvinced that Britain would gain politically or economically by participating in such an endeavour. A widespread feeling of apathy towards all forms of political integration in Europe could be made out among British officials and political leaders. This contrasted heavily with the proactive support for the Common Market by Spaak, Adenauer, and Mollet. During the Brussels negotiations,

> Britain had made it clear that to her the political aims embodied were unacceptable. Thereafter the British Government had insisted on treating relations with the Community as purely economic in nature . . . Britain had seemed to have a deep emotional commitment to the notion of independent national sovereignty and an equally strong sentiment for the unique relationships of the Commonwealth.[263]

With its frontiers unchanged since 1707, its victory in both world wars, the popularity of its institutions and 'informal constitution,' and a feeling of 'loyalty' to its wartime allies, elite beliefs in the value and merit of national sovereignty remained high in the UK.[264] Nationalism and patriotism were less tainted in Britain than on the continent, where a 'crisis of nationalism'[265] divided France and made the concept deeply problematic for Germany. Almost 'no evidence of any enthusiasm for . . . supranationalism' could be discerned among the British government.[266] Rather, the talk was of 'British commitments in the Commonwealth and . . . antipathy to supra-national organisations.'[267] Eden favoured free trade agreements and economic integration based on intergovernmental arrangements (such as the OEEC), but strongly objected to all transfers of national sovereignty. He noted in his memoirs:

> It is true that we continuously encouraged closer co-operation and unity between continental powers, but we did so from the reserve position that we would not accept a sovereign European authority, from which our Commonwealth ties precluded us.[268]

It was expected that all moves for political unification would ultimately fail due to the persistence of mutually exclusive nationalisms. When withdrawing Bretherton, the British representative at the Brussels negotiations, in late 1955, Eden was convinced the *relance* 'had no prospects.'[269] Yet Britain's withdrawal from

Spaak's committee was widely interpreted by hitherto pro-British leaders on the continent as indicative of a desire to derail the new pro-integrationist initiative.[270] Subsequently, leaders such as Spaak and Adenauer turned away from Britain and focused more on American support and French compromises in their pursuit of European policies.

The focus on the economic objectives of the *rélance* eventually overestimated the significance and impact of British concerns. Little attention was paid to the fact that, for many continental leaders, 'the Common Market represented the beginning of an irrevocable fusion of national economies, which itself was seen only as a precursor to some form of political integration.'[271] As the Brussels negotiations proceeded, Eden and Macmillan realised that they did not want to follow the EDC path to eventual failure. In consequence, Eden very belatedly began to address the proposals with 'some seriousness.'[272] Yet in the crucial first phase of the Brussels negotiations, the British had failed to steer the talks 'on lines acceptable to themselves.'[273] Eden thus faced a growing dilemma: while not wanting to participate in the proposed steps for economic – and, ultimately, political – integration, he also feared the 'possibility of political marginalisation.'[274] The situation was compounded by the fact that the United States favoured the unification of Europe and 'had little sympathy for antisupranationalist sentiment'[275] in the UK:

> The consolidation of the 'European circle' without Britain was also expected directly to undermine the special relationship. Once the plans for foreign policy coordination and ultimately political integration would come to fruition, the United States was expected to look to Europe as the preferred partner. In the longer term, the linguistic and cultural propinquity to America – so it was feared – would not suffice to offset the sheer weight of a united Europe in international diplomacy.[276]

For many observers, the 'attitude of total British indifference to Europe'[277] and the widespread 'hostility' in regard to the Brussels negotiations amounted to a 'missed opportunity' for Britain to adopt leadership on matters of European integration.[278] Eden's hesitation to use Britain's 'position of eminence' to overcome its 'unprofitable [and] prolonged retreat'[279] resulted not from self-evident economic or geopolitical necessities but from his interpretation of British interests, which in turn were shaped by personal experiences and ideas about Britain's role in the world and its engagement with Europe.

***

The creation of the Common Market and Euratom was not a predetermined and functionally necessary path of action. Spaak, Adenauer, and Mollet realised that the plans tabled at Messina could be useful for the pursuit of other, more important, political goals. Spaak sought safety from German domination and nationalism by embedding Bonn in international organisations. He fought hard to keep the negotiations afloat because he felt that a viable European institutional architecture was only possible so long as the pro-integrationists, Adenauer and Mollet, were still in office. Adenauer wanted to broaden his foreign policy options, regain the trust of his Western allies, and obtain a degree of respectability, sovereign equality, and security for West Germany. He was concerned about a revival of German nationalism, fearing this could undermine his foreign policy goals. Adenauer was adamant about immunising West Germany against nationalism by participating in European institutions. His policy of *Westintegration* depended on Franco-German reconciliation, European economic cooperation, and partnership with the United States. He chose to fully support the Common Market, as he had done with all other European initiatives to-date. Mollet, in turn, was open to the Messina proposals because he wanted a gradual economic liberalisation for the French economy, sought to keep France safe from Germany and the Soviet Union, and needed to replace the dwindling French colonial empire with new forms of economic linkages between Europe and Africa.

Adenauer and Mollet made a deliberate choice to pursue the Common Market, resolving outstanding bilateral issues and making significant concessions to each other. Yet they also chose to pursue this particular economic kind of European cooperation at home, fighting off domestic and parliamentary opposition, actively lobbying for support, and using their executive authority to overcome bureaucratic resistance. Both leaders were willing to become personally involved and identified with the *relance*. By exercising leadership in support of the Common Market and Euratom, Adenauer and Mollet contributed essential Franco-German support for the initiative.

Leadership on the Messina proposals came in different forms and modes. Spaak exercised a transactional form of leadership aimed at rescuing the Brussels negotiations from collapse. He facilitated a Franco-German compromise on the Common Market by creating a give-and-take atmosphere among these crucial states. Adenauer and Mollet exercised a direct, transformational form of leadership that aimed at altering the political parameters of European politics. It was at summit meetings that Adenauer and Mollet began to know and trust each other, and much of their leadership consisted of overcoming residual fears and incomprehension about Germany's role in Europe.

The role of Anthony Eden during the *relance* illustrates that institutional position, power, and access to resources do not automatically transfer into leadership. Eden did not dismiss the *relance* because it was in Britain's interest to do so, but because he interpreted British interests to be beyond Europe. Eden was personally uninterested in and bored by European economic integration, thinking that Britain's status as a world power and the importance of Commonwealth trade precluded it from participation in the Common Market. This attitude gave rise to an ambiguous British policy on Europe, being neither in support nor opposition to further integration. The field was therefore left to Spaak, Adenauer, and Mollet to initiate and lead one of the most important transformations of postwar European politics.

Notes

1 See K. Ruane, 'Agonizing Reappraisals: Anthony Eden, John Foster Dulles and the Crisis of European Defence, 1953–54,' *Diplomacy & Statecraft* 13 (4) (2002): 151–185.
2 C. Parsons, *A Certain Idea of Europe* (Ithaca: Cornell University Press, 2003), p. 68.
3 See T. Hörber, *The Foundations of Europe: European Integration Ideas in France, Germany, and Britain in the 1950s* (Wiesbaden: VS Verlag für Sozialwissenschaften, 2006).
4 See P. Guillen, 'Frankreich und der Europäische Wiederaufschwung. Vom Scheitern der EVG zur Ratifizierung der Verträge von Rom,' *Vierteljahrshefte für Zeitgeschichte* 28 (1) (1980): 1–19. On the attitudes of Western communist parties to European integration, see also D.S. Bell, 'Western Communist Parties and the European Union,' in *Political Parties and the European Union*, J. Gaffney ed. (London: Routledge, 1996), pp. 220–234.
5 R. Gildea, *France since 1945* (Oxford: Oxford University Press, 2002), p. 17.
6 French fears vis-à-vis a rearmed Germany with unclear eastern boundaries are treated in H. Müller-Roschach, *Die Deutsche Europapolitik: Wege und Umwege zur Politischen Union Europas* (Baden-Baden: Nomos, 1974). A comprehensive examination of French opinion on the EDC in general, and of French business leaders in particular, can be found in D. Lerner, 'French Business Leaders Look at EDC: A Preliminary Report,' *The Public Opinion Quarterly* 20 (1) (1956): 212–221. A similar account of political leaders is contained in E. Bjøl, *La France Devant l'Europe. La Politique Européenne de la IVe République* (Copenhagen: Munksgaard, 1966).
7 Müller-Roschach, *Die Deutsche Europapolitik*, pp. 34–35. See also Dulles to US Embassy, Paris, 30 August 1954: *Foreign Relations of the United States, 1952–1954*, Vol. II, National Security Affairs (Washington, DC: GPO, 1984), pp. 1114–1116 (hereafter quoted as *FRUS*). See also Adenauer to Bradford, 4 September 1954, as well as Adenauer to Schuman, 24 December 1954: K. Adenauer, *Briefe über Deutschland 1945–1955*, H.P. Mensing ed. (Munich: Siedler, 1999), pp. 172–173, pp. 180–184; H.E. Jahn, *An Adenauers Seite: Sein Berater erinnert sich* (Munich: Langen Müller, 1987); as well as Krone's diary entry for 30 August 1954 and von Brentano's letter to Teitgen of 5 October 1954, in A. Baring ed., *Sehr verehrter Herr Bundeskanzler! Heinrich von Brentano im Briefwechsel mit Konrad Adenauer 1949–1964* (Hamburg: Hoffmann und Campe, 1974), pp. 141–142.
8 On Eden's leadership in enabling the NATO/WEU deal, see D.R. Thorpe, *Eden: The Life and Times of Anthony Eden First Earl of Avon, 1897–1977* (London: Pimlico, 2004); Ruane, 'Agonizing Reappraisals'; and Jahn, *An Adenauers Seite*. On the making of the NATO system of defence arrangements, see M. Trachtenberg, *A Constructed Peace: The Making of the European Settlement, 1945–1963* (Princeton: Princeton University Press, 1999). On the rationale of German rearmament in the context of NATO/WEU, see Eisenhower to Churchill, 10 March 1955: TNA PREM 11/845.
9 See Nutting on the European context, 10 January 1956: TNA FO 371/122023/7.
10 See Spaak to Eden, 7 February 1956: TNA PREM 11/1338. The close interlinkage of European integration and the German question is elucidated in C.A. Wurm ed., *Western Europe and Germany: The Beginnings of European Integration 1945–1960* (Oxford: Berg, 1995).
11 K. Adenauer, *Erinnerungen 1953–1955* (Stuttgart: Deutsche Verlags-Anstalt, 1966), pp. 310–311. See also Eisenhower's address of 30 August 1954 at

Des Moines, and his joint statement with Adenauer of 28 October 1954, in D.D. Eisenhower, *Public Papers of the Presidents of the United States, Dwight D. Eisenhower, 1954: Containing the Public Messages, Speeches, and Statements of the President (January 1-December 31)* (Washington, DC: GPO, 1960), pp. 226, 314.

12 Spaak was convinced that the 'EDC had floundered and died on the supranational issue and the desire of some to move swiftly into more European political unity' and that 'such wishes and ideas demanded more caution since Europe was still convalescing from the fevers of the army debates'; see P.-H. Laurent, 'Paul-Henri Spaak and the Diplomatic Origins of the Common Market, 1955–1956,' *Political Science Quarterly* 85 (3) (1970): 377. For Spaak's thinking on this matter, see confidential memo prepared for the WEU Council ministerial meeting in Paris, 1 May 1956: TNA FO 371/121955/116.

13 F. Duchêne, *Jean Monnet: The First Statesman of Interdependence* (London: W.W. Norton, 1994), p. 256.

14 The claim that political integration had always been the goal behind the ECSC and EDC, and was going to remain so for other initiatives, is clearly expressed in Heinrich von Brentano's speech before the Bundestag of 7 October 1955 (von Brentano 1962: 116).

15 Duchêne, *Jean Monnet*, p. 273. Beyen had already proposed a similar plan for a customs union in a memo of 11 December 1952; see A.G. Harryvan and J. van der Harst eds., *Documents on European Union* (Basingstoke: Macmillan, 1997), pp. 71–74.

16 J. Monnet, *Memoirs* (London: Collins, 1978).

17 For a detailed overview of the negotiating positions, see: HAEU MAEF 28/25–33.

18 See S. Romano, *Guida alla Politica Estera Italiana. Da Badoglio a Berlusconi* (Milano: BUR Saggi, 2004), pp. 96–100.

19 E. Benoit, *Europe at Sixes and Sevens: The Common Market, the Free Trade Association, and the United States* (New York: Columbia University Press, 1961).

20 D. Weigall and P. Stirk eds., *The Origins and Development of the European Community* (Leicester: Leicester University Press, 1992), p. 92. The interlinkage of economic and political interests, as well as the desire to make war between Western European states unlikely, was a theme that resonated with leaders: see Adenauer's speech at the 'Grandes Conférences Catholiques,' Brussels, 25 September 1956: StBKAH 02.14/29.

21 R. Albrecht-Carrié, *The Unity of Europe: An Historical Survey* (London: Secker & Warburg, 1965), p. 297.

22 See Jebb to Selwyn Lloyd, 28 April 1957, 'The United Kingdom and the Western World': TNA PREM 11/1844.

23 O. Franks, 'Britain and Europe,' in *A New Europe?* S.R. Graubard ed. (Boston: Houghton Mifflin, 1964), pp. 98–99. This view is supported by Laurent, who reckons that 'the pragmatic construction [of the Treaties of Rome] was based on a minimum of general agreements and diplomatic negotiations that avoided "theological" assertions or doctrinaire quarrels'; see P.-H. Laurent, 'The Diplomacy of the Rome Treaty, 1956–57,' *Journal of Contemporary History* 7 (3/4) (1972): 219. A prominent German member of the Brussels negotiation committee confirms this view; see H. von der Groeben, *Aufbaujahre der Europäischen Gemeinschaft: Das Ringen um den Gemeinsamen Markt und die Politische Union (1958–1966)* (Baden-Baden: Nomos, 1982), p. 23.

24 M. Holland, 'Jean Monnet and the Federal Functionalist Approach to European Union,' in *Visions of European Unity*, P. Murray and P. Rich eds. (Boulder: Westview, 1996), p. 104.

25 Laurent, 'Paul-Henri Spaak,' p. 388.
26 Guillen, 'Frankreich'.
27 J.F. Deniau, *L'Europe Interdite* (Paris: Seuil, 1977), p. 82.
28 See P. Gerbet, *La Construction de l'Europe* (Paris: Imprimerie Nationale, 1983). Already, in a 26 May 1955 memo – prior to the Messina conference – French Foreign Ministry official Olivier Wormser concluded that the Common Market plan tabled by Beyen was unacceptable to France on economic grounds: HAEU MAEF/27/129.
29 See P. Limagne, *L'éphémère IVe République* (Paris: France-Empire, 1977). See also dispatch from US Embassy in Paris to the US Department of State, 17 January 1956, in which the decline of the French world position is illustrated: *FRUS* 1955–1957, XXVII: 21–29.
30 See Spaak to Eden, 7 February 1956: TNA PREM 11/1338.
31 As late as February 1956, Spaak continued to express deep misgivings about a post-Adenauer Federal Republic; see Macmillan to Eden, 28 February 1956: TNA PREM 11/1337.
32 H. Siegler, *Dokumentation der Europäischen Integration 1946–1961, Band 1: unter besonderer Beachtung des Verhältnisses EWG-EFTA* (Bonn: Siegler, 1961).
33 TNA PREM 11/1337.
34 F.M.B. Lynch, *France and the International Economy: From Vichy to the Treaty of Rome* (London: Routledge, 1997).
35 *FRUS* 1955–1957, IV: pp. 466–467, 473, 495. Erhard's opposition to and criticism of the Common Market in particular continued until after the Treaties of Rome had been signed in March 1957. His stance worried the French government, which feared that the compromises reached could unravel or impede the treaties' ratification (*DDF* 1957, I: doc. 127, doc. 242, doc. 245, doc. 247). See also Erhard's intervention, 171st Federal Cabinet meeting, 13 February 1957 (*KP* 1957, 10: 143–5). The rift between Adenauer and Erhard was accentuated between 1956 and 1958, when the fate of the British-sponsored plan for a free trade area was discussed: see G. Brenke, 'Europakonzeptionen im Widerstreit: Die Freihandelszonen-Verhandlungen 1956–1958,' *Vierteljahrshefte für Zeitgeschichte* 42 (4) (1994): 595–633.
36 M.P.C. Schaad, 'Plan G – A "Counterblast"? British Policy towards the Messina Countries, 1956,' *Contemporary European History* 7 (1) (1998): 39–60. Schaad (p. 44) notes that, despite his junior rank among ECSC foreign ministers, Bretherton went 'beyond the non-committal position he was instructed to adopt' and 'is even said to have displayed cynicism and amusement at the plans of the Six.'
37 See Guillen, 'Frankreich'.
38 A.S. Milward, *The European Rescue of the Nation-State*, second edition (London: Routledge, 2000), p. 120.
39 A. Moravcsik, *The Choice for Europe: Social Purpose and State Power from Messina to Maastricht* (London: Routledge, 1998), p.88.
40 Parsons, *Certain Idea*, p. 91, pp. 102–104.
41 The exact nature of Pinay's actions is controversial. Laurent suggests that 'historians still feel that France's approval of the Messina document is difficult to understand': P.-H. Laurent, 'The Diplomacy of *Junktim*: Paul-Henri Spaak and European Integration,' in *Personalities, War and Diplomacy: Essays in International History*, T.G. Otte and C.A. Pagedas eds. (London: Frank Cass, 1997), p. 193.
42 Parsons, *Certain Idea*, p. 104. See also draft article by Alain Camu highlighting the roles of Spaak and Pinay, titled 'Market fears. How the Six learned to stop worrying': TNA PREM 15/379.

43 HAEC BAC118/86 No. 5/1 (1956).
44 Laurent, 'The Diplomacy of *Junktim*'.
45 France had been in favour of Euratom from July 1955 onwards: HAEU MAEF 28/101. The Mollet government continued to favour Euratom over the Common Market until late 1956; see record of conversation between Mollet, Pineau, and Labour leader Hugh Gaitskell, 10 May 1956: TNA PREM 11/1351.
46 For German governmental reactions, see *The Times*, 'France Divided on Euratom Proposals' (29 May 1956).
47 See D.D. Eisenhower, 1958. 'Joint Statement Following Discussions with Prime Minister Eden. 1 February 1956,' in *Public Papers of the Presidents of the United States, Dwight D. Eisenhower, 1956: Containing the Public Messages, Speeches, and Statements of the President (January 1-December 31)* (Washington, DC: GPO, 1958), doc. 34.
48 Mendès-France consistently advocated for incorporating Britain into European arrangements, notably Euratom; see *The Times*, 'Big French Majority for Euratom: Right to Make Atomic Weapons' (12 July 1956).
49 See analysis of the French election of January 1956, Mollet's rise to power, and its impact on French European policy in *FRUS 1955–1957*, XXVII: 19–21, 26.
50 C. Parsons, 'Showing Ideas as Causes: The Origins of the European Union,' *International Organization* 56 (1) (2002): 69.
51 S.E.M. Charlton, *The French Left and European Integration*, Monograph Series in World Affairs, Vol. 9, Monograph No. 4–1971–1972 (Denver: University of Denver, 1972), p. 49.
52 Parsons, 'Showing Ideas,' pp. 69–70.
53 G. Bossuat, 'La Vraie Nature de la Politique Européenne de la France (1950–1957),' in *The European Integration from the Schuman Plan to the Treaties of Rome*, G. Trausch ed. (Paris: L.G.D.J, 1993).
54 *The Times* called Mollet an 'enthusiastic "European,"' noting that he wanted to conclude a treaty on Euratom before the summer of 1956: *The Times*, '"Relaunching" Europe. M. Mollet's Favour of Atom Pool' (11 February 1956).
55 See C. Tauch, 'The Testimony of an Eyewitness: Christian Pineau, Interviewed by Christian Tauch,' in *Socialist Parties and the Question of Europe in the 1950s*, R.T. Griffiths ed. (Leiden: Brill, 1993), pp. 43–57; C. Pineau and C. Rimbaud, *Le Grand Pari: L'Aventure du Traité de Rome* (Paris: Fayard, 1991).
56 D. Lefèbvre, *Guy Mollet. Le Mal Aimé* (Paris: Plon, 1992). For a detailed and insightful assessment of the new Mollet government, see *FRUS 1955–1957*, XXVII: 21–29.
57 According to Christian Pineau, many people in the SFIO were hostile to the Messina proposals. Only a few leading Socialists – including Mollet and Pineau himself – did 'in any way display enthusiasm for Europe.' In his opinion, Guy Mollet's contribution to the construction of Europe is often and unfairly 'underestimated': the 'craze for Europe was above all a thing of few men within the SFIO; it was in no way the work of party as a whole'; see Tauch, 'Testimony,' pp. 57, 62. For a concise analysis of the SFIO position see Lefèbvre, *Guy Mollet*.
58 Parsons, *Certain Idea*, pp. 106–107. On French bureaucratic opposition to supranationalism, see E. Mahant, *Birthmarks of Europe: The Origins of the European Community Reconsidered* (Aldershot: Ashgate, 2004).
59 These French efforts to open the package deal of Euratom and the Common Market, so as to delay the latter, angered Spaak: see Spaak's speech at ECSC Assembly in Strasbourg, 11 May 1956: HAEC CEAB3 No. 842/030.
60 Lynch, *France and the International Economy*, p. 178

61 Moravcsik, *Choice*, p. 115.
62 P. Guillen, 'L'Europe Remède à l'Impuissance Française? Le Gouvernement Guy Mollet et la Négociation des Traités de Rome,' *Revue d'Histoire Diplomatique* 102 (1988): 319–335.
63 For the French position and interests on Euratom, as well as the negotiation strategies it adopted, see P. Guillen, 'La France et la Négociation des Traités de Rome: L'Euratom,' in *Il Rilancio dell'Europa e i Trattati di Roma*, Enrico Serra ed. (Milan: A. Guifré, 1989), pp. 513–524; P. Guillen, 'La France et la Négociation du Traité d'Euratom,' *Relations Internationales* 44 (1985): 391–412.
64 The non-Communist Confédération Française des Travailleurs Chrétiens (CFTC) and Force Ouvrière trade unions spoke out in favour of the Common Market in July 1956, while the Communist-controlled Confédération Générale du Travail (CGT) continued to paint an 'apocalyptic vision' of the Common Market; see Guillen, 'Frankreich,' pp. 15–16.
65 See Mahant, *Birthmarks*.
66 See Guillen, 'Frankreich'.
67 Mollet consulted with the National Assembly while the treaties were still in the drafting process because he was 'mindful of the mistakes made over the [EDC] treaty, in whose early stages Parliament was never adequately consulted': *The Times*, 'Euratom Storm Brewing: Hostile Rumblings in France' (5 July 1956). He won the vote on Euratom with a majority of 342 to 183 votes: *The Times*, 'Big French Majority for Euratom: Right to Make Atomic Weapons' (12 July 1956).
68 Guillen, 'L'Europe Remède'.
69 J.G. Giauque, *Grand Designs and Visions of Unity: The Atlantic Powers and the Reorganization of Western Europe, 1955–1963* (Durham: The University of North Carolina Press, 2002).
70 See Guillen, 'L'Europe Remède'; also Guillen, 'Frankreich'.
71 Mollet followed contradictory policies on Africa and European integration; see A. Grosser, 'Suez, Hungary and European Integration,' *International Organization* 11 (3) (1957): 470–480. One reason for Adenauer's initial scepticism about Mollet came about after Mollet's 5 April 1956 interview with *U.S. News and World Report*, in which he stipulated that German unification was only possible with German disarmament. Adenauer was 'most indignant' at Mollet's declarations: H.-P. Schwarz, *Konrad Adenauer: A German Politician and Statesman in a Period of War, Revolution, and Reconstruction. Volume Two, The Statesman: 1952-1967* (Oxford: Berghahn, 1997), pp. 191–192; see also *DDF* 1956, I: doc. 218, doc. 221, doc. 228. The matter was also discussed at a Federal Cabinet special session, 12 April 1956: *KP* online.
72 While Adenauer was at first concerned about the situation in France, and the French government's commitment to the Common Market, he came to appreciate the severity of Mollet's internal difficulties, as well as his personal leadership on Europe: K. Adenauer, *Briefe 1955-1957: Rhöndorfer Ausgabe*. R. Morsey and H.-P. Schwarz eds. (Berlin: Siedler, 1998), doc. 114, doc. 116, doc. 212.
73 Schwarz, *Konrad Adenauer*, p. 232. Pineau (although being pro-European) 'showed himself distrustful of Bonn.' He was a Résistance leader who had made 'grim experiences with the Germans.' Jules Moch led a broad faction in the SFIO and was considered 'anti-German' and anti-Europe; see Federal Cabinet special session, 12 April 1956: *KP* online.
74 On Adenauer's discussions with Mollet to resolve the Saar issue, see press conference, 5 June 1956 in Bonn: StBKAH 02.14/17.
75 H. von Brentano, *Deutschland, Europa und die Welt: Reden zur Deutschen Aussenpolitik*, F. Böhm ed. (Bonn: Verlag für Zeitarchive, 1962). For von Brentano (pp. 228–229), the resolution of the Saar issue was 'convincing proof for the correctness and necessity of the policy of European reconciliation and

cooperation.' For Jahn, the Saar was a 'touchstone' of Franco-German relations; Jahn, *An Adenauers Seite*, p. 341.
76 See Adenauer to Kühn-Leitz, 18 October 1956: Adenauer, *Briefe*, doc. 220. On Adenauer's perception of the Saar compromise as a 'first rank' European issue, see Adenauer's declaration on Franco-German negotiations, 154th Federal Cabinet meeting, 3 October 1956, *KP* online. On how the Saar issue held back Franco-German relations, see A. Adenauer, *Erinnerungen 1955–1959* (Stuttgart: Deutsche Verlags-Anstalt, 1967), pp. 516–523.
77 J.G. Giauque, 'Bilateral Summit Diplomacy in Western European and Transatlantic Relations, 1956–63,' *European History Quarterly* 31 (3) (1996): 427–445.
78 On the friendly atmosphere between the two leaders, see Adenauer to Mollet, 3 October 1956: Adenauer, *Briefe*, doc. 209.
79 See Giauque, *Grand Designs*.
80 *Ibid.*, p. 28.
81 See 155th Federal Cabinet meeting, 5 October 1956: *KP* online.
82 H.-J. Küsters, 'Walter Hallstein and the Negotiations on the Treaties of Rome 1955–57,' in *Walter Hallstein: The Forgotten European?* W. Loth, W. Wallace, and W. Wessels eds. (Basingstoke: Macmillan, 1998), p. 73.
83 C. Williams, *Adenauer: The Father of New Germany* (London: Abacus, 2003), p. 441.
84 See Tauch, 'Testimony'.
85 In a 11 January 1957 letter to Adenauer, Mollet alluded to the interlinkage of their friendly relations with progress in the Brussels negotiations; quoted in Adenauer, *Briefe*, doc. 254 [fn3, 533].
86 *The Times*, 'New Structure for Europe: Less French Doubt of German Policy' (6 November 1956).
87 Britain, France, and Israel conducted military operations to recapture the Suez Canal from Egyptian control from 29 October 1956 until 6 November 1956, when heavy American pressure on Britain in particular led Eden to abandon the mission. On 5 November 1956, the Soviet Union had intervened militarily in Hungary to crush a popular uprising against Communist rule.
88 Tauch, 'Testimony,' p. 61. For the impact of Suez on French European policies, see Pineau and Rimbaud, *Le Grand Pari*.
89 See Adenauer's report on his trip to Paris, Federal Cabinet special session, 7 November 1956: *KP* online.
90 There are indications that Eden drew a similar conclusion. In his letter to Adenauer of 13 November 13, 1956, he wrote: 'If there is one conclusion which can be derived from these events [Suez] it will certainly be the one that Europe has to move closer together': quoted in Adenauer, *Erinnerungen 1955–1959*, p. 264. The lack of American support during the Suez crisis hurt Eden, whose 'lifelong lack of warmth towards the United States . . . verged on anti-Americanism': see V. Rothwell, *Anthony Eden: A Political Biography 1931–57* (Manchester: Manchester University Press, 1992), p. 4. Yet despite the fact that Eden felt let down by the US, to the point of calling them 'indignant,' it was his 'immediate purpose' to focus more on repairing the transatlantic relationship than on enhancing European integration: A. Eden, *The Memoirs of the Rt. Hon. Sir Anthony Eden K.G., P.C., M.C. Full Circle* (London: Cassell, 1960), pp. 559, 562.
91 Williams, *Adenauer*, p. 442.
92 The remaining issues concerned social policies and harmonisation: H.-J. Küsters, 'Adenauers Europapolitik in der Gründungsphase der Europäischen Wirtschaftsgemeinschaft,' *Vierteljahrshefte für Zeitgeschichte* 31 (4) (1983): 646–673. These matters were discussed at the summit of ECSC foreign ministers of 20–21

86   *Leadership and critical junctures*

      October 1956 in Paris, which had to be abandoned prematurely due to insurmountable Franco-German differences: see Lynch, *France and the International Economy*.

93 Milward, *European Rescue*, p. 215.

94 *The Times*, 'Towards a Common Market: Decision to Include French Union' (10 October 1956).

95 *The Times*, 'European Free Market: Declaration To-Day' (20 February 1957); *The Times*, 'Common Market Agreement by Six Powers: Funds for Overseas Territories' (21 February 1957).

96 See Lynch, *France and the International Economy*, pp. 204–205. An investment fund of 200,000 million francs was to be set up, to which France and Germany would each contribute 34 %, with Belgium, the Netherlands, Italy, and Luxembourg contributing the rest. The French overseas territories were to get 180,000 million francs out the fund, while the payments for the Belgian, Dutch, and Italian territories were only 10,500 million, 12,250 million, and 1,750 million francs, respectively. In this sense, Germany not only made the largest contribution, but also got no payments in return, the main share going to the French territories. The German idea of its own version of the Marshall Plan for French overseas territories was rejected by France, which feared that Germany would avoid importing agricultural produce from the French territories: On the attitude of German business leaders to the Common Market, see: G. Almond, 'The Political Attitudes of German Business,' *World Politics* 8 (2) (1956): 157–186.

97 *The Times*, 'French Plans for Common Market: Difficulties Seen by Partners' (19 February 1957).

98 Mollet got stronger support for Euratom than he had anticipated because he was able to convince right-wing parties that Euratom would not impede France's nuclear weapons programme: note of Müller-Roschach on the importance of French nuclear armament on Germany's defence and foreign policy, 7 July 1965: PAAA B130 10.096.

99 The German inexperience in African affairs is apparent in the account of Adenauer's advisor, Hans Edgar Jahn, on the German concessions on French overseas territories and the EEC: see Jahn, *An Adenauers Seite*.

100 Adenauer defended his concessions on the French overseas territories by claiming that 'the whole thing with Africa . . . has nothing to do with colonialism': see Küsters, 'Adenauers Europapolitik,' p. 668. In a 24 February 1957 letter to his son Paul, he wrote: 'We [Mollet and him] not only took another great step in the creation of the United Europe. Europe would, in my opinion, become stunted and die, if it does not exploit new resources in Africa. I hope that this will succeed. Africa is after all the complement to Europe. Dulles already pointed out to me two years ago that we should take care of Africa': Adenauer, *Briefe*, doc. 269. This idea is also discussed in Adenauer's article 'Unsere Aufgabe,' *Rheinischer Merkur*, 20 May 1950: HAEU WL 71/166-7.

101 See Küsters, 'Walter Hallstein'.

102 Adenauer had already indicated his willingness to make concessionary sidepayments to France at the Luxembourg meeting with Mollet in June 1956, when he agreed to purchase 1 billion DM worth of French arms on an annual basis: *Der Spiegel* 10 (25) (20 June 1956): 9.

103 See Moravcsik, *Choice*, p. 90.

104 *Ibid.*, p. 136.

105 See Adenauer, *Erinnerungen 1955–1959*, p. 267 as an example of how Spaak was perceived to be crucial for the successful outcome of the Brussels negotiations.

106 Adenauer's support for European integration is illustrated by the positive initial reaction to the Messina Conference during the 89th meeting of the Federal Cabinet: *KP* 1955, 8: 405–406.

107 See Maillard to Eden, 13 February 1956: TNA PREM 11/1338/24.
108 This was particularly the case in Germany, were Adenauer feared that if no progress were made on the Messina proposals, American support for European integration would vanish. German officials expected that 'isolationist tendencies' would prevail after the November 1956 elections: 154th Federal Cabinet meeting, 3 October 1956: *KP* online.
109 See H. Young, *This Blessed Plot: Britain and Europe from Churchill to Blair* (Basingstoke: Macmillan, 1998).
110 Eden's reluctance to exercise leadership on European integration has given rise to a substantial body of literature: see O. Daddow, *Britain and Europe since 1945: Historiographical Perspectives on Integration* (Manchester: Manchester University Press, 2004); also C.A. Wurm, 'Britain and European Integration, 1945–63,' *Contemporary European History* 7 (2) (1998): 246–291. Several historians suggest that Eden's attitude constituted a 'missed opportunity' for British leadership on and engagement in Europe: Thorpe, *Eden*; M.P.C. Schaad, *Bullying Bonn: Anglo-German Diplomacy on European Integration, 1955–61* (Basingstoke: Macmillan, 2000); R. Denman, *Missed Chances: Britain & Europe in the Twentieth Century* (London: Indigo, 1997); W. Kaiser, *Using Europe, Abusing the Europeans: Britain and European Integration, 1945–63* (Basingstoke: Macmillan, 1996); W. Kaiser, *Großbritannien und die Europäische Wirtschaftsgemeinschaft 1955–1961. Von Messina nach Canossa* (Berlin: Akademie Verlag, 1996); L. Bell, *The Throw that Failed: Britain's Original Application to Join the Common Market* (London: New European Publications, 1995); S. George, *Britain and European Integration since 1945* (Oxford: Blackwell, 1991); Franks, 'Britain and Europe,' pp. 89–104; Benoit, *Europe at Sixes*. Others claim that the 'refusal to join early attempts to create the European Common Market is . . . one of the greatest mistakes of British post war statesmanship': see J.W. Young, '"The Parting of the Ways?": Britain, the Messina Conference and the Spaak Committee, June-December 1955,' in *British Foreign Policy 1945–56*, M. Dockrill and J.W. Young eds. (Basingstoke: Macmillan, 1989), p. 197. A similar argument in relation to the Schuman Plan is made in E. Dell, *The Schuman Plan and the British Abdication of Leadership in Europe* (Oxford: Clarendon Press, 1995). It is also suggested that Eden's behaviour was characteristic of British governments in general: see J. Melissen and B. Zeemann, 'Britain and Western Europe, 1945–51: Opportunities Lost?' *International Affairs* 63 (19) (1986–87): 81–95. For a broader overview, see G. Clemens, 'A History of Failures and Miscalculations? Britain's Relationship to the European Communities in the Postwar Era (1945–1973),' *Contemporary European History* 13 (2) (2004): 223–232.
111 Young, 'The Parting of the Ways?' p. 197.
112 On Mollet's understanding of the Common Market as a long-term policy for economic reform, see telegram of 24 October 1956 from Paris to Foreign Office: TNA FO 371/122036/85.
113 Even in the public domain, the Common Market came to be known as 'Spaakistan,' and Spaak himself was often dubbed 'Mr. Europe' in the contemporary media: J. Huizinga, *Mr. Europe* (London: Weidenfeld and Nicolson, 1961).
114 D. Rogosch, *Vorstellungen von Europa: Europabilder in der SPD und bei den belgischen Sozialisten 1945–1957* (Hamburg: Krämer, 1996). See also D. Orlow, *Common Destiny: A Comparative History of the Dutch, French, and German Social Democratic Parties, 1945–1969* (New York: Berghahn, 2001).
115 See Nutting, 10 January 1956: TNA FO 371/122023/7.
116 *The Times*, 'Common Market Agreement by Six Powers. Funds for Overseas Territories' (21 February 1957).

117 Spaak to Eden, 7 February 1956: TNA PREM 11/1338.
118 TNA PREM 11/1338.
119 Macmillan to Eden, 28 February 1956: TNA PREM 11/1337.
120 Selkirk to Selwyn Lloyd, 20 February 1956: TNA FO 371/122023/74.
121 Laurent, 'The Diplomacy of the Rome Treaty,' p. 209.
122 See Laurent, 'Diplomacy of *Junktim*'.
123 P.-H. Spaak, *Combats Inachevés: De l'Espoir aux Decéptions* (Brussels: Fayard, 1969).
124 TNA PREM 11/1337.
125 Dumoulin, *Spaak*, p. 508.
126 TNA FO 371/121955/117.
127 P.-H. Spaak, *The Continuing Battle: Memoirs of a European 1936–1966* (London: Weidenfeld and Nicolson, 1971), p. 236.
128 *Ibid.*, p. 225.
129 Quoted in Parsons, *Certain Idea*, p. 90.
130 Laurent, 'Paul-Henri Spaak,' pp. 373–396.
131 Laurent, 'Paul-Henri Spaak,' p. 382. Seeing the Common Market as a catalyst for economic modernisation and reform was a hallmark of the Mollet government: see Valery's note of 2 February 1956 on the Common Market: DDF 1957, I: doc. 67.
132 Laurent, 'Paul-Henri Spaak,' p. 395.
133 Laurent, 'The Diplomacy of the Rome Treaty,' p. 220.
134 D. Heater, *The Idea of European Unity* (Leicester: Leicester University Press, 1992), p. 164.
135 Spaak and Monnet – who headed the influential pro-integrationist lobby group 'Action Committee for the United States of Europe' – had different ideas about the viability of the Common Market. Monnet strongly supported Euratom and used his influence to facilitate Spaak's efforts for Euratom in the Brussels negotiations: see Gerbet, *Construction*. Monnet thought that the Common Market plan was too complex and hazardous to be politically viable. His input on the Common Market initiative was therefore limited. While Spaak was convinced that only the package deal of Euratom and the EEC would be acceptable to both France and Germany, Monnet sought to sign Euratom first and delay the Common Market: Laurent, 'The Diplomacy of *Junktim*'.
136 Laurent, 'Paul-Henri Spaak,' p. 392.
137 Tauch, 'Testimony,' p. 61.
138 Laurent, 'The Diplomacy of the Rome Treaty,' p. 219.
139 On Adenauer's strategies for political survival and his means of consolidating his support base, see P.H. Merkl, 'Equilibrium, Structure of Interests and Leadership: Adenauer's Survival as Chancellor,' *The American Political Science Review* 56 (3) (1962): 634–650.
140 Poignant examples of this behaviour are illustrated in Adenauer's letters to Erhard of 5 November 1955, 19 December 1955, 13 April 1956, 16 March 1957, and 17 March 1957: K. Adenauer, *Briefe 1955–1957. Rhöndorfer Ausgabe*, R. Morsey and H.-P. Schwarz eds. (Berlin: Siedler, 1998), doc. 47, doc. 82, doc. 142, doc. 282, doc. 283.
141 On the positions and European policies of the SPD, see R. Moeller, 'The German Social Democrats,' in *Political Parties and the European Union*, J. Gaffney ed. (London: Routledge, 1996), pp. 1–30; also Rogosch, *Vorstellungen*. On the debates about whether Socialist parties should pursue a nationalist or an internationalist strategy regarding European integration, see P. Murray, 'Nationalist or Internationalist? Socialists and European Unity,' in *Visions of European Unity*, P. Murray and P. Rich eds. (Boulder: Westview, 1996), pp. 159–182.

142 See Adenauer's speech at a CDU rally, Wuppertal-Elberfeld, 5 May 1946: HAEU WL 71/040–43. Also illustrative is Adenauer's advocacy of a 'European federation' in his article 'Auf den Geist kommt es an,' *Allgemeinen Kölnischen Rundschau* (31 December 1948): HAEU WL 71/090–1.
143 See Guillen, 'Frankreich'.
144 Giauque, 'Bilateral Summit Diplomacy'. See Adenauer's article 'Klare Sicht,' *Badisches Tageblatt*, 31 December 1955: StBKAH 02.13/57.
145 See Adenauer to Kühn-Leitz, 19 February 1956, and Adenauer to Heinemann, 16 February 1956: Adenauer, *Briefe*, doc. 116, doc. 114.
146 G. von Gersdorff, *Adenauers Außenpolitik gegenüber den Siegermächten 1954. Westdeutsche Bewaffnung und internationale Politik*. Beiträge zur Militärgeschichte, Vol. 41 (Munich: Oldenbourg, 1994).
147 Adenauer to Eden, 24 October 1955: Adenauer, *Briefe*, doc. 41.
148 S.A. Kocs, *Autonomy or Power? The Franco-German Relationship and Europe's Strategic Choices 1955–1995* (Westport: Greenwood, 1995), p. 16. See also Dulles to Macmillan, 12 December 1955: TNA PREM 11/1333.
149 W. Besson, 'The Conflict of Traditions: the Historical Basis of West German Foreign Policy,' in *Britain and West Germany: Changing Societies and the Future of Foreign Policy*, K. Kaiser and R. Morgan eds. (London: Oxford University Press, 1971).
150 See Küsters, 'Adenauers Europapolitik,' and Schwarz, 'Adenauer und Europa'.
151 K. Hildebrand, *German Foreign Policy from Bismarck to Adenauer* (London: Unwin Hyman, 1989), p. 201.
152 H. von Brentano, *Germany and Europe: Reflections on German Foreign Policy* (London: André Deutsch, 1964), p. 65.
153 C. Hacke, *Die Außenpolitik Bundesrepublik Deutschland. Weltmacht wider Willen?* revised edition (Frankfurt: Ullstein, 1997), p. 65.
154 A. Deighton, 'British-West German Relations, 1945–1972,' in *Uneasy Allies: British-German Relations and European Integration since 1945*, K. Larres and E. Meehan eds. (Oxford: Oxford University Press, 2000), p. 28.
155 L. Sicking, 'A Colonial Echo: France and the Colonial Dimension of the European Economic Community,' *French Colonial History* 5 (2004): 216. Adenauer addressed the extent to which the historical past affected the dynamics of European integration in a speech, 23 October 1954: HAEC CEAB 2/178 (1955).
156 A. Döring-Manteufel, 'Rheinischer Katholik im Kalten Krieg. Das "Christliche Europa" in der Weltsicht Konrad Adenauers,' in *Die Christen und die Entstehung der Europäischen Gemeinschaft*, M. Greschat and W. Loth eds. (Stuttgart: Kohlhammer, 1994), pp. 237–246. On the fact that Adenauer's commitment to and leadership on European integration gained him trust among other European leaders, see Churchill to Adenauer, 30 March 1955: TNA PREM 11/845.
157 Schwarz, *Konrad Adenauer*, p. 245.
158 Sicking, 'A Colonial Echo'.
159 E. Forndran, 'German-American Disagreements over Arms-Control Policy,' in *The United States and Germany in the Era of the Cold War, 1945–1990: A Handbook*, Vol I: 1945–1968, D. Junker ed. (Cambridge: Cambridge University Press, 2004), pp. 243–244.
160 The extent to which Adenauer's worries about the reliability of the American engagement in Europe affected Franco-German discussion becomes obvious during a 17 September 1956 meeting between Adenauer, Hallstein, and Pineau: *DDF* 1956, II: doc. 188.
161 Schwarz, *Konrad Adenauer*.
162 D. Gowland A. Turner, and A. Wright, *Britain and European Integration since 1945: On The Sidelines* (London: Routledge, 2010), p. 49.

163 See UK Embassy Paris to Foreign Office, 24 October 1956: TNA FO 371/122036/75-6.
164 Deighton, 'British-West German Relations,' p. 34.
165 W.F. Hanrieder, 'The Foreign Policies of the Federal Republic of Germany, 1949–1989,' *German Studies Review* 12 (2) (1989): 311–332.
166 See Adenauer to Hunhold, 9 May 1951: Adenauer, *Briefe über Deutschland*, pp. 122–123; Adenauer to Döpfner, 14 January 1956: Adenauer, *Briefe 1955–1957*, doc. 92; speech at the 6th CDU party congress, Stuttgart, 29 April 1956: StBKAH 02.14/13/3; speech at the 77th German 'Katholikentag,' Cologne, 2 September 1956: StBKAH 02.14/28/5.
167 W. Loth, 'Politische Integration nach 1945. Motive und Antriebskräfte bei Konrad Adenauer und Charles de Gaulle,' in *Europäische Einigung im 19. und 20. Jahrhundert. Akteure und Antriebskräfte*, U. Lappenküper and G. Thiemeyer eds. (Paderborn: Schöningh, 2013), pp. 137–142; W. Weidenfeld, *Konrad Adenauer: Die geistigen Grundlagen der westeuropäischen Integrationspolitik des ersten Bonner Bundeskanzlers* (Bonn: Europa Union, 1976), pp. 209–215.
168 See A. Poppinga, *Konrad Adenauer: Geschichtsverständnis, Weltanschauung und politische Praxis* (Stuttgart: Deutsche Verlags-Anstalt., 1975).
169 W.E. Paterson, 'The German Christian Democrats,' in *Political Parties and the European Union*, John Gaffney ed. (London: Routledge, 1996), p. 53.
170 Quoted in P. Weymar, *Konrad Adenauer: The Authorized Biography* (Worcester: Andre Deutsch, 1957), p. 420.
171 Loth, 'Politische Integration,' p. 139.
172 Paterson, 'German Christian Democrats,' p. 53.
173 W. Loth, 'Adenauer's Final Western Choice, 1955–58,' in *Europe, Cold War, and Coexistence 1953–1965*, W. Loth ed. (London: Frank Cass, 2004), pp. 23–24.
174 K. Epstein, 'The Adenauer Era in German History,' in *A New Europe?* S.R. Graubard ed. (Boston: Houghton Mifflin, 1964), p. 107.
175 See W. Loth, 'From the "Third Force" to the Common Market: Discussions about Europe and the Future of the Nation-State in West Germany, 1945–57,' in *The Postwar Challenge: Cultural, Social, and Political Change in Western Europe, 1945–58*, D. Geppert ed. (Oxford: Oxford University Press, 2003), pp. 191–210.
176 See P.W. Wenger, 'Schuman und Adenauer,' in *Konrad Adenauer und seine Zeit. Politik und Persönlichkeit des ersten Bundeskanzlers. Beiträge von Weg- und Zeitgenossen*, D. Blumenwitz, K. Gotto, H. Maier, K. Repgen, and H.-P. Schwarz eds. (Stuttgart: Deutsche Verlags-Anstalt, 1976), pp. 395–414.
177 S. Guillaume, 'Guy Mollet et l'Allemagne,' in *Guy Mollet. Un Camarade en Republique*, B. Menager, P. Ratte, J.-L. Thiebault, R. Vandenbussche, and C.-M. Wallon-Leducq eds. (Lille: Presses Universitaires de Lille, 1987), pp. 481–497.
178 Schwarz, 'Adenauer und Europa,' p. 483.
179 See S. Lee, *Victory in Europe: Britain and Germany since 1945* (Harlow: Pearson, 2001).
180 Nutting, 10 January 1956: TNA FO 371/122023/6–9.
181 Schwarz, *Konrad Adenauer*, p. 231.
182 Weidenfeld, *Konrad Adenauer*, p. 197.
183 Hacke, *Außenpolitik*, p. 69.
184 *Ibid.*, p. 65.
185 Paterson, 'The German Christian Democrats,' pp. 53–54.
186 *Ibid.*
187 G.A. Craig, 'Konrad Adenauer and His Diplomats,' in *The Diplomats, 1939–1979*, G.A. Craig and F.L. Loewenheim eds. (Princeton: Princeton University Press, 1994), p. 202.

188 Adenauer, *Briefe 1955–1957*, doc. 212.
189 Laurent, 'The Diplomacy of the Rome Treaty,' p. 211.
190 Charlton, *The French Left*, pp. 36–37.
191 Parsons, 'Showing Ideas,' p. 71.
192 *Ibid.*, p. 72.
193 Feske, 'The Road to Suez,' p. 183.
194 Cole, 'The French Socialists,' p. 72.
195 Feske, 'The Road to Suez'.
196 Laurent, 'The Diplomacy of the Rome Treaty,' p. 212.
197 *Ibid.*
198 Parsons, 'Showing Ideas,' p. 72.
199 Lynch, 'France and European Integration,' p. 119.
200 Laurent, 'The Diplomacy of the Rome Treaty,' p. 217.
201 J.W. Young, 'Conclusion,' in *Whitehall and the Suez Crisis*, S. Kelly and A. Gorst eds. (London: Frank Cass, 2000), p. 231.
202 See Wright's memo, 31 January 1956, in response to Nutting and Jebb: TNA FO 371/122023/19–20.
203 Peters to Cairncross, 16 November 1955: TNA PREM 11/1333.
204 See Spaak, 7 February 1956: TNA PREM 11/1338; also Maillard to Eden, 13 February 1956: TNA PREM 11/1338/24. On the fact that Spaak and Eden had major 'differences of method' on European integration, see Foreign Office to UK Embassy Brussels, 25 February 1956: TNA FO 371/122023/90.
205 Peters to Cairncross, 16 November 1955: TNA PREM 11/1333.
206 Young, 'The Parting of the Ways?' p. 197.
207 J. Frankel, *British Foreign Policy 1945–1973* (London: Oxford University Press, 1975), pp. 233–234.
208 R. Lamb, *The Failure of the Eden Government* (London: Sidgwick and Jackson, 1987).
209 Eden and his government faced some parliamentary criticism over their ambiguous stance towards the Messina Conference and Britain's engagement in the Brussels negotiations: *Hansard* 5s, 542: 813–966.
210 Young, *This Blessed Plot*, p. 92, p. 96.
211 S. Burgess and R. Edwards, 'The Six Plus One: British Policy-Making and the Question of European Economic Integration, 1955,' *International Affairs* 64 (3): 413.
212 Feske, 'The Road to Suez,' p. 170.
213 Burgess and Edwards, 'Six Plus One,' p. 413.
214 Wurm, 'Britain and European Integration,' p. 255.
215 Young, 'Conclusion,' p. 231.
216 A. Sampson, *Political Leaders of the Twentieth Century: Macmillan: A Study in Ambiguity* (Harmondsworth: Penguin, 1968), p. 206.
217 J. Tratt, *The Macmillan Government and Europe: A Study in the Process of Policy Development* (Basingstoke: Macmillan, 1996), p. 198.
218 Eden to Macmillan, 3 March 1956: TNA PREM 11/1337.
219 Eden, *Memoirs*, p. 36.
220 Feske, 'The Road to Suez,' p. 171. The discussions on the Common Market were seen to 'weaken the Commonwealth relationship, both economically and politically': FO to Washington, 17 November 1955: TNA PREM 11/1333.
221 *Ibid.*, p. 172.
222 Young, *This Blessed Plot*, p. 66.
223 See Thorpe, *Eden*.
224 Feske, 'The Road to Suez,' p. 171.
225 R.G. Hughes, *Britain, Germany, and the Cold War: The Search for a European Détente 1949–1967* (Abingdon: Routledge, 2007), p. 33.

226 British disinterest turned into 'active opposition' throughout the winter of 1955–1956. Schaad, 'Plan G,' p. 44.
227 See trade charts attached to note from Fords to Rudoe, February 1958: TNA BT 70/616.
228 Steel, 'The United Kingdom and the Western World,' 22 July 1957: TNA PREM 11/1844.
229 S. George, *Britain and European Integration since 1945*, Making Contemporary Britain Series (Oxford: Blackwell, 1991), pp. 42–43.
230 *Ibid.*
231 Thorneycroft to Macmillan, 22 May 1956: TNA FO 371/122028. See Schaad, 'Plan G,' pp. 54–59.
232 In relation to Germany, a senior official noted that 'the German view is diametrically opposed to HMG': see Tebbit to Eden, 31 December 1956: TNA FO 371/122044.
233 Jebb to Selwyn Lloyd, 27 April 1957: TNA PREM 11/1844.
234 See Tennant to Kipping, 20 February 1956: TNA BT 11/5402.
235 Thorneycroft to Eden, 20 January 1956: TNA PREM 11/1333; see also British Embassy Paris to Macmillan, 15 June 1955: TNA T 232/430.
236 M. Beloff, 'Britain, Europe, and the Atlantic Community,' *International Organization* 17 (3) (1963): 574.
237 Draft report 'Political Association of the United Kingdom with Europe,' 16 January 1957: TNA CAB 21/3323.
238 H. Macmillan, *Riding the Storm 1956–1959* (London: Macmillan, 1971), p. 87.
239 S. George and D. Haythorne, 'The British Labour Party,' in *Political Parties and the European Union*, J. Gaffney ed. (London: Routledge, 1996), pp. 110–121; P. Morris, 'The British Conservative Party,' in *Political Parties and the European Union*, J. Gaffney ed. (London: Routledge, 1996); R.G. Hughes, '"We Are Not Seeking Strength for Its Own Sake": The British Labour Party, West Germany and the Cold War, 1951–64,' *Cold War History* 3 (1) (2002): 67–94; A. Forster, *Euroscepticism in Contemporary British Politics: Opposition to Europe in the British Conservative and Labour Parties since 1945* (London: Routledge, 2002); J. Turner, *The Tories and Europe* (Manchester: Manchester University Press, 2000).
240 See Nutting's letter of January 10, 1956: TNA FO 371/122023/5–11. On the incompatibility of the Common Market with the Commonwealth preferential trade agreements, see Thorneycroft's press conference, 3 October 1956: TNA BT 70/616.
241 Morris, 'The British Conservative Party,' p. 127; W. Horsfall Carter, *Speaking European: The Anglo-Continental Cleavage* (London: George Allen and Unwin, 1966), p. 104.
242 Burgess and Edwards, 'Six Plus One,' p. 396.
243 Schaad, *Bullying Bonn*, p. 3.
244 Beloff, 'Britain,' p. 578.
245 Burgess and Edwards, 'Six Plus One,' p. 412.
246 D. Sanders, *Losing an Empire, Finding a Role: British Foreign Policy since 1945* (Basingstoke: Macmillan, 1990).
247 Young, *This Blessed Plot*.
248 Quoted in *ibid*.
249 Benoit, *Europe*, p. 103.
250 Spaak, *Continuing Battle*, pp. 232–233.
251 Schaad, *Bullying Bonn*, p. 166.
252 In particular, Eden feared that the proposed common external tariff 'would seriously damage what was left of "imperial preference",' the special trade relations within the Commonwealth, which had been established at the 1932 Ottawa Conference: see Sanders, *Losing an Empire*, p. 138.

253 George, *Britain*, p. 43.
254 Spaak, *Continuing Battle*, pp. 232–233; Burgess and Edwards, 'Six Plus One,' p. 411.
255 Beloff, 'Britain,' p. 578.
256 Thorpe, *Eden*, p. 372.
257 Morris, 'British Conservative Party,' p. 127.
258 S. Hoffmann, 'De Gaulle, Europe, and the Atlantic Alliance,' *International Organization* 18 (1) (1964): 12.
259 Morris, 'British Conservative Party,' p. 125.
260 *Ibid*.
261 A. Hovey Jr, 'Britain and the Unification of Europe,' *International Organization* 9 (3) (1955): 332.
262 Schaad, *Bullying Bonn*, p. 7. Even after the Treaties of Rome had been signed, some British officials continued to speculate on whether the French would fail to ratify the treaties: see de Zulueta to Macmillan, 29 May 1957; and Macmillan's response of 3 June 1957: TNA PREM 11/1844.
263 Franks, 'Britain and Europe,' p. 89.
264 Hovey, 'Britain,' pp. 332–333.
265 Frankel, *British Foreign Policy*, p. 238.
266 Morris, 'British Conservative Party,' p. 125.
267 See Macmillan to Eden, 28 February 1956: TNA PREM 11/1337.
268 Eden, *Memoirs*, p. 29.
269 Frankel, *British Foreign Policy*, p. 239.
270 Young, 'Parting of the Ways?' p. 218.
271 Schaad, *Bullying Bonn*, pp. 166–167.
272 A. Carlton, *Anthony Eden: A Biography* (London: Allen Lane, 1981), p. 394.
273 Young, 'Parting of the Ways?' p. 204.
274 Schaad, *Bullying Bonn*, p. 167. Gladwyn Jebb hinted that Britain 'shall be unable for long to avoid the choice between closer association, political as well as economic, with Europe and increased dependence on the United States, amounting almost to becoming a forty-ninth State': see de Zulueta to Macmillan, 29 May 1957: TNA PREM 11/1844.
275 W. Yondorf, 'Monnet and the Action Committee: The Formative Period of the European Communities,' *International Organization* 19 (4) (1965): 905.
276 Schaad, *Bullying Bonn*, p. 164.
277 Quoted in Weigall and Stirk, *Origins*, p. 112.
278 Schaad, *Bullying Bonn*, p. 13.
279 Franks, 'Britain and Europe,' p. 96.

4 Changes in leadership constellations, 1969–1973

After 1957, the Common Market gradually consolidated itself as the lynchpin of European integration. Numerous officials in the British government – among them Edward Heath – began to ponder whether Britain should join the Common Market.[1] They eventually 'converted' Eden's successor, Harold Macmillan, to apply for membership.[2] Macmillan did so rather reluctantly in 1961, as did Labour's Harold Wilson again in 1967,[3] but both attempts were rejected by France. Charles de Gaulle blocked Britain's bid to join the Common Market out of the fear that the UK would dilute its cohesion and challenge France's central role in Europe.[4] In the early 1960s, the 'qualified guess' among British policy-makers was that France and de Gaulle constituted the 'main obstacle' which had to be overcome if Britain was to enter the Common Market.'[5]

Against this background of an entrenched disparity between a British-Atlanticist and a French-Gaullist vision of European integration,[6] it is surprising that Britain's accession to the Common Market unfolded so smoothly between 1969 and 1973.[7] As Douglas Hurd – then the Prime Minister's Political Secretary and later Britain's Foreign Secretary – recalls: 'Anyone who considers soberly the characters of General de Gaulle and Mr Wilson must marvel not that Britain entered the Community so late, but that she ever managed to enter at all.'[8]

Enlargement eventually came about in no small part due to a change in leadership. Between June 1969 and July 1970, new governments were elected in France, West Germany, and the UK. Georges Pompidou assumed the Presidency in June 1969 and Willy Brandt became West Germany's first social democratic chancellor in September of the same year, while Edward Heath won an unexpected victory for the Conservatives in June 1970.[9] In contrast to their predecessors they set their eyes on enlargement, albeit for different reasons.[10] On European integration, Pompidou, Brandt, and Heath – each in his own way – felt strongly about the need to break the cycle of Europe's economic stagnation and diminishing political influence in international affairs.[11]

The chances for British membership were clearly improved by these changes at the top.[12] Pompidou, Brandt, and Heath were more inclined than their predecessors to see enlargement as a solution rather than a threat to their interests.[13] Their change in tone and attitude towards European integration cannot be solely explained by material factors alone.[14] After all, the geopolitical and economic conditions did not change substantially between early 1969 (when enlargement seemed remote and unrealistic) and mid-1970 (when British membership was clearly on the political agenda). The economic conditions in France and Britain at the time did not leave Pompidou and Heath with an obvious desire for enlargement.[15] Neither was there a clear commercial case for France and West Germany to include the rapidly deteriorating British economy into the Common Market.[16]

It is therefore imperative to understand why Pompidou, Brandt, and Heath came to favour enlargement over other initiatives for institutional reforms, and economic and monetary integration, that were prominent at the time,[17] and how they managed to find a personal rapport to break the deadlock that characterised the integration process in the late 1960s.

A new generation of leaders

The story of Britain's accession to the Common Market begins with de Gaulle's resignation on 28 April 1969. In the decade since 1958, he had decisively influenced French foreign and European policies. Although his move was triggered by the fallout from his handling of the 1968 student revolts and his defeat in the 1969 constitutional referendum, de Gaulle's departure from office had a profound and immediate impact on European affairs.[18]

France's partners and allies had often found it awkward to deal with him and his rhetoric of *grandeur*.[19] Many irritations over the course and instruments of French foreign policies had ensued. In particular, de Gaulle's relations with European neighbours and the United States had become increasingly difficult.[20] To illustrate just a few points of contention: he had aborted British efforts aimed at establishing an OEEC free trade area in 1959, choosing instead to consolidate the Common Market. In 1962 and again in 1967, he had – to the dismay of many of his closest allies – blocked Britain's bid for membership in the Common Market. In 1963, de Gaulle signed a treaty of friendship with West Germany,[21] which disconcerted Britain and the United States, as well as so-called Atlanticists in Germany.[22] Throughout the 'Empty Chair crisis' of 1965–1966, France unilaterally impeded the institutionalisation of qualified majority voting in the Common Market, against the resistance of the five other member states. Last but not least, France broke ranks by recognising Communist China in 1964 and leaving the military command structure of NATO in 1966. Both moves troubled France's Western allies, and West Germany in particular.[23] In the words of one British official, 'hostility became a habit' under de Gaulle.[24]

While de Gaulle's departure from office was greeted with some relief in Western capitals, it was also acknowledged that under his tenure France had overcome the instability that characterised the Fourth Republic.[25] It was widely expected that Pompidou would provide much in terms of continuity – especially in foreign policy.[26] After all, Pompidou was a staunch Gaullist and had served as de Gaulle's Prime Minister from 1962 until July 1968.[27]

The difficult balance Pompidou sought to strike between Gaullist continuity and change manifested itself visibly in relation to European integration.[28] European integration was 'central' to Pompidou's foreign policy thinking.[29] As Alfred Grosser argues, Pompidou, who was 'little inclined to spectacular experiments in domestic affairs, [and] ill-suited to emulate General de Gaulle in the gaining of prestige through oratorical outbursts, saw action in Europe as the sole means of giving a glorious image to his reign.'[30] Pompidou was no 'ardent federalist.'[31] Yet, being a former banker and having an astute economic mind, he saw the Common Market as a useful instrument for reforming and modernising the French economy.[32] In addition, Pompidou strongly backed the Common Agricultural Policy (CAP) because it benefited French agricultural production and exports,[33] and would be beneficial in electoral terms for the Gaullist movement.[34] In fact, Pompidou insisted that the completion of the CAP's financial system was a non-negotiable French demand to be met before any movement could be expected on European integration.[35] Lastly, Pompidou continued de Gaulle's legacy of treating foreign, defence, and European policy as a *domaine réservé* of the Elysée.[36] On foreign affairs, 'it was him and only him who decided.'[37]

Yet in stark contrast to de Gaulle, he was convinced that de Gaulle's form and style had upset France's relations with its neighbours and allies. Believing that de Gaulle conducted foreign policy with great symbolic effect but often at the expense of France's long-term interests, Pompidou wanted to strike a more moderate, pragmatic, and conciliatory tone.[38] He avoided making 'dramatic gestures'[39] in foreign policy. In a 15 May 1969 interview, he noted: 'I am not General de Gaulle. I will forcefully be more persuasive and conciliate.'[40] Furthermore, he was convinced that de Gaulle pursued an inflated vision of France's role, influence, and power in international affairs. Pompidou set out to ground French foreign policy on a more 'realistic' assessment of its possibilities.[41] Pompidou was, for example, concerned about West Germany's expanding economic power, influence, and assertive foreign policy – especially as regards Brandt's *Ostpolitik*.[42] He came to see Britain 'as a useful balance against increasing German power,'[43] a move that de Gaulle had been much less explicit about.

The attitudinal change towards integration and enlargement was best illustrated by the issue of French leadership of Europe.[44] Whereas de Gaulle saw France as the natural leader of Europe,[45] Pompidou thought that France needed to build coalitions and create mechanisms so as to prevent an erosion of its influence.[46] With his previous career in finance and banking, Pompidou was especially concerned about French economic performance, productivity, and competitiveness.[47] His concern was 'less with the glory of France, more with the well-being of France.'[48] He regarded an enlarged Common Market as a crucial step towards building a greater and more influential European trading and commercial entity. Consequently, he was open to British membership so long as he received credible assurances from Britain that it would not seek to reverse the achievements of integration or challenge France's leading role in the Community.[49]

De Gaulle, by contrast, had regarded British membership as a threat to French ambitions and its privileged position in European affairs.[50] Throughout his distinguished military and political career, de Gaulle had consistently defended French independence, defended its ever-more fragile claim to world power status, and intended for it the unique role of the leader of Europe, on par with the Soviet and American superpowers.[51] By the sheer power of his personality and virtue of the prestige he had gained during Germany's occupation of France, de Gaulle came a long way in protecting and nurturing France's special role and power.[52] Although de Gaulle's successors in the Elysée – from Pompidou to Sarkozy and Hollande – have largely continued in his tradition (and its rhetoric), they have had to pay more attention to the limitations of French influence. Pompidou shared most of de Gaulle's foreign policy goals, but not necessarily his means of achieving them. This was especially the case on the question of British membership in the Common Market.

The prospects for enlargement were increased not only by Pompidou's new take on European policy, but also by the election of Willy Brandt.[53] Brandt became chancellor in September 1969, heading a SPD-FDP coalition government.[54] Having served as foreign minister in the previous SPD-CDU grand coalition cabinet (1966–1969), his pro-European inclinations were already well established.[55] Brandt supported British membership, and he backed Wilson's accession bid in 1966–1967.[56] He argued that 'without England . . . Europe cannot be, what it should and wants to be.'[57] He was clearly more favourable to enlargement than his predecessor, Kurt-Georg Kiesinger, for whom the issue had been an 'annoying nuisance' (*lästiges Problem*).[58] Brandt sought to use German support for British membership to get the support of his Western allies for his advances to Eastern Europe and the Soviet Union.[59] A Federal Chancellery document of 22 October 1969 noted that Germany 'needs a constructive relationship with France' to ensure 'a crisis-free development' of the Common Market and to 'secure our pro-active intra-German policies and *Ostpolitik* in Paris,' which were Brandt's top foreign policy and strategic concerns.[60]

As indicated in his 28 October 1969 declaration in the Bundestag, Brandt's core foreign policy objective was to establish a 'European order of peace.'[61] The two elements necessary to achieve this goal were a policy of reducing tensions with the countries of Eastern Europe (*Ostpolitik*) and a concomitant enabling policy of integration with the West (*Westpolitik*).[62] The latter aimed at garnering the goodwill, trust, and support of West Germany's European neighbours and the United States for its *Ostpolitik*.[63] *Ostpolitik*, in turn, was a way to find practical arrangements to enhance the relations between West Germany, the Soviet Union, and the Communist states of Eastern Europe,[64] and potentially reduce tension with the GDR. The quest was not only to reduce East-West tensions through improved cooperation and consultation, but also to enhance West Germany's reconciliation with those countries, which had suffered most brutally under Nazi occupation. A 'normalisation of the relations with the Eastern neighbours' was therefore necessary.[65] He was adamant that the open questions which resulted from World War II could only be resolved in the context of a common European framework, which he defined as an 'order of peace.'[66] This was not a view that was universally shared among the German political establishment at the time, as the intense controversy over *Ostpolitik* illustrated.[67]

Throughout the early 1970s, Brandt signed agreements with the Soviet Union, Poland, and Czechoslovakia, which recognised the mutual renunciation of violence and the territorial status quo.[68] Separate treaties about Berlin, the GDR – for which West Germany had to give up its claim to represent all Germans (*Alleinvertretungs anspruch*) – and commercial agreements were also signed. His European policy in general – and *Ostpolitik* in particular – were sold by Brandt in emotional and sentimental terms, both as a 'peace policy' and a 'policy of reconciliation,'[69] yet with the pragmatic aim of gradually facilitating practical contacts between Germany and its neighbours (including the GDR).[70] This policy came to be known as the 'policy of small steps' (*Politik der kleinen Schritte*),[71] and had been initiated by previous Foreign Minister, Gerhard Schröder, throughout 1961–1966.[72]

> 'Reconciliation' with the countries of the East is simply the precondition and starting point for an active West German strategy designed to set in motion, and subsequently to shape, a complex and far-reaching process of change in Europe which will lead, at some as yet indeterminate point, to the restoration of the German nation.[73]

Brandt consistently reaffirmed to his Western allies that his policies towards the USSR and the Eastern Bloc were not in any way directed against them, and that they did not signal a return to the 'Rapallo' policies of the interwar years.[74] Sensing French sensitivities on the matter, Brandt argued in a 30 January 1970 meeting with Pompidou that West Germany belonged irrevocably to the West and that it merely sought to defuse tensions and repair historical damage with the countries of the East. He wanted to establish relations with Eastern European countries similar to those which West Germany had with its Western allies.[75] For him, 'Europe neither ends at the Elbe nor at the Polish Eastern border.'[76] In his television address of 12 August 1970 he indicated that Germany's 'national interest does not allow us to stand in between East and West. Our country needs the cooperation and consultation with the West and the reconciliation with the East.'[77]

Egon Bahr, Brandt's advisor, stated that '*Ostpolitik* began in the West.'[78] For Brandt, the policy of détente and cooperation between East and West was an 'indivisible whole.'[79] Only West Germany's support for European integration and close involvement in common European institutions could assuage fears – among both its Western allies and Eastern counterparts – about its motives. Brandt's European policies had, in consequence, two sides.[80] The chancellor aimed at 'removing the rubble . . . of the recent past, in order to level the field for a secure European future.'[81] Brandt knew that Bonn's room for manoeuvre on foreign policy matters was limited, but he was determined to expand it.[82]

In return for Western support for his plans to make fundamental changes to Germany's relations with the East, Brandt was willing to boost the process of European integration. His interest in European integration touched on two issues: enlargement and economic and monetary union.

Brandt supported British membership in the Common Market as early as 1966.[83] By being so adamant to make progress on *Ostpolitik*, he offered significant concessions on *Westpolitik*. One such concession was Brandt's agreement to complete the financial arrangements of the CAP, which Pompidou demanded as a precondition for starting with enlargement negotiations. On the basis of this background, Pompidou found in Brandt a counterpart who was open to supporting new initiatives on European integration.

The 1969 summit at The Hague

The changes in the governments of France and Germany resonated on the European political agenda. Just after his inauguration as President, Pompidou proposed to hold a summit, at which new initiatives for integration were to be discussed.[84] The meeting, held in The Hague in December 1969, came to be known as the 'second *relance*.'[85] Although the conference was called in order to discuss numerous agenda points – Britain's application for membership, as well as internal problems of the Common Market and its future development – the sense of expectation about a general European breakthrough was high. Even before the summit got under way, it was deemed to be of 'historic' proportions. Brandt was eager to breathe new life into the stagnant integration process, fearing that a failure to start enlargement negotiations would make the Common Market ultimately insignificant.[86]

Many felt that the scope of the proposals made at The Hague felt short of these high expectations. It was soon realised by many that Pompidou was 'no visionary,'[87] with one Italian diplomat quoted as saying that the French President seemed like a 'de Gaulle without the same talent.'[88] *The Times* deemed Pompidou's performance 'deplorable,' commenting that his proposals had a 'distinctly pallid look about them,' and labelled it 'Pompidou's strange game.'[89] Despite these shortcomings, the summit reinvigorated the stagnating integration process, as Brandt extracted from Pompidou a firm commitment for the start of enlargement negotiations.

In his opening statement, Pompidou announced that France would now seek to make progress on three aspects of European integration: the *achèvement* (completion) of the CAP and its financial arrangements, the *approfondissement* (deepening) of the Community especially in regards to a common economic and monetary policy, as well as *élargissement* (enlargement).[90] He wanted to maintain and develop the Common Market in order to prevent it from 'slow but inexorable' decline.[91] Arguing that the Soviet Union and the United States did not consider European problems except through the lens of their own interests, Pompidou sought a 'Europe in charge of her own destiny.'[92] Turning to his fellow heads of government, he asked: 'Are we decided to pursue the construction of the European Community?'[93] In his opinion, the answer had to be positive.[94]

A face-to-face lunch-time meeting between Brandt and Pompidou on the second day of the conference paved the way for three main proposals on European integration.[95] First, on French insistence, the financial arrangements for the CAP were to be made permanent. Pompidou was adamant that without a completed CAP – which was vital to his domestic support – France would not contemplate enlargement.[96]

Yet Pompidou knew that the CAP financing system needed to be unanimously agreed to by all six member states of the Common Market. In consequence, France was pressed to support negotiations on enlargement – the second initiative to be tabled at The Hague.

Third, in the context of increasing instabilities in the Bretton Woods international financial system, both Pompidou and Brandt spoke out in favour of economic and monetary union (EMU).[97] With subsequent devaluations of the US dollar, the pressure to revalue the Deutschmark and devalue the franc mounted. Given the strength and resilience of the West German economy on the one hand, and growing balance-of-payments problems in France on the other, the disjuncture between both economies was hardening. This complicated not only the completion of a common market (because economic, fiscal, and monetary policies varied sharply), but also the French priority of completing the financial arrangements of the CAP.

The crucial outcome of the Hague summit was the opening of enlargement negotiations with Britain, Denmark, Ireland, and Norway. Brandt was adamant that the time for enlargement had now come,[98] and Pompidou was interested not only in improving France's position in the Common Market, but also in repairing its relationship with Britain.[99] Pompidou was determined to overcome the impasse in the integration process, a step for which enlargement was crucial.[100]

In Pompidou's eyes, the tensions in Anglo-French relations during de Gaulle's presidency often had to do more with a clash of personalities and policy styles than axiomatic rivalry:

> The reality is that Britain and France shared fundamental views of the Cold War and of the European Community. They both wanted the United States to remain fully engaged in the security of Europe, a European Community with limited supranational powers and a Germany firmly anchored in the western community. This fundamental agreement meant that despite periods of tension, distrust, frustration and even a degree of Machiavellian competition, they remained colleagues if not always friends.[101]

Realising that enlargement could potentially strengthen France's hand in Europe, Pompidou made a conscious effort to improve relations with Britain.

Heath's 1970 election victory

While the conference at The Hague had set the agenda for new momentum on European integration, it was Heath's surprising victory in the June 1970 general elections that transformed Britain's prospects for entering the Common Market.

On 9 June 1970, just days before the election, *The Times* still reported that Britain and the Community were 'steering a direct collision course on the Common Market.'[102] Harold Wilson's attitude to the Common Market was seen in France more as a 'consequence of a tactical approach than the product of conviction.'[103] In part due to Wilson's ambiguous stance vis-à-vis Europe, not much progress had been made to promote enlargement since December 1969, and technical experts – rather than high-level officials – were left in charge. The general mood about Britain's accession to the Common Market was sombre. It was feared that Wilson might not overcome yet another French veto.

This context was profoundly affected by the unexpected Tory victory in the 1970 general election. Heath's victory was 'warmly received' by the French government and public opinion; his 'European faith' and 'unimpeachable European conviction' carried more weight than Wilson's attitudes ever did.[104] In the run-up to the general election, both Labour and the Conservatives were in favour of – albeit split on – the issue of Common Market membership.[105] Yet unlike Labour's Harold Wilson, who held 'no particular views on the subject,'[106] Heath campaigned on an unmistakable pro-European platform. Entry into Europe would be the 'centrepiece' of the Heath government, and it was central to his 'political vision.'[107] Heath argued that a 'Europe without France in the long run makes as little sense as a Europe without Britain.'[108]

At the time of the first bid to become a member of the Common Market in 1961, Heath led the negotiations on the British side. Now, as Prime Minister, he not only sought to resurrect the compromises reached then, but was also convinced that France held the key to British membership. His strategy for accession differed substantially from the Foreign Office, which saw France as a sole obstacle and therefore attempted to isolate it. To Heath, 'this analysis was nonsense.'[109] Being 'remarkably free from bitterness against the French,' Heath thought that he needed to assuage French fears about British motives, make friends in France, and 'outmanoeuvre' enemies.[110]

Heath's strategy emphasised gaining French 'trust and support' for enlargement.[111] The elements of this strategy were testing the depth of Pompidou's commitment to enlargement, persuading him of the sincerity of Heath's pro-European policy, and building mechanisms to overcome the technical obstacles of British membership. The objective would be to steer towards a top-level diplomatic exchange between Heath and Pompidou so as to 'find a reconciliation of national interests on a higher political plane.'[112]

Already on 19 June 1970, Heath received advice suggesting that Pompidou's initiative at The Hague revealed that he 'sees the need to develop and integrate the Communities for both French and European reasons.'[113] Similarly, in a memo to Heath advisor Robert Armstrong, on 23 October 1970, it was argued that the Hague conference of December 1969 marked the 'end of the Gaullist veto.' France, it was noted, was not powerful enough anymore to 'go it alone.'[114] In the face of German economic strength and Brandt's *Ostpolitik*, Britain believed that France would need it inside the Community in order to counter-balance German influence.[115]

Being convinced that Pompidou would, unlike de Gaulle, at least countenance the British case for membership, Heath decided that gaining French trust was essential for making enlargement a success. His own personal pro-European leanings were well known across Europe, and it helped that Heath did not follow 'the native instinct of rivalry between Britain and France which was as deep-rooted in the Foreign Office as in the Quai d'Orsay.'[116]

The pro-European attitude of the new government in London became apparent from early on. A 30 June 1970 internal memo clearly revealed the new tone:

> Now there is a new government in Britain, and our determination to join the Communities as full members on fair terms, and our belief in the need for a united and strengthened Europe is proved by our presence here today.[117]

At the Luxembourg meeting of 30 June 1970, Foreign Secretary Alec Douglas-Home reaffirmed Britain's commitment to Common Market membership: 'The new British government is determined to work with you in building a Europe which has a coherent character of its own.' He also said that Britain accepted the 'Treaties and their objectives.'[118] Heath assured Brandt in late 1970 that

> the British Government will not waver in its commitment to enter the Community provided we can agree on terms which my colleagues can recommend to Parliament in good conscience and with a fair prospect of securing Parliament's approval.[119]

Apart from its public declarations, Heath's government began in earnest to assuage French fears of British motives. This was accomplished both through direct exchanges with French officials and getting Brandt to support their case in his talks with Pompidou.[120] As a record of a conversation of 9 November 1970 between French Foreign Minister Maurice Schumann and Britain's chief negotiator in the accession talks, Geoffrey Rippon, shows, it was made clear to the French that 'H.M.G. would not attempt to tamper with what the Community has achieved or seek permanent derogations from its regulations.'[121] Furthermore, by December 1970, a top-secret letter from William Nield to Heath on the effects, consequences, and lack of alternatives to Common Market membership stipulated unmistakably that '[p]resent policy is to enter the EEC if the terms are right.' British officials foresaw 'no good alternative policy to membership of the Communities,' and informed Heath of their belief that '[f]ailure of the negotiations would be a severe blow to our international standing and prospects.'[122] Yet they also warned about the potential negative side effects of joining the Common Market – namely 'devaluation and/or deflation.'[123] It was argued that '[e]conometric exercises cannot offer a reliable answer to these questions. What it involves is an act of judgement.'[124] Heath knew that the Community was 'unpopular for the moment,' but blamed this on 'extensive negative propaganda from the Labour Party.' He drew the conclusion that what was required was not an 'abdication of leadership, but more leadership.'[125]

By late 1970, the efforts of the British government to gain French trust seemed to pay off. On 12 November 1970, British Ambassador Soames reported from Paris that he was positively 'struck' by the change of Pompidou's 'demeanour':

> There was none of the scepticism I had noticed when we [Pompidou and Soames] last met in the spring. At one point he acknowledged the European orientation of our policies.[126]

Similarly, Pompidou's influential advisor, Michel Jobert, voiced his belief that Heath and Pompidou were 'two of the most "European" leaders in Europe to-day'.[127] Yet despite the progress made in persuading the French, Pompidou continued to keep his options open on enlargement. He wrote to Brandt in March 1971, saying that

> France's concern is the same as the one of . . . Germany: we believe that it would be recommendable that Great Britain adheres to the Community, but that the conditions of its adherence have to be such that we would be assured that Community would be strengthened by it . . . [I]t is not a matter for us only to defend national interests, far from it . . . We simply want to ensure that the Community, in its new dimensions, will continue to be an efficient and coherent ensemble.[128]

Pompidou's hesitancy was part of his strategy for the enlargement negotiations. He wanted to 'leave his diplomats to fight hard in Brussels, . . . test out British reactions and the reactions of the other five, while he himself could keep his options open to the last.'[129] Pompidou was convinced that he needed to sell the revocation of France's veto over British membership as part as a tough deal at home.

Given Pompidou's continuing doubts about the ultimate motives of British membership, further actions by the British were necessary.[130] As far as negotiation tactics were concerned, Heath's strategy of gaining French support for enlargement also influenced the instruments with which London sought to persuade the French. The British sought to build on the 'mild change in France's attitude':

> . . . some attempt to improve France's attitude to our entry must be considered as worthwhile and even necessary. It might take the form of consultations, culminating in a top-level meeting, aimed at reducing wherever possible the differences of attitude.[131]

From the summer of 1970 onwards, the Foreign Office had considered that a top-level meeting – either with the Six or with Pompidou alone – would be necessary in order to overcome the technical obstacles for British membership.[132] Throughout early 1971, the view crystallised that a personal summit between Heath and Pompidou would be most appropriate to win Pompidou over. Only some British officials, such as Geoffrey Rippon, worried that a bilateral summit could have 'many undesirable consequences.'¹³³ Overall, though, it was believed that Britain needed more than half-hearted French support if enlargement was to succeed. In consequence, London came to favour holding a bilateral summit with Pompidou in order to undo French demands in the negotiations with the other five member states. As a memo from Soames of 7 May 1971 argued:

> He [Pompidou] is well aware of the success which his predecessor had amongst broad sections of French opinion with his grandiose fantasy of a Europe stretching from the Atlantic to the Urals and his assiduous cult of the myth of French might. Pompidou has so far put little or nothing in their place. He has delivered a shallow treatise on confederalism (of which he is particularly proud) but apart from that has done no more than open the door like a reluctant concierge to four prospective new tenants and follow them around muttering that, if they sign the lease, the furniture must not be moved about. He needs to be persuaded that, if this deal goes through, the value of the premises will be enormously enhanced and that he will go down as the man who pulled it off for France.[134]

Heath's strategy concentrated on personally persuading Pompidou, who would then in turn order his negotiating team to surmount the technical obstacles of the negotiations. He was aware that the summit 'was not guaranteed to be a success,' yet he strongly believed that the main obstacles were political and not technical, and had to be dealt with at the highest level first.

Apart from the difficulty of persuading Paris of the sincerity and objectives of British European policy, Heath also faced increasing public and parliamentary resistance to his pro-European course. For instance, in August 1970, the Prime Minister was shown survey results which indicated that a majority of adults were opposed to joining the Common Market and that the number of people strongly against EEC membership was growing.[135] Moreover, in a 25 November 1970 memo Heath was warned about the 'ironic situation, where the veto is imposed not by any member of the Six, but by the British electorate.'[136] In consequence, Heath came to believe that only once membership became a concrete and realistic step would he be able to get public support. He was conscious that he needed – sooner rather than later – to come to an agreement with Pompidou on enlargement if his anchoring of Britain in Europe was to succeed.

The impact of summit diplomacy

The changes in government that occurred in France, Germany, and Britain throughout 1969 and 1970 facilitated British membership, but the key decisions regarding enlargement were not made until the first half of 1971. Pompidou, Brandt, and Heath all appreciated the advantages of bilateral intergovernmental consultations in which European issues could be handled. In this context, three summit meetings were of particular importance: the consultations between Pompidou and Brandt of July 1970 and January 1971, the meeting between

Brandt and Heath of early April 1971, and – most importantly – the Pompidou-Heath summit of May 1971.

For the most part, these meetings did not concentrate on hammering out the technical details of the negotiation process. Rather, they served to establish the essential political will among leaders for renewed momentum in European integration. Enlargement and economic and monetary union were considered the most pressing items.[137] It was 'inconceivable that the future of France, Britain and Europe should fail over the question of Britain's initial contribution to Community finance, over New Zealand butter or West Indian sugar.'[138] Yet what was conceivable was that Pompidou – who as late as May 1971 gave enlargement only a '50–50 chance of success'[139] – would remain unconvinced about the general motives and objectives of British policy on Europe. Pompidou wanted to be persuaded by Heath about the sincerity of Britain's commitment to Europe. Heath recalled:

> Once again, we had to convince a French President that Britain was sufficiently 'European' and would not exploit membership to disrupt or dilute the Community . . . He [Pompidou] was unsure whether the UK would be prepared to defend European interests in the face of likely economic and political onslaughts from outside . . . This trust was never going to be easy to establish, in view of traditional suspicions which permeated Anglo-French relations, the fractious state of relations throughout the 1960s and the volatile nature of public opinion in the UK at this time.[140]

Throughout late 1970, it became clear that the main bargain on enlargement would have to be struck between France and Britain.[141] The question was therefore whether Heath would be able to persuade Pompidou to overcome his distrust of British motives,[142] and whether Heath would be able to muster enough parliamentary support for a vote on Common Market membership.[143] In this context, Brandt took on the role of an intermediary between and a sounding board for both leaders.[144] In previous bilateral meetings and exchanges with Pompidou and Heath, Brandt had already explained his *Ostpolitik* at length, thereby getting to know both leaders and establishing himself as a facilitator of an Anglo-French compromise. Brandt himself recalled that the constellation of the three leaders made 'breakthroughs' on European affairs possible.[145]

An example of how Brandt mediated between French and British positions was the meeting of Pompidou and Brandt in Paris on 25 January 1971.[146] During their consultations, Pompidou and Brandt conversed extensively on the issue of enlargement. Pompidou expected that the British would join the Common Market, given that they realised that they could not destroy it and hence were more willing to accept its conditions.[147] Yet Pompidou's statements remained characterised by a high degree and distrust of British motives and policies. For instance, he regarded Britain's offer regarding its financial contributions to the Common Market as 'humorous.' He also wanted the Six to agree on a common position in the enlargement negotiations, so as to show the British that the Common Market was a 'serious matter.'[148] Brandt understood Pompidou's motives for some foot-dragging in the enlargement negotiations, knowing the difficulties of gradually moving France away from some key tenets of de Gaulle's foreign policy.

In a letter of 18 March 1971, Brandt informed Pompidou that recent contacts with London had convinced him that Britain sought 'full participation in the growing unity of Europe.' He sought an assurance from Pompidou that 'Britain would still be welcomed,' reminding him that 'creative energy' and 'willingness to compromise' were necessary now.[149] In his answer to Brandt, Pompidou noted that enlargement would only be possible if the conditions of Britain's entry would ensure that a strengthened Common Market would emerge.[150] Under no circumstances was Pompidou willing to compromise its coherence.[151]

Brandt then passed Pompidou's generally supportive attitude towards enlargement on to Heath.[152] Until his meeting with Heath in May 1971, Pompidou had often been more frank and candid with Brandt than with the British Prime Minister.

Another crucial step in the series of summit meetings facilitating Britain's membership was the Anglo-German governmental consultations held in Bonn on 5–6 April 1971. In Heath's opinion, 'there were really no bilateral matters which called for discussion between us.'[153] Seeing no pressing outstanding bilateral issues, Heath and Brandt concentrated their discussions on the question of enlargement. Heath inquired about Pompidou's attitudes and sought advice on which strategy to pursue in relation to gaining French trust. Heath noted that while the foundation of the Community was economic integration, its ultimate goal was political union.[154] They conversed on the view that European affairs should be managed through an intergovernmental (rather than a supranational) framework. Brandt pragmatically argued against the 'theological row' over how best to describe the integration process. Heath reckoned that the institutional organisation of the Community had to adapt to the necessities of Europe.[155] In his mind, what was appropriate for dealing with economic issues need not be good for resolving the difficult issues of a common foreign policy.[156]

Heath told Brandt that failure in the enlargement negotiations would affect his *Ostpolitik*, as well as allied policies on Berlin. In a similar way, in early May 1971, Heath warned about the consequences and 'danger' of excluding Britain.[157] He was convinced that the Soviet Union would only listen to and enter into agreements with the member states of a strong and cohesive. By exerting pressure on Brandt, Heath also wanted to make sure that Germany supported enlargement fully, and that Brandt would make the case for enlargement in talks with Pompidou.

Brandt, Heath, and Pompidou were convinced that an Anglo-French settlement would eventually be necessary so as to move the negotiations on enlargement forward. This elite-understanding was achieved among Heath and Pompidou at their summit meeting of 20–21 May 1971, during which both leaders cleared the way for Britain's accession. They did so by engaging in a series of private talks, to which not even their closest members of staff had access – a sort of 'staffless diplomacy.'[158] The diplomat in charge of the technical negotiations, Sir Con O'Neill, reaffirmed the view that this summit 'was the moment that decided everything'[159] when arguing that

> the whole long of our negotiations were peripheral, accidental and secondary. The general movement of events in 1969 and 1970 revived the opportunity [for enlargement], and was much more important than the negotiations themselves . . . The negotiations were concerned only with the means of achieving this objective at an acceptable price.[160]

Heath understood his task as being to convince Pompidou that he shared this European outlook.[161] He wanted to 'reverse the 1963 veto which had been a great personal setback.'[162] The core objective was 'to reconcile the national interests and philosophies of the two countries and avoid a third French veto.'[163] It was predicted that

> if the President and the Prime Minister find the agreement they both believe the other to want, then it is foreseen that the clearest instructions will be given to the French and British negotiators to sit down at the table and settle . . .[164]

In Pompidou, Heath found a leader who not only shared the political will for bringing Britain into the Common Market, but with whom he could also establish excellent personal relations.[165] In the biographical literature on Pompidou and Heath, the closeness of their relationship is attributed great importance for the development of Anglo-French relations.[166] Heath recalled:

> President Pompidou was a delightful man, and I always found him to be charming, cultured, beautifully spoken and with a splendid sense of humour . . . He and I always got on well together, at both personal and political levels. There was no Franco-British love-hate relationship in his make-up.[167]

During their first meeting, Pompidou

> had stressed that what he felt was needed was an historic change in the British attitude. If Britain was really determined to make this change, France would welcome [Britain] into the Community . . . and said quite specifically that, if the political and intellectual prestige and authority of Britain were added to those of the Six, the Community would be greatly enriched.[168]

The summit served to settle the persistent fear of failure of the enlargement negotiations. It would clarify whether Heath was prepared to take Britain into the Common Market and whether Pompidou was willing to overcome the 'residual legacy of mistrust and disbelief' about Britain which Pompidou inherited from de Gaulle.[169] The British tried to shape the summit in a way that would allow Heath 'to stand back and take a loftier view.'[170] The aim was for Heath to make the case for

> his own conception of a united Europe with a distinctive personality of its own, free of economic, political, military or monetary vassalage and deriving its cohesion from the voluntary interlocking of nation states pursuing common objectives.[171]

Far from being a foregone conclusion, a mere photo opportunity, the outcome of enlargement negotiations depended on the tone and convergence of views between Heath and Pompidou. As Soames saw the purpose of the meeting:

> The object would be to encourage [Pompidou] to see the profit and attraction in the prospect of partnership with us: to see the negotiations as an opportunity rather than a risk – an opportunity of bringing in a valuable and genuinely European ally, rather than a risk of Atlantic dilution of the Community – and to see himself as a man of destiny.[172]

It was wrong to think of the summit

> in terms of an orderly agenda, with items ticked off one after another. This was not what was happening. The President and the Prime Minister were immersing themselves in the problem as a whole, testing possibilities and each other's intention and political quality.[173]

The meeting was held in strict confidence, with no French or British officials present during the several hours of conversations. Heath did not even inform his closest advisors, Douglas Hurd and Michael Wolff, of the developments of the encounter. They learned about the successful outcome of the summit only at the press conference, at which Pompidou announced the end of France's veto.

As a summary of the meeting recalled, a 'close identity of view was established on the role and development of Europe in the event of British entry.'[174] For the British government, the summit was 'a very satisfactory outcome, which reflected the undoubted conviction on the part of . . . Pompidou that the time had come to admit Britain to the EEC.'[175] As Heath told Parliament upon his return,

> We have established that the views of the two Governments are very close over the whole range of European policies. The French President has shown his clear desire to proceed with the building of a united Europe on the basis of an enlarged Community, with Britain as a member.[176]

Turning to his understanding that Anglo-French tension over Europe was not axiomatic, he went on to say:

> . . . for so long there have been those who believed that Britain's only purpose was to try to get into the Community in order to wreck it, for so long there have been those who have believed that France's only purpose was to veto Britain's joining the Community to which she had a right to belong, and before that gathering there were two men with heavy responsibilities who have now acknowledged openly that neither of those things was true.[177]

After the summit, Pompidou reaffirmed his acceptance of enlargement:

> The conversations which I had with the Prime Minister . . . confirmed me . . . in the opinion that the British government is sincerely and resolutely determined to ensure the entry of Britain to a Community which is wholeheartedly European. Conscious of the inestimable benefit of the endeavour undertaken by the Six, and of the chances that this might carry for the future development of cooperation and union between the countries of our continent, Great Britain accedes to participate in it, not to destroy it, but to strengthen it . . . I have all reason to believe that the attitude of the British Premier did contribute to strengthen the environment of trust necessary for the success of negotiations.[178]

Brandt agreed with Pompidou's assessment of Heath's European conviction, having played a facilitating and mediating role between both decision-makers.[179] After the Heath-Pompidou summit, Brandt was 'confident that this third attempt will prove successful,' noting that 'none of us can afford failure this time.'[180] Pompidou had found that on Europe 'he could not have a better partner' than Heath.[181] Their meeting put an end to France's reluctance – so prominent under de Gaulle – to accept Britain as a European partner. After the summit, the prospects for a 'frictionless end phase to the [enlargement] negotiations' were given.[182] Subsequent meetings, such as Pompidou's 1972 meeting with Heath at Chequers, were undertaken to foster and build upon the good relations both leaders had established in May 1971.[183]

The summit of May 1971 served to bring the enlargement negotiations to a successful conclusion. Acting upon the orders of their governments, the French and British negotiation teams also settled the outstanding technical details by 23 June 1971. German Foreign Minister Walter Scheel said on this date that all negotiating partners had had 'the strong will not to fail yet again.'[184]

Although elite agreement on enlargement was reached, the compromise still hinged on parliamentary ratification. In this context, too, both Pompidou and Heath mobilised influence and personal prestige to ensure the ratification of the deal they had agreed to. Heath, knowing about the gradually diminishing public support for EEC membership, wanted to proceed as early as possible with ratification. The Labour opposition and numerous Tory backbenchers questioned the economic costs of entry and disliked Heath's 'disingenuousness' in hiding them.[185] In Parliament, Heath was accused of 'giving just about everything away' on Europe.[186] Acting upon the Chief Whip's advice, Heath not only postponed the vote until October, but also reluctantly conceded to a free vote in order to minimise the embarrassment of Tory backbench opposition to the deal.[187] It was only after the Conservative Party conference of early October 1971 that Heath saw the benefits of a free vote; it would allow pro-European Labour MPs to 'break away and vote with us.'[188] On 28 October 1971, the Commons voted 356 to 244 in favour of membership.[189] Heath personally considered this vote as his 'greatest success as Prime Minister.'[190] He had managed to secure broad parliamentary support for enlargement, but realised that the public was much less enthusiastic and supportive.

Pompidou faced a similar situation in France. Yet instead of concentrating his efforts on ratification in the National Assembly, Pompidou called a referendum on enlargement on 16 March 1972. Pompidou acted against the advice of his closest advisors, as well as other leading figures in the French political elite. He argued that the time had come to take risks. Believing that he had little room for manoeuvre, due to his personal involvement and public identification with enlargement, Pompidou deemed it necessary 'to react urgently so as to distract.'[191] In his press conference of 16 March 1972, Pompidou turned this argument around:

> Myself having taken personal responsibility first at The Hague, then in my meetings with Heath, [and] in authorising the signature of the [enlargement] treaty, I hold that it is my duty and that it is fundamentally democratic to appeal to all French who elected me directly, to pronounce themselves also directly on this policy in favour of Europe.[192]

Faced with public 'apathy,' the results of the 23 April 1972 referendum came as a great disappointment to Pompidou, who advocated a 'massive approval.'[193] Although enlargement was agreed (68.31 per cent voted in favour of enlargement) the turnout was low. Almost 12 million eligible voters (40 per cent of the electorate) did not go to vote, and over two million annulled votes were cast.[194] Having strongly advocated enlargement in the media, the indifference to and vague support for Pompidou's course on European affairs became apparent. This outcome weakened his leadership throughout 1972 and 1973, when discussions for economic and monetary union moved to the top of the European agenda.

Interpreting the purpose of British Community membership

The fact that Pompidou, Brandt, and Heath were able to move rather swiftly towards enlargement needs to be regarded in the context of their respective conceptions of Europe.

Georges Pompidou

Pompidou found in European affairs a policy terrain on which he enjoyed substantial constitutional and political autonomy.[195] On Europe, Pompidou's main departure from de Gaulle's vision of Europe regarded the question of enlargement. After agreeing to it, many wondered whether de Gaulle would 'turn around in his grave, if he knew what his epigones sacrificed in terms of [foreign policy] principles.'[196]

Pompidou's understanding of Europe differed in a number of core assumptions from de Gaulle's.[197] Pompidou advocated a 'Europe of governments,'[198] which would ensure Europe's competitiveness and its voice being heard on the international stage.[199] He spoke of Europe as a 'confederation,' in which the character of each member state would be safeguarded.[200] Whereas for de Gaulle cooperation among European nations was an expression of their organic links and cultural bonds, Pompidou was less emotive and more technocratic.[201] He accepted the premise that cooperation and integration would not stem naturally from perceived cultural commonalities among the nations of Europe. In his mind, these were not powerful enough to nurture cooperation. Rather, he talked about European commonalities in vague terms and shied away from defining their essence and meaning. He alluded to the common heritage of Christianity and rationalism, but then argued that each nation-state had shaped these in unique ways. For Pompidou, 'European Man' (*homme européen*) existed, but without a common homeland.[202] In preparation for the 1972 French referendum on enlargement, this thin understanding of European cultural commonalities was revealed in a message he sent to the National Assembly:

> Strong of more than 300 million inhabitants, of an economy in constant progress, of an ancient civilisation founded on the basis of the respect of the human being, of an affirmed desire for peace and cooperation with all, of a common conception of democratic liberties across a diversity of constitutions, Europe can play yet anew the role that falls upon it in the world, at the service of peace and justice. She will offer to all its children, our children, at the same time as economic and social progress, the pride in a great collective endeavour to accomplish.[203]

Cooperation among European nation-states was thus merely an effective way to confront shared problems, rather than an expression of a sort of European general will. Pompidou was aware that it would take significant amounts of political capital, will, and courage to accomplish even this limited approach to integration.[204] He told Brandt on 25 January 1971:

> We know the history of Europe. What constitutes Germany and France is not effaced by words, and even less by technocratic creations. For the European construction to be solid, one must not overlook the bases. The artisans of this construction will be governments, starting from national

realities. The European confederation that should take off from our common efforts is without historical precedent and cannot be defined in abstract in advance. It is a daily task to which we have to consecrate ourselves without remorse . . . and without illusions.[205]

Pompidou's more flexible attitude towards integration sought to gain practical economic and political benefits for France, even if this entailed compromising Gaullist positions on foreign policy. De Gaulle had at least rhetorically been much less inclined to set aside his principles, even though he often ended up doing so in practice.[206] Pompidou shifted his representation of Europe away from de Gaulle's geopolitical and civilisational narrative.[207]

Yet important continuities also existed with de Gaulle's policies. For instance, the achievement of cooperation would entail continuous and close consultation among European governments, in order to explore similarities of interests and concerns. This position was close to de Gaulle's 1962 Fouchet Plan. In a televised interview on 24 June 1971, Pompidou argued that 'we attempt to regroup the nations of Western Europe and to join together what they offer in terms of virtues and possibilities.'[208] Important to note is Pompidou's emphasis on intergovernmental cooperation and the step-by-step expansion of policy realms in which cooperation would make sense.[209]

Already in September 1969, Pompidou clarified that his priorities focused on economic – rather than political – integration, and that convergences of interests were most likely in the economic field. In consequence, he argued that as much as political integration was desirable, the Common Market should remain the pivot of European cooperation.[210] Pompidou used the metaphor of the Community being a city protected by the 'wall' of the common external tariff.[211] He expected that an economically viable Europe would lead to political unification, albeit slowly.[212]

Given that Pompidou was highly concerned about the fast-vanishing influence of France and Europe as a whole, he was determined to facilitate consultations and cooperation whenever possible. He noted clearly that 'France cannot guard and grow its role in the world unless it unites with other European nations.'[213] Cooperation among the nations of Europe was seen to be a necessity,[214] without which France would continue to lose its influence and freedom of action. This contrasted with Pompidou's critics on the left and right, who saw in European integration not a gain, but a loss of national influence, prestige, and sovereignty.

Pompidou sought to safeguard France's role in Europe, but his ardour for political integration or any form of federalism was minimal. He did not seek to overcome Europe's nationalisms, nor did he strive to create a federated Europe. It was his deliberate policy not to pursue political integration, but to concentrate on the enlargement and completion of the Common Market. To do so, Pompidou was aware that a departure from de Gaulle's foreign policy style was necessary. This extended not only towards opening the Common Market to Britain, but also towards realigning France's – and Europe's – relationship with the United States and the Soviet Union. He was especially concerned about the fact that in the context of the transatlantic alliance, decisions about European security and defence were taken outside of Europe.[215] Pompidou regarded the dominance exercised by the United States and the Soviet Union, as well as the emergence of new powers – China, Japan, India, and Brazil – as a challenge to Europe's influence and importance. He realised that all these 'grands ensembles' had the advantage of enjoying internal cohesion through feelings of national unity and passion.[216] These reflections framed how Pompidou put forward his case for European integration at a press conference on 16 March 1972:

> What an incentive to unite! It's all there, geography, the way of life, a certain conception of democracy and an evident political and economic interest. Only history comes to counter this evolution, in the sense that all European nations have a secular reality, a language, national pride, and the memories of their clashes.
>
> But, if one does not create Europe, the European nations will be completely eclipsed by the grands ensembles that I have just named, and from this point of view, history can come to our rescue, to the extent to which European nations have the habit and hence developed the need for playing a global role. It is about making Europe, with the condition . . . of respecting the identity (*personnalité*) of the nations of which it will be composed.[217]

In his view, a united Europe would come about neither by signing treaties nor by overestimating France's capabilities.[218] Pompidou knew about the limited policy-making instruments at France's disposal.[219] In his eyes, a united Europe could only emerge by multiplying contacts among governments.[220] Integration was premised on a top-down construction of interests by governments and technocrats. It was a governmental necessity, even if the public did not want it:

> In defiance of the difficulties, the inevitable divergences of interests, the contradictory ambitions, in defiance even of the lack of enthusiasm in public opinion, we have to persevere. It is the only way for old Europe to regain its place in the world, its personality, its influence.[221]

Being aware of the obstacles to integration, Pompidou's approach was predicated on economic modernisation. A major feature of his domestic economic policy was his efforts at modernising French industry by simultaneously enhancing competitive pressures, securing market access, and creating national industrial champions. During the first years of his presidency, this policy increased the economic performance of French industry. Pompidou wanted to support, complement, and embed this policy in the wider context of the Community.[222] In meeting with Brandt in Paris on 22 January 1973, he argued that only a common economic policy could be a viable basis for the Community on which common interests could be developed and amalgamated.[223] The development of political cooperation had to be conducted only between governments, to the exclusion of the Community's institutions.[224] This prominence of economic matters in Pompidou's approach rested on the understanding that only the Europe of the Common Market was ultimately practicable. As far as integration was concerned, Pompidou wanted not supranationalism but direct French influence over an enlarged Community's activities.

Edward Heath

Edward Heath has been called the 'nodal figure' for bringing Britain into the Common Market.[225] In doing so, he ended the UK's long period of political self-exclusion from European integration on the continent. In this sense, his tenure as Prime Minister was crucial not only for achieving British entry, but also for transforming long-established and widely held elite and public beliefs about Europe. Heath gave a clearer prominence to European integration than most other Conservative politicians at the time, and revealed an 'exceptional single-mindedness in pursuing it.'[226]

In contrast to many of his contemporaries, Heath's worldview was very much centred on Europe, and it had been his political ambition to lead Britain into Europe.[227] The *Financial Times* wrote in its obituary that he 'won his place in history as the prime minister who took Britain into Europe.'[228] This objective stemmed from his conviction that 'Britain's future would be dismal outside Europe.'[229] Heath could foresee neither a promising economic future for Britain nor possibilities for British global influence if the UK failed to join the Common Market.[230] Yet the 'overriding grounds' for getting Britain into the Community were political.[231]

Central to his desire to lead Britain into Europe were two main arguments. First, Heath argued that only by participating in the project of European integration would Britain be able to exercise a viable form of economic and political power.[232] Heath sought Community membership in order to protect the 'European voice in world affairs.'[233] Whitehall officials also felt that participating in and developing the Community would be a mechanism for Britain to preclude a 'special Franco-German relationship' which France 'would like to develop further.'[234] Second, Heath wanted to tie Britain firmly to the European continent, not only politically and economically, but also in terms of British identity and attitudes. For Heath, it was a 'fundamental truth' that 'Britain's future [lay] in Europe.'[235]

The first largely geopolitical argument rested on his aim for 'maintaining a worthwhile role for Britain in a world changing to her disadvantage.'[236] He was clearly concerned about the decreasing economic competitiveness of British industry, as well as the deterioration of Britain's relative economic and financial position in general. In his autobiography, Heath later claimed that 'Britain's influence in Europe was never lower than it was between 1964 and 1970, not least because Britain's relative economic position was deteriorating badly.'[237] From this perception of Britain's situation followed Heath's consistent efforts for making an economic case for joining the Common Market. He was convinced that 'it was only the new economic strength to be expected from EEC membership that would enable Britain to play . . . a [leading] role' in European and world affairs.[238] The objective to 'restore stability and growth in the United Kingdom economy' made it necessary to judge whether 'membership of the EEC, or . . . non-membership, provide[d] the better context for achieving these essential economic objectives.'[239] On this, Heath was more inclined than his predecessors, successors, and many Whitehall officials to go with the European option.[240]

Heath's determination to accomplish Community membership did not stem from pro-integrationist idealism but from a profound concern about Britain's role in the world.[241]

> Heath's lifelong devotion to making Britain part of a united Europe was founded on a paradox. For it derived, as much as the contrary commitment of the most determined little Englander, from sturdy English patriotism, pride in the uniqueness of Britain's history and an ardent desire to reassert British leadership in the world. He was never a European idealist, except secondarily in so far as he judged that British leadership could only be asserted through whole-hearted participation in an integrated Europe.[242]

At first sight, Heath's conception of Europe seemed similar to the mainstream Atlanticist self-understanding of Britain.[243] The difference was that Heath believed in neither Empire nor the Commonwealth and was convinced that inside the transatlantic relationship Britain would always be the less influential player. He advocated closer integration with Europe as a way of compensating for Britain's loss of its traditional sphere of influence. The referent object of Heath's approach to European integration was Britain's capacity to exercise influence – to be achieved through participation in and consolidation of the Common Market.

This approach was not self-evident or uncontroversial in Britain.[244] Heath's own understanding of the international context and Britain's role and position in it was not universally shared, even among Cabinet colleagues. His rhetoric on Europe was only marginally framed by civilisational and cultural connotations. He seldom appealed to those dimensions of European integration, which were not easily framed in terms of national interests:

> Many of you have fought in Europe, as I did, or have lost fathers, or brothers, or husbands who fell fighting in Europe. I say to you now, with that experience in my memory, that joining the Community, working together with them for our joint security and prosperity, is the best guarantee we can give ourselves of a lasting peace in Europe.[245]

Instead of focusing on sentimentalities and idealism, he honed in on the economic benefits arising from British entry, arguing that 'the Old World must now be brought together to redress the balance of the New.'[246]

Yet for all of Heath's enthusiasm about Community membership, he did not shy away from grasping its serious implications – both for Britain and his prime ministership. Community membership would not only entail the full incorporation of the *acquis* into British law, but would also mean accepting the Community's political objectives.[247] Heath knew that European integration would eventually lead to some sort of political unification in Europe, which included the controversial transfer of sovereignty to common supranational institutions.[248] He was not an advocate of supranationalism, stating in Parliament that in Europe 'no country's vital interests could be over-ruled by other members.'[249] He wanted political cooperation and consultation among European states to increase Britain's voice and influence in international affairs,[250] but understood that proper political unification was remote and that economic improvements would have to take precedence.[251]

The second of Heath's arguments for Europe – to 'realign the country's sense of identity irrevocably towards Europe'[252] – was a core theme of his time in office. He frequently repeated the mantra that 'the attitudes of mind and the hopes and aspirations which unite [Europeans] are far greater than the nationalist feelings that divide them.'[253] Yet he worried that Britain's neighbours 'have never been impressed by confused signals about our commitment to the process of union.'[254] He wanted to dispel the widespread anxiety that British membership would ultimately weaken the Community. Gaining the trust of the other European leaders was therefore an important component of his policy. Heath was determined to secure British entry, and was willing to compromise on numerous core British preferences in order to do so. His diplomatic negotiator, Sir Con O'Neill, sought to secure terms of accession that could be 'publicly shown to be reasonable, advantageous, and not too onerous.'[255] Everything else would do.

Heath was aware that he was challenging the political instincts of Whitehall and much of public opinion. In deliberately stressing Britain's European identity and interests, Heath thought he could bring about a transformational shift in how the British saw themselves in relation to Europe. He claimed that

> [w]hilst the European countries concerned were moving on from the nation state because in their view it was inadequate to meet modern requirements, the British were still thinking in terms of the power which they had previously exercised and which they believed still belonged to them. There is no doubt today that opinion in Britain has changed.[256]

Heath specifically lowered the rhetorical and political commitment to the so-called special relationship with the United States in order to dispel any fears about Britain's locus of loyalty. Campbell suggests that the 'long-cherished "special relationship" with the United States was to be abruptly ended, and sentimental allegiance to the Commonwealth briskly shelved.'[257] Heath talked instead of a 'natural relationship' with the US.[258] He told Nixon that 'there will indeed be some changes in our relations.'[259] This appeared to most observers as a downgrading of Anglo-American ties.

For his predecessors, the transatlantic alliance and the special relationship had been core elements of Britain's foreign policy. Eden, Macmillan, Douglas-Home, and Wilson nurtured – with varying degrees – close relations with the United States. In contrast, Heath was unenthusiastic about the transatlantic bond. He thought that 'there could be no special relationship between Britain and the United States, even if Britain wanted it, because one was barely a quarter the size of the other.'[260] Instead of relying on Britain's influence in Washington, he wanted to make use of European integration to enable a more balanced relationship with Washington to develop.[261] He was not anti-American, but was concerned about the imbalance of the transatlantic relationship and Nixon's increasing shift of focus away from Europe – as was the case during the Vietnam War.[262] Heath also worried that Washington would take decisions affecting European security without full and proper consideration of the needs of its European allies.[263] In consequence, he wanted Europeans 'to do more to look after their own defence,'[264] as well as to strengthen the European pillar of the asymmetric transatlantic relationship. Closer European integration and a rebalancing of the transatlantic relationship were thus seen not as mutually exclusive processes,[265] but rather as a 'modernised alliance in which national loyalty and European loyalty as well as Atlantic loyalty can find an outlet.'[266]

As far as the Commonwealth was concerned, Heath had lost patience, and treated it as a 'residual in the great equation he desired to make between Britain and Europe.'[267] His commitment to achieve Community membership made him 'intolerant' of the Commonwealth.[268] In his eyes, it amounted to 'nonsense to pretend that the amorphous, diverse, loose-knit Commonwealth could offer Britain a practical alternative to the enlarged economic opportunities of the EEC.'[269] Speaking in Zurich on 17 September 1971, Heath suggested that 'the concept held by some in my country of a cohesive political, defensive and economic Commonwealth bloc centred on Britain has never become a reality.'[270] The fact that Heath did not have personal or family ties with the Commonwealth seemingly made it easier for him to reach this point of view.

The importance and impact of Heath's leadership on Europe becomes more pronounced if one considers the constraints he faced. First, Heath's enthusiasm for Europe was not something that was widely shared among the British public or the Conservative and Labour parties.[271] He adopted an overtly 'missionary approach'[272] to advertise the expected benefits of Community membership, of which the controversial *Fanfare for Europe* campaign of early 1973 was the most visible example.

Second, especially in the early stages of the negotiations, the Treasury opposed British entry to the Community, because 'its judgement of the economic consequences was negative.'[273] The merits of the economic case that Heath made for British entry were hotly disputed and very controversial. Sir Con O'Neill, the chief official negotiator for Britain during entry negotiations, argued in his report that 'None of [the Community's] policies was essential to us; many of them were objectionable. But in order to get in we had either to accept them, or to secure agreed adaptations of them, or to negotiate acceptable transitional agreements.'²⁷⁴ Instead of the economic case put forward by Heath, the report claimed that '[w]hat mattered was to get into the Community, and thereby restore our position at the centre of European affairs which, since 1958, we had lost.'²⁷⁵ In this sense, the argument of economic urgency, which Heath often repeated, was not widely shared in Whitehall. While it was certain that Britain was facing rapidly deteriorating economic conditions, it remained unclear whether Common Market membership would alleviate or exacerbate this situation, due to increased competition. Most large companies in the Confederation of British Industry (CBI) favoured membership, expecting higher returns from technological cooperation and gains from economies of scale.²⁷⁶ Yet many remained unconvinced, and the high hopes for economic recovery connected to Common Market membership were 'quickly dashed.'²⁷⁷ The immediate period after Britain's accession brought not short-term benefits, 'but only costs,' attributed mainly to the CAP and soaring world commodity prices.²⁷⁸

Public apathy and overall lack of interest, as well as the contested nature of Heath's economic case for Europe, were serious obstacles to his European ambitions. Already, in the quest to ratify Britain's Community membership in Parliament, Heath faced increasing opposition. He was advised to push for a free, cross-party vote, in order to draw on pro-integration Labour and Liberal Democrat rebels, and also threatened to resign if his government was defeated.²⁷⁹

Despite the fact that Heath made an impassioned case for British accession to the Community – thereby challenging traditional understandings of Europe in Britain – he remained less persuasive in arguing what the enlarged Community should stand for and what role the UK should play in it.²⁸⁰

Willy Brandt

Willy Brandt's time in government – both as Foreign Minister between 1966 and 1969, and as Federal chancellor between 1969 and 1974 – is widely remembered for his *Ostpolitik*.²⁸¹ *Ostpolitik* encompassed two main components regarding European integration,²⁸² as Brandt wanted to 'decisively promote the Western European union both in terms of geography and intensity and at the same time . . . build the first bridges between Western and Eastern Europe.'²⁸³

He endeavoured to make use of the climate of détente between the United States and the Soviet Union to carve out a new foreign policy context for West Germany. Brandt told Nixon that the 'efforts of our so-called *Ostpolitik* are indeed . . . in perfect harmony with your own worldwide diplomacy.'²⁸⁴ Over time, Bonn's uncompromising stance towards the GDR had become a serious constraint on its dealings with Eastern Europe, as well as with a growing number of developing countries. Also, ever since the construction of the Berlin Wall in 1961, there was a desire to overcome the hermetic – and in Brandt's eyes artificial – division of Germany.²⁸⁵ For Brandt, any rapprochement of West Germany with the East, as well as any reorganisation of its foreign policy, would have to unfold in the context of a wider European process.[286] In his eyes, West Germany's interests would be 'best served' if the country was 'embedded' in a European institutional framework, of which the Common Market was the 'centrepiece.'[287] Writing in 1971, Brandt argued:

> Our foreign policy rests on firm principles. As things are, it has to rest in the Western alliance. It seeks peaceful compromise (*Ausgleich*) and constructive cooperation in Europe. This corresponds to the demand of our time and the wish of our peoples . . . Germany is indispensable for a settlement (*Ausgleich*) in Europe.[288]

It was essential not only to consult closely with West Germany's Western allies, but also to fine-tune foreign policy moves in order to maintain their trust and support.[289] For him it was clear that he would not be able to conduct an independent foreign policy without raising fears and objections in Western capitals. As a consequence, Brandt was cooperative and forthcoming in negotiations with the United States, France, and Britain regarding the future of European integration, as well as bilateral matters.[290] For example, as he wrote in a letter of 5 October 1970, he considered 'German-French solidarity as a precondition for a successful policy of détente in Europe.'[291] Brandt was convinced that some form of *Westpolitik* was necessary to enable *Ostpolitik*, knowing that he had to compromise on matters of European integration in order to secure allied support for his openings towards the East. The compromises, which ranged from the concession on the CAP in favour of France to undertaking first steps towards economic and monetary integration, were strongly supported by Pompidou. Brandt's support for enlargement was received positively in Britain, which in turn was by and large supportive of *Ostpolitik*.[292] Heath wrote how 'impressed' he was with Brandt's stance on *Ostpolitik*.[293]

The second European component of *Ostpolitik* stemmed from Brandt's acceptance of the de facto status quo in Europe. In contrast to his predecessors and the CDU/CSU opposition, Brandt thought the time had come to accept Europe's new territorial and political realities.[294]

Given West Germany's narrow room for foreign policy initiatives, Brandt saw European integration as an instrument which would allow Bonn to take up negotiations with Eastern European countries. His objective for European policy-making was to enable the emergence of what he called a 'European order of peace.'[295] In order to work towards this objective, and to establish diplomatic relations with the countries of Eastern Europe, West Germany needed to stop claiming revisions to Germany's eastern borders and accept the political and territorial status quo in Europe.[296]

In Brandt's understanding, the process of European integration extended to more than just the Community's dynamics of economic cooperation and integration in Western Europe. For him, European integration was a much broader endeavour. He insisted that an enlarged Community was not to be formed as a bloc against the East, but as a model for institutionalised cooperation that could one day bridge the gap between East and West:

> I never regarded the West European community as a citadel, in which we can fortify and entrench ourselves against the world around us. The Europe of the Six, and also an enlarged Western Europe, should not stand against its neighbours; it should attract them and not reject them. It has to be open and not closed.[297]

This concept of a European order of peace figured prominently in his political rhetoric. Both as foreign minister and chancellor, Brandt's foreign policy priority was to achieve practical gains to facilitate the life of Germans in a divided country.[298] In this sense, his European policy was based on distinctly German necessities, as well as the particular circumstances of Germany's limited sovereignty and territorial division. The referent object of Brandt's European policy was Germany, not Europe. Rather, Europe was seen as the only viable conduit for foreign policy.[299] Moreover, the aim of the eventual unification of both parts of Germany was only seen to be feasible in the context of more cooperative political relations with the East in general and the Soviet Union in particular.[300]

Brandt's European policy had a much more pronounced pan-European dimension than that of Heath and Pompidou.[301] Whereas Heath and Pompidou made an economic case for Europe, Brandt argued that European integration was more about long-term prospects for peace than economic utility.[302] Whereas Heath and Pompidou were concerned about the global role and economic influence of the Community, Brandt's understanding of Europe was geared towards the overcoming the continent's internal divisions and historical traumas.[303] And when Brandt did conceptualise the Community as a global actor, he did so in the context of his plans for a European peace order:

> There can be no doubt that the European peoples have to take on more responsibility for peace and progress in the world. In order to do so they have to bundle together their limited powers. This necessitates a closer European union.[304]

It was apparent that Brandt's understanding of Europe, and approach to European integration, was different not only from Heath's and Pompidou's, but also from those leaders who founded the Common Market in 1957.[305] He criticised the 'institutional perfectionism' and 'political abstractions' associated with the technocratic approach of Spaak, Monnet, and others.[306] Brandt was not an advocate of supranationalism, and he doubted that a viable foreign policy could be conducted by a European institution.[307] Instead, he argued for an extension of intergovernmental cooperation and dismissed the case for gradualism and spill-over:

> It became apparent that those were mistaken, who thought that political integration would develop more or less automatically out of economic integration. Experience teaches us that we would be well-advised to adjust to a perspective of intergovernmental cooperation.[308]

His disdain for the Brussels bureaucracies also became apparent in his 1976 book *Begegnungen und Einsichten*:

> The European *élan* of the early postwar period was . . . quickly exhausted. It is . . . true that the technocrats in Brussels – who were supposed to keep the common institutions in motion – produced not only sensible regulations, but that they contributed to bureaucratic excesses. The great European idea ran the danger of drowning in a Europe of boredom.[309]

Furthermore, his emphasis on peace and rapprochement with Eastern Europe and the Soviet Union clearly clashed with the dominant understandings of Europe in the 1950s, which treated the Communist East as Western Europe's threatening antagonist.

Culturally, Brandt's conception of Europe was informed by a largely unemotive understanding of pan-Europeanism. He was convinced that, regardless of all the continent's divisions, Europe's people would come to recognise that they shared a common fate.[310] He spoke of the existence of common European cultural values, which could be nurtured given better East-West cooperation.[311] His conception is therefore not of a common European civilisation, based on a shared religion or cultural commonalities, but more of Europe as a community of fate in which Europeans have to work together whether they like it or not.[312] In his speeches he made only few references to Europe as a cultural community. Brandt's cultural understanding of the idea of Europe was more neutral than that of the founding fathers of the Treaties of Rome, and derived from a perception of the functional necessity for cooperation and unification in the pursuit of a peaceful modus vivendi in Europe:

> Not only in the West have people begun to realise the well-understood interest in cooperation across the whole of Europe (*gesamteuropäischen Zusammenarbeit*). Slowly . . . the realisation will prevail that the cooperation and unification of Europe is aimed against nobody. In a dangerous time and a quarrelling world it could even be an example for how peoples and states, regardless of their systems of government and society, can achieve prosperity and security through peaceful cooperation.[313]

Incidentally, Brandt's long-term vision for a united Europe suffered the same problem as Heath's. Heath was unable to offer a persuasive vision of Europe after British entry had been accomplished. Similarly, Brandt's vision of a European order of peace entailed few specifics beyond West Germany's treaties with Eastern European states and the Soviet Union.

***

It has been argued in the literature that the 'major issues'[314] deadlocking Britain's accession to the Common Market were questions concerning what to do about New Zealand butter, Commonwealth sugar, and future British contributions to the Community's budget. The problem with this point of view is that it inflates the importance of technical issues in the negotiation process leading to British membership, and underestimates the peculiarity of the leadership changes that took place in 1969 and 1970.

The British, French, and West German economies were developing not only at different paces but also in opposite directions. The strength of the West German economy in global export markets vastly outpaced Paris' efforts at economic modernisation and stood in marked contrast to Britain's combined troubles of high inflation, loss of global market share, rising unemployment, and a balance of payment crisis. Keeping the ever more fragile British economy out of the Common Market was not a far-fetched proposition at the time. In this context it is even more surprising how fast the agreement to allow Britain into the Common Market ultimately came about. London's earlier bids – in 1961 and 1967 – to join the Common Market had both been opposed by France, and little had changed in terms of the structural economic and geopolitical conditions that had served as arguments to keep the UK out.

Central to overcoming the stalemate in the integration process was a fortuitous new leadership constellation. It brought together a technocratic Gaullist stalwart interested in stepping out of the General's shadow, a charismatic German chancellor whose hallmark *Ostpolitik* – for which he received the Nobel Peace Prize in 1971 – signalled a major break in West Germany's self-understanding and foreign policy posture, and arguably the most pro-integrationist British prime minister, whose enthusiastic views on Europe were 'not shared by the British public at the time, or by any of [his] successors since.'[315] What Pompidou, Brandt, and Heath managed to accomplish was not to resolve technical obstacles – in which they were all largely uninterested – but to decisively overcome the widespread anxiety about Britain not being a wholly European country, which would undermine the integration process once it was part thereof.

The archival evidence suggests that the crucial breakthrough for the negotiations was the Pompidou-Heath summit of May 1971, a classic example of personal diplomacy. At the summit, Heath was able to directly convince Pompidou of his sincerity, thereby dispelling Pompidou's residual fears about Britain's motives and commitment to the European project. Throughout the summit, Heath and Pompidou grew surprisingly fond of each other. In a tête-a-tête that excluded officials, Heath agreed to the *acquis communautaire* not because it was necessarily in the British interest to do so, but rather as an unmistakable down payment of his conviction and determination to anchor Britain in Europe. It is not coincidental that, as prime minister, Heath spared little patience for the Commonwealth and the Foreign Office's fondness for it. He was also much less enthusiastic about the transatlantic 'special relationship' with the US – and the UK's role in it – than his predecessors and successors. Heath's European priorities eclipsed other foreign policy goals. After the summit, both Pompidou and Heath instructed their officials to sort out the remaining technical obstacles.

Pompidou was well-positioned to alter the often controversial and temperamental tone, style, and substance of de Gaulle's foreign policy, without weakening the domestic public support for Gaullism as a political movement. The issue of enlargement was a policy field in which he could set himself apart from his predecessor. Brandt was a pragmatic geopolitical operator, whose interest in achieving tangible improvements in the modus vivendi between East and West led him to be largely accommodative of French interests on European integration, so as to secure Pompidou's support for *Ostpolitik*. He did so by strengthening West Germany's commitment to European integration (which would include Britain), as well as by agreeing to a number of – mainly financial – concessions (especially on agriculture).

In contrast to their predecessors, Heath, Pompidou, and Brandt staked substantial political capital on their ability to make progress on European integration. For Heath in particular, British membership in the Common Market was a primordial concern. It turned out to be the major legacy of his time in office. The three European leaders had different preferences for Europe, different personal and ideological interpretations of the idea of Europe, and different reasons for which they sought to pursue integration. Yet each in its own way, their diverging approaches all required Britain to become part of the European project. Pompidou, Brandt, and Heath were not successful leaders on enlargement because they had unique leadership capabilities or more power than their predecessors. After all, de Gaulle had illustrated his power and personal gravitas by stopping Britain from joining the Common Market. Rather, they succeeded because they regarded an enlarged Community an asset rather than an obstacle to their own political priorities, as well as a viable mechanism to raise their domestic political profiles. In contrast to their predecessors, Pompidou, Brandt, and Heath thrived on being personally involved in and publicly identified with making progress on European affairs.

Notes

1 One of the earlier voices advocating British participation in the EEC was Gladwyn Jebb, Britain's ambassador in Paris, who on 28 April 1957 had already argued that Britain would soon find itself 'faced with a choice between "coming in" to Western Europe (to some degree) and "staying out" altogether, and that the balance of advantage lies with the former': TNA PREM 11/1844. See also de Zulueta to Macmillan, 29 May 1957: TNA PREM 11/1844. Yet Christopher Steel advised Foreign Secretary Selwyn Lloyd not to follow Jebb's advice: TNA PREM 11/1844. This reinforced Macmillan's earlier ambiguity on the matter, which is illustrated by his instructions to the Secretary of State for Foreign Affairs of 3 June 1957: TNA PREM 11/1844.
2 J. Tratt, *The Macmillan Government and Europe: A Study in the Process of Policy Development* (Basingstoke: Macmillan, 1996), p. 198; S. Wall, *A Stranger in Europe: Britain and the EU from Thatcher to Blair* (Oxford: Oxford University Press, 2008), pp. 2–3.
3 On Macmillan's bid to enter the Common Market see N.J. Crowson, *Britain and Europe: A Political History since 1918* (London: Routledge, 2011);

D. Gowland, A. Turner, and A. Wright, *Britain and European Integration since 1945: On The Sidelines* (London: Routledge, 2010); M.J. Dedman, *The Origins and Development of the European Union, 1945-2008: A History of European Integration*, second edition (Abingdon: Routledge, 2010); S. Lee, *Victory in Europe: Britain and Germany since 1945* (Harlow: Pearson, 2001); D. Gowland and A. Turner, *Reluctant Europeans. Britain and European Integration, 1945-1998* (London: Longman, 2000); K. Steinnes, 'The European Challenge: Britain's EEC Application in 1961,' *Contemporary European History* 7 (1) (1998): 61–79; W. Kaiser, *Using Europe, Abusing the Europeans: Britain and European Integration, 1945-63* (Basingstoke: Macmillan, 1996); W. Kaiser, *Großbritannien und die Europäische Wirtschaftsgemeinschaft 1955-1961. Von Messina nach Canossa* (Berlin: Akademie Verlag, 1996); Tratt, *The Macmillan Government and Europe*; and L. Bell, *The Throw that Failed: Britain's Original Application to Join the Common Market* (London: New European Publications, 1995). Harold Wilson's reasons for launching a second attempt to achieve British membership are illustrated in M. Pine, *Harold Wilson and Europe: Pursuing Britain's Membership of the European Community* (London: I.B. Tauris, 2012); H. Parr, 'A Question of Leadership: July 1966 and Harold Wilson's European Decision,' *Contemporary British History* 19 (4) (2005): 437–458. British reactions to de Gaulle's vetoes are discussed in R. Davis, 'The "Problem of de Gaulle": British Reactions to General de Gaulle's Veto of the UK Application to Join the Common Market,' *Journal of Contemporary History* 32 (4) (1997): 453–464.
4 R. Gildea, *France since 1945* (Oxford: Oxford University Press, 2002).
5 Steinnes, 'The European Challenge,' p. 66. As early as 19 October 1960, Britain's new ambassador to France, Pierson Dixon, reported that de Gaulle had told him that 'Great Britain, which was an island with connexions through the Commonwealth over the world could not come into Europe': TNA PREM 11/3131. This assessment was still widely shared in early 1969: see note of conversation between von Braun and Rothschild, 21 February 1969: PAAA B130 10.096.
6 Despite the fact that both Gaullists and Atlanticists were sceptical about a federal institutional structure for Europe, they were 'parallel' conceptions of Europe, emanating out of divergent power ambitions and foreign policy traditions. See C. Hacke, *Die Außenpolitik der Bundesrepublik Deutschland. Weltmacht wider Willen?* revised edition (Frankfurt: Ullstein, 1997), p. 131. See also *Die Welt*, 'Gerhard Schröder: Die größere Gemeinschaft' (25 June 1971).
7 In August 1968 there was still no sign of any change in France's opposition to British membership in the Common Market: note of conversations between Brandt and Medici, 6 August 1968: PAAA B130 10.096.
8 D. Hurd, *An End to Promises: A Sketch of a Government 1970-74* (London: Collins, 1979), p. 57.
9 See J. Ramsden, *The Winds of Change: Macmillan to Heath, 1957-1975*, A History of the Conservative Party series (London: Longman, 1996).
10 Previous initiatives, such as the 'Kiesinger-de Gaulle Four Point Declaration' of 16 February 1968, which intended to 'bring Britain closer to the European Common Market,' ultimately faltered due to de Gaulle's hesitancy about and opposition to British membership: see comments of 17 February 1968 for Wilson attached to the Franco-German communiqué: TNA PREM 13/2107.
11 See Brandt's notes for 5–6 April 1971: WBA BK/92/46; Privy Council minute of December 1970 on the 'Ten Reasons Why Britain Should Join the Common Market': TNA PREM 15/62. On the predominant mood for intergovernmentalism, see confidential report 'Political Unification – The Davignon Report' from Michaels to Moon, 10 November 1970: TNA PREM 15/62.

12 See J. Wright, 'The Cold War, European Community and Anglo-French Relations, 1958–1998,' in *Anglo-French Relations in the Twentieth Century: Rivalry and Cooperation*, A. Sharp and G. Stone eds. (London: Routledge, 2000), pp. 324–343. See also U. Kitzinger, *Diplomacy and Persuasion: How Britain Joined the Common Market* (London: Thames and Hudson, 1973).
13 See Heath's remarks in the Commons: *Hansard*, Commons, 5th ser., 818: 32. See also E. Heath, *The Course of My Life: My Autobiography* (London: Hodder and Stoughton, 1998); Pompidou to Brandt, 28 May 1971: WBA, BK/51/92-3; Brandt's handwritten notes for 29 July 1970: WBA BK/91/100. See also notes for 25–26 January 1971: WBA BK/92/24.
14 D. Möckli, *European Foreign Policy during the Cold War: Heath, Brandt, and Pompidou and the Short Dream of Political Unity* (London: I.B. Tauris, 2009).
15 See Nield to Heath, 8 December 1970: TNA PREM 15/62; also FCO planning staff paper of 8 March 1971: TNA PREM 15/369.
16 Record of a conversation between Pompidou and Brandt, 3 July 1970: PAAA B130 10.096.
17 See the discussions of 25–26 January 1971 between Brandt and Pompidou on their preference for intergovernmentalism in *Akten zur Auswärtigen Politik der Bundesrepublik Deutschland 1971*, H.-P. Schwarz ed., Vol. I (1 January – 30 April) (Munich: Oldenbourg, 2002), doc. 27. A similar view is espoused in P. Taylor, 'Intergovernmentalism in the European Communities in the 1970s: Patterns and Perspectives,' *International Organization* 36 (4) (1982): 741–766. Brandt's handwritten notes of this meeting confirm his disdain for 'institutional perfectionism': WBA BK/92/24.
18 M. Schain, 'The Fifth Republic,' in *The French Republic: History, Values, Debates*, E. Berenson, V. Duclert, and C. Prochasson eds. (Ithaca: Cornell University Press, 2011), pp. 73–92.
19 P.G. Cerny, *The Politics of Grandeur: Ideological Aspects of de Gaulle's Foreign Policy* (Cambridge: Cambridge University Press, 1980).
20 S. Hoffmann, 'De Gaulle, Europe, and the Atlantic Alliance,' *International Organization* 18 (1) (1964): 1–28.
21 Auswärtiges Amt, *Aussenpolitik der Bundesrepublik Deutschland. Vom Kalten Krieg zum Frieden in Europa. Dokumente 1949–1989* (Munich: Verlag Bonn Aktuell, 1990), doc. 77, doc. 78.
22 J. Pinder, *Europe against De Gaulle* (London: Pall Mall Press, 1963).
23 Klaiber to AA, 3 December 1965: PAAA B130 10.096.
24 See secret memo to Robert Armstrong, 23 October 1970: TNA PREM 15/62.
25 See Schain, 'Fifth Republic'.
26 T. Barman, 'Britain, France and West Germany: The Changing Pattern of Their Relationship in Europe,' *International Affairs* 46 (2) (1970): 269–279.
27 On Pompidou's resignation as Prime Minister in 1968, and the events leading up to it, see G. Pompidou, *Pour Rétablir une Vérité* (Paris: Flammarion, 1982).
28 D. Pickles, 'The Decline of Gaullist Foreign Policy,' *International Affairs* 51 (2) (1975): 220–235. Pickles illustrates the most prominent differences between the foreign policies of de Gaulle and Pompidou. She also argues that the geopolitical and economic conditions had made de Gaulle's foreign policy objectives increasingly hard to obtain, a situation which was exacerbated after 1970. Barman talks about a gradual 'eclipse' of both de Gaulle and Gaullism: Barman, 'Britain, France and West Germany,' p. 269.
29 E. Roussel, *Georges Pompidou, 1911–1974*. Collection Tempus, Vol. 60 (Paris: Perrin, 2004); G. Pompidou, *Entretiens et Discours 1968–1974*. Vol. I (Paris: Plon, 1975), p. 18.
30 A. Grosser, 'Europe: Community of Malaise,' *Foreign Policy* 15 (1974): 169–170.

31 D. Reynolds, *Britannia Overruled: British Policy and World Power in the 20th Century*, second edition (Harlow: Pearson, 2000), p. 227. Pompidou noted that, for France, supranational institutions such as the European Parliament had only 'marginal value': *AAPD* 1970, II: doc. 293. On Pompidou's preferences for intergovernmentalism and hostility to the transfer of authority to Community institutions, see *AAPD* 1970, II: doc. 307; *AAPD* 1971, I: doc. 27. See also extract of Heath's meeting with Brandt of 6 May 1971: TNA PREM 15/371.
32 *AAPD* 1969, II: doc. 279.
33 P.N. Ludlow, 'The Making of the CAP: Towards a Historical Analysis of the EU's First Major Policy,' *Contemporary European History* 14 (3) (2005): 347–371.
34 C. Hiepel, *Willy Brandt und Georges Pompidou. Deutsch-französische Europapolitik zwischen Aufbruch und Krise* (Munich: Oldenbourg, 2012).
35 *The Times*, 'Pompidou Takes Up tough Bargaining Line at Summit' (2 December 1969).
36 On the role of the presidency in French foreign and defence policy, see J. Howorth, 'The President's Special Role in Foreign and Defence Policy,' in *De Gaulle to Mitterrand: Presidential Power in France*, J. Hayward ed. (London: Hurst, 1993), pp. 150–189.
37 Roussel, *Pompidou*, p. 417.
38 The need for a more conciliatory tone in foreign affairs was made especially with reference to Anglo-French relations. In the wake of the 'Soames affair' of early 1969, repairing the bilateral relations between Paris and London became a priority for both governments; see Wright, 'The Cold War,' pp. 324–343.
39 Kitzinger, *Diplomacy and Persuasion*, p. 60.
40 Quoted in Roussel, *Pompidou*, p. 289.
41 T. Diallo, *La Politique Étrangère de Georges Pompidou* (Paris: Librairie Général de Droit et de Jurisprudence, 1992), p. 18.
42 The extent to which Franco-German relations were affected by the change from de Gaulle to Pompidou is revealed in the notes of the German chef de cabinet in the Federal Chancellery, Paul Frank, of 22 October 1969. In them, he wrote about how Pompidou graded the Franco-German relation down from 'preferential' to 'exemplary,' a move which according to Frank suggested a return to a more realistic assessment of the state of affairs between both countries. Frank expected friction between both countries to occur as a result of the 'economic dynamism' of the FRG, France's distrust of *Ostpolitik*, the fight for the CAP financial arrangements, and West Germany's vocal support for British Community membership. Frank also notes that some Gaullists deemed it necessary for France to join with other allies so as to counteract German economic power: *AAPD* 1969, II: doc. 320.
43 Wright, 'The Cold War,' p. 331.
44 See Pine, *Harold Wilson*, pp. 132–139.
45 D.J. Mahoney, *De Gaulle: Statesmanship, Grandeur, and Modern Democracy* (New Brunswick: Transaction, 2000), pp. 132–133.
46 Pompidou struck a similar note in a speech given at the American Club in Paris in February 1964, when he argued that France was 'condemned by its geography and its history to play the role of Europe': Gildea, *France*, p. 258.
47 *AAPD* 1969, II: doc. 279. Pompidou was particularly worried that the international financial crisis of the early 1970s would threaten France's economic stability and growth: see *FRUS* 1969–1976, III: 93, 431, 595, 602, 604. He was determined to ensure that the CAP would not be affected by the economic situation or trade negotiations: *FRUS* 1969–1976, III: 600. On the recognition

that Pompidou was an expert on monetary matters, see White House memorandum of 26 February 1970: *FRUS 1969–1976*, III: 91.
48 Kitzinger, *Diplomacy and Persuasion*, p. 60. See also Pompidou's priorities for Europe as reported in *Le Figaro*, 'M. Georges Pompidou: La préoccupation no. 1 doit être la lutte contre l'inflation' (20 October 1972).
49 *AAPD* 1971, I: doc. 31.
50 De Gaulle reinforced the British understanding of its political and cultural separateness: Davis, 'The "Problem of de Gaulle,"' pp. 453–464. Yet the Gaullist exclusion of the 'Anglo-Saxons' from his understanding of Europe is less a consequence of cultural convictions than of political considerations: see Pattison de Ménil, *Who Speaks for Europe? The Vision of Charles de Gaulle* (London: Weidenfeld and Nicolson, 1977). De Gaulle's vision was not one of a Little Europe, or a Christian Abendland as it had been for Adenauer, but rather a political strategy to defend the independence and relevance of France while solving the 'German question' 'on a continental basis': Pattison de Ménil, *Who Speaks for Europe?*, p. 37. Gaullists feared that British participation in European integration would not only weaken France's position vis-à-vis Germany, but also increase the influence of the United States over French and German policies.
51 Already in a 28 July 1946 speech at Bar-le-Duc, de Gaulle discussed his understanding of Europe as a third force between the United States and the Soviet Union: see C. de Gaulle, *Discours et Messages: Dans l'Attente, Février 1946 – Avril 1958* (Paris: Plon, 1970), pp. 12–17. His view of Europe transcended the barriers that the Cold War imposed on the continent, encompassing an extensive Europe 'from Gibraltar to the Urals, from Spitzbergen to Sicily': in de Gaulle, *Discours*, p. 608. He stipulated in his memoirs that the 'French wanted to proceed towards a European Europe, in which Anglo-American influence would be kept at bay': see C. de Gaulle, *Memoirs of Hope: Renewal 1958–62, Endeavour 1962* (London: Weidenfeld and Nicolson, 1971), p. 192. The political objective for his European Europe aimed at a modus vivendi with the Soviet Union that ensured peace and safeguarded the independence of France: see E. Jouve, *Le Général de Gaulle et la Construction de l'Europe*, Vol. 1 (Paris: Librairie Générale de Droit et de Jurisprudence, 1967).
52 Crucial to de Gaulle's European policies was a collectivist and organic understanding of the nation-state. Each nation – but first and foremost France – was seen to be characterised by an 'incommunicable uniqueness': see S. Hoffmann, *Decline or Renewal? France since the 1930s* (New York: Viking Press, 1974), p. 232. In de Gaulle's eyes, the 'political independence commensurate with my country's position and aims was essential to its survival in the future': de Gaulle, *Memoirs*, pp. 178–179. From this vantage point, the values of national sovereignty and independence could not be compromised or sacrificed, because they were 'absolute values' and 'not subject to negotiation': see J. Shields, 'The French Gaullists,' in *Political Parties and the European Union*, J. Gaffney ed. (London: Routledge, 1996), p. 87.
53 Hiepel, *Brandt und Pompidou*, pp. 50–52.
54 The SPD–FDP coalition emerged in good part due to Brandt's foreign policy proposals, of which his plans for *Ostpolitik* attracted most attention: see R. Löwenthal, *Vom Kalten Krieg zur Ostpolitik* (Stuttgart: Seewald, 1974).
55 For a collection of speeches throughout Brandt's tenure as foreign minister, which highlights his commitment to European integration, see W. Brandt, *Friedenspolitik in Europa* (Frankfurt: Fischer, 1971); W. Brandt, *Außenpolitik, Deutschlandpolitik, Europapolitik: Grundsätzliche Erklärungen während des ersten Jahres im Auswärtigen Amt*, second edition (Berlin: Berlin Verlag, 1970).

56 H. Türk, *Die Europapolitik der Großen Koalition 1966–1969* (Munich: Oldenburg, 2006), pp. 57–92.
57 Quoted in H. Müller-Roschach, *Die Deutsche Europapolitik: Wege und Umwege zur Politischen Union Europas* (Baden-Baden: Nomos, 1974), p. 131.
58 T. Geiger, 'Der Streit um die deutsche Europapolitik in den 1960er Jahren,' in *Deutsche Europapolitik Christlicher Demokraten. Von Konrad Adenauer bis Angela Merkel (1945–2013)*, H.J. Küsters ed. (Düsseldorf: Droste, 2014), p. 358; see also memo to Robert Armstrong of October 23, 1970: TNA PREM 15/62.
59 Brandt's objective of building a European order of peace needs to be understood in the wider international political context, which was favourable to détente between the superpowers. Merkl suggests that 'Brandt in 1969 merely undertook to complete under more favourable terms and in a more effective manner what [former German Foreign Minister] Schroeder had attempted in vain': P. Merkl, 'The German Janus: From Westpolitik to Ostpolitik,' *Political Science Quarterly* 89 (4) (1974–75): 804.
60 *AAPD* 1969, II: doc. 320.
61 W. Brandt, 'Erklärung der Bundesregierung vom 28. Oktober 1969,' *Berühmte Reden*, Bundeskanzler Willy-Brandt-Stiftung online (1969), www.bwbs.de/Beitraege/69.html.
62 U. Lappenküper, *Die Aussenpolitik der Bundesrepublik Deutschland 1949 bis 1990*, Enzyklopädie Deutscher Geschichte, Vol. 83 (Munich: Oldenbourg, 2008), pp. 95–96; M. Herkendell, *Deutschland Zivil- oder Friedensmacht? Außen- und sicherheitspolitische Orientierung der SPD im Wandel (1982–2007)* (Bonn: Dietz, 2012), pp. 65–66.
63 WBA BK/91/72. See also W. Brandt, 'Fernsehansprache aus Moskau am 12. August 1970,' *Berühmte Reden*, Bundeskanzler Willy-Brandt-Stiftung online (1970), http://www.bwbs.de/Beitraege/70.html
64 W. Brandt, *Begegnungen und Einsichten: Die Jahre 1960–1975* (Hamburg: Hoffmann und Campe, 1976).
65 Bundesministerium für innerdeutsche Beziehungen, *Texte zur Deutschlandpolitik*, Vol. 11: 2 June – 22 December 1972 (Bonn: Bundesverlag, 1973), p. 32.
66 W. Brandt, *Ein Volk der guten Nachbarn: Außen- und Deutschlandpolitik 1966–1974*, Frank Fischer ed., Berliner Ausgabe, Vol. 6. (Bonn: Dietz, 2005), doc. 29.
67 Lappenküper, *Aussenpolitik*, pp. 97–98.
68 G. Krell, 'West German Ostpolitik and the German Question,' *Journal of Peace Research* 28 (3) (1991): 311–323.
69 W.F. Hahn, 'West Germany's Ostpolitik: The Grand Design of Egon Bahr,' *Orbis* 16 (4) (1973): 874.
70 Brimelow to Edmonds, 14 August 14, 1970: *DBPO* III, I: doc. 50.
71 F. Fischer, 'Einleitung,' in Brandt, *Ein Volk der guten Nachbarn*, p. 18.
72 Auswärtiges Amt, *Aussenpolitik*, doc. 84.
73 Hahn, 'West Germany's Ostpolitik,' pp. 874–875.
74 Brandt consistently made the case against the so-called Rapallo-complex of many Western politicians and journalists. See Brandt, *Ein Volk der guten Nachbarn*, doc. 43. He argued that Germany was not interested in conducting a rapprochement with the Soviet Union at the expense of its Western partners, as it was seen to have done with the 1922 German-Russian treaty signed at Rapallo. See also Brimelow to Edmonds, 14 August 1970: *DBPO* III, I: doc. 50; and the report by the Joint Intelligence Committee on the Soviet Threat of 14 September 1972: *DBPO* III, I: appendix.
75 Brandt, *Ein Volk der guten Nachbarn*, doc. 30.

76 Brandt, 'Fernsehansprache aus Moskau,' http://www.bwbs.de/Beitraege/70.html.
77 *Ibid.*
78 E. Bahr, 'Willy Brandts europäische Außenpolitik – Vortrag von Bundesminister a.D. Professor Egon Bahr am 9. Oktober 1998 im Rathaus Schöneberg,' *Schriftenreihe der Bundeskanzler-Willy-Brandt-Stiftung* 3 (1999): 5. Bahr notes that the reason Brandt's policy was not called 'Europapolitik' – but rather *Westpolitik* and *Ostpolitik* – was because this term was already occupied by European integration and the policies towards the Common Market. See also W. Hahn, 'West Germany's Ostpolitik: The Grand Design of Egon Bahr,' *Orbis* 16 (4) (1973): 859–880.
79 Brandt to Pompidou, 5 October 1970: WBA BK/51/28. See also Brandt, *Ein Volk der guten Nachbarn*, doc. 46.
80 See Brandt's handwritten notes for 7 June 1970: WBA/BK/91/72.
81 Bahr, 'Willy Brandts europäische Außenpolitik,' 7.
82 Brandt, *Ein Volk der guten Nachbarn*, doc. 2, doc. 9.
83 *Ibid.*, doc. 1, doc. 7.
84 The idea of holding a European summit surfaced during the 1969 presidential election campaign. Pompidou committed himself to it on 10 July 1969, a month after the elections. It is not fully established to what extent the summit idea was imposed on Pompidou as a 'condition for electoral support' by 'Gaullist vigilantes,' who were suspicious that Pompidou might abandon de Gaulle's international legacy: Kitzinger, *Diplomacy and Persuasion*, p. 62.
85 P. Gerbet, *La Construction de l'Europe* (Paris: Imprimerie Nationale, 1983).
86 Hiepel, *Brandt und Pompidou*, pp. 21–22.
87 Soames to Greenhill, 7 May 1971: TNA PREM 15/371. The view that Pompidou lacked visionary objectives is also explicit in an FCO steering brief of 11 March 1972: TNA FCO 33/1752.
88 Kitzinger, *Diplomacy and Persuasion*, p. 71
89 See *The Times*, 'Six to Prepare for Talks with Britain by End of June' (3 December 1969); 'Full Text of the Final Communiqué' (3 December 1969); 'Charles Hargrove: Pompidou's Strange Game' (3 December 1969); 'Talks on the Way' (3 December 1969).
90 Pompidou, *Entretiens*, Vol. II, p. 76.
91 *Ibid.*
92 *Ibid.*, p. 77.
93 *Ibid.*, Vol. II, p. 76.
94 This view is confirmed in the record of a conversation between Pompidou and Brandt, 3 July 1970: PAAA B130 10.096.
95 According to Brandt's account of the 1 December 1969 tête-à-tête, Pompidou wanted reassurances that enlargement would not come at the expense of Franco-German partnership. Pompidou agreed that enlargement negotiations would start throughout 1970, provided the financial arrangements for CAP were finalised: see Brandt, *Begegnungen*, p. 321.
96 Heath recalled what Pompidou had told him about his attachment to CAP on a visit to Chequers in 1972: 'If you ever want to know what my policy is, don't bother to call me on the telephone. I do not speak English and your French is awful. Just remember that I am a peasant, and my policy will always be to support the peasants': in Heath, *Course of My Life*, p. 368.
97 After the Hague summit, talks about EMU gained momentum, leading to the publication of the Werner Plan in October 1970: see C. Parsons, *A Certain Idea of Europe* (Ithaca: Cornell University Press, 2003), pp. 161–162; Auswärtiges Amt, Auswärtige Politik 1949–1989, doc. 131; P. Ludlow, *The Making*

of the European Monetary System: A Case Study of the Politics of the European Community (London: Butterworth Scientific, 1982); K. McNamara, *The Currency of Ideas: Monetary Politics in the European Union* (Ithaca: Cornell University Press, 1998), p. 96.
98 Brandt, *Begegnungen*.
99 Heath to Brandt, 27 May 1971: WBA BK/52/93.
100 Gerbet, *Construction*, p. 348.
101 Wright, 'The Cold War,' p. 324.
102 *The Times*, 'David Howell: Collision course for Britain and the Six?' (9 June 1970).
103 *The Times*, 'Paris Ready to Trust Heath' (25 June 1970).
104 *Ibid*. The same was true for Brandt. He had been both politically and personally close to Wilson, but had also known Heath, with whom he established 'uncomplicated, trustful, and . . . friendly' relations: Brandt, *Begegnungen*, pp. 325–326.
105 Ramsden, *Winds of Change*.
106 Hurd, *End to Promises*, p. 57.
107 Ramsden, *Winds of Change*, p. 336; J. Campbell, *Edward Heath: A Biography* (London: Jonathan Cape, 1993), p. xvii.
108 Heath, *Course of My Life*, p. 364.
109 Hurd, *End to Promises*, p. 58.
110 *Ibid*.
111 Heath, *Course of My Life*, p. 365.
112 *The Times*, 'David Wood: What Britain Hopes to Gain from the Summit' (10 May 1971).
113 Nield to Heath, 19 June 1970: TNA PREM 15/62.
114 Secret memo of October 23, 1970 to Robert Armstrong, titled "The EEC Negotiations – Strategic Review: The Need for a Negotiating Strategy and Programme to July 1971": TNA PREM 15/62.
115 Memo to Armstrong, 23 October 1970: TNA PREM 15/62.
116 Hurd, *End to Promises*, p. 59.
117 Secret draft memo 'for ministers for a statement (to be presented by a senior minister) at the Inaugural Conference of the Ten on June 30, 1970' in Luxembourg: TNA PREM 15/62.
118 See draft for Douglas-Home's Luxembourg speech on 30 June 1970: TNA PREM 15/62.
119 Heath to Brandt, 2 December 1970: TNA PREM 15/62.
120 Brandt to Pompidou, 18 March 1971: WBA BK/51/51; Brandt to Pompidou, 6 April 1971: WBA BK/51/81–2.
121 Record of conservation between Schumann and Rippon, 9 November 1970: TNA PREM 15/62.
122 FCO planning staff paper 'Options for British External Policies if our Application for Membership of the European Communities fails,' 8 March 1971: TNA PREM 15/369.
123 Nield to Heath, 8 December 1970: TNA PREM 15/62
124 *Ibid*.
125 Heath, *Course of My Life*, p. 362.
126 Soames to FCO, 12 November 1970: TNA PREM 15/370.
127 Soames to FCO, 6 May 1971: TNA PREM 15/371.
128 Pompidou to Brandt, 27 March 1971: WBA BK/51/54–6.
129 Kitzinger, *Diplomacy and Persuasion*, p. 107.
130 For Pompidou's worries about Britain's commitments beyond Europe, see press conference of 2 July 1970: in Pompidou, *Entretiens*, Vol. II.
131 Memo FCO to Armstrong, 23 October 1970: TNA PREM 15/62.

132 Letter to Moon, 11 November 1970: TNA PREM 15/62.
133 Heath, *Course of My Life*, p. 365.
134 Soames to Greenhill: 7 May 1971: TNA PREM 15/371.
135 Survey of the *Opinion Research Centre* carried out for Conservative Central Office, ORC 777, between 5–9 August 1970, titled "Britain and the Common Market": TNA PREM 15/30.
136 Memo by Tufton Beamish on 'Party Policy on the Common Market,' which Heath noted to be a 'v. good paper': TNA PREM 15/30.
137 Record of conversation between Pompidou and Brandt, 3 July 1970: PAAA B130 10.096.
138 *The Times*, 'Summit Is Viewed with Hope' (11 May 1971).
139 *Ibid.*
140 Heath, *Course of My Life*, p. 364.
141 Brandt noted on June 4–5, 1971, when Heath visited Bonn, that bilateral consultations between France and Britain would facilitate the overall agreement between Britain and the Six: WBA BK/92/46.
142 See record of conversation between Pompidou and Brandt, 3 July 1970: PAAA B130 10.096.
143 *AAPD*, 1971, II: doc. 228.
144 This intermediary role is also apparent in a newspaper article which highlights Brandt's view that without Pompidou and Heath – and their agreement – enlargement would not have occurred: *Frankfurter Zeitung*, 'Brandt begrüßt Englands Beitritt als Sieg des europäischen Gedankens' (25 Juni 1971).
145 W. Brandt, *Erinnerungen: Mit den 'Notizen zum Fall G'* (Munich: Ullstein, 2003), p. 456.
146 See, for instance, Brandt's advocacy of a compromise position between French and British proposals regarding the UK's contributions to the EEC budget: *AAPD* 1971, I: doc. 31.
147 *AAPD* 1971, I: doc. 31.
148 *Ibid.*
149 WBA BK/51/51.
150 WBA BK/51/54.
151 WBA BK/51/56.
152 Heath to Brandt, 15 February 1971: WBA BK/52/79.
153 Heath to Brandt, 8 April 1971: WBA BK/52/84.
154 *AAPD* 1971, I: doc. 121.
155 *Ibid.*
156 *Ibid.*
157 *The Times*, 'Mr Heath lays stress on friendship with France and warns Europe of the danger of excluding Britain' (6 May 1971).
158 H. Young, *This Blessed Plot: Britain and Europe from Churchill to Blair* (Basingstoke: Macmillan, 1998), p. 237.
159 *Ibid.*, p. 234.
160 C. O'Neill, *Britain's Entry into the European Community: Report on the Negotiations of 1970–1972*, D. Hannay ed. (London: Frank Cass, 2000), p. 355.
161 *The Times*, 'M Pompidou Says the Basic Issue in Talks is Britain's Will to Join Europe' (18 May 1971).
162 Young, *This Blessed Plot*, p. 260.
163 *The Times*, 'What Britain Hopes to Gain from the Summit' (10 May 1971).
164 *Ibid.*
165 Pompidou informed Brandt that he was now convinced that Heath wanted to turn Britain towards Europe without any other 'ulterior motives' (*ohne Hintergedanken*): *AAPD* 1971, II, doc. 228.
166 See Roussel, *Pompidou*; Young, *This Blessed Plot*; Campbell, *Heath*.

167 Heath, *Course of My Life*, p. 369.
168 *Ibid.*, p. 370.
169 Soames to Greenhill, 7 May 1971: TNA PREM 15/371.
170 Wolff to Heath, 10 May 1971: TNA PREM 15/372.
171 Soames to Greenhill, 7 May 1971: TNA PREM 15/371.
172 *Ibid.*
173 Hurd, *End to Promises*, p. 63.
174 See Robert Armstrong's summary of the Heath-Pompidou meeting of 20–21 May 1971: TNA PREM 15/372.
175 Conclusions of Cabinet meeting of 24 May 1971 (CM(71), 27th conclusions, copy no. 13): TNA CAB 128/49.
176 *Hansard*, Commons, 5th ser., 818: 34–5.
177 *Ibid.*, 818: 40.
178 Pompidou to Brandt, 28 May 1971: WBA BK/51/92
179 Brandt to Pompidou, 26 April 1972: WBA BK/51/131.
180 *The Times*, 'Herr Brandt says "We cannot afford failure this time"' (27 May 1971).
181 *Le Figaro*, 'La page tournée' (24 June 1971).
182 *Die Zeit*, 'Endlich vor Anker in Europa. Nach stürmischer Fahrt: England gehört zur EWG' (25 June 1971).
183 Soames to Heath, 16 February 1972: TNA FCO 59/721. See also steering brief for Pompidou's UK visit, 11 March 1972: TNA FCO 33/1752.
184 Auswärtiges Amt, *Aussenpolitik der Bundesrepublik Deutschland. Vom Kalten Krieg zum Frieden in Europa. Dokumente 1949-1989* (Munich: Verlag Bonn Aktuell, 1990), doc. 137.
185 Reynolds, *Britannia*, p. 228.
186 *Hansard*, Commons, 5th ser., 818: 1229.
187 Reynolds, *Britannia*, p. 228–229.
188 Heath, *Course of My Life*, p. 379.
189 The government was equally successful in the Lords: see *Hansard*, Lords, 5th ser., 324: 533–536.
190 Heath, *Course of My Life*, p. 380.
191 Roussel, *Pompidou*, p. 497.
192 Pompidou, *Entretiens*, Vol. II, p. 146.
193 Roussel, *Pompidou*, p. 509.
194 J.-P. Maury, 'Référendum sur l'élargissement de la Communauté européenne,' *Digithèque de matériaux juridiques et politiques de l'Université de Perpignan* online (1998), http://mjp.univ-perp.fr/france/ref1972.htm.
195 Diallo, *Politique Étrangère*.
196 *Frankfurter Rundschau*, 'De Gaulles Prinzipien' (24 June 1971).
197 *L'Aurore*, 'Roland Faure' (24 June 1971).
198 *AAPD* 1970, II: doc. 307.
199 P. Taylor, 'The Politics of the European Communities: The Confederal Phase,' *World Politics* 27 (3) (1975): 336–360.
200 The protection of the character (*personnalité*) of individual nations is a recurrent theme in Pompidou's public interventions: see Pompidou, *Entretiens*, Vol. II, pp. 143–144, 149.
201 *Ibid.*, p. 80.
202 *Ibid.*, p. 145.
203 *Ibid.*, p. 147.
204 *Ibid.*, p. 143.
205 *Ibid.*, p. 158.
206 W. Loth, 'Politische Integration nach 1945. Motive und Antriebskräfte bei Konrad Adenauer und Charles de Gaulle,' in *Europäische Einigung im 19. und*

20. *Jahrhundert. Akteure und Antriebskräfte*, U. Lappenküper and G. Thiemeyer eds. (Paderborn: Schöningh, 2013), p. 146.
207 Pompidou, *Entretiens*, Vol. II, p. 162.
208 *Ibid.*, p. 127.
209 *Ibid.*, p. 125.
210 *AAPD* 1969, II: doc. 279.
211 *Ibid.*: doc. 352.
212 *Ibid.*
213 Quoted in Diallo, *Politique Étrangère*, pp. 73–74.
214 *Ibid.*, p. 70.
215 *AAPD* 1971, II: doc. 228.
216 Pompidou, *Entretiens*, Vol. II, p. 142.
217 *Ibid.*, pp. 142–143.
218 Roussel, *Pompidou*, p. 658.
219 Diallo, *Politique Étrangère*, p. 26.
220 Roussel, *Pompidou*, p. 658.
221 Pompidou, *Entretiens*, Vol. II, pp. 97–98.
222 Roussel, *Pompidou*, p. 337.
223 *AAPD* 1972, III: doc. 16.
224 *Ibid.*
225 Young, *This Blessed Plot*, p. 215.
226 *Ibid.*, pp. 214–215.
227 P. Ziegler, *Edward Heath: The Authorised Biography* (London: Harper Press, 2010), pp. 271–297; Campbell, *Heath*, p. 352.
228 *Financial Times*, 'A Gifted Leader with Euro Vision' (18 July 2005).
229 Heath, *Course of My Life*, p. 363; D. Allen, 'Britain and Western Europe,' in *British Foreign Policy: Tradition, Change, and Transformation*, M. Smith, S. Smith, and B. White eds. (London: Unwin Hyman, 1988), pp. 168–192. See also 'Texte Complet Consacré au Marché Commun – Le Royaume Uni et les Communautés Européennes' (French translation): HAEU FMM/42.
230 See Heath's speech of 5 April 1971 in Bonn: TNA FCO 30/1149.
231 See FCO guidance note by Douglas-Home, 30 July 1973: TNA PREM 15/1894.
232 *La Libre Belgique*, 'La grandeur et les larmes' (24 June 1971).
233 Draft for discussions for upcoming Heath-Pompidou summit, attached to letter from Nield to Armstrong, 13 May 1971: TNA PREM 15/372.
234 FCO note on Heath's upcoming visit to Bonn, 7 February 1973: TNA FCO 59/934.
235 Heath's dinner speech in Bonn, 5 April 1971: TNA FCO 30/1149.
236 Campbell, *Heath*, p. 334.
237 Heath, *Course of My Life*, p. 359.
238 Campbell, *Heath*, p. 336. On the economic and industrial benefits of enlargement, see Heath's interview with *Paris Match*, 14 May 1973: TNA FCO 26/1295.
239 Nield to Heath, 3 December 1970: TNA PREM 15/62.
240 C. Hill, 'The Historical Background: Past and Present in British Foreign Policy,' in *British Foreign Policy: Tradition, Change, and Transformation*, M. Smith, S. Smith, and B. White eds. (London: Unwin Hyman, 1988), pp. 24–49.
241 On the perceived need to use accession to build up the Community's external relations and a common foreign policy, see secret draft from Cable to Permanent Under-Secretary's Planning Committee, 9 November 1973: TNA FCO 30/1646.
242 Campbell, *Heath*, pp. 334–335.

134 Leadership and critical junctures

243 R. Nixon, *Public Papers of the Presidents of the United States, Richard Nixon, 1971: Containing the Public Messages, Speeches, and Statements of the President (January 2-December 30)* (Washington, DC: GPO, 1972), doc. 403.
244 On British debates about whether or not to 'join' Europe, see Younger (1972), as well as the contributions to Evans' (1971) edited volume.
245 Quoted in Ramsden, *Winds of Change*, p. 337.
246 E. Heath, *Old World, New Horizons: Britain, the Common Market, and the Atlantic Alliance* (London: Oxford University Press, 1970), p. 11.
247 See Heath's speech in Bonn, 22 March 1971: TNA FCO 33/1422; minutes of a meeting between Heath and Brandt in Bonn, 5 April 1971: TNA FCO 30/1149/2.
248 Minute to non-cabinet members, 'Ten Reasons Why Britain Should Join the Common Market,' December 1970: TNA PREM 15/62.
249 *Hansard*, Commons, 5th ser., 818: 1236.
250 See Heath's interview with *Paris Match*, 14 May 1973: TNA FCO 26/1295; *Hansard*, Commons, 5th ser., 818: 38–9.
251 Cubbon to Denman, 3 December 1973: TNA FCO 30/1646.
252 Campbell, *Heath*, p. 336.
253 Heath, *Old World*, pp. 11–12.
254 Heath, *Course of My Life*, p. 358.
255 O'Neill, *Britain's Entry*, p. 356.
256 Heath, *Old World*, p. 19.
257 Campbell, *Heath*, p. 336.
258 See Heath's speech in Zurich, 17 September 1971: TNA FCO 33/1655.
259 *PPPUS 1971*: doc. 403.
260 Heath, *Course of My Life*, p. 370.
261 Heath, *Old World*, p. 67.
262 *The New York Times*, 'Transatlantic Gaullism' (22 October 1971).
263 Steering brief for the Heath-Nixon summit at Bermuda, 25 November 1971: TNA PREM 15/712.
264 Heath, *Old World*, p. 74.
265 This is apparent in FCO ('Johny'?) letter to Moon titled 'Relations with the United States,' 5 November 1971: TNA PREM 15/712.
266 Heath, *Old World*, pp. 70–71.
267 Young, *This Blessed Plot*, p. 222.
268 Campbell, *Heath*, p. 337.
269 *Ibid*.
270 TNA FCO 33/1655.
271 See FCO confidential steering brief by James, 15 February 1973: TNA FCO 59/934.
272 Young, *This Blessed Plot*, p. 221.
273 Ryrie to Heath, 10 November 1970: TNA PREM 15/62. See also Young, *This Blessed Plot*, p. 225.
274 O'Neill, *Britain's Entry*, p. 355.
275 *Ibid*.
276 Young, *This Blessed Plot*, p. 261; also CBI document C384A 72, 5 May 1972: HAEU FMM 42.
277 Campbell, *Heath*, p. 555.
278 *Ibid.*, p. 556.
279 Ramsden, *Winds of Change*, p. 337.
280 Young, *This Blessed Plot*, p. 238. On Heath's vague plans for the Community after enlargement, see Heath's speech at Gymnich Palace, 1 March 1973: TNA FCO 26/1295. On EMU see Hunt to Armstrong, 14 April 1973: TNA PREM 15/1529.

281 B. Marshall, *Willy Brandt: A Political Biography* (Basingstoke: Macmillan, 1997).
282 Notes of 7 June 1970: WBA BK/91/72.
283 Translation of Brandt's speech at the *Friedrich-Ebert-Stiftung*, Bonn, 13 April 1972: TNA FCO 33/1807.
284 R. Nixon, *Public Papers of the Presidents of the United States, Richard M. Nixon, 1973: Containing the Public Messages, Speeches, and Statements of the President (January 2-December 31)* (Washington, DC: GPO, 1975), doc. 136.
285 Bundestag address, 28 October 1969: www.bwbs.de/Beitraege/69.html.
286 See Brandt's handwritten notes, 29 July 1970: WBA BK/91/100.
287 WBA BK/91/100.
288 Brandt, *Friedenspolitik*, p. 52.
289 Brandt's notes, 4 July 1970: WBA BK/91/92. See also A. Deighton, 'British-West German Relations, 1945–1972,' in *Uneasy Allies: British-German Relations and European Integration since 1945*, K. Larres and E. Meehan eds. (Oxford: Oxford University Press, 2000), pp. 27–44.
290 http://www.bwbs.de/Beitraege/70.html
291 Brandt to Pompidou, 5 October 1970: WBA BK/51/28.
292 FCO steering brief by James, 15 February 1973: TNA FCO 59/934.
293 Heath to Brandt, 2 December 1970: TNA PREM 15/62. See also Heath to Brandt, 8 April 1971: WBA BK/52/84.
294 Auswärtiges Amt, *Aussenpolitik der Bundesrepublik Deutschland. Vom Kalten Krieg zum Frieden in Europa. Dokumente 1949–1989* (Munich: Verlag Bonn Aktuell, 1990), doc. 140; see also Palliser to Wright, 15 February 1973: TNA FCO 59/934.
295 Brandt, *Friedenspolitik*, p. 16.
296 Auswärtiges Amt, *Aussenpolitik 1949–1989*, doc. 140; Brandt, *Friedenspolitik*, p. 52.
297 Brandt, *Friedenspolitik*, p. 59.
298 *Ibid.*, p. 17.
299 Auswärtiges Amt, *Aussenpolitik 1949–1989*, doc. 146.
300 G. Schöllgen, *Willy Brandt: Die Biographie* (Munich: Ullstein, 2003), p. 171.
301 Brandt, *Erinnerungen*, p. 478.
302 Brandt's 1971 Nobel Peace Prize speech, Oslo, 11 December 1971: Auswärtiges Amt 1949-1989, doc. 141.
303 Brandt to Pompidou, January 1973: WBA BK/52/230.
304 Brandt, *Friedenspolitik*, p. 53.
305 On Bonn's commitment to intergovernmentalism, see Walter Scheel's interview with *Frankfurter Rundschau*, 24 June 1971. In it, Scheel describes discussions about an 'ideal Europe' as 'phantasies' which have not led to 'practical progress': *Frankfurter Rundschau*, 'Scheel: Nur der Verputz felt noch,' 24 June 1971.
306 See Brandt's notes for 25–26 January 1971: WBA BK/91/24.
307 This is implicit in his handwritten notes of 4 July 1972: WBA BK/92/120. He did contemplate the case for strengthening the role of the European Parliament, as a record of a conversation with Heath on 18 October 1972 reveals: TNA FCO 33/1804. See also Lappenküper, *Aussenpolitik*, p. 100.
308 Brandt, *Friedenspolitik*, p. 58.
309 Brandt, *Begegnungen*, p. 318.
310 Brandt, *Friedenspolitik*, p. 258.
311 *Ibid.*, p. 239.
312 See notes of 30 September 1970: WBA BK/91/130.
313 Brandt, *Friedenspolitik*, p. 96.
314 Reynolds, *Britannia*, p. 227.
315 Wall, *A Stranger in Europe*, p. 3.

5 Problem-solving leadership, 1990–1993

The democratic revolutions of 1989–1990 and the end of the Cold War marked a watershed moment in European history. It not only affected Germany and the countries in Central and Eastern Europe that were freed from Soviet domination, but also transformed the course of European integration. In the late 1980s, European integration had mainly been about technical issues – reviving the integration process, changing voting procedures, and completing the Common Market. In 1989, the sudden end of the division of Europe raised a whole new set of geopolitical challenges. For the first time, it became possible to turn the project of European integration into a truly pan-European endeavour. What emerged out of this unsettled historical period was an ambitious agenda for deeper integration that would tie a unified Germany into a tight network of European institutions and governance arrangements. While negotiations on a common currency had garnered pace before (at the Stuttgart summit in 1983 and again after the Hannover summit in 1988),[1] there had been no sign of an imminent breakthrough.[2] Yet all of this changed in the wake of the dismantlement of the Austrian-Hungarian border, the Polish elections of 4 June 1989, and the fall of the Berlin Wall. The 'German question' again came to preoccupy Europe. What would become of the two German states? How realistic was unification? What role would and should a unified Germany play in Europe? What should a future European governance architecture look like and how could it be achieved?

In November 1989, it was far from given that a peacefully reunited Germany, a fully fledged European Union (EU), and a common currency would be a reality only a few years later.[3] What the events of 1989–1990 illustrate, even more than those in the preceding chapters, is the degree to which opportunities for the exercise of leadership often emerge in moments of crisis and upheaval. In these circumstances, the public looks to its elected representatives for guidance, and statesmen look closely at each other to see what they are thinking and doing. The fact that decision-makers have to react – rather paradoxically and often without much premeditation – to rapidly unfolding events can enhance their ability to decisively influence the course of events. This is what I call 'problem-solving leadership.' Leadership and political will are not mono-causal explanations of events and processes, but need to be understood as constitutive elements for changes in times when political priorities and institutional designs are called into question.[4]

What I illustrate in this chapter is the extent to which the personal rapport of French President François Mitterrand and German Chancellor Helmut Kohl made this ambitious pro-integrationist agenda possible. Their main contribution was the design of a grand bargain – which was codified in the Maastricht Treaty – for concurrent economic and monetary union (EMU), political integration, and the prospect of extending enlargement to countries behind the former Iron Curtain. The creation of a common currency in particular would be the ultimate manifestation of Germany's commitment to the European cause.

Starting from very different conceptions of Europe – shaped in great part by their own personal biographical experiences – the two leaders converged on this pro-integrationist set of policies, which would have been unlikely in the years before 1989. Their aim was to strengthen the common European institutions and preclude a dilution of the *acquis communautaire* in the future. European integration was to be anchored around a 'hard core' of member states with the Franco-German alliance at its centre, even if doing so would alienate the UK.

Kohl and Mitterrand realised soon in early 1990 that the end of the Cold War in Europe was a unique window of opportunity to push for deeper economic, monetary, and political integration, which would entail significant and unpopular curtailments of national sovereignty. The idea behind this was to make integration irreversible and irrevocable before it would be too late to do so.

It is important to examine and elucidate how these developments came about. Beyond the explanations structural and institutionalist accounts offer,[5] it was also the problem-solving leadership of Kohl and Mitterrand that created a sense of urgency and purpose for European integration while overcoming the resistance against deeper integration that had foiled similar initiatives before.[6] While Kohl and Mitterrand could not single-handedly create the kind of Europe they wanted, their interventions impacted significantly on the integration process. Their leadership consisted of overcoming strong domestic opposition – which almost derailed the Maastricht Treaty in the wafer-thin victory for Mitterrand in the 1992 referendum – as well as advocating a powerful vision of the future direction and purpose of Europe. Autonomy was necessary to push their vision of a politically unified Europe centred on a hard core of pro-integrationist member states through political opposition and reluctant officialdom. After initial hesitation and apprehension, both leaders came to wholly invest their political capital and prestige in this pro-integrationist agenda to the extent that they became personally identified with the initiatives under consideration.

But leadership did not come automatically to Europe's statesmen. The push for deeper integration gained saliency at the same time that feelings of scepticism and outright rejection of Europe as a political community became more widespread. While this paradox affected all European decision-makers, it particularly shaped British Prime Minister John Major's position on Europe. He succeeded Margaret Thatcher in November 1990 and immediately faced strong domestic opposition and growing anti-integrationist sentiment from Parliament and the public alike. Major had to balance the ambitious agenda of his fellow European heads of government with the increasingly hostile public attitudes to monetary and political integration that were widely shared among Tories.[7] Major's efforts at advocating his own compromise on Europe failed. His lack of autonomy on European affairs greatly reduced the possibilities for advocating an alternative to the Kohl-Mitterrand vision of European integration.

The personal diplomacy of Mitterrand and Kohl

In 1990–1993, European integration began to diverge from the format that Adenauer, Spaak, and Mollet had in mind in 1957. Sectoral and economic integration were to be complemented by a much more comprehensive institutional architecture for political cooperation, coordination, and integration. The Maastricht Treaty – the first major institutional reform after the end of the Cold War – clearly framed unequivocal political objectives for the newly established EU. In its wake, the European Parliament (EP) gained more power, a European form of citizenship was created, the Euro was introduced, cooperation on foreign and security policies was strengthened, and – despite the controversy surrounding the 2005 Constitutional Treaty and its subsequent failed referendums – a new institutional base for the EU was found in the form of the 2007 Lisbon Treaty.

Neither political nor monetary integration followed easily from the prevailing structural circumstances or institutional dynamics of the time. For example, only few Germans regarded the adoption of the Euro as being necessary and in their national economic interest.[8] Similarly, few French wanted to see a further pooling of their national sovereignty.[9] It took a lot of political will, skill, and determination to move towards monetary and political union.[10] Both projects encountered strong opposition and counted only on moderate, if not reluctant, public and electoral support.[11] These circumstances make it even more pertinent to explore what motivated these leaders to embark on such potentially risky projects. It is in this sense that leaders' personal conceptions of Europe play a significant explanatory role. These ideas provide an important linkage between the motivations for and conduct of French, German, and British European policies.

Europe and the personal relationship between Mitterrand and Kohl

Throughout the 1980s, François Mitterrand – elected as French President in May 1981 – and Helmut Kohl – who became chancellor in October 1982 – established a close working relationship.[12] Kohl was an ideologically committed Christian Democrat and Mitterrand a rather opportunistic Socialist, but the two politicians soon discovered a meeting of minds on European affairs. Prior to coming to office, Mitterrand and Kohl did not share much in terms of political and ideological convictions, and were not bound by a close friendship as their predecessors, Valéry Giscard d'Estaing and Helmut Schmidt, had been.[13] In his memoirs, Kohl remembers that he did not believe at first that he would develop a good rapport with Mitterrand.[14] Yet from their early meetings onwards, it became clear that the cause of European unification was something they both espoused. Kohl later characterised his 'relationship of confidence' (*Vertrauensverhältnis*) with Mitterrand as a 'stroke of luck' for their countries and the European project.[15] Crucially, both leaders understood Europe as a long-term political project, legitimated by historical necessity and the need for reconciliation.[16] Both were strongly committed to the Franco-German partnership,[17] regarding it as the 'motor' of European integration.[18]

Especially for Mitterrand, who undertook a conscious effort to shape his image as the European statesman,[19] European policy became a closely guarded personal domain of statecraft. In his study of the first Socialist president of the Fifth Republic, Alistair Cole argues that Mitterrand used his European credentials as a way to foster his domestic electoral chances.[20] He wanted to carefully cultivate 'his image as a *grand européen* within France, [as] a prelude to the presidential campaign of 1988.'[21] In the 1988 presidential campaign, 'Mitterrand made "the construction of Europe" the leitmotif of his presidency.'[22]

Mitterrand's conversion to the European cause began in earnest in March 1983, when he was forced to abandon – under significant economic and fiscal pressure – his signature socialist economic programme. At the time, it was the wholehearted embrace of European affairs which enabled him to regain his political standing.[23] Cole suggests that far

> from occupying a secondary role, Europe became the means through which Mitterrand could internalise and rationalise the shift in domestic economic policy, as well as claim a leading role for France in European affairs, and for himself as partisan of European integration. This necessitated an unambiguous, even an emphatic concentration on European issues, the counterpart to a withdrawal from the finer details of domestic policy after 1983. However sincerely felt, Mitterrand's European conviction was not devoid of domestic considerations.[24]

In the subsequent years, Mitterrand played a crucial role in all key developments of European integration, such as the solution to the Community budget crisis that was found at the 1984 Fontainebleau summit and the 1985 negotiations for the Single European Act.[25] European integration after 1984 became literally 'associated with the personality of François Mitterrand himself.'[26] Despite this instrumental use of European affairs for domestic purposes, Mitterrand's commitment to European integration was nonetheless a genuine and long-standing concern throughout his political career.[27]

In his determination to push the integration process forward, Mitterrand received crucial support from his former finance minister, Jacques Delors, who assumed the presidency of the European Commission in January 1985.[28] Delors is widely credited for his leadership on revitalising the Community and for embarking on a concise programme aimed at completing the single market.[29] Michel Gueldry suggests that 'Delors was animated by a bold vision of European unity, which met the needs of the times.'[30] The Single European Act, proposed and negotiated in 1985, initiated the reform of the Community's voting system, abolished many national vetoes, established directives for finalising the single market by 1992, granted more competences to the European Parliament, and overcame the sense of 'Eurosclerosis' which had emerged in the late 1970s.[31] Delors' negotiating skills also helped to pave the way for a compromise on the membership applications of Portugal and Spain, which joined in January 1986.[32] For a brief period in the mid-1980s, Mitterrand's and Delors' desire to move ahead on European integration struck a popular chord in France, when public opinion supported reforms to the Community so long as Paris retained its powerful influence.[33]

Kohl encouraged Mitterrand's European initiatives on two grounds. First, he felt a sense of historical responsibility to nurture the continent's unification. He told Mitterrand already at their first meeting in Paris in 1982 that 'I may be the last Chancellor with whom you can build Europe.'[34] This sentiment was fuelled by 'deeply felt family memories,' making European integration a 'generational as well as personal matter.'[35] Second, Kohl was convinced that the Franco-German partnership was crucial in order to expand Germany's room for manoeuvre on foreign policy. Like Helmut Schmidt, he saw that only a strong Paris-Bonn axis would produce trust of, confidence in, and the respectability of West Germany. Kohl argued that 'with Franco-German cooperation and European integration, the frightening spectre of a Fourth Reich would vanish.'[36] By working closely with Mitterrand on European integration, Kohl managed to make progress on Franco-German defence cooperation efforts (such as the Eurobrigades) which would later serve as a basis for creating a joint European defence architecture.[37] It certainly helped that Mitterrand liked Kohl and appreciated his advice, which stood in stark contrast to Mitterrand's personal dislike of Schmidt, whom he called a 'faulty character' (*foutu caractère*).[38]

While Mitterrand was most active and visible on European affairs throughout the 1980s, the nature and equilibrium of the Mitterrand-Kohl relationship shifted as a consequence of the democratic revolutions of 1989–1990.[39] From November 1989 onwards, it was Kohl who emerged as the primary European statesman, propelled into this exposed role by the dramatic events of German unification.[40] These did not determine Kohl's European choices, but gave him the opportunity and exposure to strengthen his leadership on European affairs.

In 1989, Mitterrand – concerned about the rise in power and influence of a unified Germany – wanted to 'channel and slow down German unification.'[41] Despite his failure to delay unification, Mitterrand's first impulse of hesitancy and resistance against German unification temporarily soured the Franco-German relationship.[42] This was particularly the case due to Mitterrand's visit to East Berlin on 20–22 December 1989, where he tried to reaffirm the viability of the GDR as a separate nation-state.[43] Mitterrand was criticised for his failing (*le plus grand faux pas*)[44] to use the 'historic opportunity'[45] and 'great historic gesture'[46] to join Kohl in walking through a newly opened Brandenburg Gate. David Bell provides the following explanation:

> In public, Mitterrand's reaction to the prospect of reunification (just before the Wall came down) was supportive of Chancellor Kohl, who in turn gave the President much credit. However, in other accounts he was hostile to reunification until the meeting with Gorbachev at Kiev [in March 1990] and then, when it became unstoppable, he reacted by accelerating European integration.[47]

Mitterrand's preference was to throttle the dynamics of integration and strengthen the Community before German unification took place.[48] At a press conference in Strasbourg on 9 December 1989, he said:

> I believe that these two movements [German and European unification] fit in to the becoming of Europe, but not just any time or anyhow . . . I would say right away that it would be wise to develop, strengthen and accelerate the structures of the Community before any further steps . . . Had it [the Community] not been there, things would not have happened the same way. There would have been a rapid approach to European anarchy, such as we knew before the 1914 War . . . If the Community is first strengthened, the movement of peoples and States that do not belong to it will organise around this reality. The new German equilibrium that Germans are aiming for will fit into the European equilibrium . . . .[49]

After meeting with Kohl in early January 1990, he concluded that it would be 'stupid' to be against German unification.[50] What was happening to Europe and Germany called for a strengthening of European integration, but nonetheless he was, like Thatcher, wary of German power in the future.[51] Thatcher advocated a more traditional solution, based on an Anglo-French éntente designed to balance Germany's influence.[52]

Kohl, in turn, was convinced that German unification was driven by the force of history and that a dynamic of its own was unfolding, which made it imperative to act swiftly.[53] Crucial for Kohl's response to the fast-paced events was the American support he received, along with what he interpreted to be positive signals from Moscow.[54] In its *Four Points on the German Question*, published in December 1989, the Bush administration signalled its backing for German unification. Kohl proceeded to spell out his own *Ten-Point-Programme* to overcome the division of Germany, which he presented to the Bundestag without consulting his Western allies and in which he noted that the unification of the country could be a realistic political option.[55] In a speech in Paris on 17 January 1990, which Mitterrand famously boycotted, Kohl addressed the fears of his allies and argued that German unification could only be viable if all of West Germany's partners were behind it.[56] He knew that for the sake of German unification he needed to gain the trust of his Western allies and assuage their concerns.[57] Mitterrand was highly concerned about German recognition of the Oder-Neisse line as its Eastern boundary, and annoyed Kohl by insisting on a comprehensive treaty between Germany and Poland.[58] The British and the Americans were pushing to ensure that a united Germany would stay in NATO, something which complicated Kohl's relations with Gorbachev.[59] Kohl had to stick to Germany's 'approved Cold-War convictions.'[60] If Germany wanted to 'encase its existence' as a unified nation, it required 'a European framework as a safeguard against any return of national hubris.'[61]

Kohl sought to achieve this by combining German with European unification and garnering French support.[62] He promised Mitterrand that a reunified Germany would not harbour irredentist ambitions or become a 'military power.'[63] William Paterson reckons that

> trust [was] a key value since support by successive German governments for European integration had created the external trust which rendered unity possible, but the maintenance of that trust required that the unified Germany had to support deeper integration.[64]

After their consultations at Mitterrand's country home at Latché on 4 January 1990, Kohl became convinced that 'Mitterrand's endorsement of unification would only be gotten by the way of closer cooperation [with France] and a strengthening of the EC.'[65] This also entailed a permanent legal recognition of Germany's Eastern borders, and the Oder-Neisse line in particular.[66]

Knowing that Kohl lobbied for his support on German unification, Mitterrand managed to wring a series of crucial concession from Kohl. Kohl consented to EMU under pressure from Mitterrand, Delors and others, 'in order to demonstrate Germany's commitment to building European unity; this went further than any previous German administration.'[67] The German chancellor was driven by the 'perception that integration could be used to achieve [a] primary geo-political goal, embedding Germany in European institutions to dismantle the security dilemma with is European neighbours, particularly with France.'[68] Mitterrand wanted EMU as a means to 'counterbalance Germany within Europe' under the guidance of a close Franco-German partnership.[69] The birth of the Euro needs to be seen in this cross-linking of German reunification with anxieties about the nature, power, and foreign political orientation of unified Germany, which took place between Kohl and Mitterrand in early 1990.

Their previous personal dispositions towards, interests in, and commitments to the European project made this move more likely, but did not predetermine it. Instead of choosing a balance-of-power policy, Mitterrand pushed for more European integration and Franco-German cooperation,[70] even though Thatcher warned him against it and French domestic opinion was not very enthusiastic.[71] Kohl could have chosen to ally Germany closer to the United States and seek a new relationship with Russia, but he also favoured deeper integration with

France. Thatcher and other European leaders who did not share these commitments and European conceptions, and advocated more intergovernmentalist, less pro-integrationist, and more transatlantic approach to European affairs, found themselves outmanoeuvred by Kohl and Mitterrand.[72]

Kohl benefited in two major ways from the transformations of German and European politics after 1989. First, he was catapulted into the position of being the key decision-maker in Europe. While the danger of reactive politics persisted – given the speed at which events were moving – this also gave him a strengthened platform from which he could pursue his preferred European policies. Second, Kohl realised that he might just – if it all went well – pull off what Adenauer always wanted: a vision of a united Germany securely anchored in the West, and a decisive victory against the opposition of the Left to such an agenda.[73]

In the new context of European politics after 1989, Kohl's conception of Europe became 'the defining European vision in relation to which all other visions respond,' whereas before it was merely one of several competing approaches.[74] From December 1989 onwards, 'Kohl reinvented his political persona – in a manner not dissimilar to Mitterrand after March 1983.'[75] He embraced EMU as a top priority, located its management within the scope of his constitutional executive authority (*Richtlinienkompetenz*), and was determined 'to seize a political leadership role on EMU, [making] the project his own.'[76]

By investing his political leadership in the twin projects of monetary and political union, Kohl's plans for Europe began to overlap with Mitterrand's.[77] In the period just after the settlement on German unification and just before the disintegration of Yugoslavia and the collapse of the Soviet Union, the two leaders turned their whole attention to the pursuit of a pro-integrationist agenda. By mid-1990 it was agreed, on Kohl's insistence, to open two parallel intergovernmental conferences (IGC) – one on EMU and one on political union. These were eventually merged in the Maastricht Treaty, which was finalised in December 1991 and signed in February 1992.

Economic and monetary union

On the basis of the recommendations of a committee chaired by Delors in 1988–1989, the Maastricht Treaty established a three-staged plan for EMU.[78] Convergence criteria stipulating the economic parameters for the introduction of a single currency were added into the treaty. Moreover, on Germany's insistence, it was decided that the future European Central Bank (ECB) would be independent and modelled on the institutional format and mandate of the Bundesbank. In 1997, an additional 'Stability and Growth Pact' was signed at German insistence in order to ensure that the new single currency would be a hard currency, based on sound macroeconomic foundations. The Stability Pact defined sanctions against any member states violating the convergence criteria. At the Maastricht, Britain secured an opt-out clause from the EMU plans, for reasons which will be analysed below.

For the 'Mitterrand-Delors-Kohl leadership trio,'[79] EMU became a major focus of visions for a united Europe. EMU was first and foremost a political issue, with Kohl and Mitterrand showing little interest in the technical and economic details.[80] The impetus for EMU gained new saliency as a consequence of the Single European Act. It was widely held that a functioning single market would ultimately require a common currency and some form of Community macroeconomic management.[81] Delors, Mitterrand, and Kohl – aided by Hans-Dietrich Genscher – were the 'key players' on the issue.[82] Delors sought EMU mainly on economic and financial grounds, arguing that it would complete the single market and strengthen Europe's position in the global financial architecture.

Mitterrand's leadership emerged clearly in two instances. First, Mitterrand personally decided on French pursuit of full EMU, 'over objections from some his closest allies and advisors.'[83] Second, Mitterrand 'stepped beyond his domestic support' so as to advance this ambitious pro-integrationist project.[84] He did so because he was convinced that a common currency would bring double benefits.[85] On the one hand, it would satisfy long-standing French economic interests in a common currency capable of counterbalancing French weakness vis-à-vis the US dollar and an 'overmighty' Deutschmark.[86] EMU was about 'recreating scope for French leadership by sharing power at the European level, harnessing Germany's economic strengths to European objectives.'[87] On the other hand, EMU was an essential part of Mitterrand's conception of Europe as a political instrument.[88] Achieving it would be an important step towards consolidating common institutions in which France could exercise significant power – together with and over Germany.[89] The Euro would therefore be the ultimate test of Germany's commitment to Europe.[90] Mitterrand's support for EMU not only derived not only from economic and geopolitical considerations, but also from the fact that it would cement the Franco-German partnership at the helm of the integration process. Mitterrand was convinced that 'Europe as built above all on the Franco-German couple, more importantly than anything else; Europe would never be built if they waited for the British.'[91]

EMU became the central part of Kohl's European policies and vision only gradually and somewhat reluctantly. In a similar fashion to Mitterrand, he was only marginally interested in the economic implications of EMU, animated instead by a powerful historical narrative based on personal experiences and beliefs. Kohl was fully aware that abandoning the Deutschmark would be hugely unpopular and risky, not only in financial terms but also because it was a powerful national symbol of postwar Germany.[92] His leadership on the Euro proved to be essential for its eventual success.

Kohl's determination to see EMU succeed becomes apparent on three different issues. First, he conceded to Mitterrand's pressure on EMU, seeing monetary union as the price Germany would have to pay for unification. Once convinced of this necessity, Kohl invested significant political capital in EMU.[93] Second, he was instrumental in railroading Theo Waigel's Finance Ministry and the Bundesbank to support the project, both of which were notoriously sceptical about the endeavour. Third, Kohl was determined to elaborate compelling benchmarks for the future Eurozone (which later became the 'Stability and Growth Pact') and to secure the independence of the ECB. Kohl faced powerful domestic opposition, although the main Bundestag parties – notably the SPD – supported EMU.[94]

For the two leaders, EMU was a risky strategy because they quickly came to be personally identified with the project. What emerged was a complex web of leader-follower interactions, in which the influential leaders were constrained by expectations about the success of their own policy programmes. Major obstacles, or even failure, would have had serious consequences for their political careers. According to Kenneth Dyson, 'EMU imposed requirements on his [Kohl's] political leadership, emerging as the focal point of his strategic thinking about the EU.'[95] Kohl made EMU his top European priority, deflecting attention away from Kohl's original vision for Europe – political union.

Deepening and enlargement

The project of political union encompassed institutional reforms, more powers for the European Parliament, the democratisation of European decision-making, the creation of a common foreign and security policy, and a European form of citizenship. The enlargement of the EU to Eastern and Central Europe was part of this political project, given that the future membership of former Eastern bloc states would require a period of economic and political adjustment and would be a financial burden.[96]

In contrast with its attitude towards EMU, Britain strongly supported enlargement. Whereas some scholars argue that the project for political union was essentially a Franco-German bargain over geopolitics,[97] others suggest that it was mainly a framework for containing Germany's growing economic influence.[98] Both positions attribute significant causal weight to either geopolitical or economic factors. This focus tends to disregard not only the impact of individual policy-makers, but also the way in which the project of political union corresponded to Mitterrand's and Kohl's historical conception of Europe. By illustrating the importance of leadership and elite-conceptions of Europe in relation to political union, it becomes clear that both Mitterrand and Kohl framed their respective understandings of national economic and political interests as part of a wider vision of their countries' roles in a united Europe. The same was true for the John Major's advocacy of enlargement. In their understandings, domestic, national, and European interests overlapped, and can therefore not be as easily separated as some scholars suggest.

The plans for political union were another consequence of the democratic revolutions of 1989. As the common declaration by Mitterrand and Kohl of 18 April 1990 attested, both leaders regarded German unification as a catalyst for speeding up the political construction of Europe.[99] Mitterrand came to support the project of political union not because of his belief in the desirability of supranational institutions but because it was a way to ensure that a unified

Germany would remain committed to the process of European integration.[100] It did, however, remain 'secondary' to Mitterrand's interest in successfully concluding EMU.[101]

Kohl, in turn, being the driving force behind the project for political union, was convinced that German and European unification were closely related and needed each other: 'The future architecture of Germany has to fit into the future architecture of the whole of Europe. The "house Germany" has to be built under a European roof.'[102] Political union not only meant expanding the role, voting mechanisms, and competences of the EP and the other institutions, but also encompassed the EU's plans for Eastern enlargement. Both dimensions were politically controversial in most member states, yet Kohl was convinced that political union was both necessary and advantageous.[103]

On the one hand, at least paying lip service to the cause of political union was necessary for gaining the trust of Germany's allies and neighbours. In this sense, Kohl's 'policy of self-restraint'[104] served to 'reassure externally and mobilise internally.'[105] While succeeding in gaining the trust of his foreign partners, he failed to win over public opinion of the merits of political union. In this sense, political union remained an elite-driven project in Germany. Kohl's case for political union had yet to strike a chord with the public, although today it remains 'strikingly effective at the level of the German elite who continue to be committed to multilateralism, to a Europeanised identity and to the integration project.'[106]

On the other hand, Kohl was convinced that political union could be advantageous for Germany in a more narrow sense. He saw the pursuit of German interests to be viable only within the framework of European cooperation, because doing otherwise would resuscitate fears about German domination. Kohl knew that the German economy benefited from European integration, and yet he was prepared to make significant financial concessions in order to push this integration further than the Bundesbank, the Finance Ministry, and many business leaders wanted.[107] Political union made sense to Kohl because it corresponded and added to his historically framed conception of Europe. It demonstrated 'a close emotional commitment to a vision of a Europe within which war is impossible.'[108] Given that his was a long-term approach to European integration, and that Kohl was sure that history would prove him right, he would – 'on the central aspects of his European policy' – favour 'vision over public opinion.'[109] After the setbacks of the Maastricht ratification process in France and Britain in 1992, it was clear that political union had only thin elite support and that it aroused little enthusiasm among the public. Therefore, it is all the more striking that Kohl and Mitterrand continued to reaffirm their support in the project.

Personal diplomacy and conceptions of Europe

Effective leadership often becomes apparent only in hindsight. Yet leaders do not have the benefit of hindsight, and therefore it is important to study how they perceived the possibilities for change and leadership at the time. Mitterrand and Kohl were not free from the constant interplay of agency and structure, of opportunity and constraints. Yet in the case of Mitterrand's and Kohl's perception, external events affected the balance of possibility and constraint in such a way that innovative interventions on European policy became more viable. In their quest to advance their specific conceptions of a desirable Europe, the two politicians opted to secure elite support rather than popular backing. Both EMU and political union were very controversial, as the 1992 French referendum on the Maastricht Treaty revealed. Yet Mitterrand and Kohl gambled that the public's tacit agreement and 'permissive consensus'[110] would prevail.

As far as the styles of and circumstances for leadership are concerned, some notable differences existed between Kohl, Mitterrand, and Major. In the wake of the fall of the Berlin Wall, Kohl's stature as Europe's 'key statesman' increased his authority and leverage.[111] The democratic revolutions of 1989 sharpened Kohl's conviction that there were significant possibilities for transforming the European order. He reminded his audience at a speech in Königswinter on 3 April 1992 that

> we humans are not a playing ball, not a passive object of so-called 'historical laws', but we are active subjects of history. If we do not make ourselves conscious of this over and over again, then we will have no reason to fear freedom, but all reason to celebrate and embrace the possibilities of the present.[112]

Kohl was convinced that a substantial transformation of the old European order of nation-states was possible if the political will and leadership to this end existed. Speaking in Speyer on 2 July 1991, he recalled that

> only a few decades ago, during my time in school, we taught children in France and Germany in the evil spirit of an alleged hereditary rivalry. But hatred and animosity were overcome because people wanted it that way.[113]

His sensitivity to the possibilities of transformative leadership was strengthened by his experiences in 1989–1990, and boosted his historically framed long-term view for reforming the basis of European policy-making.[114] During the fluid period when German unification was negotiated, Kohl realised he could exercise meaningful leadership not only to bring about the unity of his country but also to make Germany's commitment to the West and integration a *fait accompli*. In this sense, an external event (the opening of the Berlin Wall in November 1989) strengthened the German public's goodwill vis-à-vis Kohl, endowing him with new opportunities for leadership but forcing him to formulate his vision for Germany and Europe. Through his position as chancellor, his influence would be most crucial for diffusing the 'German question.' He understood his role as being to alter the existing political framework from Germany and Europe alike.

The opposite was true of John Major, who struggled to step out of the Thatcherite shadow over European policy throughout his time in office. With the Tories divided on Europe, he was left with little room for policy compromises.¹¹⁵ Major found it difficult to oppose a political direction for Europe of which he was not convinced. He sought to balance the diverging opinions at home in a transactional form of leadership. Yet as his failure to achieve such balance became apparent, he grew frustrated with the dynamics, direction, and outcome of EU negotiations. He recalls in his *Autobiography*:

> I had now seen the Union in action from the inside. It was a dispiriting experience. Europe's heads of government met several times a year in the European Council. Always, there was a distinct hierarchy in these discussions. Delors, Kohl, and Mitterrand mattered, and were referred to *ad nauseam* in other countries' contributions. 'I agree with Helmut' became an intensely irritating *leitmotif* in round-table discussions.¹¹⁶

The informal, personal, and consensual nature of European negotiations clashed with his own executive experiences from Westminster:

> Only Britain was the grit in the oyster. I saw how and why Margaret Thatcher had become so unpopular among her fellow European heads of government. She was used to a democratic system in which criticism was harsh and often unfair, and where people spoke their mind. The pussy-footing of the European Council would not have been at all to her taste. Nor was it to mine. But when British ministers spoke the language of Westminster in Brussels it was like spitting in church. Others shied away from our 'non-consensual' approach, and the club closed ranks against us. Britain was isolated again. It was immensely frustrating.¹¹⁷

The attitudes of Kohl, Mitterrand, and Major illustrate different styles and contingent circumstances for leadership. It is necessary not only to distinguish different motives their choices on Europe, but also to ascertain in which way their understandings of national interests merged or mismatched with European considerations.

One of the main conclusions Mitterrand and Kohl drew from their analysis of the possibilities for a transformation of the political order in Europe was that integration – if necessary – could not proceed uniformly. For instance, in Mitterrand's and Kohl's eyes, the scepticism of British, Danish, and Greek policy-makers vis-à-vis EMU and political union should not be allowed to determine the pace and scope of Franco-German initiatives. Both Mitterrand and Kohl came to endorse – hesitantly – the vision of a hard core of pro-integrationist countries which would be at the vanguard of European integration. Yet, as Hubert Védrine recalls, while Mitterrand and Kohl were keen advocates of integration, they never foresaw or intended an ultimate absorption of their nation-states into a larger federal structure.¹¹⁸ Mitterrand's conception of Europe was one of a confederation of states centred on a hard core of like-minded countries, with Paris and Bonn in the driving seat. Mitterrand disliked supranationalism and accepted it only reluctantly, belatedly, and as a mechanism for extending – rather than curtailing – France's international profile and influence. Kohl had a more supranationalist and pro-American outlook, and framed 'Europe' emotionally in terms of history and memory.

François Mitterrand

Mitterrand, writing in his posthumously published memoirs, described his conversion to Europe in the following terms:

> At the end of the last and most bloody of our internecine wars, Europe appeared to me, as it did to the largest part of those who survived, as the fertile idea, the driving idea, the necessary idea of the second half of the twentieth century. To be more precise, it was neither in 1992 nor 1989 nor 1983 nor 1957, nor even in 1945, but in 1940, on the 14th of June . . . that it came to me with a blinding clarity that the foundations of Europe could only be Franco-German and that we would have to find other occasions for us to meet, than in each generation, out in the fields . . . with a rifle in hand.[119]

In biographical material on Mitterrand,[120] his commitment to European integration is often posited as one of few continuities throughout his political career. At all major junctures in the history of European integration, Mitterrand supported deeper European integration, thereby accepting – at least implicitly – the logic of the Common Market and some form of pooling of national sovereignty.[121] One can find an illustrative quote from Spinelli, which highlights Mitterrand's longstanding involvement with the cause of European unification:

> He [Mitterrand] was a man who had been there at the beginning and supported the first steps . . . At the Hague Congress (1948) he could say I was there and I believed in it. When Schuman began (1950) he could say I was there and I believed in it. And this has lain dormant in his spirit, but it existed. When it awakened in his mind he discovered again that he believed in it.[122]

One such moment of rediscovery came in March 1983, when Mitterrand's Socialist demand-side economic reforms had to be abandoned under immense financial and economic pressure.[123] The failure of the signature policy on which he was elected convinced him of the need to seek solutions to France's economic problems on a broader European level.[124] The experiences of his 'U-turn' strengthened his belief in the necessity and benefit of advancing European integration for France's sake, especially in the economic realm. He came to believe in, and make the case for, the 'historical necessity of Europe.'[125] Mitterrand's closer involvement in European affairs was a mixture of sincere commitment to closer European integration, an aversion to the avarices of domestic policy, and a far-sighted recognition of the importance of Europe for the pursuance of French objectives. Throughout the course of 1982–84, Mitterrand redefined his European vision, which combined a mixture of idealism, realism, and self-interest.[126]

It was Mitterrand's instrumentalisation of the idea of Europe for the pursuit of what he perceived French interests to be which became a key element of his approach to European integration in the 1990s. He very consciously cultivated an image of himself as a 'historic European statesman,'[127] but he was not an advocate of supranationalist integration or a federal idealist.[128] Rather, he saw himself as an *animateur*, seeking

> to encourage and enthuse his negotiators, to ensure that he remained their central point of reference, and to do so by placing his views and actions in an historic vision of the interests of the French state.[129]

In his mind, national and European interests could overlap and national interests could be defined in relation to a particular vision of Europe. For Mitterrand,

> European integration had become . . . a permanent French national interest . . . Mitterrand's presidency produced a centre-Left/centre-Right consensus that 'more' Europe was good for France. All the rest became policy questions about how much and at what speed.[130]

In consequence, the major concerns of Mitterrand's conception of Europe were not about whether integration was desirable, but about the modalities, mechanisms, and objectives of integration. The question was not one of choosing between national interests on the one hand and European integration on the other, but one of selling deeper integration as being in the interest of France.[131] Given that Mitterrand had been forced to conduct a sharp change in macroeconomic policy due to economic pressures, it was in this field that he saw the most pressing need for European remedial action.[132] He therefore initiated and supported the Single European Act (SEA), supported EMU, and wanted to develop plans for a European social model. He also tied France closely to West Germany, thinking that 'France could not stand alone either economically or politically in a world where other nations were becoming more competitive.'[133] For Mitterrand, 'at the heart of Europe, there is the Franco-German knot.'[134]

With the fall of the Berlin Wall, Mitterrand was forced to recalibrate France's foreign policy position in Europe. His first instincts were fear of increasing German influence and a recourse to traditional balance-of-power diplomacy, trying to conspire with Gorbachev to derail or delay German unification.[135] This approach had to be abandoned not only in face of the pace of events but also because of France's inability to determine European outcomes. Eventually, Mitterrand's pragmatism overcame his 'latent mistrust of a unified Germany.'[136]

Ronald Tiersky sums up Mitterrand's trial-and-error approach to European affairs in the following terms:

> For Mitterrand as for de Gaulle . . . France's main problem . . . – how to deal with Germany's strength – required a European-level solution. France alone could not balance Germany, nor could it match Germany's economic strength, above all unified Germany's economic and demographic size, by itself.
>
> The solution was not to organise with other countries against Germany but to organise European integration around Franco-German cooperation, a Franco-German tandem or special partnership whose leadership would be the political fuel and the economic engine of European development.[137]

By March 1990, Mitterrand had chosen to 'tame'[138] and 'Europeanise Germany'[139] but not with a traditional balance-of-power response to Germany's unification.[140] This meant securing Kohl's support for EMU, which he saw as a mechanism for Germany's future engagement in the making of Europe.[141] Mitterrand came to believe that French political, economic, and security interests would only be viable in a European framework. The national interest of France could no longer be separable from European considerations, but would need to be closely linked to the viability of Europe as a political, economic, and defence community.[142] During his last years in the Elysée, this understanding of European integration became a widespread consensus among the main political actors in France. Rather than a threat to France, European integration came to be perceived as a vital necessity for advancing Frances's influence. On this point, Mitterrand was neither an 'intransigent nationalist nor a dreamer of federal utopias,' yet his 'pragmatic "gaullo-mitterrandism"' achieved such a wide consensus in French society that it ended up being criticised domestically as a new form of orthodoxy, a *penseé unique*.'[143]

The vigour of Mitterrand's engagement in European affairs thus resulted from the conviction that integration overlapped with the national interest, and that France had to lead in the creation of common institutions so as to secure its influence. The premises of Mitterrand's decision-making on Europe did not arise solely out of economic necessity or fear of German power.[144] They arose also out of the deliberate merger of perceived national interests with a broader political agenda for Europe.[145] This point of view did not engrain itself automatically in French politics, but was made popular by Mitterrand.

Since Mitterrand's conception of Europe was so innately linked to his vision of France, he came to want a politically and economically unified Europe which could speak forcefully with one voice on the international scene. Yet this also meant jealously protecting those mechanisms in the European web of institutions (such as the Council of Ministers) in which nation-states remained the 'locus of power.'[146] Plans for further integration remained punctuated by traditional foreign policy considerations. For instance, on the plans for creating a common foreign and security policy, 'France had been . . . verbally favourable . . . and politically ambivalent, because of a strong attachment to an independent security and above all foreign policy.'[147] In speeches and public declarations, Mitterrand repeated the theme of a confederation of Europe, which became the code word for an intergovernmental institutional structure.[148] For example, in his address to the Council of Europe in October 1993, he noted: 'For a long time, I have thought to create a Confederation of the democratic states of Europe: I still think so today. I am indifferent to the word, what interests me is the thing itself.'[149]

Mitterrand's conception of a confederation encompassed significant differences with the Gaullist-intergovernmentalist conception of Europe.[150] It also drew stark distinctions with the vision of a loosely knit Europe, centred on free trade and intergovernmental consultations, which was prevalent mainly in British political discourse. In contrast to de Gaulle, Mitterrand did not reject supranational institutions *per se*, but embraced them if they could help to address those economic and political challenges which France could not adequately cope with on its own. In short, 'for de Gaulle Europe was an option, for Mitterrand it was a necessity.'[151] Yet the difference between de Gaulle's and Mitterrand's conception of Europe was not only about the intensity of commitment to the European cause. It was also about how – by what mechanisms – a European framework beneficial for France could be constructed.

In contrast to the British attitude to Europe, Mitterrand regarded a loose framework of cooperation among European states as inadequate for the effective defence of French interests. Hence, the difference between these conceptions was one about what kind of Europe would be ultimately desirable. In Mitterrand's eyes, only a strongly integrated – meaning institutionalised – Europe would ensure cohesiveness and influence as a global player.

Mitterrand's approach to European integration was therefore heavily predicated on the construction of common institutions in which France would command a crucial influence.[152] In a speech delivered in Vienna on 8 October 1993, Mitterrand clarified the importance of institutions: 'Without institutions there is no liberty, without institutions there is no democracy, without institutions worthy of that name, there will be no Europe.'[153] The creation of common institutions at the European level, albeit along intergovernmental lines, would have the effect of establishing a political framework in which no single member state could dominate and to which all member states had equal access. Post-1945 France was faced with a

> choice between a 'bad solution' and a 'very bad solution'. The bad solution means operating within the constraints born of growing regional interdependence. The very bad solution . . . would have required France to face globalisation and other challenges . . . alone. Since the 1980s, France has consistently, if often half-heartedly, opted for the first alternative because it has been able, to a degree, to use integration for its own benefit.[154]

Mitterrand shared this assessment and strongly supported the understanding that integration was beneficial for France. However, in order to be so, the

European institutions would have not only to address and help to remedy France's economic and social needs, but also to allow for cooperation on foreign and security policy. Therefore, Mitterrand was strongly committed to deepening the Community, and pushed for a pro-integrationist agenda on EMU and political union.

His approach to European integration hinged upon the notion of a European confederation. The plans for a confederation were distinct from both de Gaulle's notion of a Europe of nation-states and Pompidou's notion of a Europe of governments.[155] In contrast to his predecessors, Mitterrand framed integration in a historical narrative, seeking to commit France 'beyond a point of no return' to the integration project.[156] Unlike de Gaulle and Pompidou, integration was not a matter of 'diplomatic necessity,'[157] but rather of economic and political need, as well as ideational commitment. In this sense, Mitterrand moved from the perception that European integration was but one of several realms of French foreign policy-making to an understanding that integration was the only viable mechanism for France to play an international role. His support for a pro-integrationist agenda thus entailed the narrowing of foreign political alternatives. The fact that Mitterrand's conception was an elite understanding of Europe revealed itself clearly throughout the 1992 referendum on the Maastricht Treaty, which he had called at his own initiative. Although he only narrowly secured a 'yes vote' in the referendum, the heated debates about the vote revealed a core tenet of Mitterrand's thinking on Europe, which was geared at seeking elite agreement. He asked: 'One cannot make Europe advance faster than Europeans want? That is a matter of governmental will. Europe will exist if one makes it exist.'[158]

At the centre of Mitterrand's notion of a confederation rested, as mentioned, the concept of a tightly integrated Community formed around a 'hard core' of pro-integrationist countries. At the outset, this concept did not appeal to Mitterrand. He feared that if some countries integrated more than others it would ultimately lead to disunity and a weakened Community. Yet in the face of hesitancy of other European leaders – notably Thatcher and Major – Mitterrand rejected the idea that the pace and scope of integration should be set by the most integration-reluctant country. He came to advocate a certain degree of flexibility in the process of European unification, which would allow France and Germany in particular to place themselves at the vanguard of integration, while tying Eastern European countries into a process of ever-closer cooperation and integration with the EU.[159] He liked the so-called 'federation-within-a-confederation idea,'[160] because it made it easier to make a decision about widening versus deepening the Community. Speaking on 11 April 1991, he argued:

> I await a common organisation in which each of the countries of Europe can see its dignity equal in relation to those of others, its future assured by perhaps different means – not yet present – but with an equal voice, as it already is the case in the Europe of the Twelve. That is what I called the confederation.[161]

The confederation Mitterrand had in mind could accommodate various groupings of countries participating in different aspects, creating a stratified community at several speeds. This signified 'a departure from the "everyone participates in everything" principle,'[162] which had been a characteristic of the integration process. Mitterrand ultimately embraced the notions of 'variable geometry' Europe or 'two or three-speed Europe.' While these did not figure in Mitterrand's original plans, he nonetheless came to appreciate the effectiveness of these notions in order to combine the three objectives of his European policies: making European integration irreversible, enhancing the Franco-German partnership, and opening a long-term prospect for Eastern enlargement so as to prevent a new division of Europe.[163] Furthermore, by concentrating on the notion of a hard-core Community, Mitterrand came to see British reluctance to participate in EMU and political union as less of a threat to French interests.

Helmut Kohl

German and European unification have come to be closely identified with the person and the politics of Helmut Kohl, who is seen as a 'father' of the Euro, at least in Germany. Kohl's conception of Europe – his emotive-sentimental vision of European integration as an historical responsibility and a choice between war and peace – derived from two key influences. First, Kohl's personal commitment to European unification was based on tragic and emotional personal memories of World War II, which he experienced in his youth. His brother Paul died in the war and Kohl himself experienced the war as a teenager, when he had to serve in an anti-aircraft battery.[164] In his speeches and public declarations, as well as during bilateral meetings and summits, Kohl recalled his own memories of the war, and placed in them a broader narrative of reconciliation and integration.[165] Despite the fact that Kohl lacked notable oratory skills, his recollection of personal experiences created an impression of his sincerity and commitment to the European cause.

The second – political – influence on Kohl's conception of Europe was borrowed from Adenauer. Already as leader of the Christian-Democratic opposition throughout the late 1970s, as well as in his first years as chancellor, Kohl consistently alluded to Adenauer's European legacy. In a speech in Zurich on 18 June 1992, he said:

> It has always been my policy to inseparably connect the unity of Germany and the unification of Europe. To me both are – as was for Konrad Adenauer – the two sides of the same coin.[166]

He incorporated the key features of Adenauer's vision of Europe into his own management of European affairs. One the one hand, Kohl followed Adenauer's cultural-civilisational discourse of Europe, with its emphasis on philosophy,

Christianity, and humanism.[167] He also reaffirmed the notion that Europe formed a community of common values and culture (*Werte- und Kulturgemeinschaft*), which separated it from other regions and cultures.[168]

On the other hand, Kohl followed Adenauer's prescriptions for embedding Germany into the Western alliance, safeguarding the Franco-German partnership as the engine of European integration, and committing solidly to the Atlantic partnership with the United States. Like Adenauer, Kohl regarded Europe as the only outlet for conducting a viable German foreign policy. He remained convinced that West Germany could only act in conjunction with its Western allies, which in turn demanded that German be a reliable, predictable, and reassuring partner. Under Kohl, more than under any of his predecessors, Germany adopted a multilateralist, compromising, and cooperative form of foreign policy-making.[169] Emboldened by some notable successes, especially in Franco-German defence cooperation,[170] Kohl's European policy continued in Adenauer's legacy.

The end of the Cold War and the dramatic events of 1989/90 were a turning point in Kohl's approach to European integration. By combining the processes of German and European unification, Kohl committed himself more than rhetorically towards making significant progress in the direction of European unity. In a similar fashion to Mitterrand, Kohl framed the national interest in European terms. This became a recurring feature of his political rhetoric and thinking about Europe: 'The future architecture of Germany has to fit into the future overall architecture of the whole of Europe.'[171] The linkage of national and European interests not only served to secure German unification, but also provided the arguments for an ambitious pro-integrationist agenda. The strength of Kohl's pro-European convictions, and the investment of his leadership, prestige, and political capital into EMU and political union, went beyond what the economic or political situation demanded.

Kohl took the deliberate and calculated decision to attempt to transform Germany's role in Europe, making integration irreversible, and thereby embedding Germany permanently into a political community with its neighbours. These long-term goals called for a transformative form of leadership. Its aim would be to determine the overall direction of European integration, rather than winning beneficial concessions on individual political and economic issues. The transformative leadership style characterised Kohl's understanding of his role and influence, and derived from a conception of Europe informed by historical memory.

Kohl stipulated that for Germany the construction of a politically unified Europe was not only a matter of fate (*Schicksal*),[172] but also one of historical responsibility for the future of Germany and Europe.[173] Speaking in Paris on 17 January 1990, Kohl argued: 'The Federal Republic of Germany stands without doubt or hesitancy to its European responsibilities – because especially for us Germans it is valid to say: Europe is our fate!'[174] This was not just exaggerated rhetoric, but Kohl's 'genuine historical belief.'[175] He characterised European integration as a logical continuation of the dynamic of German unification and framed it in terms of a historical duty for Germany as a nation:

> We Germans also know that the unification of Europe is a historic task for our people. Therefore, we Germans dedicate ourselves fully, also after the reunification of our fatherland, towards contributing to the construction of the 'United States of Europe.'[176]

Kohl understood his own role as a facilitator of German and European unification. In 1992, he stated this intention clearly: 'If something moves me now, it is the opportunity as German Federal Chancellor to contribute my part for a reunified Germany in a politically united Europe.'[177] His public declarations and rhetoric on Europe not only indicated that he saw opportunities for innovative leadership available to him, but also elucidated what kind of Europe he envisaged. Influenced by historical memory and Adenauer's legacy, Kohl developed three main themes of his conception of the idea of Europe. These were the necessity for making integration irreversible, the argument for parallel deepening and widening, and the further 'federalisation' of the Community through the principle of subsidiarity. Kohl was 'much more interested in giving new form to political Europe' than Mitterrand.[178]

The chancellor's primordial concern, both before and after 1989–1990, aimed to preserve German unification within the framework of European unification. Prior to the end of the Cold War, Kohl was convinced that Germany's orientation towards the West was the only viable way to secure his country's security, democracy, and prosperity. He sought opportunities to nurture and strengthen Germany's commitment to the Atlantic alliance as well as the EC. The collapse of the Eastern bloc merely reaffirmed Kohl's conviction that the twin policies of embedding Germany into common institutions (*Einbindung*) and tying it into the Western alliance (*Westbindung*) had been beneficial foreign policy cornerstones. It also strengthened his understanding that they were the only normatively acceptable options available.[179] As the prospects for German unification became clearer, Kohl thus argued for continuity in foreign policy. Speaking at the *World Economic Forum* in Davos on 3 February 1990, he made his case for continuity on foreign affairs and mentioned the key elements of his vision of a desirable Europe:

> Human rights and human dignity; free self-determination; a free societal order (*freiheitliche Gesellschaftsordnung*); private initiative; market economy. These goals are the building blocks of a future European order of peace, which overcomes the division of Europe and the division of Germany. We are therefore well advised to stay the course. We have to continue to prescribe these tested political bases, both soberly yet oriented towards the future.[180]

He wanted at all costs to prevent Europe from regressing into a political state-of-affairs characterised by power-rivalries and nationalist antagonisms. For him, it was necessary to set

> ... a clear, unmistakable sign that in Western Europe there is no way back to the power political rivalries of past times. The lesson of this experience consisted and consists of the ever closer joining together of the peoples of Europe.[181]

To make the achievements of European integration irreversible, Kohl pursued two main policies. First, he reaffirmed and strengthened his commitment to EMU, having been talked into the project by Mitterrand. EMU evolved into the main project for European unification with which Kohl's political career and persona came to be closely identified. Second, he argued that the processes of deepening and widening should run parallel to each other.[182] In Kohl's historically informed and legitimated understanding of Europe, both further integration and Eastern enlargement were equally necessary challenges.[183]

Kohl's advocacy of these two policies cannot be fully accounted for without paying attention to his conception of the idea of Europe. He started from the premise that integration was ultimately a question of war and peace.[184] In a speech in Bonn on 31 May 1994, he claimed that

> peace and freedom cannot be taken for granted. They have to be secured on a daily basis. It is without question that European unity is the most effective insurance against a resurgence of chauvinism and ethnic conflicts also in our part of the continent.[185]

In 1991, the First Gulf War and the civil wars in Yugoslavia revealed the precariousness of peace and stability in Europe, and thus strengthened Kohl's vision of the Community as an 'anchor of stability' for the continent. The question that posed itself to Kohl was how to enhance and secure the Community, and how to adapt it to the new circumstances of the post-Cold War era. It was clear for him that a regression to traditional Realpolitik would be catastrophic for Germany and Europe:

> We cannot be indifferent to the path Europe will take – if it irrevocably commits itself to political and economic unification or if it falls back into the rivalries of past times. This, in actual fact, is the central question of European politics.[186]

From his point of view, the founding fathers of the Common Market in the 1950s already sought to move European nation-states beyond the point of detrimental nationalistic rivalries and competition. In consequence, power politics and traditional mechanisms of interstate diplomacy carried little appeal.

Instead, Kohl embraced the idea of common institutions and rejected the notion that the Common Market would be sufficient to stabilise Europe.[187] In his mind, the Community had to be more than 'a loose alliance exposed to the ups and downs of daily politics'[188] if it was to remain the anchor of stability for Europe. In consequence, Kohl developed his vision of a hard-core Europe (*Kerneuropa*).

Similarly to Mitterrand, Kohl understood the EU to be only one part – though the crucial one – of a wider European framework of cooperation. In this sense, the EU in general and the Franco-German partnership in particular formed the bases of this hard core.[189] In their 1994 paper *Reflections on European Policy*, Wolfgang Schäuble and Karl Lamers, who as his foreign policy advisors influenced Kohl's thinking on Europe, argued that

> [t]he quality of Franco-German relations must be raised to a new level if the historic process of European unification is not to peter out before it reaches its political goal. Therefore, no significant action in the foreign or EU policy fields should be taken without prior consultation between France and Germany. Following the end of the East-West conflict, the importance of Franco-German cooperation has not diminished; on the contrary, it has increased yet further. Germany and France form the core of the hard core. From the outset, they were the driving force behind European unification.[190]

Yet Kohl's conception of *Kerneuropa* was more ambitious than Mitterrand's pragmatic interpretation. Not only did Kohl strongly advocate the principle of subsidiarity for the EU and the creation of federal institutions,[191] but he was also more adamant not to make the EU into a 'fortress Europe' (*Festung Europa*).[192] In his view, the EU was neither a permanent 'exclusive club'[193] nor a little Europe (*Klein-Europa*),[194] but a precondition for securing the future viability of an enlarged – and undiluted – Community: 'This is no rejection of a greater Europe, but we will only be able to achieve that Europe, if we push ahead with today's hard core of Europe.'[195] Given his intention to make European integration irreversible, he did want to be held back by the most integration-reluctant states. Kohl eventually accepted – like Mitterrand – that European integration had to proceed at different speeds among different members. Speaking in Oxford on 11 November 1992, he noted: 'We do not want a Europe of two or three speeds – but I add in similar clarity: we also do not want a Europe, which orients itself by the slowest ship in the convoy.'[196]

This belated recognition that some member states – notably Britain and Denmark – chose not to participate in Kohl's initiatives was not unproblematic for the German chancellor. He feared that a two-speed Europe would increasingly lead to a less coherent and ultimately less unified Community, losing its capacity to prevent a re-emergence of national antagonisms and rivalries. German government officials argued for a rapid institutionalisation of the multi-speed approach, so as to allow a less rigid timetable for EMU and political union, but thereby preventing some EU members from not taking part in major integration initiatives.[197]

This view reveals that Kohl balanced geopolitical considerations of Realpolitik with the objectives derived from his historically informed conception of Europe. The pursuit of EMU, even at the expense of toning down the plans for political union, became Kohl's main tool for making the integration project irreversible. The explanation for this approach and commitment to integration lies more in Kohl's own understanding of Europe, and Europe's capacity to provide him with an international leadership role, rather than in the economic merits of EMU or the institutional dynamics of the Common Market as accelerated by the SEA. Much later, in a speech to the Council of Europe on 28 September 1995, Kohl hinted at the fact that economic integration was a means to a larger – ideationally conceived – end rather than an end in itself:

> The building of the European house has many reasons, but for me the most decisive one is more important than all economic data. For me it is decisive that we in the twenty-first century in Europe live together in peace and freedom and that we never fall back into that period of barbarism which we left behind.[198]

It is through our analytical focus on personal diplomacy, leadership, and conceptions of Europe that this interlinkage of ideas, political resources, and structural constraints can be brought to the fore.

John Major

In contrast to the pro-integrationist agenda pursued by Mitterrand and Kohl, British prime ministers – with the exception of Heath – remained torn over diverging approaches to integration. Even after joining the Common Market in 1973, British political and public debate on Europe was characterised by profound divisions and an overall lack of elite consensus on the issue. Throughout the 1970s and 1980s, elite attitudes not only hardened vis-à-vis the Community, but also led to serious party political rifts and conflict. In both the Labour and Conservative parties, influential internal pro- and anti-European wings consolidated.[199]

The end of the Cold War did not fundamentally alter the nature of the British public debate on Europe and required no significant adjustments to British policy on Europe.[200] It did, however, strengthen the position of those politicians who were opposed to pro-integrationist projects, fearing that Britain's influence would diminish in a more integrated institutional structure.[201] More specifically, the negotiations (and ratification debates) for the Maastricht Treaty set the context for a more vigorous attempt by many politicians to prevent the absorption of the UK into an increasingly federal European framework.[202] Euroscepticism became particularly accentuated inside the governing Conservative Party, while the opposition Labour Party turned slowly away from its traditional anti-European views. Ironically for Major, it was his own party, rather than the Labour opposition, that most constrained his policy options.[203]

Throughout his tenure as Prime Minister, Major managed to secure important victories for Britain by negotiating opt-outs from EMU and the Social Charter and resisting – as much as possible – compromising federalist language in the Maastricht Treaty.[204] The plans for EMU and political union accentuated the contestation between pro- and anti-Community sentiments in Britain. The Maastricht ratification debate in November 1993 was characterised by concerns about the potential loss of British national and parliamentary sovereignty, independence, and identity to European integration.[205]

While structuralist accounts of integration argue that Major's position was based on concerns about economic convergence and the defence of British national economic interests, his hesitancy on political integration requires further analytical examination. Rather than emanating solely from domestic party political or economic considerations, British opposition to continental pro-integrationist projects touched upon significant contestation about diverging visions for Europe. In Britain, the public and parliamentary debate was split between those who advocated a closer engagement with Europe, and those seeking to reaffirm British national interests, identity, and independence.[206] This cleavage cut across the political spectrum, beyond party-political affiliations and ideologies. In consequence, Major's leadership consisted largely in balancing the conflicting groups and interests on Europe, while at the same time developing an alternative approach to integration, which he labelled 'Euro-realism.'[207]

The Tories were split over what kind of Europe was desirable.[208] As Philip Cowley and John Garry's analysis of the 1990 Conservative Party leadership contest suggests, the European attitudes of Tory MPs were especially important for determining their voting behaviour in the contest.[209] Major was elected Prime Minister in part because he was not a Euro-enthusiast along the lines of Michael Heseltine and Douglas Hurd.[210] Yet while the internal divisions over Europe among the Tories helped Major to office, they also undermined his stature on European affairs as Prime Minister, since everybody knew that he was unable to count on explicit or tacit support from his own party.[211] Given that Major had 'acquired the premiership through good fortune and a sustained application of a consensus building approach to political management,'[212] much of his time in office was spent on mustering internal support for his government. The close interlinkage between leadership on the one hand, and elite-conceptions of Europe on the other, was highly visible throughout the Major government. Due to the differences over the purpose, goals, and mechanisms of European integration, Major lacked the essential autonomy from domestic electoral and parliamentary politics to effectively pursue a coherent policy on the European level.[213] Even his unexpected victory in the 1992 general elections did not afford him more autonomy on European policy.

Despite achieving notorious successes, such as securing significant concessions at the Maastricht negotiations, Major's hands on European affairs were tied – for two reasons. First, by lacking autonomy (or at least tacit support) at home, Major's room for compromises in European negotiations was severely limited.[214] Without being able to compromise, Major had to adopt stringent requirements in European negotiations, which in turn put him at odds with his European counterparts. During the his government, Major's limited options on Europe and the differences over which conception of Europe to advocate were not only close linked but exacerbated each other.[215]

The preceding Thatcher government had already defined a vision of Europe which was sharply distinct from Mitterrand's and Kohl's, so much so that it was labelled 'the Thatcher crusade on Europe.'[216] Her Bruges speech of 20 September 1988 had laid out her rejection of plans for ever-deeper integration:

> The Community is not an end in itself. Nor is it an institutional device to be constantly modified according to the dictates of some abstract intellectual concept. Nor must it be ossified by endless regulation. The European Community is the practical means by which Europe can ensure the future prosperity and security of its people in a world in which there are many other powerful nations and groups of nations. We Europeans cannot afford to waste our energies on internal disputes or arcane institutional debates.[217]

Instead, she provided brief and general indications of an alternative vision of Europe, which would strongly protect sovereign prerogatives of the Community's member states:

> My first guiding principle is this: willing and active cooperation between independent sovereign states is the best way to build a successful European Community. To try to suppress nationhood and concentrate power at the centre of a European conglomerate would be highly damaging and would jeopardise the objectives we seek to achieve.[218]

At Bruges, Thatcher effectively set the cornerstones of an alternative British vision of Europe, against which other British decision-makers measured their own declarations and preferences.[219] Subsequently, the debate about Europe came to be framed much more by the issues of federalism, sovereignty, national identity, independence, and patriotism, rather than technical concerns about the economic merits of EMU.

Major characterised his own approach to Europe as a form of 'Euro-realism,' situating it in between the Thatcherite and the pro-integrationist wings of the Conservative Party. As he recalls in his *Autobiography*,

> I had no instinctive animosity towards the Community, nor was I a starry-eyed supporter of it. I was a friendly agnostic. I might have wished the European issue was not there, but it was. It could not be avoided.[220]

Major, born in 1943, did not share the same personal historical memories of World War II which weighed so heavily on both Mitterrand's and Kohl's vision of Europe. Also, as a Conservative politician, his economic instincts tended to follow a liberal laissez-faire and supply-side economic model.[221] He was therefore wary of the *dirigiste* impulses of the European Commission and the activist approach, which motivated the pro-integrationist initiatives for deeper integration.[222] Moreover, as Kavanagh and Seldon claim,

> Major travelled light in terms of political ideology and dogma . . . He was a Prime Minister for harmony, for whom leadership was an opportunity to find common ground rather than strike out on a strong line of his own . . . His lack of ideological moorings may have contributed to the perception even more among some of his own staff that he was primarily a tactician and lacked sense of overall strategy . . . He had no burning desire to lead his followers into a promised land.[223]

Seen from the point of view of Major's ideological commitments, further plans for European integration were neither a primordial political objective nor an interest. Unlike Mitterrand and Kohl, he had not developed a coherent European vision which informed his thinking and policies. Rather, the key elements of Major's approach to Europe encompassed the articulation of specific themes: the defence of the national interest, the quest for Conservative Party unity, and the pursuit of intergovernmental cooperation and Eastern enlargement. All were geared at minimising the effects of increasing political unification and preventing Britain's participation in the most ambitious integration projects. He wanted to 'reposition' Britain within the Community.[224] For Major, a choice existed between a heavily institutionalised and a less institutionalised, free-market model for integration:

> The question is, what sort of Europe is it that we wish to help build? The Community today is at a crossroads. No one should duck, dodge or weave around that question. There are important decisions to be made, now and in the immediate future, about the way in which the Community develops. We can develop as a centralist institution, as some might want, or we can develop as a free-market, free-trade, wider European Community more responsive to its citizens. I am unreservedly in favour of the latter form of the Community, and I believe that that is the overwhelming view of this country.[225]

Crucially, what set Major's conception of Euro-realism apart from both Mitterrand and Kohl was the fact that, in his mind, the national and the European interests did not necessarily overlap. Integration could therefore only be supported if it served Britain's direct and tangible interests. Major told the Commons that Britain did and could benefit from Community membership.[226] Yet on numerous issues, Britain's interests were defined not as part of a broader European theme, but rather in contrast to Europe. This was especially the case with the projects for EMU and political union.[227] Major's approach was characterised by the attempt to calculate the merits of each issue at stake: 'From the beginning of my premiership, I tried to maximise the advantages to Britain of our membership, and to minimise the concessions we had to make.'[228]

For Mitterrand and Kohl, European solutions to national economic, security, or political challenges had to be sought, because the nation-state was only partially capable of addressing them. For instance, Mitterrand advocated EMU in order to cope with France's growing financial and economic difficulties. Similarly, Kohl sought EMU and political union to safeguard Germany's stability and security, believing that Germany could only dispel fears about its intentions by being integrated into a European political community.

Major was more reluctant to frame and define the British national interest through European means. He told the Commons:

> I have made it clear that I believe that the way forward for Europe is as a Europe of nation states built upon co-operation. Key decisions affecting this nation must be taken here in this House. My guiding principle is to do what I believe is in our national interest – to argue for Britain's interest in Europe, and to build a Europe which carries the trust of the British people. That I will continue to do.[229]

Major's pragmatism on Europe meant that European policy was conducted on a case-by-case basis.[230] Rather than aiming to influence the overall direction of the European project in the long term, Major gave priority to specific issues, which were of particular importance either for safeguarding the national interest, or for assuaging the divergent wings of the Conservative Party. This approach is exemplified in a statement about his programme for the December 1991 Maastricht negotiations:

> No federalism. No commitment to a single currency. No Social Chapter. No Community competence on foreign or home affairs or defence. Cooperation in the areas, yes; compulsion, no. It could not have been clearer. I set out too what we hoped to gain at Maastricht. More power for the European Parliament to control the Commission and investigate fraud. A more open Community that enlarged its borders to the east. Treaty acknowledgement of 'subsidiarity' – the principle that Europe should only do what the nation state could not do equally well – so that we could end the creep of increasing Commission power.[231]

In this sense, his leadership style entailed delineating 'red lines,' which Britain would defend at all costs, and achieving immediate concessions and benefits.[232]

Another difference with Mitterrand and Kohl concerned the degree to which each leader pursued his European ambitions. Both Mitterrand and Kohl aimed at identifying themselves with the nascent EU. Major did not share this personal European ambition. Instead, his main point of reference was the Conservative Party itself, which had been a crucial element of his personal and political formation.[233] Young claims that Major actually liked the Conservative Party. Long before he became its leader, it was by far the most important influence in his life. Keeping it one and whole was to be the defining task of his leadership.[234]

Major was concerned that Europe might pose an existential threat to the medium-term electoral chances for the party, believing that 'Europe had the capacity to split the Conservative Party and hurl it into the wilderness.'[235] This view impacted on his European policies because it implicitly meant that controversial issues on Europe would have to be circumvented.[236] Major wanted to pursue a line that would 'keep both the pro-Europeans and sceptics on board, hence the position of "wait and see," or negotiate and then decide.'[237] His 'preferred posture was that of a facilitator,' who wanted to 'finesse the divisions within the party by compromise and party management.'[238] Yet Major could not really achieve this balancing act between diverging party factions:

> Major's leadership style, of leniency with Cabinet ministers, and leaving the whips to strong-arm recalcitrant backbenchers, was not ideal in building unity and loyalty. Above all, Cabinet ministers were in no mood to follow a central lead: they had their own agendas, personal and political, to be weighed against pleas from Number Ten to behave and toe the line.[239]

The Prime Minister's leadership style thus opened the possibility for powerful challenges to his European policy to emerge from within the Cabinet and the parliamentary party. In this sense, Major exacerbated the existing disagreements over Europe, thereby undermining his autonomy on European affairs even further.

Apart from the charged domestic political debate about Europe, and the constant need to reconcile party political and European considerations, Major's conception of the idea of Europe nonetheless delineated an alternative to the ambitious pro-integrationist projects of Mitterrand and Kohl. His March 1991 speech at the Konrad-Adenauer-Stiftung in Bonn, as well as his September 1993 article, published in *The Economist*, indicated his conception of Europe.[240] Both pronouncements illustrated the core elements of his Euro-realism.

For Major, Europe had to develop 'by evolution, [and] not some treaty-based revolution provoking disunity in the cause of unity.'[241] He was wary of further institutionalising the Community. Rather than understanding common institutions as an extension of the national interest, he feared they would unnecessarily close off political options and alternatives, and lead to a lack of democratic accountability. Major told the Commons that he did not want to be 'placed in a position in which a more intrusive European Union overrides the instinctive wishes, habits and traditions of the United Kingdom.'[242] Common institutions were a 'straightjacket,'[243] seeking to engineer cohesion and convergence in areas where they were not viable. Major took issue with the perceived artificial nature of the Community in general, and with the twin projects of EMU and political union in particular. He challenged the view that 'we had to march forward to ever greater political and economic uniformity.'[244] For him, as he told the House of Commons at the end of his premiership in 1997,

> the whole tradition and manner of government in the United Kingdom, and our history throughout much of this century, are almost the polar opposite of those of continental Europe. Our traditions and instincts are different. What is commonplace for those in Europe is not remotely what has been seen traditionally to be in our interests.[245]

The delineation of historical, cultural, and political differences with continental Europe underlined his conviction that integration was only viable if it would result in tangible benefits which could be sold to the Conservative Party and the British electorate. He argued that 'Europe should focus on what its people wanted, not the institutional reforms that so attracted its leaders.'[246]

Faced with the polarised British sentiments about Europe, the notion of 'Euro-realism' came to be increasingly determined by the need to balance sharply diverging elite-conceptions of Europe. The fault-lines of the British debate about Europe were marked by stark contestation about how to define and pursue the national interest. In this context, the leadership style of John Major comprised more transactional rather than transformative elements. Unlike the explanation put forward by structural theories of integration, it was not the incompatibility of British interests with EMU and political union which prevented its participation in both projects. Rather, Major's hesitancy was due to the fact that he could neither set the tone of public debate on Europe nor achieve the public's and Parliament's tacit support (autonomy).

Domestically, he sought to remain a 'European pragmatist,'[247] playing the role of an honest broker so as to adjudicate when integration would or would not be in Britain's interest. On the international stage, Major sought to win 'compensating advantages'[248] or opt-outs from the more ambitious integration projects, whose merits he did not believe in:

> I was not an integrationist or a federalist. I did not favour the further large-scale transfer of powers from London to Brussels. I believed in a Europe of sovereign nation states. I was . . . prepared to be isolated in Europe on points of principle . . . I was not enthusiastic about the single currency, and had ensured that Britain was not committed to joining it. But these beliefs about what was best for our nation's future did not turn me against the European Union as a whole. I knew too, because I talked to them that many of my hopes for Europe were also those of other European leaders. I was proud of the economic and social benefits Britain gained from membership, and aware how difficult our future would be should we decide to leave.[249]

Yet the balancing act on both domestic and international fronts increasingly failed to cater to his various audiences. Major was 'painfully unsuccessful' at striking 'a middle way between the anti-Europe passion of its most vocal minority of politicians and the pro-European necessities that came with the task of government.'[250]

On the one hand, his European policies were undermined through 'lamentable misreporting of European issues by an increasingly Eurosceptic press.'[251] On the other hand, Mitterrand and Kohl came to accept that Major was not prepared to support either EMU or the Community's political unification, but proceeded with both projects regardless. For Major this was a significant setback, given that it rendered his vision of a desirable Europe ineffectual. This vision, as laid out in his 1993 article in *The Economist*, aimed at preventing the progressive institutionalisation and deepening of the EU, and instead advocated enlargement and intergovernmental cooperation:

> It is for nations to build Europe, not for Europe to attempt to supersede nations. I want to see the Community become a wide union, embracing the whole of democratic Europe, in a single market and with common security arrangements . . . A Community which ceases to nibble at national freedoms, and so commands the enthusiasm of its member nations . . . Such a Community would be a more genuine and lasting European Union than anything we have now . . . It is an ambition for the new century that dwarfs the dreams of the founders of the Community. The Treaty of Rome is not creed. It is an instrument.[252]

Major never shared Mitterrand's and Kohl's enthusiasm for European unification. He did not subscribe to the historical conception of Europe which characterised especially Kohl's behaviour on European affairs. Yet despite having the influence, power, and prestige of a British prime minister, Major's leadership on Europe remained ineffective. He could neither find support for his desirable vision of Europe nor prevent integration from taking a direction which he disagreed with.[253]

***

The EU and the Euro were responses to the end of the Cold War in Europe. Why would Germany give up its strong Deutschmark, why would France willingly forfeit its ability to devalue, and why would Britain would want to left out of a European monetary bloc? Kohl could have prevented the Euro had he wanted to, and still have acted in Germany's interest, and Major could have embraced political and monetary union while acting in Britain's.

The dynamics among leaders matter. The close personal relationship between Kohl and Mitterrand had the effect of dominating the pace and direction of European negotiations at a watershed moment in European history. Major, who was often opposed to the initiatives under consideration, was frustrated by his inability to break this personal relationship. He did not share their historical understanding of the idea of Europe. Mitterrand and Kohl consistently defined their national interests in relation to broader European considerations – to the point that these often overlapped. Their conception of Europe influenced the manner in which their material, ideational, and rhetorical power was deployed. By subscribing to a historical interpretation of the idea of Europe, Mitterrand and Kohl came to favour long-term success in shaping the direction of European integration over short-term gains on single issues of negotiation. Major, by contrast, couched his European policies in a cost-and-benefit rhetoric, and his negotiation style and tactics were at odds with Mitterrand's and Kohl's.

For Mitterrand and Kohl, the exogenous shock of the end of the Cold War was both a challenge and an opportunity, and both dealt with the fast-moving events, uncertainty, and anxiety about German unification by embracing proposals to make European integration irrevocable. In early 1990, key decisions were taken to simultaneously pursue both German and European unification, to create a common currency, and to secure the continuity of the Franco-German alliance even at the expense of sidelining Britain. This pathway cannot fully accounted for by simply claiming that it was in France's and Germany's national interest to do so. As the increasing politicisation and polarisation over European integration exemplified – the French and Danish Maastricht referenda were cases in point – Kohl and Mitterrand's choices were not universally shared or popular.

Major's troubles in forcefully advocating his own 'Euro-realist' approach to the developments in Europe highlight the other side of the claim that leadership is a social relationship. In Major's case, his autonomy on European affairs was severely curtailed because he lacked support – and could not generate it – among his own party, British public opinion, and his fellow heads of government. His de facto power as Prime Minister was reduced because he could not entice, coerce, convince, or marshal others to follow his preferences.

Notes

1. H.-D. Heumann, *Genscher. Die Biographie* (Paderborn: Schöningh, 2012), pp. 213–216.
2. J.W. Friend, *Unequal Partners: French-German Relations 1989–2000* (Westport: Praeger, 2001), pp. 18–19; M. Sutton, *France and the Construction of Europe, 1944–2007: The Geopolitical Imperative* (Oxford: Berghahn, 2007), pp. 240–243.
3. S. Hoffmann, 'Towards a Common Foreign and Security Policy,' *Journal of Common Market Studies* 38 (2) (2000): 191.
4. P. Murray. 'European Integration Studies: The Search for Synthesis,' *Contemporary Politics* 6 (1) (2000): 19–28.
5. See D.W. Urwin, *A Political History of Western Europe since 1945*, fifth edition (London: Longman, 1997); R.O. Keohane, J. Nye, and S. Hoffmann eds. *After the Cold War: International Institutions and State Strategies in Europe, 1989–1991* (Cambridge: Harvard University Press, 1993); R.O. Keohane and S. Hoffmann, 'Institutional Change in Europe in the 1980s,' in *The New European Community: Decisionmaking and Institutional Change*, R.O. Keohane and S. Hoffmann eds. (Boulder, CO: Westview, 1991), pp. 1–40.
6. F. Bozo, *Mitterrand, the End of the Cold War, and German Unification* (Oxford: Berghahn, 2009).

7 R. Self, *British Foreign and Defence Policy since 1945: Challenges and Dilemmas in a Changing World* (Basingstoke: Palgrave, 2010), pp. 134–135.
8 K. Kaltenthaler, 'German Interests in European Monetary Integration,' *Journal of Common Market Studies* 40 (1) (2002): 69–87.
9 A.V. Menéndez-Alarcón, *The Cultural Realm of European Integration: Social Representations in France, Spain, and the United Kingdom* (Westport: Praeger, 2004).
10 W.E. Paterson, 'Helmut Kohl, "The Vision Thing," and Escaping the Semi-Sovereignty Trap,' in *The Kohl Chancellorship*, C. Clemens and W.E. Paterson eds. (London: Frank Cass, 1998), pp. 17–36.
11 On elite support for European federalism, see: L.K. Hallstrom, 'Support for European Federalism? An Elite View,' *European Integration* 25 (2003): 51–72.
12 See P. McCarthy ed. *France-Germany, 1983–1993: The Struggle to Cooperate* (Basingstoke: Macmillan, 1993).
13 D.S. Bell, *François Mitterrand: A Political Biography* (Cambridge: Polity, 2005).
14 H. Kohl, *Erinnerungen, 1982–1990* (Munich: Droemer, 2005).
15 *Ibid.*, p. 104.
16 See E. Pond, *The Rebirth of Europe* (Washington, DC: Brookings Institution Press, 1999).
17 Illustrative is Kohl's speech in Davos, 3 February 1990: H. Kohl, 'Europa – Die Zukunft aller Deutschen,' *Bulletin* 21 (1990): 165–169.
18 D. Dinan, *Europe Recast: A History of European Union* (Boulder: Lynne Rienner, 2004), p. 236.
19 On Mitterrand's use of symbols for political ends, see: W. Northcutt, 'François Mitterrand and the Political Use of Symbols: The Construction of a Centrist Republic,' *French Historical Studies* 17 (1) (1991): 141–158.
20 W. Northcutt, *Mitterrand: A Political Biography* (New York: Holms and Meier, 1992).
21 A. Cole, *François Mitterrand: A Study in Political Leadership*, second edition (London: Routledge, 1997), p. 124.
22 Dinan, *Europe Recast*, p. 236.
23 Eric Roussel traces Mitterrand's 'decisive zeal for integration dates to the events of 1983/84, when he decided that support for European integration was "the priority of priorities"': see E. Roussel, *Mitterrand ou la Constance du Funambule* (Mesnil-sur-l'Estrée: Éditions Lattès, 1991), pp. 108–109.
24 On the domestic dimension, Cole suggests that Mitterrand's concentration on Europe also 'reflected the depths of unpopularity an interventionist President had reached during his first three years of the presidential mandate. Europe offered a less controversial, potentially more glamorous terrain for political activity': Cole, *Mitterrand*, pp. 122–123.
25 G. Saunier, '"J'y étais, j'y croyais." Les origines de l'engagement européen de François Mitterrand,' *La lettre de l'Institut François Mitterrand* 8 (June 2004): 10–11.
26 Cole, *Mitterrand*, pp. 122–123.
27 R. Tiersky, *François Mitterrand: A Very French President* (Lanham: Rowman and Littlefield, 2000), p. 166.
28 Cole, *Mitterrand*, p. 124. On the role, influence, and leadership of Jacques Delors on European integration, see K. Endo, *The Presidency of the European Commission under Jacques Delors: The Politics of Shared Leadership* (Basingstoke: Macmillan, 1999); C. Grant, *Delors: Inside the House Jacques Built* (London: Nicholas Brealey, 1994).
29 M.J. Hillenbrand, 'An Assessment of the EC Future,' *Annals of the American Academy of Political and Social Science* 531 (1994): 168–177.
30 M.R. Gueldry, *France and European Integration: Toward a Transnational Polity?* (Westport: Praeger, 2001), p. 34.

31 For a structural explanation of the SEA negotiations, see A. Moravcsik, 'Negotiating the Single European Act: National Interests and Conventional Statecraft in the European Community,' *International Organization* 45 (1) (1991): 651–688.
32 Dinan, *Europe Recast*, p. 208.
33 On French conceptions of Europe in the 1980s and 1990s, see: R. Joas, *Zwischen Nation und Europa: Die europapolitischen Vorstellungen der Gaullisten 1978 bis 1994* (Bochum: Universitätsverlag Dr. N. Brockmeyer, 1996).
34 Quoted in K. Dyson and K. Featherstone, *The Road to Maastricht: Negotiating Economic and Monetary Union* (Oxford: Oxford University Press, 1999), p. 309.
35 *Ibid.*, p. 308.
36 Kohl, *Erinnerungen*, p. 1076.
37 C. Hacke, *Die Außenpolitik der Bundesrepublik Deutschland. Weltmacht wider Willen?* revised edition (Frankfurt: Ullstein, 1997).
38 Heumann, *Genscher*, p. 213.
39 Roussel, *Mitterrand*.
40 Mitterrand's health started to deteriorate as a consequence of his suffering from cancer: E. Guigou, 'Le Traité de Maastricht: la Dernière Oeuvre Européen de François Mitterrand,' *La lettre de l'Institut François Mitterrand* 8 (June 2004): 22–23. Mitterrand's close adviser, Hubert Védrine, claims that the French President was most active on the European scene between 1984 and 1992, with Kohl following in his footsteps: H. Védrine, 'L'Europe de Mitterrand,' *La lettre de l'Institut François Mitterrand* 8 (June 2004): p. 1.
41 Tiersky, *Mitterrand*, p. 13.
42 Powell to Wall, 20 January 1990: *DBPO* III, VII: doc. 103.
43 Auswärtiges Amt, *Aussenpolitik der Bundesrepublik Deutschland. Vom Kalten Krieg zum Frieden in Europa. Dokumente 1949–1989* (Munich: Verlag Bonn Aktuell, 1990), doc. 307.
44 Quoted in J. Howorth, 'France and the Unification of Germany: Clio's Verdict?' *French Politics, Culture & Society* 29 (1) (2011): 123.
45 R. Fritsch-Bournazel, *Europe and German Unification* (New York: Berg, 1992): 177.
46 Hacke, *Außenpolitik*, p. 367.
47 Bell, *Mitterrand*, p. 139.
48 Fergusson to Hurd, 2 February 1990: *DBPO* III, VII: doc. 118.
49 Reproduced in Fritsch-Bournazel, *Europe*, p. 174.
50 Powell to Wall, 20 January 1990: *DBPO* III, VII: doc. 103.
51 *Ibid.*
52 Mallaby to Hurd, 1 February 1990: *DBPO* III, VII: doc. 115. See also J. Wright, 'The Cold War, European Community and Anglo-French Relations, 1958–1998,' in *Anglo-French Relations in the Twentieth Century: Rivalry and Cooperation*, A. Sharp and G. Stone eds. (London: Routledge, 2000), pp. 324–343.
53 H. Mayer, 'Early at the Beach and Claiming Territory? The Evolution of German Ideas on a New European Order,' *International Affairs* 73 (4) (1997): 721–737. For a comprehensive overview and documentation of the diplomatic activity surrounding German unification, see Auswärtiges Amt, *Deutsche Aussenpolitik 1990/91: Auf dem Weg zu einer Europäischen Friedensordnung. Eine Dokumentation* (Munich: Verlag Bonn Aktuell, 1991).
54 S. Szabo, 'The United States and German Unification,' in *The United States and Germany in the Era of the Cold War, 1945–1990: A Handbook*, Volume 2: 1968–1990, D. Junker ed. (Cambridge: Cambridge University Press, 2004), pp. 104–110. On US President Bush's personal engagement with and support for German unification, see: M. Cox and S. Hurst, '"His Finest Hour?" George

Bush and the Diplomacy of German Unification,' *Diplomacy & Statecraft* 13 (4) (2002): 123–150. Illustrative are also Bush's speeches in Bonn, 31 May 1989, and at the NATO Council in Brussels, 4 December 1989: Auswärtiges Amt, *Aussenpolitik*, doc. 277; doc. 300.
55 Auswärtiges Amt, *Aussenpolitik*, doc. 299. See also J. Anderson, *German Unification and the Union of Europe: The Domestic Politics of European Integration* (Cambridge: Cambridge University Press, 1999), pp. 26–27.
56 H. Kohl, 'Die deutsche Frage und die europäische Verantwortung,' *Bulletin* 9 (1990): 61.
57 Kohl, 'Europa – Die Zukunft,' p. 168.
58 Bozo, *Mitterrand*, pp. 227–235; Friend, *Unequal Partners*, pp. 30–31.
59 U. Herbert, *Geschichte Deutschlands im 20. Jahrhundert* (Munich: C.H. Beck, 2014), pp. 1121–1123.
60 Mayer, 'Early at the Beach,' p. 722. Throughout November 1989, Kohl and Genscher used interviews and press conferences to make the case for Germany's continuing commitment to its *Westintegration* or Western foreign policy: see Auswärtiges Amt, *Aussenpolitik*: doc. 298.
61 Hoffmann, 'Towards a Common Foreign and Security Policy,' p. 193.
62 Hacke, *Außenpolitik*, p. 368.
63 Kohl, *Erinnerungen*, p. 1076.
64 Paterson, 'Helmut Kohl,' p. 28.
65 Kohl, *Erinnerungen*, p. 1077. At Latché, Kohl already agreed to the 'necessary deepening and associated institutional reforms.' This commitment limited Germany's subsequent foreign political options when doubts emerged in Germany about the direction of European integration and the question of whether EMU was in Germany's interest: Mayer, 'Early at the Beach,' p. 723.
66 By his own admission, the question of the Oder-Neisse line and the consolidation of Germany's borders was a great concern for Mitterrand throughout late 1989 and early 1990: F. Mitterrand, *De l'Allemagne, de la France* (Paris: Poches Odile Jacob, 2001).
67 A. Cole, 'Political Leadership in Western Europe: Helmut Kohl in Comparative Context,' in *The Kohl Chancellorship*, C. Clemens and W.E. Paterson eds. (London: Frank Cass, 1998), p. 129.
68 Kaltenthaler, 'German Interests,' p. 69.
69 D. Vernet, 'The Dilemma of French Foreign Policy,' *International Affairs* 68 (4) (1992): 658.
70 See Howorth, 'France,' pp. 118–129.
71 Powell to Thatcher, 9 February 1990: *DBPO* III, VII: doc. 136. On the influence of ideas and identities on German foreign policy after 1989, see J.P.G. Bach, *Between Sovereignty and Integration: German Foreign Policy and National Identity after 1989* (New York, NY: St. Martin's Press, 1999); H. Kundnani, *The Paradox of German Power* (London: Hurst, 2014).
72 J. Campbell, *Margaret Thatcher, Volume Two: The Iron Lady* (London: Pimlico, 2003).
73 U. Lappenküper, 'Helmut Kohl als europapolitischer Netzwerker: Seine Zusammenarbeit mit François Mitterrand, Felipe González und Jacques Chirac,' in *Deutsche Europapolitik Christlicher Demokraten. Von Konrad Adenauer bis Angela Merkel (1945–2013)*, H.-J. Küsters ed. (Düsseldorf: Droste, 2014), pp. 203–231.
74 Paterson, 'Helmut Kohl,' p. 27.
75 K. Dyson, 'Chancellor Kohl as Strategic Leader: The Case of Economic and Monetary Union,' in *The Kohl Chancellorship*, C. Clemens and W.E. Paterson eds. (London: Frank Cass, 1998), p. 38.
76 *Ibid.*, p. 40.

77 Mitterrand's and Kohl's common letter to the Irish EC Council President of 18 April 1990 is evidence of a renewal of their commitment to each other: Auswärtiges Amt, *Gemeinsame Aussen- und Sicherheitspolitik der Europäischen Union (GASP). Dokumentation* (Bonn: Auswärtiges Amt, 1994), pp. 492–493.
78 On the detailed history of the Euro, see K. Dyson ed. *European States and the Euro: Europeanization, Variation, and Convergence* (Oxford: Oxford University Press, 2002); M. Kaelberer, *Money and Power in Europe: The Political Economy of the European Monetary Cooperation* (Albany: State University of New York Press, 2001); K.R. McNamara, *The Currency of Ideas: Monetary Politics in the European Union* (Ithaca: Cornell University Press, 1998).
79 Védrine, 'L'Europe,' p. 1.
80 Gueldry, *France and European Integration*, p. 123.
81 W.I. Hitchcock, *The Struggle for Europe: The History of the Continent since 1945* (London: Profile Books, 2003), pp. 441–442.
82 Dinan, *Europe Recast*, p. 236.
83 C. Parsons, *A Certain Idea of Europe* (Ithaca: Cornell University Press, 2003), p. 203.
84 *Ibid*. Major French political parties were divided on Europe. Despite Mitterrand's advocacy that deeper European integration was in France's interest, the 1992 Maastricht referendum revealed the unexpectedly large extent of elite and public resistance to further transfers of national sovereignty: Menéndez-Alarcón, *Cultural Realm*, pp. 25–35.
85 See C. de Boissieu and J. Pisani-Ferry, 'The Political Economy of French Economic Policy in the Perspective of EMU,' in *Forging an Integrated Europe*, B. Eichengreen and J. Frieden eds. (Ann Arbor: University of Michigan Press, 1998), pp. 49–89.
86 Dyson and Featherstone, *Road to Maastricht*, p. 65; J.-J. Roche, 'Une Politique Étrangère Malmenée par l'Histoire,' in *État Politique de la France*, D. Chagnollaud ed. (Paris: Quai Voltaire, 1992), pp. 127–144.
87 Dyson and Featherstone, *Road to Maastricht*, p. 65.
88 D. Howarth, 'The French State in the Euro-Zone: "Modernization" and Legitimizing *Dirigisme*,' in *European States and the Euro: Europeanization, Variation, and Convergence*, K. Dyson ed. (Oxford: Oxford University Press, 2002), pp. 145–172.
89 In order to 'multilateralise' the Deutschmark and its zone of influence, Mitterrand was willing to compromise France's interventionist economic model and accept the creation of an independent European Central Bank along Bundesbank lines. This move, criticised by numerous analysts and some business leaders in France, came to be seen as an 'inevitable concession' by Paris: Roche, 'Politique Étrangère,' p. 140.
90 Parsons, *Certain Idea*, p. 209.
91 *Ibid.*, p. 218.
92 Hacke, *Außenpolitik*, p. 429. On the shaky foundations of the European monetary system, see Hillenbrand, 'Assessment.'
93 Kenneth Dyson claims that Kohl 'seized every opportunity to be bold on EMU. He was bold in gaining Mitterrand's agreement to couple EMU with political union negotiations; in endorsing the communiqué on EMU at Rome 1 in October 1990; in setting a final date for stage 3 at Maastricht; and in taking a strong strand at Dublin European Council in December 1996 on the nature of sanctions within the Stability Pact. On none of these issues was Kohl passively reactive': Dyson, 'Chancellor Kohl,' p. 50.
94 For SPD position on EMU see SPD internal position paper on Europe of 25 May 1993: HIA ESC/12. See also SPD leaflet for 1994 EP elections:

'Europa. Eine historische Chance. 10 vernünftige Gründe die für Maastricht sprechen': HIA ESC/12.
95 Dyson and Featherstone, *Road to Maastricht*, p. 39.
96 On the reasons for, difficulties of, and debates on enlargement, see A. Bieler, 'The Struggle over EU Enlargement: A Historical Materialist Analysis of European Integration,' *Journal of European Public Policy* 9 (4) (2002): 575–597; H. Grabbe, 'Europeanization Goes East: Power and Uncertainty in the EU Accession Process,' in *The Politics of Europeanization*, K. Featherstone and C. Radoelli eds. (Oxford: Oxford University Press, 2003), pp. 303–327; P.-H. Laurent, 'Widening Europe: The Dilemmas of Community Success,' *Annals of the American Academy of Political and Social Science* 531 (1994): 124–140; N. Pautola, 'Toward European Union Eastern Enlargement: Progress and Problems in Pre-Accession,' *Russian and East European Finance and Trade* 35 (6) (2000): 45–67; F. Schimmelpfennig, 'Liberal Identity and Postnational Inclusion: The Eastern Enlargement of the European Union,' in *Constructing Europe's Identity: The External Dimension*, L.-E. Cederman ed. (Boulder: Lynne Rienner, 2001), pp. 165–186; G. Verheugen, 'The Enlargement of the European Union,' *European Foreign Affairs Review* 5 (2000): 439–444.
97 M.J. Baun, 'The Maastricht Treaty as High Politics: Germany, France, and European Integration,' *Political Science Quarterly* 110 (4) (1995): 605–624.
98 A. Moravcsik, *The Choice for Europe: Social Purpose and State Power from Messina to Maastricht* (London: Routledge, 1998).
99 Auswärtiges Amt, *Gemeinsame Aussen- und Sicherheitspolitik*.
100 P.J. Katzenstein ed. *Tamed Power: Germany in Europe* (Ithaca: Cornell University Press, 1997).
101 Parsons, *Certain Idea*, p. 216.
102 Kohl, 'Die deutsche Frage und die europäische Verantwortung,' pp. 61–66.
103 Lappenküper, 'Helmut Kohl,' pp. 217–220.
104 S. Bulmer, C. Jeffery, and W.E. Paterson, *Germany's European Diplomacy: Shaping the Regional Milieu* (Manchester: Manchester University Press, 2000), p. 1.
105 Paterson, 'Helmut Kohl,' p. 30.
106 *Ibid*.
107 K. Dyson, 'Germany and the Euro: Redefining EMU, Handling Paradox, and Managing Uncertainty and Contingency,' in *European States and the Euro: Europeanization, Variation, and Convergence*, K. Dyson ed. (Oxford: Oxford University Press, 2002), pp. 173–211.
108 Cole, 'Political Leadership,' p. 139.
109 Paterson, 'Helmut Kohl,' p. 32.
110 L.N. Lindberg and S.A. Scheingold eds. *Regional Integration: Theory and Research* (Cambridge: Harvard University Press, 1971).
111 For an example of Kohl's cultivation of this image, see CDU campaign leaflet for 1994 EP elections: HIA ESC/12.
112 H. Kohl, 'Zielvorstellungen und Chancen für die Zukunft Europas,' *Bulletin* 38 (1992): 353.
113 H. Kohl, 'Unterwegs zu einem versöhnten Europa,' *Bulletin* 75 (1991): 603.
114 With the benefit of hindsight, Kohl claimed that this instinct for transformative leadership on integration was proven right: 'The revitalisation of the EC also contributed significantly to the victory of freedom in the European revolutions of 1989/90. Just as everybody else, François Mitterrand and I neither foresaw this epochal turning point, nor expected its force and speed. But when it came, we gave the only right answer: not a renationalisation of the European Community was called for – as some continue to believe until today – but its further

development towards a European Union': H. Kohl, 'Präsident François Mitterrand – ein großer Europäer verabschiedet sich' [first published in *Le Monde*, 11 May 1995], *Bulletin* 41 (1995): 357.
115 D. Kavanagh and A. Seldon eds. *The Powers behind the Prime Minister: The Hidden Influence of Number Ten* (London: Harper Collins, 1999).
116 J. Major, *The Autobiography* (London: Harper Collins, 1999), p. 582.
117 *Ibid.*, p. 583.
118 H. Védrine, *Dans la Mêlée Mondiale 2009–2012* (Paris: Fayard, 2012), p. 265.
119 F. Mitterrand, *Mémoires pour Servir à l'Histoire de Ma Vie* (Paris: Bartillat, 1997), p. 198.
120 See J. Lacouture, *Mitterrand: Une Histoire de Français: 1. Les Risques de l'Escalade* (Paris: Seuil, 1998); S. Baumann-Reynolds, *François Mitterrand: The Making of a Socialist Prince in Republican France* (Westport: Greenwood, 1995).
121 For an overview of the origins of Mitterrand's commitment to the cause of European unification, see: Saunier, '"J'y étais, j'y croyais." Les origines de l'engagement européen de François Mitterrand'.
122 Quoted in M. Burgess, *Federalism and European Union: Political Ideas, Influences and Strategies in the European Community, 1972–1987* (London: Routledge, 1989), p.186.
123 The economic causes of Mitterrand's heightened interest in European integration are disputed: see Parson, *Certain Idea*, p. 183; and, in contrast, J.W. Friend, *The Long Presidency: France in the Mitterrand Years, 1981–1995* (Boulder: Westview, 1998), p. 204.
124 *Ibid.*
125 F. Mitterrand, *Réflexions sur la Politique Extérieure de la France: Introduction à vingt-cinq Discours (1981–1985)* (Paris: Fayard, 1986), pp. 260–266.
126 Cole, *François Mitterrand*, pp. 121–122.
127 Dyson and Featherstone, *Road to Maastricht*, p. 63.
128 Regarding Mitterrand's lack of idealism on European affairs, see: Tiersky, *Mitterrand*, p. 168.
129 Dyson and Featherstone, *Road to Maastricht*, p. 62.
130 Tiersky, *François Mitterrand*, p. 167.
131 *Ibid.*, p. 162. Tiersky suggests that 'Mitterrand's federalist inclinations regarding the long-term future of European integration arose out of French patriotism, from an absolutely traditional, in a sense *gaullien*, idea of national interest. It was no abstract internationalist, let alone socialist, shift of loyalty from France to a supranational "Europe."'
132 See Mitterrand's speech of 7 February 1984 at The Hague: Mitterrand, *Reflexions*.
133 Friend, *Long Presidency*, p. 212.
134 Mitterrand, *Mémoires*, pp. 199–200.
135 Pond, *Rebirth*, p. 37.
136 *Financial Times*, 'In defence of Mitterrand' (4 January 2001).
137 Tiersky, *François Mitterrand*, p. 162.
138 Pond, *Rebirth*, p. 42.
139 Gueldry, *France*, p. 34.
140 Bozo, *Mitterrand*, pp. 233–243.
141 Friend, *Long Presidency*, p. 212.
142 See F. Mitterrand, *Mémoires Interrompus, Entretiens avec Georges-Marc Benamou* (Paris: Odile Jacob, 1996).
143 Tiersky, *Mitterrand*, p. 11.
144 See U. Lappenküper, *Mitterrand und Deutschland, Die enträtselte Sphinx* (Munich: Oldenbourg, 2011).

145 See Roussel, *Mitterrand*.
146 Bell, *Mitterrand*, p. 141.
147 Hoffmann, 'Towards,' p. 193.
148 Auswärtiges Amt, *Aussenpolitik*, doc. 310.
149 See HAEC BAC 212/2000.1/6.
150 Northcutt, *Mitterrand*, p. 342.
151 J. Musitelli, 'François Mitterrand, l'européen,' *La lettre de l'Institut François Mitterrand* 8 (June 2004): 3.
152 Tiersky, *Mitterrand*, p. 12.
153 See HAEC BAC 212/2000.1/8.
154 Gueldry, *France*, p. 7.
155 Mitterrand's conception of Europe started to distinguish itself more clearly from Delors,' who had – to Mitterrand's 'displeasure' – called for an openly federalist and political agenda for European integration: see Friend, *Long Presidency*, p. 218; J. Delors, *Mémoirs* (Paris: Plon, 2004).
156 Tiersky, *Mitterrand*, p. 11.
157 Dyson and Featherstone, *Road to Maastricht*, p. 74.
158 Mitterrand, *Mémoires*, p. 199.
159 For Mitterrand, Eastern enlargement was only viable in the long term: see Friend, *Long Presidency*, p. 221.
160 Tiersky, *Mitterrand*, p. 166.
161 HAEC D/François Mitterrand, April 11, 1991, p.9.
162 Tiersky, *Mitterrand*, p. 164.
163 *Ibid.*, p. 165.
164 Pond, *Rebirth*, p. 24.
165 See Kohl's speech of 27 May 1993: HIA, ESC/12.
166 H. Kohl, 'Politik der konsequenten Verwirklichung der Europäischen Union,' *Bulletin* 73 (1992): 697–701.
167 For an example of this cultural-civilsational discourse, see H. Kohl, 'Für ein gemeinsames Europa in Frieden und Freiheit,' *Bulletin* 76 (1995): 745–751.
168 Kohl, 'Unterwegs,' p. 605.
169 Katzenstein, *Tamed Power*.
170 Hacke, *Außenpolitik*, p. 300.
171 Kohl, 'Die deutsche Frage,' p. 65.
172 H. Kohl, 'Europas politische Agenda für die neunziger Jahre,' *Bulletin* 94 (1993): 1051.
173 H. Kohl, 'Aktuelle Entwicklungen in der Europapolitik,' *Bulletin* 103 (1992): 968.
174 Kohl, 'Die deutsche Frage,' p. 66.
175 Mayer, 'Early,' p. 726.
176 Kohl, 'Politik,' p. 697.
177 *Ibid.*, p. 701.
178 Friend, *Long Presidency*, p. 218.
179 In a declaration in the Bundestag of 27 May 1994, Kohl disputed that viable alternatives to a continuation of European integration had existed: H. Kohl, 'Aktuelle Fragen der Europapolitik,' *Bulletin* 51 (1994): 477–481.
180 Kohl, 'Europa – Die Zukunft aller Deutschen,' p. 166.
181 Kohl, 'Aktuelle Entwicklungen,' p. 965.
182 This view was clearly stated in the so-called Schäuble-Lamers paper on Europe of September 1994, which sketched German interests and strategies regarding European integration: see B.F. Nelsen and C.-G. Stubb eds. *The European Union: Readings on the Theory and Practice of European Integration*, second edition (Basingstoke: Macmillan, 1998), p. 73.

183 See Lappenküper, 'Helmut Kohl,' pp. 217–220.
184 Kohl, 'Aktuelle Fragen,' p. 478.
185 H. Kohl, 'Zukunftssicherung des Standorts Deutschland im geeinten Europa,' *Bulletin* 57 (1994): p. 537.
186 H. Kohl, 'In der europäischen Einigung liegt unsere nationale Zukunft,' *Bulletin* 125 (1992): 1142.
187 H. Kohl, 'Perspektiven Deutschlands im erweiterten Europa,' *Bulletin* 42 (1994): 367.
188 H. Kohl, 'Fundamente und Strukturen einer gemeinsamen europäischen Zukunft,' *Bulletin* 60 (1991): 474.
189 H. Kohl, 'Declaration Delivered in Maastricht, December 13,' *Bulletin* 142 (1991): 1153.
190 Quoted in Nelsen and Stubb, *European Union*, p. 77.
191 See Kohl, 'Politik,' p. 701. Kohl described himself as a 'convinced partisan of federalism' (*überzeugter Anhänger des Föderalismus*): H. Kohl, 'Die deutschamerikanischen Beziehungen – Garantie für Frieden und Freiheit,' *Bulletin* 12 (1994): 103.
192 *Ibid.*, p. 102.
193 Kohl, 'Europas politische Agenda,' p. 1051.
194 H. Kohl, 'Press Briefing Delivered in Birmingham, October 16,' *Bulletin* 115 (1992): 1061.
195 Kohl, 'Zielvorstellungen,' p. 354.
196 Kohl, 'In der europäischen Einigung,' p. 1142.
197 In Nelsen and Stubb, *European Union*, p. 76.
198 Kohl, 'Für ein gemeinsames Europa,' p. 748.
199 D. Gowland, A. Turner and A. Wright, *Britain and European Integration since 1945: On the Sidelines* (London: Routledge, 2010), pp. 109–113.
200 N.J. Crowson, *Britain and Europe: A Political History since 1918* (London: Routledge, 2011), pp. 120–125.
201 On Conservative Euroscepticism, see G. Morgan, *The Idea of a European Superstate: Public Justification and European Integration* (Princeton: Princeton University Press, 2005), pp. 58–64.
202 Kavanagh and Seldon suggest that on Europe the 'mood of the party changed after the 1992 election. A number of sceptics had suppressed their distaste for Maastricht in 1991 out of loyalty to Major and the need for unity before the general election . . . The Danish rejection of Maastricht in a referendum in June 1992 only emboldened the critics': Kavanagh and Seldon, *The Powers*, p. 235. In this sense, the Maastricht ratification debates were arguably more of a critical juncture for the debate on Europe in the UK than the events of 1989–1990. This increase in Euroscepticism in 1992 occurred despite the fact that, during the 1992 election campaign, Major's role in the Maastricht negotiations was hailed as a triumph: H. Young, *This Blessed Plot: Britain and Europe from Churchill to Blair* (Basingstoke: Macmillan, 1998), p. 435.
203 Forster, *Britain*, p. 170.
204 Buller, *National Statecraft*, pp. 146–149. On the difficulties for Major in resisting deeper European integration while participating in, and even chairing, the European Council, see *Le Monde*, 'L'Europe de Maastricht,' special supplement (August–September 1992), pp. 11–16.
205 See D. Hurd, *Memoirs* (London: Abacus, 2003), pp. 413–429.
206 See Crowson, *Britain*, pp. 122–123.
207 See Hurd, *Memoirs*, pp. 458–462.
208 J. Turner, *The Tories and Europe* (Manchester: Manchester University Press, 2000), pp. 142–143.

209 P. Cowley and J. Garry, 'The British Conservative Party and Europe: The Choosing of John Major,' *British Journal of Political Science* 28 (3) (1998): 473–499.
210 *Ibid.*
211 Cole, 'Political Leadership,' p. 137.
212 M. Foley, *John Major, Tony Blair and a Conflict of Leadership: Collision Course* (Manchester: Manchester University Press, 2002), p. 25.
213 A. Forster, *Britain and the Maastricht Negotiations* (Basingstoke: Palgrave, 1999), pp. 161–164.
214 J. Buller, *National Statecraft and European Integration: The Conservative Government and the European Union, 1979–1997* (London: Pinter, 2000), pp. 161–163.
215 See K. Larres, 'Schwierige Verbündete: Margaret Thatcher, John Major und die Politik Helmut Kohls,' in *Deutsche Europapolitik Christlicher Demokraten. Von Konrad Adenauer bis Angela Merkel (1945–2013)*, H.-J. Küsters ed. (Düsseldorf: Droste, 2014), pp. 267–269.
216 See Conservative Party manifesto titled 'Leading Europe into the 1990s. The Conservative manifesto for Europe 1989': HIA ESC/3.
217 Quoted in Nelsen and Stubb, *European Union*, p. 51.
218 *Ibid.*, p. 52.
219 M. Pugh, *State and Society: A Social and Political History of Britain since 1870*, fourth edition (London: Bloomsbury, 2012), pp. 359–361.
220 Major, *Autobiography*, p. 579.
221 P. Hennessy, *The Prime Minister: The Office and Its Holders since 1945* (London: Penguin, 2000), pp. 437–444.
222 Buller, *National Statecraft*, pp. 154–157.
223 Kavanagh and Seldon, *The Powers*, p. 207.
224 Hennessy, *Prime Minister*, p. 455.
225 *Hansard*, Commons, 6th ser., 213: 284–5.
226 *Ibid.*, 295.
227 *Ibid.*, 288.
228 Major, *Autobiography*, p. 580.
229 *Hansard*, Commons, 6th ser., 262: 895.
230 See Paterson, 'Helmut Kohl,' pp. 28–29.
231 Major, *Autobiography*, p. 274.
232 For this wait-and-see approach to European affairs, see Major's intervention in the House of Commons of 18 December 1992: *Hansard*, Commons, 6th ser., 216: 277.
233 See A. Seldon, *Major: A Political Life* (London: Phoenix, 1997).
234 Young, *This Blessed Plot*, p. 413.
235 Major, *Autobiography*, p. 584.
236 Turner, *Tories*, pp. 161–165.
237 Kavanagh and Seldon, *The Powers*, p. 230. This view is strengthened by Major's own assessment in his *Autobiography* (p. 585): 'My concern was twofold. First, what was right for Britain? Here I believed my policy of cautious engagement with Europe, but hostility to federalism, was the right approach. My second concern was whether this policy could unite the Conservative Party and prevent it from splintering.'
238 Foley, *John Major*, p. 33.
239 Seldon, *Major*, p. 360.
240 S. Hogg and J. Hill. 1995. *Too Close to Call: Power and Politics–John Major in No. 10* (London: Little, Brown and Company, 1995).
241 *Ibid.*, p. 78.

242 *Hansard*, Commons, 6th ser., 295: 819.
243 Hogg and Hill, *Too Close*, p. 78.
244 Major, *Autobiography*, pp. 586–587.
245 *Hansard*, Commons, 6th ser., 295: 814.
246 Major, *Autobiography*, pp. 586–587.
247 *Ibid.*, p. 585.
248 *Ibid.*, p. 580.
249 *Ibid.*, pp. 697–698.
250 Young, *This Blessed Plot*, p. 417.
251 Major, *Autobiography*, p. 585.
252 Quoted in *Ibid.*, pp. 586–587.
253 On Major's objective of preventing the project of political union, see *Hansard*, Commons, 6th ser., 216: 277.

6 What's next? From leadership to crisis management

In *Contesting Democracy*, Jan-Werner Müller writes that

> the creators of the European Community followed an indirect way of gaining legitimacy for their project: rather than having the peoples of the initial member states vote for supranational arrangements, they relied on technocratic and administrative measures agreed among elites to yield what Monnet time and again called 'concrete achievements' – which were eventually to persuade citizens that European integration was a good thing.[1]

Over the last six decades, much of European integration has occurred 'by stealth,'[2] through elite agreements, judicial decisions, and a deliberate focus on technical political matters – the so-called low politics.[3] In a context in which European integration was built in the shadow of the public's interest and approval, leaders, from Adenauer and Mollet to Mitterrand and Kohl, were able to exert a decisive influence over the construction of the EU. Today, it has become obvious that a focus on low politics is no longer enough.[4] While European integration has survived many challenges, none have been as existential as the current set of simultaneous crises: British withdrawal from the EU, the economic dysfunction inside the Eurozone, the refugee crisis, and the security threats emanating from Europe's immediate neighbourhood.[5] The Eurozone crisis in particular has blurred the differentiation between 'high' and 'low' politics and revealed profound inadequacies within the EU's governance architecture.[6] It laid bare the uneasy balance between competing supranational institutions on the one side and member states – each with different interests – on the other.[7] It also illustrated the growing economic and social divergence within the EU, with some member states struggling with massive unemployment, debts, and loss of productivity and global market share, while others – notably Germany – have almost full employment and run high current account and trade surpluses.[8] The 'concrete achievements' that were to garner public support have become costly burdens, and many Europeans ask: What for? Robert Kaplan claims that the very edifice of the EU is unravelling and that the old historic tensions in Europe risk reappearing.[9]

My purpose is not to recount the events of the Eurozone and migration crises, analyse the structural technical flaws of EMU that have now become apparent, or pass judgement on the recent institutional and policy responses.[10] Rather, it is to reflect on the changes in the modes of decision-making that are taking place in the EU, and what this means for the future of leadership in Europe.

Since the Maastricht Treaty came into force in 1993, much has changed as far as European integration is concerned. The Community of 12 has become a fully fledged European Union of 28 member states with a common currency (albeit not used by all), influential institutions with competences over ever more policy fields, a joint diplomatic service, and the profile of a global player on issues such as the mitigation of global climate change, development assistance, preventive diplomacy, and international justice. Yet these achievements cannot dispel the unsettling gradual erosion of the foundations of the EU, both in terms of public support and political legitimacy.[11] The irony is that this erosion is a result of the determined push for deeper integration and enlargement by national leaders and elites in the past, who then paid scant attention to the growing apathy and opposition among the public, or to the multiple economic and political warnings against premature integration and enlargement (notably by Thatcher, Major, and Tory Eurosceptics). Paradoxically, the proactive leadership of Mitterrand and Kohl in favour of integration and rapid enlargement in the 1990s and early 2000s has now turned into a full-blown leadership and confidence crisis, as EU and national leaders seem incapable of coming to terms with the economic, financial, and political fallout of the challenges now engulfing the EU.[12]

The challenges for the EU are significant and numerous. The most obvious indication that something is wrong is the fact that, in June 2016, the UK – Europe's most significant military power and its second-largest economy – decided to leave the EU altogether. That David Cameron felt compelled to call for a public vote illustrates both the continuity of the deep divide in Britain over Europe and a widespread sense of frustration with and disbelief in the workings of the EU.[13] It is also indicative of a major leadership gamble that went wrong. Just as a small majority of Britons voted for Brexit, the apprehension over what many perceive as a bureaucratisation and centralisation of power in Brussels and the erosion of meaningful national self-determination and sovereignty is likely to fester in other parts of Europe as well.[14]

Moreover, since 2010, the Eurozone financial and debt crisis has been unraveling the economic foundations of the European project, highlighting with unmistakable clarity the lack of economic convergence among EU economies as well as their vastly diverging degrees of fiscal health and competitiveness.[15] Due to prolonged recession and economic stagnation, calls for protectionism, which are anathema to the idea of a common market, have proliferated in Italy and other underperforming economies.[16]

Its legal foundations have been weakened by the way in which key European norms and pieces of legislation have been bent, ignored, and sidelined – by member states and EU bodies (such as the European Central Bank) alike – not only to allow for the emergency rescue bailouts for Greece and others but also to supersede and circumvent painful and politically undesirable adjustments and sanctions. The deception by Greek authorities to get into the Euro, Germany and France's dilution of the Stability Pact in 2004, and the insistence not to accept the Irish people's rejection – in a 2008 referendum – of the Lisbon Treaty, are cases in point of the gradual hollowing out of common norms.

The social foundations of the European project have come under severe duress as a consequence of the high levels of unemployment, the austerity measures imposed as a condition for bailout rescues, and the necessity of pulling a number of European economies – Greece, Ireland, Portugal, Spain, Italy, and Cyprus – back from the brink of insolvency by drastically reducing budget deficits. European integration promised stability and prosperity, but now the Eurozone's monetary and economic framework makes socially explosive structural adjustments to governmental spending, welfare systems, and public services unavoidable.

The political foundations of the European project have been challenged by the way in which independent judicial systems and democratic rules and institutions have been twisted by populist governments in new member states such as Hungary, Romania, Bulgaria, and, more recently, Poland.

Last but not least, the ideational foundations of European unity have been called into question through the emergence of overtly anti-EU, anti-immigrant, and anti-Islamic political movements all across the continent, ranging from the *Perussuomalaiset* (True Finns) and the *Danske Folkeparti* (Danish People's Party) in the north, to Geert Wilders's *Partij voor de Vrijheid* (Party of Freedom) and France's *Front National* in the west, Hungary's *Jobbik* in the east, and Greece's neo-fascist Χρυσή Αυγή (Golden Dawn) in the south. All across Europe, political movements are gaining traction advocating values which are diametrically opposed to those espoused by the EU.[17] Even in Germany, where Euroscepticism has traditionally been only a marginal political force, the *Alternative für Deutschland* (AfD) is making inroads while calling into question both the Euro and the freedom of movement within the EU. The populist and Eurosceptic challenge to the project of European integration has been exacerbated by the rapid increase in arrivals of refugees and asylum-seekers fleeing from multiple conflicts in Syria, Iraq, and elsewhere.

A perception that the EU is in a deep crisis has gained ground among public opinion and elites alike.[18] Commission President Jean-Claude Juncker warned in his 2015 *State of the Union* address that the EU cannot go on 'with business as usual': 'There is not enough Europe in this Union. And there is not enough Union in this Union.'[19] The enthusiasm that emerged in parallel with the integration milestones marked throughout the 1990s and early 2000s has dissipated. Even the academic commentary that embraced the optimism about and prospects for European unity – T.R. Reid's *The United States of Europe*, Jeremy Rifkin's *The European Dream*, and Stephen Hill's *Europe's Promise* – has aged rapidly and now seems oddly misplaced.[20]

Since May 2009, European leaders have time and again held emergency summits to stem the crisis. Large emergency rescue funds – the 440 billion Euro *European Financial Stability Facility* and the 500 billion Euro *European Stability Mechanism* – have been created to provide the financial wherewithal to counter doubts about the potential insolvency of Eurozone member states. The European Central Bank has kept interests at record lows, initiated a controversial bond purchase programme, and provided almost one trillion Euro in three-year low-interest loans to banks as part of two *Long-Term Refinancing Operations*.[21] Governments all across Europe have adopted emergency austerity packages, cutting public spending and raising taxes even in the face of the public's fierce opposition.

Arguably, given these determined efforts to solve the financial and economic crisis, it would seem counterintuitive to speak of a 'leadership crisis.'[22] But despite the efforts of Europe's leaders – Angela Merkel in Germany; Nicolas Sarkozy and François Hollande in France; Mario Monti, Enrico Letta, and Matteo Renzi in Italy; Mariano Rajoy in Spain; and the ECB's Mario Draghi – little has been achieved in terms of solving the underlying reasons for the disarray.[23] The question is: Why have their sustained efforts not led to significant improvements? Why has so much concentrated EU policy-making and diplomacy been considered so inadequate by citizens and investors alike? What are the origins of the 'leadership crisis' and what does this mean for Europe?

Finding an answer to these questions makes it necessary to revisit the elements that made for successful leadership interventions in the past and assess how the opportunities for the exercise of leadership on the European stage have diminished.

From leadership to leadership crisis

Since its inception, European integration has resulted from key agreements and compromises among member states that were produced, engineered, or brokered by a few determined leaders. I maintain that we are now witnessing a shift within European diplomacy and EU decision-making that has the effect of diminishing the incentives politicians have to exercise leadership at the highest level.[24] Without this leadership the European integration process stalls.

Ironically, it can be argued that the EU has become a victim of its own success. The very enabling conditions for integration have begun to unravel over time. Because of numerous rounds of enlargement, the informal decision-making channels that lay at the heart of the leadership constellations in the past have become less effective. Giving purpose and direction to the process of European integration was difficult enough with six, 12, or 15 members, but it has proved to be almost unmanageable with 28 member states. The costs of integration – and EMU in particular – remained hidden in times of economic growth but are visible and palpable in times of recession and stagnation. The emotional attachment to integration has waned as Europe has become more peaceful and less threatened by external powers. In addition, the institutional architecture of the EU has evolved in ways that were not foreseen when it were first established. Progressively, the EU as a system of regional governance has become a much more overtly political and ideological project, gradually distancing itself from its sectoral, technical, and functional origins. Many Europeans have come to actively dislike this centralisation of competences in Brussels and the idea of an ever-closer union.[25] Yet there are also other transformations in European politics that have important effects on exercise of leadership and deserve closer analytical scrutiny.

Enhanced cooperation

The first transformation that has limited the opportunities for leadership came in the wake of EMU. The creation of the Euro was a departure from the conventional pathway of European integration insofar as it set a precedent for the emergence of an *Europe à deux vitesses* (two-speed Europe).[26] Until 1991, all member states operated on a shared *acquis communautaire*, or what Jean-Claude Piris calls a 'unity dogma.'[27] But as was illustrated in the previous chapter, Mitterrand and Kohl did not want to be constrained in their ambitions by the most integration-reluctant member states (which at the time were the UK and Denmark). In consequence, they accommodated Major's requests for opt-outs to the single currency, the Social Chapter, and other provisions on justice and home affairs cooperation. By doing so, all leaders got what they wanted: Mitterrand got Kohl to give up the Deutschmark, Kohl got acceptance of German unification, and Major got the retention of significant national sovereignty. This way, a lengthy and acrimonious negotiation process that would have ended badly for Major was avoided. Yet ever since, the EU has been divided into separate camps of member states.

This is not only about some member states using the Euro while others do not. The opt-outs have the effect of fragmenting the institutional, legal, and normative cohesion of the EU as multi-level system of governance.[28] Article 10 of the Lisbon Treaty codified this form of 'enhanced cooperation' into EU law.[29] While this allows for higher degrees of flexibility in the instruments of integration among like-minded member states (at least nine), it concurrently enhances the ability of governments to pick and choose which integration initiative they want to be part of. Furthermore, it leads to a less clear-cut application of common legal norms to all member states. To give an example: do the rules governing the economic management of the Eurozone also apply to non-Eurozone states when they affect the common market? The trend towards enhanced cooperation exacerbates the distance in terms of preferences between Eurozone and non-Eurozone member states and increases the likelihood of legal disputes.

The structure of multi-level governance within the EU has become more and more complex as more and more instances of enhanced cooperation are created. The unintended effect of this growing lack of cohesion is the consolidation of subgroups of member states that push for or block major EU policy initiatives.

Germany and other countries with a high influx of refugees and asylum-seekers are interested in the creation of a common EU immigration and asylum-processing system, but Poland, Hungary, Slovenia, Croatia, and others are vehemently opposed. The outcome might well be a form of enhanced cooperation on immigration and asylum policy in some parts of Western Europe (Denmark has an opt-out) but not in Central and Eastern Europe. What results from this growing policy heterogeneity is the formation of smaller 'coalitions of the willing,' with a more pronounced absence among heads of government of a sense of responsibility for the EU as a whole. Even if leadership constellations emerge at the European level, they are increasingly confined to these subgroups rather than the EU as a common entity. The 'Merkozy' tandem became influential in the initial phase of the Eurozone crisis, but was less able to exert influence in non-Eurozone countries.[30]

Referendums

The second major transformation that has altered the effectiveness of leadership constellations in the management of EU affairs is the usage of national referendums on core issues about the EU. The Brexit referendum was a veritable watershed moment in the history of postwar European integration. In Britain the call for a referendum on EU membership had been a long-standing *cause célèbre* of Eurosceptic backbenchers and conservative commentators in the media. In France, the September 1992 Maastricht referendum set a benchmark for public involvement in major treaty revisions and transfers of sovereignty. François Hollande committed France to a referendum on Turkish EU membership, thereby de facto reducing the likelihood of future EU enlargement. In 2005, a number of national referendums were held across Europe to ratify the European Constitutional Treaty. In Spain and Luxembourg a majority voted in favour, but in France and the Netherlands it was rejected. In Denmark and Ireland, where referendums are constitutionally mandated, majorities voted against EU treaties in the past (the Danes voted against the Maastricht Treaty in June 1992 and the Irish against the Lisbon Treaty in June 2008), only to be asked to vote again after cosmetic concessions and further opt-outs were arranged.

Since the debacle of the 1992 Maastricht referendum, it has become apparent that whenever consulted, majorities of national electorates tend to favour the status quo over new integration initiatives. Referendums thus illustrate a significant dichotomy between elite and public support for European integration. In a similar fashion to the Brexit vote, in the 2003 Swedish referendum on the Euro, virtually all major political parties, leaders, and influential media outlets advocated a 'yes' vote for the Euro. Yet it was rejected by an ample majority of over 56 per cent.[31] The same happened in the Dutch and French plebiscites in 2005, when the electorate rejected a ratification of the Constitutional Treaty that was favoured by all major political actors. Increasingly, elite and public sentiments about the EU no longer overlap.

The effect of referendums on the integration process are twofold. On the one hand, if referendums are held, the chance of a rejection of further steps to deepen or enlarge the EU is very high. On the other hand, if major initiatives are agreed to without a referendum, through a parliamentary vote, this increases the cynical view among many voters that integration takes place 'by stealth,' i.e. that the parliamentary route was chosen with the intention of overriding the public's likely disapproval. This exacerbates the public's emotive perception that the EU is 'undesirable' and 'out of control.'[32]

Referendums are a major gamble for Europe's politicians. David Cameron had called for a referendum on EU membership in order to escape the same stranglehold within the Conservative Party that hamstrung Major's government in the 1990s. Yet the risks are significant: he lost both the referendum and his political career. By contrast, had he won the referendum, his stature at home and in Europe would have been much enhanced. Most politicians are too risk-averse to take such a gamble. The spectre of a lost referendum diminishes the opportunities for leadership because it forces politicians to take unequivocal sides on a specific issue and sets them up for the prospect of failure.

The growing use of national referendums in EU matters means that a negative vote in one country can block all measures requiring unanimity, such as enlargement, treaty changes, or free trade agreements. This contributes to an acute immobilism when it comes to reforming fundamental aspects of EU governance. In consequence, there is a significant incentive for politicians to engineer changes to EU governance in such a way that they do not require referendums to be held. This leads to a vicious circle: it exacerbates the public's perception of pursuing 'integration by stealth' and reinforces the calls for future referendums. This sentiment has increased in the wake of the ratification process for the Lisbon Treaty, when Denmark, Britain, and France painstakingly tried to prevent another public vote.

French public opinion

The third transformation that has diminished the opportunities for leadership in Europe is the growing disillusionment with European integration in French public opinion.[33] Ever since Robert Schuman first tabled his idea for a joint Franco-German authority for the coal and steel industries on 9 May 1950, France has been the major political driving force of the integration process. The major innovations and compromises in the history of European integration reflect outcomes that were acceptable to France and its leaders. The French public has been broadly supportive of European integration, as long as France's central leadership role in European affairs was safeguarded. Yet the 1992 Maastricht referendum signalled a change in underlying perceptions of France's position in the EU among the French public. Many French have since become more apprehensive about the language of federation, the degree of institutional supranationalism, and the palpable loss of meaningful French national sovereignty. The 'permissive consensus' for the gradual construction of an integrated Europe has noticeably diminished.

The shift in French public opinion is due to a variety of reasons.[34] Economic stagnation, unemployment, disaffection with establishment politicians and parties, and the fear of a loss of national sovereignty and cultural identity have combined to reduce the popular acclaim for the EU and its institutions. Since the early 2000s, a significant part of the French electorate has given support to the *Front National*, which advocates policies and values that stand in diametrical opposition to the aspirations and activities of the EU. While its electoral success has been limited, it is nonetheless worrying that approximately one third of French voters voted for the FN in the first round of the 2015 regional elections.[35]

Political populism and extremism is not confined to France, but its impact on the nature of European politics is more significant than elsewhere because of France's centrality in European affairs. The more French public opinion becomes apathetic to and divided over the EU and the desirability of further integration, the less likely it is that French politicians will decide to invest their political capital and personal prestige in the pursuit of leadership on EU affairs. In the future, it will be increasingly difficult to build a united Europe against the wishes of the French electorate.

Power disequilibrium

The third transformation that has taken place in European politics is the return of power imbalances within the EU. Christopher Bickerton *et al.* identity a 'profound state of disequilibrium' within the EU, with moments of instability and contradiction becoming more frequent and pronounced than in the past.[36] Partially, this is a result of significant divergences in terms of relative financial power and economic competitiveness among EU member states. But it is also due to a differentiation among member states in their ability to exert influence over EU policy-making as a whole. To put it in a nutshell: France is willing but no longer able to lead, Britain is neither willing nor interested in leading, and Germany is capable but reluctant to lead, and clueless on how to do so Paradoxically, Germany's growing position of strength in Europe risks reactivating old animosities and mistrust about Germany's role in Europe, while its indecision leads to questions about whether it does indeed have the will and capacity for leadership in Europe.

Jürgen Habermas wrote in 2013 that the Eurozone crisis is first and foremost 'a crisis of the German political class' which is not grasping its own responsibility for the effects its handling of the crisis has on the rest of continent.[37] Yet Germany's relative strength sits uncomfortably next to French weakness to balance German interests. The Franco-German partnership at the heart of the integration process is becoming more asymmetrical as a response to the fragility of the French economy, high unemployment, and social fragmentation.[38] Germany has emerged as the more prominent and influential of the two partners not by design but by default. In fact, Germany's postwar history and evolution as a democratic society mitigate against the prospect of German domination in

European affairs, even though its national identity is gradually changing.[39] The German political establishment may be uncomfortable with its growing influence in Europe, but events elsewhere require Germany to make difficult choices that affect the rest of Europe as well.

The Russian annexation of Crimea in March 2014, the ongoing conflicts in Syria, Iraq, Libya, and Yemen, and the threat of Jihadi terrorism have accentuated geopolitical rifts within Europe itself. EU member states struggle to find common ground on these challenges. To give just a few examples: Britain has been largely inactive over the Ukrainian conflict, while Germany's traditional closeness to Russia has nurtured suspicions, particularly in Central and Eastern Europe. The German handling of the refugee crisis has occurred without much coordination and consultation with Paris, London, and Rome. After two major terrorist attacks in Paris in 2015, President Hollande has come to favour punitive military action against targets in the Middle East, which elicited only scant support from Germany and other member states.

In a way not dissimilar to 1989, geopolitical events are heightening the global stature and visibility of Germany as Europe's preeminent power. While this is beneficial for Angela Merkel – since it entails a broader potential horizon of leadership opportunities – it also comes with the expectation that she can deliver viable solutions to Europe's challenges. In fact, as Gerd Langguth claims, she comes across in Europe as the 'Madame No'[40] who insists on economic austerity, is reluctant and indecisive on security matters, and is disillusioned by the lack of European support for her migration and asylum policy.

Lessons

The question arising from these transformations in Europe is: What does this mean for the future exercise of political leadership on European integration? David Dunn notes in his analysis of summit diplomacy that meetings of heads of government serve the purpose of 'breaking down the barriers of mutual suspicion which inevitably exist between two parties who are unfamiliar with each other.'[41] Summits are the backdrop where leaders meet each other, explore possibilities for negotiations, and gain or lose trust in each other. In the EU, summit diplomacy has become an institutionalised form of decision-making, yet the sheer proliferation of summits has also undermined its effectiveness. Summits have become more formal and less personal. The discussions at summits have gradually moved away from 'big picture' meetings of minds to more detailed and technical policy briefs. Increasingly, summits have become role-play for Europe's heads of government. In these meetings of 28 leaders, it is all too easy to slip into a routine of speeches and declarations rather than purposeful guidance of policy-making.

Ever more, the summit diplomacy that used to be the backdrop and conduit for the emergence of leadership constellations in support of European integration has evolved into a routinised platform for reactive crisis management. A tougher economic environment, a more apprehensive public, a more complex and fragmented legal and institutional system for decision-making, and a growing disparity among the power of EU member states diminishes the incentives and opportunities for individual leaders to take substantial risks on EU affairs.

As we have seen in the previous chapters, leadership opportunities often arise at times of turmoil and crisis. Joseph Nye notes that leaders can harness the generative power of crises to enhance their prospects for leadership by nurturing a 'visible dramatisation of urgency' to increase the willingness of others to 'grant leaders exceptional powers.'[42] In Europe's current circumstances, its leaders have tried to do the opposite: they have attempted to calm markets, restore confidence in the viability of the Eurozone, and display a high degree of policy and institutional continuity. The consequence of the current combination of a protracted economic crisis and the heightened risks of leadership is a shift away from transformational leadership towards transactional and reactive crisis management. Rather than seeking autonomy on EU affairs in order to reform, recalibrate, and redesign the purpose and mechanisms of European integration, the political energies of Europe's heads of government are channelled towards maintaining the status quo.

This bodes ill for the future of purposeful political leadership in the context of European integration. The ability of politicians to generate enthusiasm and support is easier when the purpose is to build and generate something rather than preserve something from decay. The former mantra, that European integration leads to peace, stability, consolidation of democracy, and prosperity, no longer reflects the day-to-day realities of many Europeans. A significant portion of Europeans feels threatened by economic insecurity, high levels of immigration, Jihadi terrorism, Russian aggression, and the indifference of their political elites. They turn to what they know best – the nation-state. The rise in nativist populism in Europe is in no small part due to the growing fear that European integration will gradually erase the uniqueness of Europe's nations and national cultures. Incidentally, the rhetoric of European integration exacerbates this sense of dis-belonging because it positions the cause of European unification in opposition to the narrowness of nationalism. The transformative leadership that shaped so many critical junctures of European integration will not reappear as long as the stated purpose of leadership is to merely prevent the growing fragmentation of the EU as a system of governance.

Notes

1 J.-W. Müller, *Contesting Democracy: Political Ideas in Twentieth-Century Europe* (New Haven, CT: Yale University Press, 2011), p. 142.
2 *Ibid.*
3 See G. Majone, *Dilemmas of European Integration: The Ambiguities and Pitfalls of Integration through Stealth* (Oxford: Oxford University Press, 2005). On the role of elites, see H. Best, G. Lengyel, and L. Verzichelli eds., *The Europe of Elites: A Study into the Europeanness of Europe's Political and Economic Elites* (Oxford: Oxford University Press, 2012).
4 D. Marquand, *The End of the West: The Once and Future Europe* (Princeton: Princeton University Press, 2011), pp. 108–109.

5. *Frankfurter Allgemeine Zeitung:* 'Die Fundamente der EU sind bedroht' (23 June 2015). On European security, see A. Menon, 'The Other Euro Crisis: Why Europe Desperately Needs Military Collaboration,' *Foreign Affairs* (13 December 2013): https://www.foreignaffairs.com/articles/western-europe/2013-12-10/other-euro-crisis
6. C.J. Bickerton, D. Hodson, and U. Puetter, 'The New Intergovernmentalism and the Study of European Integration,' in *New Intergovernmentalism: States and Supranational Actors in the Post-Maastricht Era*, C.J. Bickerton, D. Hodson, and U. Puetter eds. (Oxford: Oxford University Press, 2015), p. 35. See also N. Berggruen and N. Gardels, *Intelligent Governance for the 21st Century: A Middle Way between West and East* (Cambridge: Polity, 2013), pp. 164–165.
7. Y. Doutriaux and C. Lequesne, *Les Institutions de l'Union Européenne Après la Crise Euro* (Paris: La Documentation Française, 2013).
8. J. Pisani-Ferry, *The Euro Crisis and Its Aftermath* (Oxford: Oxford University Press, 2014).
9. *The Wall Street Journal*: 'Robert Kaplan: Europe's New Medieval Map' (15 January 2016).
10. On the Eurozone crisis, see J. van Overtveldt, *The End of the Euro: The Uneasy Future of the European Union* (Chicago: B2 Books, 2011); F.M. Bongiovanni, *The Decline and Fall of Europe* (Basingstoke: Palgrave Macmillan, 2012); C. Lapavitsas, A. Kaltenbrunner, G. Labrindis, D. Lindo, J. Meadway, J. Michell, J.P. Painceira, E. Pires, J. Powell, A. Stenfords, N. Teles, and L. Vatikotis, *Crisis in the Eurozone* (London: Verso, 2012).
11. V.A. Schmidt, 'The Eurozone's Crisis of Democratic Legitimacy: Can the EU Rebuild Public Trust and Support for European Economic Integration?' European Commission, *Fellowship Initiative 2014–2015*, Discussion paper 015 (September 2015): 1–56: http://ec.europa.eu/economy_finance/publications/eedp/pdf/dp015_en.pdf
12. M. Sandbu, *Europe's Orphan: The Future of the Euro and the Politics of Debt* (Princeton: Princeton University Press, 2015).
13. R. Liddle, *The Europe Dilemma: Britain and the Drama of EU Integration* (London: I.B. Tauris, 2014).
14. See A. Giddens, *Turbulent and Mighty Continent: What Future for Europe?* (Cambridge: Polity, 2014).
15. D. Marsh, *The Euro: The Battle for the New Global Currency* (New Haven, CT: Yale University Press, 2011); R. Herzog, C. Mestre, and Y. Petit, *La Crise Financière et Budgétaire en Europe. Un Moment de Verité pour la Construction Européenne* (Nancy: Presses Universitaires de Nancy, 2013).
16. See A. Somma, *La Dittatura dello Spread. Germania, Europa e Crisi del Debito* (Milano: Derive Approdi, 2014).
17. See T. Pauwels, *Populism in Western Europe: Comparing Belgium, Germany, and the Netherlands* (London: Routledge, 2014).
18. *Frankfurter Allgemeine Zeitung*: 'Ach, Europa' (31 January 2016).
19. J.-C. Juncker, 'State of the Union: Time for Honesty, Unity, and Solidarity' (9 September 2015): http://europa.eu/rapid/press-release_SPEECH-15-5614_en.htm
20. T.R. Reid, *The United States of Europe: From Euro to Eurovision–the Superpower Nobody Talks About* (London: Penguin, 2004); J. Rifkin, *The European Dream: How Europe's Vision of the Future Is Quietly Eclipsing the American Dream* (Cambridge: Polity, 2004); S. Hill, *Europe's Promise: Why the European Way Is the Best Hope in an Insecure Age* (Berkeley: University of California Press, 2010). See also U. Beck and E. Grande, *Das kosmopolitische Europa* (Frankfurt: Suhrkamp, 2004).
21. See D. Marsh, *Europe's Deadlock: How the Euro Crisis Could Be Solved–and Why It Won't Happen* (New Haven, CT: Yale University Press, 2013).

22 For a critical view of the evolution of EU governance, see C. Joerges and C. Glinski eds., *The European Crisis and the Transformation of Transnational Governance: Authoritarian Managerialism versus Democratic Governance* (Oxford: Hart, 2014).
23 Ibid.
24 T. Chopin, *La Fracture Politique de l'Europe: Crise de Légitimité et Déficit Politique* (Paris: Promoculture, 2015).
25 On the problem of EU legitimacy and the disjuncture between positive and negative integration, see: F. Scharpf, *Governing in Europe: Effective and Democratic?* (Oxford: Oxford University Press, 1999), pp. 11–13.
26 J. Pisani-Ferry, 'L'Europe à géométrie variable: une analyse économique,' *Politique Étrangère* 60 (2) (1995): 447–465.
27 J.-C. Piris, 'The Acceleration of Differentiated Integration and Enhanced Cooperation,' *Fondation Robert Schuman–European Issues* 328 (13 October 2014): 1–5. See also J.M. Beneyto, J. Baquero, B. Becerril, M. Bolle, M. Cremona, S. Ehret, V. Lopez-Ibor, and J. Mallo, *Unity and Flexibility in the Future of the European Union: The Challenge of Enhanced Cooperation* (Madrid: CEU Ediciones, 2009).
28 R. Adler-Nissen, *Opting Out of the European Union: Diplomacy, Sovereignty, and European Integration* (Cambridge: Cambridge University Press, 2014), pp. 25–46; A. Hinarejos, *The Euro Area Crisis in Constitutional Perspective* (Oxford: Oxford University Press, 2015).
29 Treaty of Lisbon (2007/C 306/01): http://eur-lex.europa.eu/legal-content/EN/TXT/?uri=uriserv:OJ.C_.2007.306.01.0001.01.ENG&toc=OJ:C:2007:306:TOC.
30 U. Guérot and T. Klau, 'After Merkozy: How France and Germany Can Make Europe Work,' *European Council of Foreign Relations Policy Brief* 56 (May 2012): 1–11: http://www.ecfr.eu/page/-/ECFR56_FRANCE_GERMANY_BRIEF_AW.pdf
31 European Commission, 'Post-Referendum in Sweden,' *Flash Eurobarometer* 149 (October 2003): http://ec.europa.eu/public_opinion/flash/fl149_en.pdf
32 See J. Garry, 'Emotions and Voting in EU Referendums,' *European Union Politics* 15 (2) (2014): 235–254; M. Maier, J. Maier, A. Baumert, N. Jahn, S. Krause, and S. Adam, 'Measuring Citizens' Implicit and Explicit Attitudes towards the European Union,' *European Union Politics* 16 (3) (2015): 369–385.
33 A comprehensive overview of changes in public opinion can be found at: Pew Research Centre, Global Attitudes & Trends, *A Fragile Rebound for the EU Image on Eve of European Parliament Elections* (12 May 2014): http://www.pewglobal.org/2014/05/12/a-fragile-rebound-for-eu-image-on-eve-of-european-parliament-elections/.
34 S. Bornschier, 'France: The Model Case of Party System Transformation,' in *West European Politics in the Age of Globalisation*, H. Kriesi, E. Grande, R. Lachat, M. Dolezal, S. Bornschier, and T. Frey eds. (Cambridge: Cambridge University Press, 2008), pp. 85–90.
35 See Ministère de l'Intérieur: http://www.interieur.gouv.fr/Elections/Elections-regionales-2015/Resultats-du-premier-tour-des-elections-regionales-2015
36 Bickerton, Hodson, and Puetter, 'New Intergovernmentalism,' pp. 37–38.
37 *Der Spiegel:* 'Jürgen Habermas: Ein Fall von Elitenversagen' (5 August 2013). See also *Süddeutsche Zeitung:* 'Jürgen Habermas: Merkels von Demoskopie geleiteter Opportunismus' (7 April 2011).
38 D. Vernet, 'Le Lack ist ab. Warum die deutsch-französische Zusammenarbeit nicht mehr das ist, was sie einmal war,' *Internationale Politik und Gesellschaft* (22 December 2014), http://www.ipg-journal.de/kommentar/artikel/le-lack-ist-ab-704/

39 R. Vogt and C. Li, 'German National Identity: Moving beyond Guilt,' in *European National Identities: Elements, Transitions, Conflicts*, R. Vogt, W. Cristaudo, and A. Leutzsch eds. (New Brunswick: Transaction, 2014), pp. 71–93.
40 G. Langguth, 'Die Europapolitik Angela Merkels,' in *Deutsche Europapolitik Christlicher Demokraten. Von Konrad Adenauer bis Angela Merkel (1945–2013)*, H.J. Küsters ed. (Düsseldorf: Droste, 2014), p. 289.
41 D. Dunn, 'How Useful Is Summitry?,' in *Diplomacy at the Highest Level: The Evolution of International Summitry*, D. Dunn ed. (Basingstoke: Macmillan, 1996), p. 248.
42 J.S. Nye, *The Powers to Lead* (Oxford: Oxford University Press, 2008), p. 103.

Conclusion

Leadership and the fragility of institutions

Since the end of World War II, the growth of international organisations and regimes has become one of the most characteristic and enduring features of our contemporary international order.[1] European integration is part of this larger trend towards ever-denser institutionalised forms of cooperation and coordination between states.

The proliferation and consolidation of international organisations, treaties, regimes, and agreements has profoundly affected the governance of modern states and the way states interact – in Europe and elsewhere. It has also influenced both public perceptions of and scholarship on what institutions can and should deliver and accomplish. In Europe, the rhetoric of integration, unity, and a common destiny meant that the bar of expectations was set very high. European integration has been sold to a frequently apathetic and largely disinterested public as a preferable path to securing Europe's peace, prosperity, and power in the world. The institutional edifice of the EU has been invoked as a bulwark against petty nationalisms, the temptations of populism, and the dangers of dictatorship. In 2012, the EU was even awarded the Nobel Peace Prize for its contribution to making war a distant memory for most Europeans.

Yet much of the shine has come off the quest for ever-closer union since the economic and financial crisis began to bite in 2010. Ever since, and in rapid succession, many deficiencies in the EU's institutional, legal, and political architecture have become apparent. Austerity, economic stagnation, and unemployment have greatly reduced the enthusiasm for deeper integration – both in those countries (like Greece) that suffer most from the economic crisis and those (like France) who will have to make substantial financial commitments to secure the survival of the Eurozone and the EU.[2] The EU has also been caught on the back-foot by Russian aggression in Ukraine, turmoil in the Middle East, and the challenge of a major global refugee crisis.

From the diplomatic historian's point of view, the faith we place in institutions seems premature, if not naive. After all, empires and states have come and gone, companies have emerged and disappeared, and international organisations have flourished and withered away. To believe that the institutions of the state or the EU are capable of growing stronger through every crisis, and that they are always capable of solving the continent's most pressing concerns, is to overestimate the extent to which institutions have to be continuously socially reproduced through behaviour, political support, and economic necessity.

Institutions atrophy and decay when they lose track of or outgrow their purpose and fail to inspire significant elite and public support. In the case of the EU, there is a growing mismatch between what the EU – as a network of institutions and a system of governance – aspires to do and is capable of doing, and what is politically acceptable and desirable. It has been pointed out that it is unlikely that a return to economic growth in Europe is going to save the EU from the problems of its thin legitimacy and democratic accountability, rising anti-Islamic populism, and ever-deeper discrepancies between rich and poor Europeans.[3] To many Europeans, the EU is surprisingly ill-prepared and hamstrung when it comes to addressing the continent's most urgent challenges: the structural imbalances within the Eurozone, the collapse of the Middle East and the refugee flows this gives rise to, and the dual threats of terrorism and Russian expansionism. As the British referendum on EU withdrawal has shown, substantial parts of the European electorate have turned against the project of ever-closer union as the costs of integration have become apparent at a personal level.

My point is not to apportion blame and responsibility for the current state of affairs, but merely to illustrate that these problems will not just solve themselves. Addressing them will require – just as in the past – determined and innovative leadership at the highest level. Institutions thrive and flourish when they are backed up by the support of key constituents, but they stumble and fail when key constituents lose faith in them. The resurgence of Germany as the major power in Europe, the British referendum on EU membership, and the growing opposition to the EU among the French electorate are tell-tale signs of significant structural shifts inside the EU.[4] The fact that relatively new EU member states, such as Hungary and Poland, have powerful political movements that seek to distance themselves from the core values of European integration should give pause for thought. Why have large segments of the public, even in countries which euphorically embraced the EU only a few years ago, and which have benefited from EU membership in economic terms, turned against the project of European integration so quickly? The growing dissatisfaction with the state of affairs in the EU is palpable, and is something that needs to be addressed.[5] There is a fundamental tension between what people expect of the EU and what the EU is and does.[6]

Leadership, political will, and personal diplomacy are not a magic wand that can be applied to remedy every challenge Europe faces. They are not a *sufficient* condition for change to occur in the EU but a *necessary* one. Institutions and the law have the effect of constraining the autonomy of the actors within any given political system. In the early years of European integration, when the degree of institutionalisation was low and major parameters of the EU's legal system had yet to form, Adenauer, Mollet, Spaak, Eden, de Gaulle, and others had ample possibilities to make a substantial imprint on the course of the integration process if they chose to. But as the network of institutions has grown thicker, as the body of law, jurisprudence, and precedent has increased, and as more and more national vetoes have been abolished, the opportunities for the exercise of leadership at the highest level have diminished. In an EU with 28 diverse member states, powerful institutions guarding their prerogatives, and a multitude of influential interest groups, the difference individual leaders can make is much smaller than when the EU was a club of six relatively like-minded countries whose main challenge was to work out deep-seated differences between Paris and Bonn. Today, even when the leaders of France and Germany agree – after a bout of personal diplomacy – the effects of their decision-making are much less significant than in the past.

This inverted correlation between the density of institutions and leadership opportunities is something that both the structuralist and institutionalist literatures have not paid enough attention to. Institutions have unintended outcomes and consequences. It was certainly not the rationale of the Euro to increase political tensions and socio-economic divergences among Eurozone members rather than bringing them together.[7] It was certainly not the intention of successive rounds of enlargements to create a cumbersome and unwieldy governance structure which is capable of high levels of bureaucratic activity but unable to effectively address the continent's urgent challenges.[8] Fixing these problems requires leadership, but the reduction of leadership opportunities is precisely one of the side-effects of higher degrees of institutionalisation.

The broader point to be made about the role of institutions in international affairs is that they are durable but fragile. They are durable because they are quite 'sticky' (i.e. they tend not to disappear), but fragile because they run the risk of becoming irrelevant. In their study of international organisations and the growing bureaucratisation of world politics, Michael Barnett and Martha Finnemore cast doubt on a number of the conceptual premises of structuralist and institutionalist literature. International organisations do not always serve the interests of powerful states or do what states want them to do. Likewise, they are also prone to produce 'inefficient, self-defeating outcomes and turn their backs on those whom they are supposed to serve.'[9]

This is a central danger for the whole project of European unification. The decay of international organisations begins when major states decide to no longer follow the agreed-upon procedures. The 'spirit' of many of the key compromises on which the EU is built has long been violated. For all their professions of loyalty to the European cause, governments of the EU's most powerful member states have bent or ignored major rules. While this behaviour is common in international organisations, it nonetheless sets a problematic precedent when the most powerful countries decide not to follow the rules whenever doing so is politically expedient. This is particularly the case for the EU, whose main foundation is a shared body of law and norms. The Stability Pact for the Eurozone, the Schengen and Dublin agreements, and many of the rules for macroeconomic and fiscal management introduced since 2010 are already being watered down or ignored.

The EU has become entangled in a Gordian knot. Fundamental reforms to its system of governance and its institutional competences require treaty change. Yet treaty change is highly unlikely, since it requires unanimous ratification, which it is all too easily unpicked in one of the 28 member states.[10] Given that the prospect for a major reconfiguration of the EU's tasks and purpose is blocked, other, more flexible, kinds of avenues for decision-making are being explored. Since the Eurozone crisis, most of the policy instruments to tackle Europe's economic and financial problems have been established within the remit of Eurozone countries and under the authority of the Council of the European Union, where member states are in charge. This 'new intergovernmentalism'[11] becomes a problem not only because it separates Eurozone and non-Eurozone states but also because it falters whenever member states begin to deviate from agreements. Fearing precedents and tit-for-tat reprisals, member states are structurally reluctant to agree to sanctioning infractions, preferring instead to compromise the agreed-upon rules. The outcome is that member states begin to pick and choose which agreements to follow and when to ignore them. Meanwhile, the European Commission, which could exercise a more muscular executive authority to enforce the implementation of agreements, has been shut out from many new decision-making processes.

In 1957, 1969, and 1990, a grand bargain among key leaders was able to break the knot in which the integration process had become stuck. Today, this form of grand bargain is not only much less likely to emerge in the first place, but would also be less influential even if it does come about. It has been argued that what Europe needs, now more than ever, is a decisive push for a fully fledged federation.[12] Yet this line of argumentation is flawed for two reasons. On the one hand, it overestimates the desire for federalism among European leaders. On the other, it is blind to the dangerous consequences this will have: a choice between integration and democracy.[13] As the push for federal Europe currently lacks popular support, any movements to pursue higher degrees of integration and federalisation by stealth will have the direct effect of undermining democracy in Europe.[14]

In the preface to his book *The End of Power*, Moisés Naím writes about the dichotomy between the widespread perception of politicians as being powerful and the actual constraints and limitations of the offices they hold.[15] Naím is correct in asserting that most people who find themselves in positions of power can ultimately do and change very little. Yet this renders the leadership of those who can and do change the environments they encounter even more remarkable.

As I have argued throughout this book, the belief in the geopolitical origins or functional viability of international organisations underestimates the extent to which the institutions of the EU were themselves products of political will and leadership. Those individuals who are willing to take substantial risks to lead face the prospect of major failure. For most European politicians, the risks of too close an identification with the state of affairs in the EU outweigh the opportunities. From our vantage point today it is easily forgotten how vulnerable the Fourth Republic and Mollet's coalition government were in 1956–1957, how deep Britain's economic malaise was in 1970, how volatile and unpredictable were the events in late 1989 and early 1990. Yet at these critical junctures, European integration had a sense of historical purpose and responsibility that has over the years lost traction with elites and the public alike. Guy Mollet, Paul-Henri Spaak, Konrad Adenauer, Willy Brandt, Georges Pompidou, Edward Heath, Helmut Kohl, and François Mitterrand all managed – each in their own way – to mobilise support for integration by invoking the emotive idea of European unity as a long-term historical project.

Nowadays, one reason why the chances are slim for the emergence of determined leadership on the European scene is that the highest decision-makers in Europe struggle to personally believe in and publicly articulate the cause of European integration. The leaders even say it publicly: Angela Merkel does not want the 'transfer union' that a federal Europe would entail. Matteo Renzi does not want the European Commission to run the Italian economy. François Hollande does not want 'Brussels' to pick apart the social achievements of the French Republic. Beata Sydło does not want to be part of European immigrant-distribution system. The *Taoiseach* does not want the European Commission or Parliament to decide tax rates. Despite his advocacy for Britain to remain a member state of the EU, David Cameron was openly against the idea of an ever-closer union. Almost no one wants Turkey to become an EU member, though accession negotiations continue with no end in sight. Everybody wants better European defence capabilities but military budgets all across the EU are being cut. The expectation that the leaders of Europe should go out of their way to advocate something of uncertain utility to their own political careers and something they do not believe in is misguided.

In *World Order*, Henry Kissinger posits that the EU has become 'a hybrid, constitutionally something between a state and a confederation, operating through ministerial meetings and a common bureaucracy.'[16] He casts doubt on the expectation that European unification can ever be achieved by 'primarily administrative procedures' and suggests that unification in Europe has 'required a unifier – Prussia in Germany, Piedmont in Italy – without whose leadership (and willingness to create *faits accomplis*) unification would have remained stillborn.'[17]

Today, the most likely candidate to effectively marshal this kind of leadership is Germany. The Eurozone crisis has weakened France more than Germany – both in economic and political terms – leaving Berlin in the uncomfortable position of being Europe's reluctant 'half-hegemon' or leader-by-default.[18] The Franco-German 'tandem' at the helm of the EU is much diminished.[19] Yet in today's EU, Germany is not strong enough to lead Europe.[20] Berlin might be able to block initiatives it does not like, but it struggles to garner support for its own preferences. Angela Merkel did not want repeated bailouts for Greece, but had to accept them since she did not want to see a rupture of the Eurozone under her watch.[21] She is in favour of an EU-wide asylum system but is not able to get backing from her fellow leaders. The consequence of this form of

German preeminence is a dilemma for Berlin in trying either to impose its preferences on others or doing its own thing altogether.[22] In June 2011, Merkel's *Energiewende* decision to withdraw from nuclear power occurred without her consulting her European counterparts, just as her decision in 2015 to allow refugees from the Hungarian border to move to Germany in contravention of the Dublin agreements was not coordinated with other capitals.

It is seemingly ironic that the institutional edifice of European integration – whose core purpose it was to control Germany – has now become so dependent on Berlin. There is a gradual 'renationalisation of European politics' under way, as Charles Kupchan puts it.[23] This renationalisation is taking a toll in several forms. The prominent influence of Germany has already sharpened opposition against what many outside of Germany perceive as the *diktat* from Berlin. In addition, there is a gap between people's discontent with 'unwanted immigration, growing inequality, fraying welfare states, stagnant wages, bailout and austerity packages' and EU policies that require the freedom of movement, fiscal consolidation, unfettered economic competition, and a mix of bailouts and austerity.[24] There is also a disjuncture between voters – notably in the UK and France – wanting to repatriate political control and restore national autonomy, and EU institutions that are growing in competence and authority.[25] Last but not least, the renationalisation of European politics is making it more difficult to reform the EU in more fundamental way, as it rewards European leaders for a 'tough stance' against Brussels and punishes painful compromises. The case of the UK's renegotiation of its relationship with the EU in the run-up to the referendum on British membership is a case in point.

With the withdrawal of the UK, a resurgent Germany, an aggressive Russia, and widespread turmoil in the Middle East, the structural-geopolitical imperative for further integration is arguably strong. The same applies to the institutional imperative for integration. Now could be the time to establish a common economic government, create Eurobonds, consolidate tax rates across Europe, set up a European army, and build up a common immigration policy. Yet I maintain that these expectations are unrealistic because of a lack of political will among Europe's leaders. Without it, no change or innovation in European integration will occur automatically. Since international organisations – from the EU to the UN – lack the emotive affection and loyalty that nation-states can muster among a population, they depend not only on the goodwill of states but also on the determination of national leaders to find them useful and abide by their authority. The EU as we know it today would have been unlikely without the leadership interventions that I analysed throughout this book. The future success of European integration depends more on the political will, guidance, and leadership of Europe's current and future leaders than we care to admit.

Notes

1 M. Mazower, *Governing the World: The History of an Idea* (London: Allen Lane, 2012).

2 See G. Tremonti, *La Paura e la Speranza. Europa: La Crisi Globale che si Avvicina e la Via per Superarla* (Milan: Mondadori, 2008), pp. 31–58.
3 *Financial Times*, 'Growth will not save Europe from extremists' (24 March 2015); *The Economist*, 'A flawed temple' (16 March 2013); *Frankfurter Allgemeine Zeitung:* 'Nicht noch einmal' (7 August 2012); *Corriere Della Sera*: 'La Tentazione Nazionalista (12 June 2012).
4 H. Kundnani, *The Paradox of German Power* (London: Hurst, 2014), pp. 2–4.
5 *Corriere Della Sera*: 'Se la gente d'Europa reclama il ritorno della politica' (13 June 2012).
6 A. Möller, 'Die Europäische Union vor der Zerreißprobe,' in *Außenpolitik in der Wirtschafts-und Finanzkrise*, J. Braml, S. Mair, and E. Sandschneider eds. (Munich: Oldenburg, 2012), pp. 306–307.
7 See E. Jones, 'Merkels Folly,' *Survival* 52 (3) (2010): 21–38.
8 B. Lippert, 'Glanzloser Arbeitserfolg von epochaler Bedeutung: eine Bilanz der EU-Erweiterungspolitik 1989–2004,' in *Bilanz und Folgeprobleme der EU-Erweiterung*, B. Lippert ed. (Baden-Baden: Nomos, 2004), pp. 13–72.
9 M. Barnett and M. Finnemore, *Rules for the World: International Organisations in Global Politics* (Ithaca: Cornell University Press, 2004), p. 2.
10 See J. Janning, 'Leadership Constellations and Change: the Role of States in the European Union,' International Affairs 81 (4) (2005): 821–834.
11 C.J. Bickerton, D. Hodson, and U. Puetter eds., *The New Intergovernmentalism: States and Supranational Actors in the Post-Maastricht Era* (Oxford: Oxford University Press, 2015).
12 See *Die Zeit:* 'Der Euro erzwingt den europäischen Superstaat' (28 Juni 2012).
13 See *Der Spiegel:* 'Herfried Münkler: Alle Macht dem Zentrum' (4 July 2011).
14 See P. Mair, *Ruling the Void: The Hollowing of Western Democracy* (London: Verso, 2013), pp. 115–142.
15 M. Naím, *The End of Power: From Boardrooms to Battlefield and Churches to States, Why Being in Charge Isn't What It Used to be* (New York: Basic Books, 2013), pp. xi–xii.
16 H. Kissinger, *World Order* (London: Penguin, 2015), p. 92.
17 *Ibid.*, p. 94.
18 S. Bierling, *Vormacht Wider Willen. Deutsche Außenpolitik von der Wiedervereinigung bis zur Gegenwart* (Munich: C.H. Beck, 2014); M. Hüther, *Die Junge Nation: Deutschlands neue Rolle in Europa* (Hamburg: Murmann, 2014); H. Münkler, *Macht in der Mitte. Die neuen Aufgaben Deutschlands in Europa* (Hamburg: Körber Stiftung, 2015).
19 C. Calla and C. Demesmay, *Que Reste-t-il du Couple Franco-Allemand?* (Paris: La Documentation Française, 2013).
20 See H. Stark, *La Politique Internationale de l'Allemagne. Une Puissance Malgré Elle* (Paris: Septentrion, 2011), p. 306.
21 See G. Langguth, 'Die Europapolitik Angela Merkels,' in *Deutsche Europapolitik Christlicher Demokraten. Von Konrad Adenauer bis Angela Merkel (1945–2013)*, H.J. Küsters ed. (Düsseldorf: Droste, 2014), pp. 271–293.
22 S. Mair, 'Deutschland: Gestaltungsmacht Wider Willen,' in *Außenpolitik in der Wirtschafts-und Finanzkrise*, J. Braml, S. Mair, and E. Sandschneider eds. (Munich, Oldenburg, 2012), p. 136.
23 C. Kupchan, 'Centrifugal Europe,' *Survival* 54 (1) (2012): 111.
24 *Ibid.*
25 *Ibid.*

Glossary and abbreviations

AA	Auswärtiges Amt
AAPD	Akten zur Auswärtigen Politik der Bundesrepublik Deutschland
AfD	Alternative für Deutschland
CAP	Common Agricultural Policy
CBI	Confederation of British Industry
CDU	Christlich-Demokratische Union
CFTC	Confédération Française des Travailleurs Chrétiens
CGT	Confédération Général du Travail
Common Market	Term referring to the European Economic Community
CSU	Christlich-Soziale Union
DBPO	Documents on British Policy Overseas
DDF	Documents Diplomatiques Français
DM	Deutschmark
EC	European Communities (1965–1986), European Community (1986–1992)
ECB	European Central Bank
ECJ	European Court of Justice
ECSC	European Coal and Steel Community
EDC	European Defence Community
EEC	European Economic Community
EFTA	European Free Trade Association
EMS	European Monetary System
EMU	Economic and Monetary Union
EP	European Parliament
EU	European Union (1992-present)
Euratom	European Nuclear Energy Community
Euro	European single currency
FCO	Foreign and Commonwealth Office
FDP	Freie Demokratische Partei
FO	Foreign Office
FRG	Federal Republic of Germany
FRUS	Foreign Relations of the United States

GDR	German Democratic Republic
HAEC	Historical Archives of the European Commission, Brussels
HAEU	Historical Archives of the European Union, Florence
HIA	Hoover Institution Archives, Stanford
IGC	Intergovernmental Conference (of EU heads of government)
IR	International Relations (academic discipline)
KP	Kabinettsprotokolle der Bundesregierung
NATO	North Atlantic Treaty Organisation
OEEC	Organisation for European Economic Cooperation
SEA	Single European Act
SFIO	Section Française de l'Internationale Ouvrière
SPD	Sozialdemokratische Partei Deutschlands
StBKAH	Stiftung Bundeskanzler Adenauer Haus, Rhöndorf
TEU	Treaty of European Union
TNA	The National Archives, Kew
UK	United Kingdom
US	United States
USSR	Union of Socialist Soviet Republics
WBA	Willy Brandt Archive, Bonn-Bad Godesberg
WEU	Western European Union

Bibliography

I Primary sources

Archives

Historical Archives of the European Commission, Brussels (quoted as HAEC)
BAC
CEAB
D
Historical Archives of the European Union, Florence (quoted as HAEU)
FMM
MAEF
WL 71
Hoover Institution Archives, Palo Alto (quoted as HIA)
ESC/12
ESC/3
Politisches Archiv des Auswärtigen Amtes, Berlin (quoted as PAAA)
B130
The National Archives, Kew (quoted as TNA)
BT 11
BT 70
CAB 21
CAB 128
FO 371
FCO 26
FCO 30
FCO 33
FCO 59
PREM 11
PREM 13
PREM 15
T 232
Stiftung Bundeskanzler Adenauer Haus, Rhöndorf (quoted as StBKAH)
02.14
02.13
Willy Brandt Archiv im Archiv der deutschen Sozialdemokratie, Bonn-Bad Godesberg
  (quoted as WBA)
BK/51
BK/52

BK/91
BK/92

Published sources

Parliamentary debates

Hansard, Commons, 6th series
Hansard, Commons, 5th series
Hansard, Lords, 5th series

Diplomatic sources

Akten zur Auswärtigen Politik der Bundesrepublik Deutschland
(quoted as AAPD)

AAPD 1973, Vol. I: 1 January – 30 April 1973.
AAPD 1973, Vol. II: 1 May – 30 September 1973.
AAPD 1972, Vol. II: 1 June – 30 September 1972.
AAPD 1972, Vol. III: 1 October – 31 December 1972.
AAPD 1971, Vol. I: 1 January – 30 April 1971.
AAPD 1971, Vol. II: 1 May – 30 September 1971.
AAPD 1971, Vol. III: 1 October – 31 December 1971.
AAPD 1970, Vol. II: 1 May – 31 August 1970.
AAPD 1970, Vol. III: 1 September – 31 December 1970.
AAPD 1969, Vol. II: 1 July – 31 December 1969.

Die Kabinettsprotokolle der Bundesregierung (quoted as KP online)

Bundesarchiv: available at www.bundesarchiv.de/kabinettsprotokolle/web/index.jsp

Documents on British policy overseas (quoted as DBPO)

DBPO, Series III, Vol. VII: German Unification 1989–1990.
DBPO, Series III, Vol. I: Britain and the Soviet Union 1968–1972.

Documents diplomatiques Français (quoted as DDF)

DDF 1957, Vol. I: 1 January – 30 June 1957.
DDF 1956, Vol. I: 1 January – 30 June 1956.
DDF 1956, Vol. II: 1 July – 23 October 1956.
DDF 1956, Vol. III: 24 October – 31 December 1956.

Foreign relations of the United States (quoted as FRUS)

FRUS 1969–1976, Vol. III: Foreign Economic Policy, 1969–1972.
FRUS 1955–1957, Vol. IV: Western European Security and Integration.

FRUS 1955–1957, Vol. XXVII: Western Europe and Canada.
FRUS 1952–1954. Vol. II: National Security Affairs.

Public papers of the presidents of the United States (quoted as PPUS)

PPUS, Dwight D. Eisenhower, 1954: Containing the Public Messages, Speeches, and Statements of the President: 1 January – 31 December 1954.

PPUS, Dwight D. Eisenhower, 1956: Containing the Public Messages, Speeches, and Statements of the President: 1 January – 31 December 1956.

PPUS, Richard M. Nixon, 1971: Containing the Public Messages, Speeches, and Statements of the President: 2 January-30 December 1971.

PPUS, Richard M. Nixon, 1973: Containing the Public Messages, Speeches, and Statements of the President: 2 January – 31 December 1973.

Other document editions

Auswärtiges Amt, *Gemeinsame Aussen- und Sicherheitspolitik der Europäischen Union (GASP). Dokumentation* (Bonn: Auswärtiges Amt, 1994).

———, *Deutsche Aussenpolitik 1990/91: Auf dem Weg zu einer Europäischen Friedensordnung. Eine Dokumentation* (Munich: Verlag Bonn Aktuell, 1991).

———, *Aussenpolitik der Bundesrepublik Deutschland. Vom Kalten Krieg zum Frieden in Europa. Dokumente 1949–1989* (Munich: Verlag Bonn Aktuell, 1990).

———, *Die Auswärtige Politik der Bundesrepublik Deutschland* (Cologne: Verlag Wissenschaft und Politik, 1972).

Brandt, W. 'Fernsehansprache aus Moskau am 12. August 1970,' *Berühmte Reden*, Bundeskanzler Willy-Brandt-Stiftung online (1970), http://www.bwbs.de/Beitraege/70.html

———, 'Erklärung der Bundesregierung vom 28. Oktober 1969,' *Berühmte Reden*, Bundeskanzler Willy-Brandt-Stiftung online (1969), www.bwbs.de/Beitraege/69.html

Bundesministerium für innerdeutsche Beziehungen, *Texte zur Deutschlandpolitik*, Vol. 11: 2 June – 22 December 1972 (Bonn: Bundesverlag, 1973).

Ministère de l'Intérieur: http://www.interieur.gouv.fr/Elections/Elections-regionales-2015/Resultats-du-premier-tour-des-elections-regionales-2015

Treaty of Lisbon (2007/C 306/01): http://eur-lex.europa.eu/legal-content/EN/TXT/?uri=uriserv:OJ.C_.2007.306.01.0001.01.ENG&toc=OJ:C:2007:306:TOC

Newspapers and periodicals

Corriere Della Sera
Der Spiegel
Die Welt
Die Zeit
Frankfurter Allgemeine Zeitung
Frankfurter Rundschau
Frankfurter Zeitung
Financial Times
L'Aurore

La Libre Belgique
Le Figaro
Le Monde
Süddeutsche Zeitung
The Economist
The New York Times
The Wall Street Journal
The Times

II Secondary sources

Adenauer, K. *Briefe über Deutschland 1945–1955*. H.P. Mensing ed. (Munich: Siedler, 1999).
———, *Briefe 1955–1957. Rhöndorfer Ausgabe*. R. Morsey and H.-P. Schwarz eds. (Berlin: Siedler, 1998).
———, *Erinnerungen 1955–1959* (Stuttgart: Deutsche Verlags-Anstalt, 1967).
———, *Erinnerungen 1953–1955* (Stuttgart: Deutsche Verlags-Anstalt, 1966).
———, *Erinnerungen 1945–1953* (Stuttgart: Deutsche Verlags-Anstalt, 1965).
Adler-Nissen, R. *Opting Out of the European Union: Diplomacy, Sovereignty, and European Integration* (Cambridge: Cambridge University Press, 2014).
Albrecht-Carrié, R. *The Unity of Europe: An Historical Survey* (London: Secker & Warburg, 1965).
Allen, D. 'Britain and Western Europe,' in *British Foreign Policy: Tradition, Change, and Transformation*, M. Smith, S. Smith, and B. White eds. (London: Unwin Hyman, 1988), 168–192.
Almond, G. 'The Political Attitudes of German Business,' *World Politics* 8 (2) (1956): 157–186.
Anderson, J. *German Unification and the Union of Europe: The Domestic Politics of Integration Policy* (Cambridge: Cambridge University Press, 1999).
Axelrod, R. and R.O. Keohane, 'Achieving Cooperation under Anarchy: Strategies and Institutions,' *World Politics* 38 (1) (1985): 226–254.
Bach, J.P.G. *Between Sovereignty and Integration: German Foreign Policy and National Identity After 1989* (New York: St. Martin's Press, 1999).
Bahr, E. 'Willy Brandts europäische Außenpolitik – Vortrag von Bundesminister a.D. Professor Egon Bahr am 9. Oktober 1998 im Rathaus Schöneberg,' *Schriftenreihe der Bundeskanzler-Willy-Brandt-Stiftung* 3 (1999): 1–13.
Balassa, B. *The Theory of Economic Integration* (London: Allen and Unwin, 1961).
Baring, A. ed. *Sehr verehrter Herr Bundeskanzler! Heinrich von Brentano im Briefwechsel mit Konrad Adenauer 1949–1964* (Hamburg: Hoffmann und Campe, 1974).
Barman, T. 'Britain, France and West Germany: The Changing Pattern of Their Relationship in Europe,' *International Affairs* 46 (2) (1970): 269–279.
Barnett, M. and M. Finnemore, *Rules for the World: International Organisations in Global Politics* (Ithaca: Cornell University Press, 2004).
Baumann-Reynolds, S. *François Mitterrand: The Making of a Socialist Prince in Republican France* (Westport: Greenwood, 1995).
Baun, M.J. 'The Maastricht Treaty as High Politics: Germany, France, and European Integration,' *Political Science Quarterly* 110 (4) (1995): 605–624.

Beach, D. *The Dynamics of European Integration: Why and When EU Institutions Matter* (Basingstoke: Palgrave Macmillan, 2005).
Beck, U. and E. Grande, *Das kosmopolitische Europa* (Frankfurt: Suhrkamp, 2004).
Bell, D.S. *François Mitterrand: A Political Biography* (Cambridge: Polity, 2005).
———, 'Western Communist Parties and the European Union,' in *Political Parties and the European Union*, J. Gaffney ed. (London: Routledge, 1996), 220–234.
Bell, L. *The Throw that Failed: Britain's Original Application to Join the Common Market* (London: New European Publications, 1995).
Beloff, M. 'Britain, Europe, and the Atlantic Community,' *International Organization* 17 (3) (1963): 574–591.
Beneyto, J.M., J. Baquero, B. Becerril, M. Bolle, M. Cremona, S. Ehret, V. Lopez-Ibor, and J. Mallo, *Unity and Flexibility in the Future of the European Union: The Challenge of Enhanced Cooperation* (Madrid: CEU Ediciones, 2009).
Benoit, E. *Europe at Sixes and Sevens: The Common Market, the Free Trade Association, and the United States* (New York: Columbia University Press, 1961).
Berggruen, N. and N. Gardels, *Intelligent Governance for the 21st Century: A Middle Way between West and East* (Cambridge: Polity, 2013).
Besson, W. 'The Conflict of Traditions: The Historical Basis of West German Foreign Policy,' in *Britain and West Germany: Changing Societies and the Future of Foreign Policy*, K. Kaiser and R. Morgan eds. (London: Oxford University Press, 1971), 61–80.
Best, H., G. Lengyel, and L. Verzichelli eds. *The Europe of Elites: A Study Into the Europeanness of Europe's Political and Economic Elites* (Oxford: Oxford University Press, 2012).
Bickerton, C.J., D. Hodson, and U. Puetter eds. *The New Intergovernmentalism: States and Supranational Actors in the Post-Maastricht Era* (Oxford: Oxford University Press, 2015).
———, 'The New Intergovernmentalism and the Study of European Integration,' in *The New Intergovernmentalism: States and Supranational Actors in the Post-Maastricht Era*, C.J. Bickerton, D. Hodson, and U. Puetter eds. (Oxford: Oxford University Press, 2015), 1–50.
Bieler, A. 'The Struggle Over EU Enlargement: A Historical Materialist Analysis of European Integration,' *Journal of European Public Policy* 9 (4) (2002): 575–597.
Bierling, S. *Vormacht Wider Willen. Deutsche Außenpolitik von der Wiedervereinigung bis zur Gegenwart* (Munich: C.H. Beck, 2014).
Bjøl, E. *La France Devant l'Europe. La Politique Européenne de la IVe République* (Copenhagen: Munksgaard, 1966).
Bongiovanni, F.M. *The Decline and Fall of Europe* (Basingstoke: Palgrave Macmillan, 2012).
Bornschier, S. 'France: The Model Case of Party System Transformation,' in *West European Politics in the Age of Globalisation*, H. Kriesi, E. Grande, R. Lachat, M. Dloezal, S. Bornschier, and T. Frey (Cambridge: Cambridge University Press, 2008), 77–104.
Bossuat, G. 'La Vraie Nature de la Politique Européenne de la France (1950–1957),' in *The European Integration From the Schuman Plan to the Treaties of Rome*, G. Trausch ed. (Paris: L.G.D.J, 1993), 191–230.
Bozo, F. *Mitterrand, the End of the Cold War, and German Unification* (Oxford: Berghahn, 2009).

Brandt, W. *Ein Volk der guten Nachbarn: Außen- und Deutschlandpolitik 1966–1974*, F. Fischer ed., Berliner Ausgabe, Vol. 6. (Bonn: Dietz, 2005).
———, *Erinnerungen: Mit den 'Notizen zum Fall G'* (Munich: Ullstein, 2003).
———, *Begegnungen und Einsichten: Die Jahre 1960–1975* (Hamburg: Hoffmann und Campe, 1976).
———, *Friedenspolitik in Europa* (Frankfurt: Fischer, 1971).
———, *Außenpolitik, Deutschlandpolitik, Europapolitik: Grundsätzliche Erklärungen während des ersten Jahres im Auswärtigen Amt*, second edition (Berlin: Berlin Verlag, 1970).
Brenke, G. 'Europakonzeptionen im Widerstreit: Die Freihandelszonen-Verhandlungen 1956–1958,' *Vierteljahrshefte für Zeitgeschichte* 42 (4) (1994): 595–633.
Brinkley, D. and C.B. Hackett eds. *Jean Monnet: The Path to European Unity* (London: Macmillan, 1991).
Bromberger, M. and S. Bromberger, *Jean Monnet and the United States of Europe* (New York: Coward-McCann, 1969).
Buller, J. *National Statecraft and European Integration: The Conservative Government and the European Union, 1979–1997* (London: Pinter, 2000).
Bulmer, S., C. Jeffery, and W.E. Paterson, *Germany's European Diplomacy: Shaping the Regional Milieu* (Manchester: Manchester University Press, 2000).
Bunse, S. *Small States and EU Governance: Leadership Through the Council Presidency* (Basingstoke: Palgrave, 2009).
Burgess, M. *Federalism and European Union: Political Ideas, Influences and Strategies in the European Community, 1972–1987* (London: Routledge, 1989).
Burgess, S. and R. Edwards, 'The Six Plus One: British Policy-Making and the Question of European Economic Integration, 1955,' *International Affairs* 64 (3) (1988): 393–413.
Burley, A.-M. and W. Mattli, 'Europe Before the Court: A Political Theory of Legal Integration,' *International Organization* 47 (1) (1993): 41–76.
Burns, J.M. *Transforming Leadership: A New Pursuit of Happiness* (New York: Grove, 2004).
———, *Leadership* (New York, NY: Harper and Row, 1978).
Calla, C. and C. Demesmay, *Que Reste-t-il du Couple Franco-Allemand?* (Paris: La Documentation Française, 2013).
Campbell, J. *Margaret Thatcher, Volume Two: The Iron Lady* (London: Pimlico, 2003).
———, *Edward Heath: A Biography* (London: Jonathan Cape, 1993).
Carlton, A. *Anthony Eden: A Biography* (London: Allen Lane, 1981).
Cerny, P.G. *The Politics of Grandeur: Ideological Aspects of de Gaulle's Foreign Policy* (Cambridge: Cambridge University Press, 1980).
Charlton, S.E.M. *The French Left and European Integration*. Monograph Series in World Affairs, Vol. 9, Monograph No. 4–1971–1972 (Denver: University of Denver, 1972).
Checkel, J. 'International Institutions and Socialization in Europe: Introduction and Framework,' *International Organization* 59 (2005): 801–826.
———, 'Why Comply? Social Learning and European Identity Change,' *International Organization* 55 (3) (2001): 553–588.
———, 'The Constructivist Turn in International Relations Theory,' *World Politics* 50 (2) (1998): 324–348.
Chopin, T. *La Fracture Politique de l'Europe: Crise de Légitimité et Déficit Politique* (Paris: Promoculture, 2015).

Christiansen, T., K.E. Jørgensen, and A. Wiener eds. *The Social Construction of Europe* (London: Sage, 2001).
Clemens, G. 'A History of Failures and Miscalculations? Britain's Relationship to the European Communities in the Postwar Era (1945–1973),' *Contemporary European History* 13 (2) (2004): 223–232.
Cohen, R. *Theatre of Power: The Art of Diplomatic Signalling* (Harlow: Longman, 1987).
Cole, A. 'Political Leadership in Western Europe: Helmut Kohl in Comparative Context,' in *The Kohl Chancellorship*, C. Clemens and W.E. Paterson eds. (London: Frank Cass, 1998), 120–142.
Cole, A. 'The French Socialists' in *Political Parties and the European Union*, J. Gaffney ed. (London: Routledge, 1996), 71–85.
———, *François Mitterrand: A Study in Political Leadership*, second edition (London: Routledge, 1997).
Cornett, L. and J.A. Caporaso, '"And Still It Moves!" State Interests and Social Forces in the European Community,' in *Governance Without Government: Order and Change in World Politics*, J.N. Rosenau and E.-O. Czempiel eds. (Cambridge: Cambridge University Press, 1992), 219–249.
Cowley, P. and J. Garry, 'The British Conservative Party and Europe: The Choosing of John Major,' *British Journal of Political Science* 28 (3) (1998): 473–499.
Cox, M. and S. Hurst, '"His Finest Hour?" George Bush and the Diplomacy of German Unification,' *Diplomacy & Statecraft* 13 (4) (2002): 123–150.
Craig, G.A. 'Konrad Adenauer and His Diplomats,' in *The Diplomats, 1939–1979*, G.A. Craig and F.L. Loewenheim eds. (Princeton: Princeton University Press, 1994), 201–227.
Crowson, N.J. *Britain and Europe: A Political History Since 1918* (London: Routledge, 2011).
Daddow, O. *Britain and Europe Since 1945: Historiographical Perspectives on Integration* (Manchester: Manchester University Press, 2004).
Davis, R. 'The "Problem of de Gaulle": British Reactions to General de Gaulle's Veto of the UK Application to Join the Common Market,' *Journal of Contemporary History* 32 (4) (1997): 453–464.
de Boissieu, C. and J. Pisani-Ferry, 'The Political Economy of French Economic Policy in the Perspective of EMU,' in *Forging an Integrated Europe*, B. Eichengreen and J. Frieden eds. (Ann Arbor: University of Michigan Press, 1998), 49–89.
de Gaulle, C. *Memoirs of Hope: Renewal 1958–62, Endeavour 1962* (London: Weidenfeld and Nicolson, 1971).
———, *Discours et Messages: Dans l'Attente, Février 1946 – Avril 1958* (Paris: Plon, 1970).
Dedman, M.J. *The Origins and Development of the European Union, 1945–2008: A History of European Integration*, second edition (Abingdon: Routledge, 2010).
Deighton, A. 'British-West German Relations, 1945–1972,' in *Uneasy Allies: British-German Relations and European Integration Since 1945*, K. Larres and E. Meehan eds. (Oxford: Oxford University Press, 2000), 27–44.
Dell, E. *The Schuman Plan and the British Abdication of Leadership in Europe* (Oxford: Clarendon Press, 1995).
Deniau, J.F. *L'Europe Interdite* (Paris: Seuil, 1977).
Denman, R. *Missed Chances: Britain & Europe in the Twentieth Century* (London: Indigo, 1997).

Deutsch, K. *Political Community and the North Atlantic Area* (Princeton: Princeton University Press, 1957).
Diallo, T. *La Politique Étrangère de Georges Pompidou* (Paris: Librairie Général de Droit et de Jurisprudence, 1992).
Dinan, D. *Europe Recast: A History of European Union* (Boulder: Lynne Rienner, 2004).
Döring-Manteufel, A. 'Rheinischer Katholik im Kalten Krieg. Das "Christliche Europa" in der Weltsicht Konrad Adenauers,' in *Die Christen und die Entstehung der Europäischen Gemeinschaft*, M. Greschat and W. Loth eds. (Stuttgart: Kohlhammer, 1994), 237–246.
Doutriaux, Y. and C. Lequesne, *Les Institutions de l'Union Européenne Après la Crise Euro* (Paris: La Documentation Française, 2013).
Duchêne, F. *Jean Monnet: The First Statesman of Interdependence* (London: WW Norton, 1994).
Dumoulin, M. *Spaak* (Brussels: Editions Racine, 1999).
Dunn, D. 'How Useful Is Summitry?,' in *Diplomacy at the Highest Level: The Evolution of International Summitry*, D. Dunn ed. (Basingstoke: Macmillan, 1996), 247–268.
Dunn, D.H. ed. *Diplomacy at the Highest Level: The Evolution of International Summitry* (Basingstoke: Macmillan, 1996).
Dutton, D. *Anthony Eden: A Life and Reputation* (London: Arnold, 1997).
Dyson, K. ed. *European States and the Euro: Europeanization, Variation, and Convergence* (Oxford: Oxford University Press, 2002).
———, 'Germany and the Euro: Redefining EMU, Handling Paradox, and Managing Uncertainty and Contingency,' in *European States and the Euro: Europeanization, Variation, and Convergence*, K. Dyson ed. (Oxford: Oxford University Press, 2002), 173–211.
———, 'Chancellor Kohl as Strategic Leader: The Case of Economic and Monetary Union,' in *The Kohl Chancellorship*, C. Clemens and W.E. Paterson eds. (London: Frank Cass, 1998), 37–63.
Dyson, K. and K. Featherstone, *The Road to Maastricht: Negotiating Economic and Monetary Union* (Oxford: Oxford University Press, 1999).
Eden, A. *The Memoirs of the Rt. Hon. Sir Anthony Eden K.G., P.C., M.C. Full Circle* (London: Cassell, 1960).
Edinger, L.J. 'Political Science and Political Biography,' in *Political Leadership: Readings for an Emerging Field*, G.D. Paige ed. (New York: Free Press, 1972), 213–239.
Eilstrup-Sangiovanni, M. and D. Verner, 'European Integration as a Solution to War,' *European Journal of International Relations* 11 (1) (2005): 99–135.
Endo, K. *The Presidency of the European Commission under Jacques Delors: The Politics of Shared Leadership* (Basingstoke: Macmillan, 1999).
Epstein, K. 'The Adenauer Era in German History,' in *A New Europe?* S.R. Graubard ed. (Boston: Houghton Mifflin, 1964), 105–139.
European Commission, 'Post-Referendum in Sweden,' *Flash Eurobarometer* 149 (October 2003): http://ec.europa.eu/public_opinion/flash/fl149_en.pdf
Feske, V.H. 'The Road to Suez: The British Foreign Office and the Quai d'Orsay, 1951–1957,' in *The Diplomats, 1939–1979*, G. Craig and F.L. Loewenheim eds. (Princeton: Princeton University Press, 1994), 167–200.

Finnemore, M. *National Interests in International Society* (Ithaca: Cornell University Press, 1996).
Fligstein, N. and A. Stone Sweet, 'Constructing Polities and Markets: An Institutionalist Account of European Integration,' *American Journal of Sociology* 107 (5) (2002): 1–33.
Foley, M. *Political Leadership: Themes, Contexts and Critiques* (Oxford: Oxford University Press, 2013).
———, *John Major, Tony Blair and a Conflict of Leadership: Collision Course* (Manchester: Manchester University Press, 2002).
Forndran, E. 'German-American Disagreements over Arms-Control Policy,' in *The United States and Germany in the Era of the Cold War, 1945–1990: A Handbook*, Vol I: 1945–1968, D. Junker ed. (Cambridge: Cambridge University Press, 2004), 240–247.
Forster, A. *Euroscepticism in Contemporary British Politics: Opposition to Europe in the British Conservative and Labour Parties Since 1945* (London: Routledge, 2002).
———, *Britain and the Maastricht Negotiations* (Basingstoke: Palgrave, 1999).
Frankel, J. *British Foreign Policy 1945–1973* (London: Oxford University Press, 1975).
Franks, O. 'Britain and Europe,' in *A New Europe?*, S.R. Graubard, ed. (Boston: Houghton Mifflin, 1964), 89–104.
Fransen, F.J. *The Supranational Politics of Jean Monnet: Ideas and Origins of the European Community* (Westport: Greenwood, 2001).
Freeman, C.W. *Arts of Power: Statecraft and Diplomacy* (Washington, DC: United States Institute of Peace Press, 1997).
Friedrich, C.J. 'Political Leadership and the Problem of the Charismatic Power,' *The Journal of Politics* 23 (1) (1961): 3–24.
Friend, J.W. *Unequal Partners: French-German Relations 1989–2000* (Westport: Praeger, 2001).
———, *The Long Presidency: France in the Mitterrand Years, 1981–1995* (Boulder: Westview, 1998).
Fritsch-Bournazel, R. *Europe and German Unification* (New York: Berg, 1992).
Gardner, H. *Leading Minds: An Anatomy of Leadership* (New York: Basic Books, 1995).
Garry, J. 'Emotions and Voting in EU Referendums,' *European Union Politics* 15 (2) (2014): 235–254.
Gehler, M. and H. Meyer, 'Konrad Adenauer, Europa und die Westintegration der Bundesrepublik Deutschland im Kontext von privaten und politischen Netzwerken,' in *Deutsche Europapolitik Christlicher Demokraten. Von Konrad Adenauer bis Angela Merkel (1945–2013)*, H.J. Küsters ed. (Düsseldorf: Droste, 2014), 117–156.
Geiger, T. 'Der Streit um die deutsche Europapolitik in den 1960er Jahren,' in *Deutsche Europapolitik Christlicher Demokraten. Von Konrad Adenauer bis Angela Merkel (1945–2013)*, H.J. Küsters ed. (Düsseldorf: Droste, 2014), 331–362.
George, S. *Britain and European Integration Since 1945* (Oxford: Blackwell, 1991).
George, S. and D. Haythorne, 'The British Labour Party,' in *Political Parties and the European Union*, J. Gaffney ed. (London: Routledge, 1996), 110–121.
Gerbet, P. *La Construction de l'Europe* (Paris: Imprimerie Nationale, 1983).
Giauque, J.G. *Grand Designs and Visions of Unity: The Atlantic Powers and the Reorganization of Western Europe, 1955–1963* (Durham: The University of North Carolina Press, 2002).

———, 'Bilateral Summit Diplomacy in Western European and Transatlantic Relations, 1956–63,' *European History Quarterly* 31 (3) (1996): 427–445.
Giddens, A. *Turbulent and Mighty Continent: What Future for Europe?* (Cambridge: Polity, 2014).
Gildea, R. *France Since 1945* (Oxford: Oxford University Press, 2002).
Gillingham, J. *European Integration 1950–2003: Superstate or New Market Economy?* (Cambridge: Cambridge University Press, 2003).
Ginsberg, R.H. *Demistifying the European Union: The Enduring Logic of Regional Integration*, second edition (Lanham: Rowman and Littlefield, 2010).
Gowland, D. and A. Turner, *Reluctant Europeans: Britain and European Integration, 1945–1998* (London: Longman, 2000).
Gowland, D., A. Turner, and A. Wright, *Britain and European Integration Since 1945: On the Sidelines* (London: Routledge, 2010).
Grabbe, H. 'Europeanization Goes East: Power and Uncertainty in the EU Accession Process,' in *The Politics of Europeanization*, K. Featherstone and C. Radoelli eds. (Oxford: Oxford University Press, 2003), 303–327.
Grant, C. *Delors: Inside the House Jacques Built* (London: Nicholas Brealey, 1994).
Grieco, J.M. 'State Interests and Institutional Rule Trajectories: A Neorealist Interpretation of the Maastricht Treaty and European Economic and Monetary Union,' *Security Studies* 5 (3) (1996): 277–307.
———, 'The Maastricht Treaty, Economic and Monetary Union and the Neo-Realist Research Programme,' *Review of International Studies* 21 (1995): 21–40.
Grosser, A. 'Europe: Community of Malaise,' *Foreign Policy* 15 (1974): 169–170.
———, 'Suez, Hungary and European Integration,' *International Organization* 11 (3) (1957): 470–480.
Gueldry, M.R. *France and European Integration: Toward a Transnational Polity?* (Westport: Praeger, 2001).
Guérot, U. and T. Klau, 'After Merkozy: How France and Germany Can Make Europe Work,' *European Council of Foreign Relations Policy Brief* 56 (May 2012): 1–11: http://www.ecfr.eu/page/-/ECFR56_FRANCE_GERMANY_BRIEF_AW.pdf
Guigou, E. 'Le Traité de Maastricht: la Dernière Oeuvre Européen de François Mitterrand,' *La lettre de l'Institut François Mitterrand* 8 (June 2004): 22–23.
Guillaume, S. 'Guy Mollet et l'Allemagne,' in *Guy Mollet. Un Camarade en Republique*, B. Menager, P. Ratte, J.-L. Thiebault, R. Vandenbussche, and C.-M. Wallon-Leducq eds. (Lille: Presses Universitaires de Lille, 1987), 481–497.
Guillen, P. 'La France et la Négociation des Traités de Rome: L'Euratom,' in *Il Rilancio dell'Europa e i Trattati di Roma*, Enrico Serra ed. (Milan: A. Guiffré, 1989), 513–524.
———, 'L'Europe Remède à l'Impuissance Française? Le Gouvernement Guy Mollet et la Négociation des Traités de Rome,' *Revue d'Histoire Diplomatique* 102 (1988): 319–335.
———, 'La France et la Négociation du Traité d'Euratom,' *Relations Internationales* 44 (1985): 391–412.
———, 'Frankreich und der Europäische Wiederaufschwung. Vom Scheitern der EVG zur Ratifizierung der Verträge von Rom,' *Vierteljahrshefte für Zeitgeschichte* 28 (1) (1980): 1–19.
Haas, E.B. *The Uniting of Europe: Political, Social, and Economic Forces, 1950–1957* (Palo Alto: Stanford University Press, 1958).

Hacke, C. *Die Außenpolitik der Bundesrepublik Deutschland. Weltmacht wider Willen?* revised edition (Frankfurt: Ullstein. 1997).

Hahn, W. 'West Germany's Ostpolitik: The Grand Design of Egon Bahr,' *Orbis* 16 (4) (1973): 859–880.

Hallstrom, L.K. 'Support for European Federalism? An Elite View,' *European Integration* 25 (2003): 51–72.

Hamilton, K. and R. Langhorne, *The Practice of Diplomacy: Its Evolution, Theory and Administration* (London: Routledge, 1996).

Hanrieder, W.F. 'The Foreign Policies of the Federal Republic of Germany, 1949–1989,' *German Studies Review* 12 (2) (1989): 311–332.

Hargrove, E.C. and J.E. Owens, 'Introduction: Political Leadership in Context,' in *Leadership in Context*, E.C. Hargrove and J.E. Owens eds. (Lanham, MD: Rowman and Littlefield, 2003), 1–16.

Harryvan, A.G. and J. van der Harst eds. *Documents on European Union* (Basingstoke: Macmillan, 1997).

Hasenclever, A., P. Mayer and V. Rittberger, *Theories of International Regimes* (Cambridge: Cambridge University Press, 1997).

Hay, C. and D. Wincott, 'Structure, Agency and Historical Institutionalism,' *Political Studies*, 47 (1998): 954.

Hayward, J. ed. *Leaderless Europe* (Oxford: Oxford University Press, 2008).

Heater, D. *The Idea of European Unity* (Leicester: Leicester University Press, 1992).

Heath, E. *The Course of My Life: My Autobiography* (London: Hodder and Stoughton, 1998).

———, *Old World, New Horizons: Britain, the Common Market, and the Atlantic Alliance* (London: Oxford University Press, 1970).

Helms, L. *Presidents, Prime Ministers, and Chancellors: Executive Leadership in Western Democracies* (Basingstoke: Palgrave Macmillan, 2005).

Hennessy, P. *The Prime Minister: The Office and Its Holders Since 1945* (London: Penguin, 2000).

Herbert, U. *Geschichte Deutschlands im 20. Jahrhundert* (Munich: C.H. Beck, 2014).

Herkendell, M. *Deutschland Zivil- oder Friedensmacht? Außen- und sicherheitspolitische Orientierung der SPD im Wandel (1982–2007)* (Bonn: Dietz, 2012).

Hermann, M.G. 'Leaders, Leadership, and Flexibility: Influences on Heads of Government as Negotiators and Mediators,' *Annals of the American Academy of Political and Social Science* 542 (1995), Flexibility in International Negotiation and Mediation: 148-167.

Herzog, R., C. Mestre and Y. Petit, *La Crise Financière et Budgétaire en Europe. Un Moment de Verité pour la Construction Européenne* (Nancy: Presses Universitaires de Nancy, 2013).

Heumann, H.-D. *Genscher. Die Biographie* (Paderborn: Schöningh, 2012).

Hiepel, C. *Willy Brandt und Georges Pompidou. Deutsch-französische Europapolitik zwischen Aufbruch und Krise* (Munich: Oldenbourg, 2012).

Hildebrand, K. *German Foreign Policy From Bismarck to Adenauer* (London: Unwin Hyman, 1989).

Hill, C. 'The Historical Background: Past and Present in British Foreign Policy,' in *British Foreign Policy: Tradition, Change, and Transformation*, M. Smith, S. Smith, and B. White eds. (London: Unwin Hyman, 1988), 24–49.

Hill, S. *Europe's Promise: Why the European Way Is the Best Hope in an Insecure Age* (Berkeley: University of California Press, 2010).

Hillenbrand, M.J. 'An Assessment of the EC Future,' *Annals of the American Academy of Political and Social Science* 531 (1994): 168–177.

Hinarejos, A. *The Euro Area Crisis in Constitutional Perspective* (Oxford: Oxford University Press, 2015).

Hitchcock, W. *The Struggle for Europe: The History of the Continent Since 1945* (London: Profile Books, 2003).

Hoffmann, S. 'Towards a Common Foreign and Security Policy,' *Journal of Common Market Studies* 38 (2) (2000): 189–198.

———, 'The Case for Leadership,' *Foreign Policy* 81 (1990–1991): 20–38.

———, *Decline or Renewal? France Since the 1930s* (New York: Viking Press, 1974).

———, 'De Gaulle, Europe, and the Atlantic Alliance,' *International Organization* 18 (1) (1964): 1–28.

Hogg, S. and J. Hill, *Too Close to Call: Power and Politics – John Major in No. 10* (London: Little, Brown and Company, 1995).

Holland, M. 'Jean Monnet and the Federal Functionalist Approach to European Union,' in *Visions of European Unity*, P. Murray and P. Rich eds. (Boulder: Westview, 1996), 93–108.

Hooghe, L. *The European Commission and the Integration of Europe: Images of Governance* (Cambridge: Cambridge University Press, 2002).

Hopf, T. *Social Construction of International Politics: Identities and Foreign Policies, Moscow, 1955 & 1999* (Ithaca: Cornell University Press, 2002).

Hörber, T. *The Foundations of Europe: European Integration Ideas in France, Germany, and Britain in the 1950s* (Wiesbaden: VS Verlag für Sozialwissenschaften, 2006).

Horsfall Carter, W. *Speaking European: The Anglo-Continental Cleavage* (London: George Allen and Unwin, 1966).

Hovey Jr, A. 'Britain and the Unification of Europe,' *International Organization* 9 (3) (1955): 332–337.

Howarth, D. 'The French State in the Euro-Zone: "Modernization" and Legitimizing *Dirigisme*,' in *European States and the Euro: Europeanization, Variation, and Convergence*, K. Dyson ed. (Oxford: Oxford University Press, 2002), 145–172.

Howorth, J. 'France and the Unification of Germany: Clio's Verdict?,' *French Politics, Culture & Society* 29 (1) (2011): 118–129.

———, 'The President's Special Role in Foreign and Defence Policy,' in *De Gaulle to Mitterrand: Presidential Power in France*, J. Hayward ed. (London: Hurst, 1993), 150–189.

Hughes, R.G. *Britain, Germany, and the Cold War: The Search for a European Détente 1949–1967* (Abingdon: Routledge, 2007).

———, '"We Are Not Seeking Strength for Its Own Sake": The British Labour Party, West Germany and the Cold War, 1951–64,' *Cold War History* 3 (1) (2002): 67–94.

Huizinga, J. *Mr. Europe* (London: Weidenfeld and Nicolson, 1961).

Hurd, D. *Memoirs* (London: Abacus, 2003).

———, *An End to Promises: A Sketch of a Government 1970–74* (London: Collins, 1979).

Hüther, M. *Die Junge Nation. Deutschlands neue Rolle in Europa* (Hamburg: Murmann, 2014).

Isaacson, W. ed. *Profiles in Leadership: Historians on the Elusive Quality of Greatness* (New York: Norton, 2010).

Jackson, P.T. 'Making Sense of Making Sense: Configurational Analysis and the Double Hermeneutic,' in *Interpretation and Method: Empirical Research Methods and the Interpretive Turn*, second edition, D. Yanow and P. Schwartz-Shea eds. (Armonk: M.E. Sharpe, 2014).
Jahn, H.E. *An Adenauers Seite: Sein Berater erinnert sich* (Munich: Langen Müller, 1987).
Joas, R. *Zwischen Nation und Europa: Die europapolitischen Vorstellungen der Gaullisten 1978 bis 1994* (Bochum: Universitätsverlag Dr. N. Brockmeyer, 1996).
Joerges, C. and C. Glinski eds. *The European Crisis and the Transformation of Transnational Governance: Authoritarian Managerialism versus Democratic Governance* (Oxford: Hart, 2014).
Jones, E. 'Merkels Folly,' *Survival* 52 (3) (2010): 21–38.
Jouve, E. *Le Général de Gaulle et la Construction de l'Europe*, Vol. 1 (Paris: Librairie Générale de Droit et de Jurisprudence, 1967).
Juncker, J.-C. 'State of the Union: Time for Honesty, Unity, and Solidarity' (9 September 2015): http://europa.eu/rapid/press-release_SPEECH-15-5614_en.htm
Jupille, J. and J.A. Caporaso, 'Institutionalism and the European Union: Beyond International Relations and Comparative Politics,' *Annual Review of Political Science* 2 (1999): 409–425.
Kaelberer, M. *Money and Power in Europe: The Political Economy of the European Monetary Cooperation* (Albany: State University of New York Press, 2001).
Kaiser. W. *Großbritannien und die Europäische Wirtschaftsgemeinschaft 1955–1961. Von Messina nach Canossa* (Berlin: Akademie Verlag, 1996).
———, *Using Europe, Abusing the Europeans: Britain and European Integration, 1945–63* (Basingstoke: Macmillan, 1996).
Kaltenthaler, K. 'German Interests in European Monetary Integration,' *Journal of Common Market Studies* 40 (1) (2002): 69–87.
Kalyvas, S.N. *The Rise of Christian Democracy in Europe* (Ithaca: Cornell University Press, 1996).
Katzenstein, P.J. ed. *Tamed Power: Germany in Europe* (Ithaca: Cornell University Press, 1997).
———, *The Culture of National Security: Norms and Identity in World Politics* (New York: Columbia University Press, 1996).
Kavanagh, D. and A. Seldon eds. *The Powers behind the Prime Minister: The Hidden Influence of Number Ten* (London: Harper Collins, 1999).
Keck, M.E. and K. Sikkink, *Activists beyond Borders: Advocacy Networks in International Politics* (Ithaca: Cornell University Press, 1998).
Keohane, N.O. *Thinking about Leadership* (Princeton: Princeton University Press, 2010).
Keohane, R.O. 'Governance in a Partially Globalized World: Presidential Address, American Political Science Association, 2000,' *American Political Science Review* 95 (1) (2000): 1–13.
———, *After Hegemony: Cooperation and Discord in the World Political Economy* (Princeton: Princeton University Press, 1984).
Keohane, R.O. and J.S. Nye, *Power and Interdependence*, third edition (New York: Longman, 2001).
———, 'Introduction: The End of the Cold War in Europe,' in *After the Cold War: International Institutions and State Strategies in Europe, 1989–1991*, R.O. Keohane, J. Nye, and S. Hoffmann eds. (Cambridge: Harvard University Press, 1993), 1–19.

Keohane, R.O. and S. Hoffmann, 'Institutional Change in Europe in the 1980s,' in *The New European Community: Decisionmaking and Institutional Change*, R.O. Keohane and S. Hoffmann eds. (Boulder, CO: Westview, 1991), 1–40.

Keohane, R.O., J. Nye, and S. Hoffmann eds. *After the Cold War: International Institutions and State Strategies in Europe, 1989–1991* (Cambridge: Harvard University Press, 1993).

Kirkeby, O.F. *The Virtue of Leadership* (Copenhagen: Copenhagen Business School Press, 2008).

Kissinger, H. *World Order* (London: Penguin, 2015).

Kitzinger, U. *Diplomacy and Persuasion: How Britain Joined the Common Market* (London: Thames and Hudson, 1973).

Klotz, A. 'Norms Reconstituting Interests: Global Racial Equality and U.S. Sanctions against South Africa,' *International Organization* 49 (3) (1995): 451–478.

Kocs, S.A. *Autonomy or Power? The Franco-German Relationship and Europe's Strategic Choices 1955–1995* (Westport: Greenwood, 1995).

Kohl, H. *Erinnerungen, 1982–1990* (Munich: Droemer, 2005).

———, 'Für ein gemeinsames Europa in Frieden und Freiheit,' *Bulletin* 76 (1995): 745–751.

———, 'Präsident François Mitterrand – ein großer Europäer verabschiedet sich' [first published in *Le Monde*, 11 May 1995], *Bulletin* 41 (1995): 356–357.

———, 'Aktuelle Fragen der Europapolitik,' *Bulletin* 51 (1994): 477–481.

———, 'Die deutsch-amerikanischen Beziehungen – Garantie für Frieden und Freiheit,' *Bulletin* 12 (1994): 101–103.

———, 'Perspektiven Deutschlands im erweiterten Europa,' *Bulletin* 42 (1994): 365–368.

———, 'Zukunftssicherung des Standorts Deutschland im geeinten Europa,' *Bulletin* 57 (1994): 537–540.

———, 'Europas politische Agenda für die neunziger Jahre,' *Bulletin* 94 (1993): 1051–1052.

———, 'Aktuelle Entwicklungen in der Europapolitik,' *Bulletin* 103 (1992): 965–968.

———, 'In der europäischen Einigung liegt unsere nationale Zukunft,' *Bulletin* 125 (1992): 1141–1145.

———, 'Press Briefing Delivered in Birmingham, October 16,' *Bulletin* 115 (1992): 1060–1061.

———, 'Politik der konsequenten Verwirklichung der Europäischen Union,' *Bulletin* 73 (1992): 697–701.

———, 'Zielvorstellungen und Chancen für die Zukunft Europas,' *Bulletin* 38 (1992): 353–356.

———, 'Declaration Delivered in Maastricht, December 13,' *Bulletin* 142 (1991): 1153–1158.

———, 'Fundamente und Strukturen einer gemeinsamen europäischen Zukunft,' *Bulletin* 60 (1991): 473–378.

———, 'Unterwegs zu einem versöhnten Europa,' *Bulletin* 75 (1991): 603–608.

———, 'Die deutsche Frage und die europäische Verantwortung,' *Bulletin* 9 (1990): 61–66.

———, 'Europa – Die Zukunft aller Deutschen,' *Bulletin* 21 (1990): 165–169.

Krell, G. 'West German Ostpolitik and the German Question,' *Journal of Peace Research* 28 (3) (1991): 311–323.

Kuhnert, K.W. and P. Lewis, 'Transactional and Transformational Leadership: A Constructive/Developmental Analysis,' *The Academy of Management Review* 12 (4) (1987): 648–657.

Kundnani, H. *The Paradox of German Power* (London: Hurst, 2014).

Kupchan, C. 'Centrifugal Europe,' *Survival* 54 (1) (2012): 111–118.

Küsters, H.-J. 'Walter Hallstein and the Negotiations on the Treaties of Rome 1955-57,' in *Walter Hallstein: The Forgotten European?*, W. Loth, W. Wallace, and W. Wessels eds. (Basingstoke: Macmillan, 1998), 60–81.

———, 'Adenauers Europapolitik in der Gründungsphase der Europäischen Wirtschaftsgemeinschaft,' *Vierteljahrshefte für Zeitgeschichte* 31 (4) (1983): 646–673.

Lacouture, J. *Mitterrand: Une Histoire de Français: 1. Les Risques de l'Escalade* (Paris: Seuil, 1998).

Lamb, R. *The Failure of the Eden Government* (London: Sidgwick and Jackson, 1987).

Langguth, G. 'Die Europapolitik Angela Merkels,' in *Deutsche Europapolitik Christlicher Demokraten. Von Konrad Adenauer bis Angela Merkel (1945–2013)*, H.J. Küsters ed. (Düsseldorf: Droste, 2014), 271–293.

Lapavitsas, C., A. Kaltenbrunner, G. Labrindis, D. Lindo, J. Meadway, J. Michell, J.P. Painceira, E. Pires, J. Powell, A. Stenfords, N. Teles, and L. Vatikotis, *Crisis in the Eurozone* (London: Verso, 2012).

Lappenküper, U. 'Helmut Kohl als europapolitischer Netzwerker: Seine Zusammenarbeit mit François Mitterrand, Felipe González und Jacques Chirac,' in *Deutsche Europapolitik Christlicher Demokraten. Von Konrad Adenauer bis Angela Merkel (1945–2013)*, H.-J. Küsters ed. (Düsseldorf: Droste, 2014), 203–232.

———, *Mitterrand und Deutschland, Die enträtselte Sphinx* (Munich: Oldebourg, 2011).

———, *Die Aussenpolitik der Bundesrepublik Deutschland 1949 bis 1990*, Enzyklopädie Deutscher Geschichte, Vol. 83 (Munich: Oldenbourg, 2008).

Larres, K. 'Schwierige Verbündete: Margaret Thatcher, John Major und die Politik Helmut Kohls,' in *Deutsche Europapolitik Christlicher Demokraten. Von Konrad Adenauer bis Angela Merkel (1945–2013)*, H.-J. Küsters ed. (Düsseldorf: Droste, 2014), 233–270.

———, *Churchill's Cold War: The Politics of Personal Diplomacy* (New Haven: Yale University Press, 2002).

Laurent, P.-H. 'The Diplomacy of *Junktim*: Paul-Henri Spaak and European Integration,' in *Personalities, War and Diplomacy: Essays in International History*, T.G. Otte and C.A. Pagedas eds. (London: Frank Cass, 1997), 186–212.

———, 'Widening Europe: The Dilemmas of Community Success,' *Annals of the American Academy of Political and Social Science* 531 (1994): 124–140.

———, 'The Diplomacy of the Rome Treaty, 1956-57,' *Journal of Contemporary History* 7 (3/4) (1972): 209–220.

———, 'Paul-Henri Spaak and the Diplomatic Origins of the Common Market, 1955-1956,' *Political Science Quarterly* 85 (3) (1970): 373–396.

Lee, S. *Victory in Europe: Britain and Germany Since 1945* (Harlow: Pearson, 2001).

Lefèbvre, D. *Guy Mollet. Le Mal Aimé* (Paris: Plon, 1992).

Lerner, D. 'French Business Leaders Look at EDC: A Preliminary Report,' *The Public Opinion Quarterly* 20 (1) (1956): 212–221.

Liddle, R. *The Europe Dilemma: Britain and the Drama of EU Integration* (London: I.B. Tauris, 2014).

Limagne, P. *L'éphémère IVe République* (Paris: France-Empire, 1977).
Lindberg, L.N. *The Political Dynamics of European Economic Integration* (Palo Alto: Stanford University Press, 1963).
Limberg, L.N. and S.A. Scheingold eds. *Regional Integration: Theory and Research* (Cambridge: Harvard University Press, 1971).
Lippert, B. 'Glanzloser Arbeitserfolg von epochaler Bedeutung: eine Bilanz der EU-Erweiterungspolitik 1989-2004,' in *Bilanz und Folgeprobleme der EU-Erweiterung*, B. Lippert ed. (Baden-Baden: Nomos, 2004), 13–72.
Lord, C. *British Entry to the European Community under the Heath Government of 1970–74* (Aldershot: Dartmouth, 1993).
Loth, W. 'Politische Integration nach 1945. Motive und Antriebskräfte bei Konrad Adenauer und Charles de Gaulle,' in *Europäische Einigung im 19. und 20. Jahrhundert. Akteure und Antriebskräfte*, U. Lappenküper and G. Thiemeyer eds. (Paderborn: Schöningh, 2013), 137–154.
———, 'Adenauer's Final Western Choice, 1955–58,' in *Europe, Cold War, and Coexistence 1953–1965*, W. Loth ed. (London: Frank Cass, 2004), 23–33.
———, 'From the "Third Force" to the Common Market: Discussions about Europe and the Future of the Nation-State in West Germany, 1945–57,' in *The Postwar Challenge: Cultural, Social, and Political Change in Western Europe, 1945–58*, D. Geppert ed. (Oxford: Oxford University Press, 2003), 191–210.
Löwenthal, R. *Vom Kalten Krieg zur Ostpolitik* (Stuttgart: Seewald, 1974).
Ludlow, P.N. 'The Making of the CAP: Towards a Historical Analysis of the EU's First Major Policy,' *Contemporary European History* 14 (3) (2005): 347–371.
———, *The Making of the European Monetary System: A Case Study of the Politics of the European Community* (London: Butterworth Scientific, 1982).
Lynch, F.M.B. 'France and European Integration: From the Schuman Plan to Economic and Monetary Integration,' *Contemporary European History* 13 (1) (2004): 117–121.
Lynch, F.M.B. *France and the International Economy: From Vichy to the Treaty of Rome* (London: Routledge, 1997).
Macmillan, H. *Riding the Storm 1956–1959* (London: Macmillan, 1971).
Mahant, E. *Birthmarks of Europe: The Origins of the European Community Reconsidered* (Aldershot: Ashgate, 2004).
Mahoney, D.J. *De Gaulle: Statesmanship, Grandeur, and Modern Democracy* (New Brunswick: Transaction, 2000).
Maier, M., J. Maier, A. Baumert, N. Jahn, S. Krause, and S. Adam., 'Measuring Citizens' Implicit and Explicit Attitudes towards the European Union,' *European Union Politics* 16 (3) (2015): 369–385.
Mair, P. *Ruling the Void: The Hollowing of Western Democracy* (London: Verso, 2013).
Mair, S. 'Deutschland: Gestaltungsmacht Wider Willen,' in *Außenpolitik in der Wirtschafts- und Finanzkrise*, J. Braml, S. Mair, and E. Sandschneider eds. (Munich: Oldenburg, 2012), 125–136.
Majone, G. *Dilemmas of European Integration: The Ambiguities and Pitfalls of Integration Through Stealth* (Oxford: Oxford University Press, 2005).
Major, J. *The Autobiography* (London: Harper Collins, 1999).
Marquand, D. *The End of the West: The Once and Future Europe* (Princeton: Princeton University Press, 2011).

Marsh, D. *Europe's Deadlock: How the Euro Crisis Could Be Solved – and Why It Won't Happen* (New Haven: Yale University Press, 2013).
———, *The Euro: The Battle for the New Global Currency* (New Haven: Yale University Press, 2011).
Marshall, B. *Willy Brandt: A Political Biography* (Basingstoke: Macmillan, 1997).
Martin, L. 'The Rational Choice of Multilateralism,' in *Multilateralism Matters: The Theory and Praxis of an Institutional Form*, J.G. Ruggie ed. (New York: Columbia University Press, 1993), 91–124.
Massip, R. *De Gaulle et l'Europe* (Paris: Garimard, 1963).
Mattli, W. *The Logic of Regional Integration: Europe and Beyond* (Cambridge: Cambridge University Press, 1999).
Maury, J.-P. 'Référendum sur l'élargissement de la Communauté européenne,' *Digithèque de matériaux juridiques et politiques de l'Université de Perpignan* online (1998), http://mjp.univ-perp.fr/france/ref1972.htm
Mayer, H. 'Early at the Beach and Claiming Territory? The Evolution of German Ideas on a New European Order,' *International Affairs* 73 (4) (1997): 721–737.
Mayne, R. 'The Role of Jean Monnet,' *Government and Opposition* 2 (1966): 350–360.
Mazower, M. *Governing the World: The History of an Idea* (London: Allen Lane, 2012).
McCarthy, P. ed. *France-Germany, 1983–1993: The Struggle to Cooperate* (Basingstoke: Macmillan, 1993).
McNamara, K.R. *The Currency of Ideas: Monetary Politics in the European Union* (Ithaca: Cornell University Press, 1998).
Mearsheimer, J.J. *The Tragedy of Great Power Politics* (New York: WW Norton, 2001).
———, 'The False Promise of International Institutions,' *International Security* 19 (3) (1994–5): 5–49.
———, 'Back to the Future: Instability in Europe After the Cold War,' *International Security* 15 (1) (1990): 5–56.
Melissen, J. and B. Zeemann, 'Britain and Western Europe, 1945–51: Opportunities Lost?,' *International Affairs* 63 (19) (1986–87): 81–95.
Menéndez-Alarcón, A.V. *The Cultural Realm of European Integration: Social Representations in France, Spain, and the United Kingdom* (Westport: Praeger, 2004).
Menon, A. 'The Other Euro Crisis: Why Europe Desperately Needs Military Collaboration,' *Foreign Affairs* (13 December 2013): https://www.foreignaffairs.com/articles/western-europe/2013-12-10/other-euro-crisis
Merkl, P. 'The German Janus: From Westpolitik to Ostpolitik,' *Political Science Quarterly* 89 (4) (1974–75): 803–824.
———, 'Equilibrium, Structure of Interests and Leadership: Adenauer's Survival as Chancellor,' *The American Political Science Review* 56 (3) (1962): 634–650.
Milward, A.S. *The European Rescue of the Nation-State*, second edition (London: Routledge, 2000).
Mitterrand, F. *De l'Allemagne, de la France* (Paris: Poches Odile Jacob, 2001).
———, *Mémoires pour Servir à l'Histoire de Ma Vie* (Paris: Bartillat, 1997).
———, *Mémoires Interrompus, Entretiens avec Georges-Marc Benamou* (Paris: Odile Jacob, 1996).

———, *Réflexions sur la Politique Extérieure de la France: Introduction à vingt-cinq Discours (1981–1985)* (Paris: Fayard, 1986).
Möckli, D. *European Foreign Policy During the Cold War: Heath, Brandt, and Pompidou and the Short Dream of Political Unity* (London: I.B. Tauris, 2009).
Moeller, R. 'The German Social Democrats,' in *Political Parties and the European Union*, J. Gaffney ed. (London: Routledge, 1996), 1–30.
Möller, A. 'Die Europäische Union vor der Zerreißprobe,' in *Außenpolitik in der Wirtschafts- und Finanzkrise*, J. Braml, S. Mair, and E. Sandschneider eds. (Munich: Oldenburg, 2012), 306–311.
Monnet, J. *Memoirs* (London: Collins, 1978).
Moravcsik, A. 'The Future of European Integration Studies: Social Science or Social Theory,' *Millennium* 28 (2) (1999): 371–391.
———, *The Choice for Europe: Social Purpose and State Power From Messina to Maastricht* (London: Routledge, 1998).
———, 'Negotiating the Single European Act: National Interests and Conventional Statecraft in the European Community,' *International Organization* 45 (1) (1991): 651–688.
Morgan, G. *The Idea of a European Superstate: Public Justification and European Integration* (Princeton: Princeton University Press, 2005).
Morris, P. 'The British Conservative Party,' in *Political Parties and the European Union*, J. Gaffney ed. (London: Routledge, 1996), 122–138.
Müller, H. 'Arguing, Bargaining and All That: Communicative Action, Rationalist Theory and the Logic of Appropriateness in International Relations,' *European Journal of International Relations* 10 (3) (2004): 395–435.
Müller, J.-W. *Contesting Democracy: Political Ideas in Twentieth-Century Europe* (New Haven: Yale University Press, 2011).
Müller-Roschach, H. *Die Deutsche Europapolitik: Wege und Umwege zur Politischen Union Europas* (Baden-Baden: Nomos, 1974).
Münkler, H. *Macht in der Mitte. Die neuen Aufgaben Deutschlands in Europa* (Hamburg: Körber Stiftung, 2015).
Murray. P. 'European Integration Studies: The Search for Synthesis,' *Contemporary Politics* 6 (1) (2000): 19–28.
———, 'Nationalist or Internationalist? Socialists and European Unity,' in *Visions of European Unity*, P. Murray and P. Rich eds. (Boulder: Westview, 1996), 159–182.
Murray, P. and P. Rich eds. *Visions of European Unity* (Boulder: Westview, 1996).
Musitelli, J. 'François Mitterrand, l'européen,' *La lettre de l'Institut François Mitterrand* 8 (June 2004), 2–6.
Naím, M. *The End of Power: From Boardroom to Battlefields and Churches to States, Why Being in Charge Isn't What It Used to Be* (New York: Basic Books, 2013).
Nelsen, B.F. and Alexander C.-G. Stubb eds. *The European Union: Readings on the Theory and Practice of European Integration*, second edition (Basingstoke: Macmillan, 1998).
Northcutt, W. *Mitterrand: A Political Biography* (New York: Holms and Meier, 1992).
———, 'François Mitterrand and the Political Use of Symbols: The Construction of a Centrist Republic,' *French Historical Studies* 17 (1) (1991): 141–158.
Nye, J.S. *The Powers to Lead* (Oxford: Oxford University Press, 2008).

O'Neill, C. *Britain's Entry Into the European Community: Report on the Negotiations of 1970–1972.* D. Hannay ed. (London: Frank Cass, 2000).

Orlow, D. *Common Destiny: A Comparative History of the Dutch, French, and German Social Democratic Parties, 1945–1969* (New York: Berghahn, 2001).

Otte, T.G. 'Eyre Crowe and British Foreign Policy: A Cognitive Map,' in *Personalities, War, and Diplomacy: Essays in International History*, T.G. Otte and C.A. Pagedas eds. (London: Frank Cass, 1997), 14–37.

Packer, G. 'The Quiet German: The Astonishing Rise of Angela Merkel, the Most Powerful Woman in the World,' *The New Yorker* (1 December 2014): http://www.newyorker.com/magazine/2014/12/01/quiet-german

Paige, G. *Political Leadership: Readings for an Emerging Field* (New York: Free Press, 1972).

Parr, H. 'A Question of Leadership: July 1966 and Harold Wilson's European Decision,' *Contemporary British History* 19 (4) (2005): 437–458.

Parsons, C. *A Certain Idea of Europe* (Ithaca: Cornell University Press, 2003).

———, 'Showing Ideas as Causes: The Origins of the European Union,' *International Organization* 56 (1) (2002): 47–84.

Parsons, C. and M. Matthijs, 'European Integration Past, Present and Future: Moving Forward Through Crisis' and M. Matthijs and M. Blyth, 'Conclusion: The Future of the Euro: Possible Futures, Risks, and Uncertainties,' in *The Future of the Euro*, M. Matthijs and M. Blyth eds. (Oxford: Oxford University Press, 2015), 210–232.

Paterson, W.E. 'Helmut Kohl, "The Vision Thing," and Escaping the Semi-Sovereignty Trap,' in *The Kohl Chancellorship*, C. Clemens and W.E. Paterson eds. (London: Frank Cass, 1998), 17–36.

———, 'The German Christian Democrats,' in *Political Parties and the European Union*, John Gaffney ed. (London: Routledge, 1996), 53–70.

Pattison de Ménil, L. *Who Speaks for Europe? The Vision of Charles de Gaulle* (London: Weidenfeld and Nicolson, 1977).

Pautola, N. 'Toward European Union Eastern Enlargement: Progress and Problems in Pre-Accession,' *Russian and East European Finance and Trade* 35 (6) (2000): 45–67.

Pauwels, T. *Populism in Western Europe: Comparing Belgium, Germany, and the Netherlands* (London: Routledge, 2014).

Peele, G. 'Leadership and Politics: A Case for a Closer Relationship?,' *Leadership* 1 (2) (2005): 187–204.

Peterson, J. and E. Bomberg, *Decision-Making in the European Union* (Basingstoke: Palgrave, 1999).

Pew Research Centre, Global Attitudes & Trends, *A Fragile Rebound for the EU Image on Eve of European Parliament Elections* (12 May 2014): http://www.pewglobal.org/2014/05/12/a-fragile-rebound-for-eu-image-on-eve-of-european-parliament-elections/

Pfeffer, J. 'The Ambiguity of Leadership,' *The Academy of Management Review* 2 (1) (1977): 104–112.

Pickles, D. 'The Decline of Gaullist Foreign Policy,' *International Affairs* 51 (2) (1975): 220–235.

Pierson, P. 'The Path to European Integration: A Historical Institutionalist Analysis,' *Comparative Political Studies* 29 (2) (1996): 123–163.

Pinder, P. *Europe against De Gaulle* (London: Pall Mall Press, 1963).

Pine, M. *Harold Wilson and Europe: Pursuing Britain's Membership of the European Community* (London: I.B. Tauris, 2012).

Pineau, C. and C. Rimbaud, *Le Grand Pari: L'Aventure du Traité de Rome* (Paris: Fayard, 1991).

Piris, J.-C. 'The Acceleration of Differentiated Integration and Enhanced Cooperation,' *Fondation Robert Schuman – European Issues* 328 (13 October 2014): 1–5.

Pisani-Ferry, J. *The Euro Crisis and Its Aftermath* (Oxford: Oxford University Press, 2014).

———, 'L'Europe à géométrie variable: une analyse économique,' *Politique Étrangère* 60 (2) (1995): 447–465.

Pollack, M.A. *The Engines of European Integration: Delegation, Agency and Agenda Setting in the EU* (Oxford: Oxford University Press, 2003).

———, 'International Relations Theory and European Integration,' *Journal of Common Market Studies* 39 (2) (2001): 221–244.

Pomper, P. 'Historians and Individual Agency,' *History and Theory* 35 (3) (1996): 281–308.

Pompidou, G. *Pour Rétablir une Vérité* (Paris: Flammarion, 1982).

———, *Entretiens et Discours 1968–1974. Vol. I* (Paris: Plon, 1975).

———, *Entretiens et Discours 1968–1974. Vol. II* (Paris: Plon, 1975).

Pond, E. *The Rebirth of Europe* (Washington, DC: Brookings Institution Press, 1999).

Poppinga, A. *Konrad Adenauer: Geschichtsverständnis, Weltanschauung und politische Praxis* (Stuttgart: Deutsche Verlags-Anstalt, 1975).

Post, J.M. *Leaders and Their Followers in a Dangerous World: The Psychology of Political Behavior* (Ithaca: Cornell University Press, 2004).

Price, T.L. *Leadership Ethics: An Introduction* (Cambridge: Cambridge University Press, 2008).

Pugh, M. *State and Society: A Social and Political History of Britain Since 1870*, fourth edition (London: Bloomsbury, 2012).

Ramsden, J. *The Winds of Change: Macmillan to Heath, 1957–1975*. A History of the Conservative Party series (London: Longman, 1996).

Reid, T.R. *The United States of Europe: From Euro to Eurovision–the Superpower Nobody Talks about* (London: Penguin, 2004).

Reus-Smit, C. 'The Idea of History and History With Ideas,' in *Historical Sociology of International Relations*, S. Hobden and J.M. Hobson eds. (Cambridge: Cambridge University Press, 2002), 120–140.

———, *The Moral Purpose of the State: Culture, Social Identity, and Institutional Rationality in International Relations* (Princeton: Princeton University Press, 1999).

Reynolds, D. *Summits: Six Meetings That Shaped the Twentieth Century* (Philadelphia: Perseus, 2007).

Rhodes James, R. *Anthony Eden* (London: Weidenfeld and Nicholson, 1986).

Rifkin, J. *The European Dream: How Europe's Vision of the Future Is Quietly Eclipsing the American Dream* (Cambridge: Polity, 2004).

Risse, T. '"Let's Argue!": Communicative Action in World Politics,' *International Organization* 54 (1) (2000): 1–39.

Roche, J.-J. 'Une Politique Etrangère Malmenée par l'Histoire,' in *État Politique de la France*, D. Chagnollaud ed. (Paris: Quai Voltaire, 1992), 127–144.

Rogosch, D. *Vorstellungen von Europa: Europabilder in der SPD und bei den belgischen Sozialisten 1945–1957* (Hamburg: Krämer, 1996).

Romano, S. *Guida alla Politica Estera Italiana. Da Badoglio a Berlusconi* (Milano: BUR Saggi, 2004).
Rosato, S. *Europe United: Power Politics and the Making of the European Community* (Ithaca: Cornell University Press, 2011).
———, 'Europe's Troubles: Power Politics and the State of the European Project,' *International Security* 35 (4) (2011): 45–86.
Rost, J.C. *Leadership for the Twenty-First Century* (Westport: Praeger, 1993).
Rothwell, V. *Anthony Eden: A Political Biography 1931–57* (Manchester: Manchester University Press, 1992).
Roussel, E. *Georges Pompidou, 1911–1974.* Collection Tempus, Vol. 60 (Paris: Perrin, 2004).
———, *Jean Monnet, 1888–1979* (Paris: Arthème Fayard, 1996).
———, *Mitterrand ou la Constance du Funambule* (Mesnil-sur-l'Estrée: Éditions Lattès, 1991).
Ruane, K. 'Agonizing Reappraisals: Anthony Eden, John Foster Dulles and the Crisis of European Defence, 1953–54,' *Diplomacy & Statecraft* 13 (4) (2002): 151–185.
Sampson, A. *Political Leaders of the Twentieth Century: Macmillan: A Study in Ambiguity* (Harmondsworth: Penguin, 1968).
Sandbu, M. *Europe's Orphan: The Future of the Euro and the Politics of Debt* (Princeton: Princeton University Press, 2015).
Sanders, D. *Losing an Empire, Finding a Role: British Foreign Policy Since 1945* (Basingstoke: Macmillan, 1990).
Sandholtz, W. and A. Stone Sweet eds. *European Integration and Supranational Governance* (Oxford: Oxford University Press, 1998).
Saunier, G. '"J'y étais, j'y croyais." Les origines de l'engagement européen de François Mitterrand,' *La lettre de l'Institut François Mitterrand* 8 (June 2004): 10–11.
Schaad, M.P.C. *Bullying Bonn: Anglo-German Diplomacy on European Integration, 1955–61* (Basingstoke: Macmillan, 2000).
———, 'Plan G – A "Counterblast"? British Policy towards the Messina Countries, 1956,' *Contemporary European History* 7 (1) (1998): 39–60.
Schain, M. 'The Fifth Republic,' in *The French Republic. History, Values, Debates*, E. Berenson, V. Duclert, and C. Prochasson eds. (Ithaca: Cornell University Press, 2011), 83–92.
Scharpf, F. 'Monetary Union, Fiscal Crisis and the Disabling of Democratic Accountability,' in *Politics in the Age of Austerity*, A. Schäfer and W. Streeck eds. (Cambridge: Polity, 2013), 108–147.
———, *Governing in Europe: Effective and Democratic?* (Oxford: Oxford University Press, 1999).
Schimmelpfennig, F. 'Liberal Identity and Postnational Inclusion: The Eastern Enlargement of the European Union,' in *Constructing Europe's Identity: The External Dimension*, L.-E. Cederman ed. (Boulder: Lynne Rienner, 2001), 165–186.
Schmidt, V.A. 'The Eurozone's Crisis of Democratic Legitimacy: Can the EU Rebuild Public Trust and Support for European Economic Integration?,' European Commission, *Fellowship Initiative 2014–2015*, Discussion paper 015 (September 2015): 1–56: http://ec.europa.eu/economy_finance/publications/eedp/pdf/dp015_en.pdf
Schneider, G. and M. Aspinwall eds. *The Rules of Integration: The Institutionalist Approach to European Studies* (Manchester: Manchester University Press, 2001).

Schöllgen, G. *Willy Brandt: Die Biographie* (Munich: Ullstein, 2003).
Schwarz, H.-P. *Konrad Adenauer: A German Politician and Statesman in a Period of War, Revolution, and Reconstruction. Volume Two, The Statesman: 1952-1967* (Oxford: Berghahn, 1997).
Segers, M. 'Der Streit um die deutsche Europapolitik in den 1950er Jahren,' in *Deutsche Europapolitik Christlicher Demokraten. Von Konrad Adenauer bis Angela Merkel (1945–2013)*, H.J. Küsters ed. (Düsseldorf: Droste, 2014), 295–330.
Seldon, A. *Major: A Political Life* (London: Phoenix, 1997).
Seligman, L.G. 'The Study of Leadership,' *The American Political Science Review* 44 (4) (1950): 904–915.
Shamir, B., H. Dayan-Horesh, and D. Adler, 'Leading by Biography: Towards a Life-Story Approach to the Study of Leadership,' *Leadership* 1 (1) (2005): 13–30.
Shaw, M. *Theory of the Global State: Globality as an Unfinished Revolution* (Cambridge: Cambridge University Press, 2000).
Sheffer, G. ed. *Innovative Leaders in International Politics* (Albany: State University of New York Press, 1993).
Shields, J. 'The French Gaullists,' in *Political Parties and the European Union*, J. Gaffney ed. (London: Routledge, 1996), 86–109.
Sicking, L. 'A Colonial Echo: France and the Colonial Dimension of the European Economic Community,' *French Colonial History* 5 (2004): 207–228.
Siegler, H. *Dokumentation der Europäischen Integration 1946–1961, Band 1: unter besonderer Beachtung des Verhältnisses EWG-EFTA* (Bonn: Siegler, 1961).
Smaghi, L.B. *Morire di Austerità. Democrazie europee con le spalle al muro* (Bologna: Il Mulino, 2013).
Smith, K.E. *European Union Foreign Policy in a Changing World* (Cambridge: Polity, 2003).
Somma, A. *La Dittatura dello Spread. Germania, Europa e Crisi del Debito* (Milano: Derive Approdi, 2014).
Spaak, P.-H. *The Continuing Battle: Memoirs of a European 1936–1966* (London: Weidenfeld and Nicolson, 1971).
———, *Combats Inachevés: De l'Espoir aux Deceptions* (Brussels: Fayard, 1969).
Stark, H. *La Politique Internationale de l'Allemagne. Une Puissance Malgré Elle* (Paris: Septentrion, 2011).
Steinnes, K. 'The European Challenge: Britain's EEC Application in 1961,' *Contemporary European History* 7 (1) (1998): 61–79.
Stogdill, R.M. *Handbook of Leadership: A Survey of Theory and Research* (New York: Free Press, 1974).
Stone Sweet, A. and T.L. Brunell, 'Constructing a Supranational Constitution: Dispute Resolution and Governance in the European Community,' *The American Political Science Review* 92 (1) (1998): 63–81.
Stone Sweet, A. and J.A. Caporaso, 'From Free Trade to Supranational Polity: The European Court and European Integration,' in *European Integration and Supranational Governance*, W. Sandholtz and A. Stone Sweet eds. (Oxford: Oxford University Press, 1998), 92–133.
Stone Sweet, A. and W. Sandholtz, 'Integration, Supranational Governance, and the Institutionalization of the European Polity,' in *European Integration and Supranational Governance*, W. Sandholtz and A. Stone Sweet eds. (Oxford: Oxford University Press, 1998), 1–26.
Sutton, M. *France and the Construction of Europe, 1944–2007: The Geopolitical Imperative* (Oxford: Berghahn, 2007).

Szabo, S. 'The United States and German Unification,' in *The United States and Germany in the Era of the Cold War, 1945–1990: A Handbook*, Volume 2: 1968–1990, D. Junker ed. (Cambridge: Cambridge University Press, 2004), 104–110.

Tallberg, Jonas, *Leadership and Negotiation in the European Union* (Cambridge: Cambridge University Press, 2006).

———, 'The Power of the Presidency: Brokerage, Efficiency and Distribution in EU Negotiations,' *Journal of Common Market Studies* 42 (5) (2004): 999–1022.

Tauch, C. 'The Testimony of an Eyewitness: Christian Pineau, Interviewed by Christian Tauch,' in *Socialist Parties and the Question of Europe in the 1950s*, R.T. Griffiths ed. (Leiden: Brill, 1993), 43–57.

Taylor, P. 'The Politics of the European Communities: The Confederal Phase,' *World Politics* 27 (3) (1975): 336–360.

Thorpe, D.R. *Eden: The Life and Times of Anthony Eden First Earl of Avon, 1897–1977* (London: Pimlico, 2004).

Tiersky, R. *François Mitterrand: A Very French President* (Lanham: Rowman and Littlefield, 2000).

Trachtenberg, M. *A Constructed Peace: The Making of the European Settlement, 1945–1963* (Princeton: Princeton University Press, 1999).

Tratt, J. *The Macmillan Government and Europe: A Study in the Process of Policy Development* (Basingstoke: Macmillan, 1996).

Tremonti, G. *La Paura e la Speranza. Europa: La Crisi Globale che si Avvicina e la Via per Superarla* (Milan: Mondadori, 2008).

Tsebelis, G. and G. Garrett, 'The Institutional Foundations of Intergovernmentalism and Supranationalism in the European Union,' *International Organization* 55 (2) (2001): 357–390.

Tsoukalis, L. *The Politics and Economics of European Monetary Integration* (London: George Allen and Unwin, 1977).

Tucker, R.C. *Politics as Leadership* (Columbia: University of Missouri Press, 1981).

———, 'Personality and Political Leadership,' *Political Science Quarterly* 92 (3) (1977): 383–393.

Türk, H. *Die Europapolitik der Großen Koalition 1966–1969* (Munich: Oldenburg, 2006).

Turner, J. *The Tories and Europe* (Manchester: Manchester University Press, 2000).

Urwin, D.W. *A Political History of Western Europe Since 1945*, fifth edition (London: Longman, 1997).

van Overtveldt, J. *The End of the Euro: The Uneasy Future of the European Union* (Chicago: B2 Books, 2011).

Védrine, H. *Dans la Mêlée Mondiale 2009–2012* (Paris: Fayard, 2012).

———, 'L'Europe de Mitterrand,' *La lettre de l'Institut François Mitterrand* 8 (June 2004): 1.

Verheugen, G. 'The Enlargement of the European Union,' *European Foreign Affairs Review* 5 (2000): 439–444.

Vernet, D. 'Le Lack ist ab. Warum die deutsch-französische Zusammenarbeit nicht mehr das ist, was sie einmal war,' *Internationale Politik und Gesellschaft* (22 December 2014).

———, 'The Dilemma of French Foreign Policy,' *International Affairs* 68 (4) (1992): 655–664.

Vogt, R. and L. Chong, 'German National Identity: Moving beyond Guilt,' in *European National Identities: Elements, Transitions, Conflicts*, R. Vogt, W. Cristaudo, and A. Leutzsch eds. (New Brunswick: Transaction, 2014), 71–94.

von Brentano, H. *Germany and Europe: Reflections on German Foreign Policy* (London: André Deutsch, 1964).

———, *Deutschland, Europa und die Welt: Reden zur Deutschen Aussenpolitik*, F. Böhm ed. (Bonn: Verlag für Zeitarchive, 1962).

von der Groeben, H. *Aufbaujahre der Europäischen Gemeinschaft: Das Ringen um den Gemeinsamen Markt und die Politische Union (1958–1966)* (Baden-Baden: Nomos, 1982).

von Gersdorff, G. *Adenauers Außenpolitik gegenüber den Siegermächten 1954. Westdeutsche Bewaffnung und internationale Politik*. Beiträge zur Militärgeschichte, Vol. 41 (Munich: Oldenbourg, 1994).

Wall, S. *A Stranger in Europe: Britain and the EU From Thatcher to Blair* (Oxford: Oxford University Press, 2008).

Waltz, K.N. 'Political Structures,' in *Neorealism and Its Critics*, R.O. Keohane ed. (New York: Columbia University Press, 1985), 70–97.

Weidenfeld, W. *Konrad Adenauer und Europa: Die geistigen Grundlagen der westeuropäischen Integrationspolitik des ersten Bonner Bundeskanzlers* (Bonn: Europa Union, 1976).

Weigall, D. and P. Stirk eds. *The Origins and Development of the European Community* (Leicester: Leicester University Press, 1992).

Wendt, A. *Social Theory of International Politics* (Cambridge: Cambridge University Press, 1999).

Wenger, P.W. 'Schuman und Adenauer,' in *Konrad Adenauer und seine Zeit. Politik und Persönlichkeit des ersten Bundeskanzlers. Beiträge von Weg- und Zeitgenossen*, D. Blumenwitz, K. Gotto, H. Maier, K. Repgen, and H.-P. Schwarz eds. (Stuttgart: Deutsche Verlags-Anstalt, 1976), 395–414.

Wessels, W. 'The EC Council: The Community's Decisionmaking Center,' in *The New European Community: Decisionmaking and Institutional Change*, R.O. Keohane and S. Hoffmann eds. (Boulder: Westview, 1991), 133–154.

Weymar, P. *Konrad Adenauer: The Authorised Biography* (Worcester: Andre Deutsch, 1957).

Williams, C. *Adenauer: The Father of New Germany* (London: Abacus, 2003).

Wright, J. 'The Cold War, European Community and Anglo-French Relations, 1958–1998,' in *Anglo-French Relations in the Twentieth Century: Rivalry and Cooperation*, A. Sharp and G. Stone eds. (London: Routledge, 2000), 324–343.

Wurm, C.A. 'Britain and European Integration, 1945–63,' *Contemporary European History* 7 (2) (1998): 246–291.

Wurm, C.A. ed., *Western Europe and Germany: The Beginnings of European Integration 1945–1960* (Oxford: Berg, 1995).

Yondorf, W. 'Monnet and the Action Committee: The Formative Period of the European Communities,' *International Organization* 19 (4) (1965): 885–912.

Young, H. *This Blessed Plot: Britain and Europe From Churchill to Blair* (Basingstoke: Macmillan, 1998).

Young, J.W. 'Conclusion,' in *Whitehall and the Suez Crisis*, S. Kelly and A. Gorst eds. (London: Frank Cass, 2000), 221–231.

———, '"The Parting of the Ways?": Britain, the Messina Conference and the Spaak Committee, June-December 1955,' in *British Foreign Policy 1945–56*, M. Dockrill and J.W. Young eds. (Basingstoke: Macmillan, 1989), 197–224.

Young, O.R. *Governance in World Affairs* (Ithaca: Cornell University Press, 1999).

———, 'The Politics of International Regime Formation: Managing Natural Resources and the Environment,' *International Organization* 43 (3) (1989): 349–375.

Ziegler, P. *Edward Heath: The Authorised Biography* (London: Harper Press, 2010).

Index

Acquis communautaire 116, 122, 137, 182
Adenauer, Konrad: and *Auswärtiges Amt* 65; and Catholic social theory 10, 66, 68; and de Gaulle 10, 127, 192; and Erhard 3, 32, 36, 70, 82; and Franco-German partnership 58–9, 65, 68, 70, 79, 84–5; and German rearmament 67; as influenced on Kohl 156; and Mollet 9, 11, 30, 33, 57–62, 65–72, 74, 77–9, 84–6, 138, 178, 192, 195; and 'order to integrate' 3, 65; and 'rush to Rome' 62; and Saar agreement 57–9, 67, 71, 84, 85; and United States 67–9, 78, 87, 89; and *Westintegration* 66–7, 79
Adenauer, Paul 86
Africa 60, 79, 84, 99
agency 9, 12, 27, 38–9, 146
agriculture 55, 57, 86, 96, 123
Algerian crisis 3, 47, 55–6, 61, 63, 65, 67, 70
Alleinvertretungsanspruch 98
Alternative für Deutschland (AfD) 180
anti-Americanism 85, 117
anti-Communism 10, 65, 68
appeasement 44
Armstrong, Robert 101
atheism 69
Atlanticism 58, 63, 73, 94–5, 115, 124
atomic energy *see nuclear energy*
austerity 2, 6, 180–1, 191, 196
Austria 136

Bahr, Egon 98, 129
bailout 4, 180, 195–6
behaviour 2, 7, 10, 12, 20–3, 26, 37, 39, 41, 43, 46, 47, 60–2, 66, 72, 75, 77, 87, 160, 166, 192–3; as an outcome of institutional dynamics 192–3; as an outcome of interests 12, 62; as an outcome of structural conditions 21; of decision-makers 7, 12, 20, 27, 37, 39, 41, 47, 60–2, 66, 72, 75, 87, 166; of states 2, 23, 26, 77
Belgium 53–4, 62–3, 65, 86
beliefs 7, 10, 42, 46, 77, 114, 144, 165
Berlin 98, 106, 195–6; Berlin Wall 118, 136, 147, 150; and Brandenburg Gate 141; East Berlin 140
Beyen, Johan 54, 81–2
Board of Trade 55
Bonn 58, 60, 78, 84, 98, 106, 118–19, 131, 135, 140, 148, 157, 164, 193
Brandt, Willy 10, 11, 19, 94–106, 109–11, 113, 118–23, 125, 127–31, 195; and EMU 100; and enlargement 19, 94–5, 97, 102, 106, 118, 122; and European Order of Peace 97, 119–21, 128; and Hague summit (1969) 99–101, 110; and Heath 94–5, 100–6, 109–10, 118–23, 130, 131, 195; and Nixon 118; and Nobel Peace Prize 122; and *Ostpolitik* 96–8, 101, 105–6, 118–19, 122–3, 126, 127, 129; and 'Politik der kleinen Schritte' 98; and Pompidou 11, 19, 94–106, 109–11, 113, 119–20, 122–3, 125, 131, 195; and *Westpolitik* 97, 99, 119, 129
Brazil 113
Bretherton, Russell 55
Bretton Woods system 100
Brexit 2, 5, 8, 12, 179, 183, 192
Britain 2–5, 7–9, 19, 28–9, 32, 55–7, 61–3, 66–9, 71–9, 82, 83, 85, 87, 91–110, 112, 114–19, 121–4, 126, 127, 131, 134, 137–8, 142–6, 148,

152, 154, 158–63, 165–7, 176, 178–9, 183–6, 192, 195–6; and attitudes to European integration 28, 63, 73–4, 76–9, 87, 101–3, 107, 114, 116, 138, 148, 152, 159–60; and French veto to British accession 101, 103–4, 107–9, 124; and great power status 74, 114, 116
Bruges 161
Brussels 4, 6, 27, 103, 121, 148, 165, 179, 182, 195, 196; Brussels negotiations 55–9, 61, 64, 66, 70–1, 73–4, 76–9, 86, 91
Bundesbank 25, 143, 144, 146, 171
Bundeswehr 53, 67
Bush, George H.W. 141, 169

cabinet viii; in Britain 115, 164; in France 56, 57, 70; Germany 3, 36, 97
Cameron, David 179, 184, 195
Catholic Church *see* Roman Catholicism
Catholicism *see* Roman Catholicism
Chamberlain, Neville 44
Chequers 109, 129
China 8, 55, 95, 113
Christian democracy 66, 138, 154
Christianity 66, 68–9, 111, 127, 155
Christlich-Demokratische Union (CDU) 97, 119, 172
Christlich-Soziale Union (CSU) 119
civilisation 10, 46, 68, 111–12, 115, 121, 154
Cold War 19, 100, 127, 136–8, 142, 155–7, 159, 166, 167, 169
Common Agricultural Policy (CAP) 96, 99, 100, 118, 126
Common Market *see* European Economic Community
Commonwealth 73–7, 91, 115–17, 122, 124; and preferential trade with Britain 79, 92, 121
Communism 10, 53, 57, 65, 68, 69, 80, 84, 85, 95, 97, 121
Confédération Française des Travailleurs Chrétiens (CFTC) 84
Confédération Générale du Travail (CGT) 84
Confederation of British Industry (CBI) 118
Conservative Party (UK) 74, 94, 101, 110, 114, 117, 138, 148, 159–65, 175, 184
constitutionalism 76

constructivism (theory of International Relations) 12, 39, 45, 48
cooperation 3, 6, 10, 12, 19, 22–4, 31, 45, 47, 53–4, 56, 58, 64, 70–1, 79, 85, 97–8, 109, 111–12, 114, 116, 118–21, 138, 140, 142, 146, 151–3, 155, 158, 161–2, 166, 182–3, 191
Coty, René 56
Council of Europe 152, 159
Council of the European Union 194
Crimea 186
crisis management 4, 6, 178, 186–7
culture 47, 155, 187
customs union 29, 31, 32, 46–7, 54, 65, 81
Cyprus 4, 180
Czechoslovakia 98

Danske Folkeparti (DF) 180
Davignon Report 124
Davos 156
De Gaulle, Charles 10, 19, 20, 29, 37, 42, 94–7, 99–101, 106, 108–9, 111–12, 123, 124, 125, 126, 127, 129, 151–3, 192; and British veto 101, 108–9, 124; and Empty Chair Crisis 45, 95; and Gaullism 45, 53, 69, 94–6, 101, 112, 122–3, 124, 125, 126, 127, 152; and *grandeur* 95; and NATO 95; and OEEC 95; resignation 95; and 'Third Force' Europe 127
Delors, Jacques 139, 140, 148, 168, 174; and EMU 142–4; and Single European Act 140
Denmark 100, 158, 183, 184
détente 98, 118, 119, 128
determinism 11, 20, 25–7, 38
diplomacy viii, 1–2, 4, 9, 11–12, 22, 27, 30, 32, 37, 53, 58–9, 61, 64, 76, 78, 104, 107, 118, 138, 146, 150, 157, 159, 179, 181, 186, 192–3; and autonomy 4, 9, 11, 40–1, 45, 47, 111, 137–8, 160, 164, 167, 187, 192, 196; and closed diplomacy 64; and personal diplomacy 22, 27, 30, 32, 37, 53, 59, 122, 138, 146, 159, 192–3; and preventive diplomacy 179; and staffless diplomacy 107; and summit diplomacy 2, 9, 58–9, 79, 104, 107, 122, 129, 130, 186
Dirigisme see France
Douglas-Home, Alec 102, 117
Draghi, Mario 4, 181

Dublin agreement 193, 196
Dulles, John F. 86

East Germany *see* German Democratic Republic
Economic and Monetary Union (EMU) 4, 5, 11, 25, 27, 95, 98–100, 105, 119, 129, 137–8, 142–8, 150–1, 153–5, 157–66, 170, 171, 179–82; and Bundesbank 25, 143, 144, 146, 171; and convergence criteria 143; and Euro (single currency) 2, 5, 10–11, 24–5, 27, 136–8, 142–4, 154, 163, 165–7, 180–3, 193; and European Financial Stability Facility 181; and European Stability Mechanism 181; and Eurozone viii, 2, 4–6, 8, 11–12, 25, 145, 178–83, 185, 187, 191–5; and Maastricht Treaty 137, 143, 146–7, 159–60, 163, 171, 179; and 'rush to EMU,' 11; and Stability and Growth Pact 143, 145; and Werner Plan 129
economic stagnation 2, 5, 94, 179, 181, 185, 191
Eden, Sir Anthony 11, 57, 59, 61–2, 71–9, 80, 85, 87, 94, 117, 192; and Anglo-French Union 57, 71; and Britain's world power status 74–5, 79; and Commonwealth 73–7, 79; and European Defence Community 61; and German rearmament 61; and 'missed opportunity' thesis 72, 78, 87; and Mollet 57, 59, 61, 71–2, 74, 75, 77, 78–9; and Suez crisis (1956) 59, 75, 85; and United States 73–4, 117
Eisenhower, Dwight D. 37, 75, 80
elites 28, 42, 44–7, 53–6, 63–4, 70, 74, 77, 106, 109–10, 114, 145–7, 153, 159–60, 165, 168, 171, 178–80, 183, 187, 192, 195
Elysée Palace 96, 97, 151
Empty Chair crisis (1965) 45, 95
enlargement 2, 94–112, 119, 123, 129, 131, 134, 137, 145–6, 154, 157, 162, 166, 172, 174, 179, 181, 184, 193
Erhard, Ludwig 3, 32, 36, 55, 70, 82, 88
Eurafrique see France
Euratom 54, 56, 57, 60, 63–5, 72, 78, 79, 83, 84, 86, 88
Euro *see* Economic and Monetary Union

Eurobrigades 140
European Central Bank (ECB) 4, 143
European integration viii, 1–23, 25–33, 37–40, 42–3, 45–7, 53–9, 61–75, 77–9, 84, 85, 86, 87, 88, 89, 94–100, 105–6, 111–20, 122–3, 127, 129, 136–44, 146–62, 164–7, 168, 170, 171, 172, 173, 174, 175, 178–87, 191–6; and common norms 1, 179–80, 182, 193; and confederation 104, 111–12, 148, 152–4, 195; and critical junctures 2, 4, 12, 19, 27, 175, 187, 195; and democracy 113, 152, 156, 187, 194; and elite support 45, 47, 53–6, 63, 70, 77, 106, 146–7, 153, 160, 165, 178–9, 183, 192, 195; and *Europe à deux vitesses* 182; and Euroscepticism 6, 69, 159, 166, 175, 179, 180, 183; and Eurosclerocis 140; and exogenous shocks 20, 167; and ex post facto explanations 8, 32; and federalism 1, 30, 53, 64, 69, 71, 76, 96, 112, 156, 160–1, 163, 165, 174, 175, 176, 194; and 'fortress Europe,' 158; and intergovernmental conference (IGC) 143; irreversibility 4, 8, 137, 154–9; and *Kerneuropa* 158; and law 1, 5, 7, 179, 182, 187, 191–3; and multi-level governance 182; and multi-speed integration 158; and renationalisation 172, 196; by stealth 54, 178, 187; and supranationalism 19, 22, 24, 27, 29, 32, 45, 47, 54–5, 57, 62–4, 66, 73–4, 77, 83, 100, 106, 114, 116, 120, 126, 145, 149–50, 173, 178, 184; and unity dogma 182; and variable geometry 154
European Central Bank (ECB) 4, 143; and Long-Term Refinancing Operations 181
European Coal and Steel Community (ECSC) 54, 60, 73, 81, 82; and High Authority 54
European Commission 163, 180, 194, 195
European Community (EC) 26, 31, 42, 139–41, 144, 153–8, 160–4, 166, 178, 179
European Constitution (Constitutional Treaty) 26, 138, 183
European Council 36, 42, 148, 175
European Court of Justice (ECJ) 26

European Defence Community (EDC) 53–6
European Economic Community (EEC) (Common Market) 9, 19, 29–32, 54–79, 81, 82, 83, 84, 86, 87, 88, 91, 92, 94, 99–110, 112–23, 124, 126, 129, 133, 134, 149, 157, 159; and community finance/budget 122, 139; and Hague summit (1969) 99–101, 110, 129; and Messina conference (1955) 3, 54–5, 68, 72, 78–9, 82, 83, 86, 87, 91; and Noordwijk conference (1955) 56; and Treaties of Rome (1957) 4, 29, 55–6, 60–1, 64, 81, 82, 84, 93, 121, 166; and Venice conference (1956) 56
European Parliament (EP) 6, 126, 138, 140, 145, 163, 195
European Union (EU) 1–12, 20–3, 26–7, 29, 47, 136, 138, 145–6, 148, 153, 158–9, 163, 166, 178–87, 191–6; and citizenship 138, 145; and climate change 179; and Common Foreign and Security Policy 145, 151, 163; as a global player 152, 179; and joint diplomatic service 179
Euroscepticism *see* European integration
Eurozone *see* Economic and Monetary Union

Faure, Edgar 56
Faure, Maurice 56, 71
federalism *see* European integration
Federal Republic of Germany *see* Germany
Fontainebleau 139
Force Ouvrière 84
Fouchet Plan 112
France ix, 2–8, 19, 27–9, 32, 53–60, 64–71, 73, 75, 77–80, 82, 83, 84, 85, 86, 88, 93, 94–114, 119, 122–3, 124, 125, 126, 127, 129, 131, 137–44, 146–7, 149–54, 158, 163, 166–7, 169, 171, 173, 180–1, 183–5, 191–3, 195–6; and Algerian crisis 3, 47, 55–6, 61, 63, 65, 67, 70; and colonies 55; and *dirigisme* 54, 161; and *Eurafrique* 67; and Fifth Republic 139; and Fourth Republic 3, 54, 56, 58, 64, 70, 95, 195; and gaullo-mitterrandism 151; and *immobilisme* 70, 184; and Poujadism 69
Franco-German partnership 28, 56, 58–60, 68–71, 79, 114, 126, 137, 139–40, 142, 144–5, 148–51, 154–5, 158, 167, 185, 195
Frank, Paul 126
Freie Demokratische Partei (FDP) 97, 127
French Union *see* France
Front National 180, 185
functionalism 22, 25

Gaitskell, Hugh 83
game theory 22
Gandhi, Mohandas Karamchand (Mahatma) 42
Gare de l'Est 59
Gaullism *see* France
Genscher, Hans-Dietrich 144, 170
geopolitics viii, 4, 6, 20–2, 30, 56, 68, 78, 94, 112, 114, 123, 136, 144, 145, 159, 186, 194, 196
German Democratic Republic (also East Germany) 97, 98, 118, 140
German question 62, 127, 136, 141
Germany (Federal Republic of, also West Germany) ix, 2–8, 10, 19, 21, 25, 27–9, 31–2, 44, 53–60, 62–71, 73, 77–8, 80, 81, 83, 84, 85, 86, 87, 88, 89, 92, 94–101, 103–4, 106, 109, 111, 114, 118–23, 126, 127, 128, 129, 136–51, 153–8, 163, 166–7, 169, 170, 174, 178, 180–6, 192–3, 195–6; and *Alleinvertretungsanspruch* 98; and Eurozone crisis 5, 25, 185; and half-hegemony 195; and irreversibility of European integration 5, 25, 185; and *Richtlinienkompetenz* 65, 143; and unification 27, 66, 69–70, 84, 120, 136, 140–7, 150–1, 154–8, 167, 182; and Western allies 3, 6, 62–70, 79, 81, 96–9, 100, 118–21, 123, 141–3, 147, 150, 155–6, 158
Giscard d'Estaing, Valérie 139
global financial crisis 5, 179, 191
Gorbachev, Mikhail 141, 142, 150
Greece 4, 5, 6, 148, 180, 191, 195
Gulf War 157

Haas, Ernst 25
Habermas, Jürgen 185
Hague Congress (1948) 149
Hague summit (1969) *see* European Economic Community
Hallstein, Walter 89
Hannover 136

Heath, Edward 9, 94–5, 100–10, 114–23, 129, 130, 131, 134, 159, 195; and Brandt 94–5, 100–6, 109–10, 118–23, 130, 131, 195; and Commonwealth 115–17, 121–2; and 1970 general elections 94, 100–1, 104; and Nixon 116–18; and Pompidou 9, 95–5, 100–10, 114, 119, 122–3, 129, 131; and United States 116–18
Heseltine, Michael 160
High Authority *see* European Coal and Steel Community
High politics 22, 178
Hitler, Adolf 44
Hollande, François 29, 97, 181, 183, 186
Hungary 59, 180, 183, 192; uprising and Soviet intervention (1956) 59, 85

ideas viii, 2, 5, 8, 10–12, 28–30, 37, 44–6, 61, 71, 78, 81, 88, 138, 159, 170
ideology 2, 30, 58, 66, 69, 123, 138–9, 160, 162, 182
immigration viii, 2, 183, 196
Immobilisme see France
immunity 67
independence 56, 97, 127, 145, 160, 161
India 113

Jahn, Hans Edgar 85, 86
Japan 113
Jebb, Gladwyn 74, 93, 123
Jobert, Michel 103
Juncker, Jean-Claude 180

Kiesinger, Kurt-Georg 97, 124
King, Martin Luther 42
Kissinger, Henry 195
Kohl, Helmut 6, 9–10, 24, 27, 137–49, 151, 154–9, 161–4, 166–7, 169, 170, 171, 172, 174, 175, 178–9, 182, 195; and Adenauer 6, 9, 10, 138, 143, 154–6, 178, 195; and Bundesbank 143–4, 146; and EMU 27, 137, 142–8, 151, 155, 157–9, 163, 166, 170, 171, 182; and German unification 27, 140–7, 154–8, 167, 182; and Gorbachev 141–2; and Major 138, 145, 148–9, 159, 161–4, 166–7, 179, 182; and Mitterrand 6, 9–10, 137–49, 151, 155–9, 161–4, 166–7, 170, 171, 172, 178–9, 195; and Oder-Neisse-line 142, 170; and Single European Act 140, 144, 159; and Ten Point Programme 141
Kohl, Paul 154
Königswinter 147
Konrad-Adenauer-Stiftung 164

Labour Party (UK) 83, 102, 110, 118, 159, 160
Lamers, Karl 158, 174
language 46, 74, 113, 148, 160, 184
Latché 142, 170
leadership 1–2, 4–6, 8–12, 20–2, 27–8, 30, 32–3, 37–47, 56, 58–63, 65–6, 68–9, 71–2, 78–9, 80, 84, 87, 89, 94, 96, 102, 110, 115, 117, 122–3, 136–7, 140, 143–8, 151, 155–6, 159–60, 162–7, 172, 178–9, 181–7, 191–6; and agency 9, 12, 27, 38–9, 146; and autonomy 4, 6, 9, 11, 40–1, 45, 47, 111, 137–8, 160, 164–5, 167, 187, 192; and biography 10–11, 39, 45, 137; and choice 4, 7–8, 10, 19, 21, 24–5, 27–9, 37, 39–40, 45, 61, 66, 71, 79, 93, 123, 140, 148, 152, 154, 167, 186, 194; and crisis 1, 2, 4–6, 9, 40, 43, 136, 178–87; definition of 28, 38–41, 47; and followership 38–41; and management 9, 43–4; moral 38, 41–3; and power 10, 20–2, 39–47, 71–2, 79, 97, 123, 166–7, 194; opportunity 4, 6, 10, 20, 40, 42–3, 62, 71–2, 78, 87, 108, 136–7, 140–1, 147, 156, 162, 167, 171, 181–2, 184, 186–7, 193–4; and purpose 44–7; and risk 2, 4, 6, 25, 27, 38, 43–4, 47, 110, 138, 144–5, 184–5, 187, 194; and skill 38–40, 42, 61–2, 138, 140; as a social relationship 10–12, 37, 39, 47, 167; traits 9, 38–9; transactional 27, 41–2, 62–3, 65, 79, 148, 165; transformational 9, 41–2, 79, 116, 147, 155, 165, 172, 187
legitimacy 2, 6, 31, 40, 44, 76, 139, 178, 179, 189, 192
Letta, Enrico 181
Liberal Democratic Party (UK) 118
Liberal-intergovernmentalism 22, 29–30
Libya 186
Lloyd, Selwyn 74, 123

low politics 6, 22, 178
Luxembourg 58, 86, 102, 183
Luxembourg compromise *see* Empty Chair Crisis

Maastricht Treaty *see* European Union
Macmillan, Harold 62, 72–4, 78, 94, 123
Major, John 137–8, 145, 147–8, 153, 159–67, 175, 177, 179, 182
Mandela, Nelson 43, 44
Mendès-France, Pierre 56, 83
Merkel, Angela 4, 9, 10, 181, 183, 186, 195, 196
Messina conference *see* European Economic Community
Middle East 12, 60, 72, 186, 191, 192, 196
Mitterrand, François 6, 9, 10, 137–59, 161–4, 166–7, 168, 169, 170, 171, 172, 173, 178–9, 195; and European confederation 152–4; and Gaullism 152; and German unification 140–1, 143; and Kohl 6, 9–10, 137–49, 151, 155–9, 161–4, 166–7, 171, 172, 178–9, 195; and Maastricht referendum (1992) 137, 147, 153, 171; and Major 138, 145, 147–8, 153, 159, 161–4, 166, 167, 179; and 1983 economic crisis 139, 149; and Oder-Neisse-line 142, 170; and Thatcher 141–3, 148, 153, 161, 179
Moch, Jules 58, 84
Mollet, Guy 9, 11, 30, 33, 47, 56–63, 65–79, 83, 84, 85, 86, 87, 88, 138, 178, 192, 195; and Adenauer 9, 11, 30, 33, 56–62, 65–71, 72, 74, 77–9, 84, 85, 86, 138, 178, 192, 195; and Algerian crisis 47, 55–6, 61, 63, 65, 67, 70; and Suez crisis (1956) 57, 59, 61, 63, 67–8, 70–1
Monnet, Jean 6, 30, 42, 54, 63, 88, 120, 178
Monti, Mario 181
Mother Teresa 42

National Assembly (France) 53, 56–7, 60, 65–6, 69, 84, 110, 111
national identity 74, 113, 114, 116, 160, 161, 185, 186
national interest 2, 3, 5, 7–8, 11–12, 19–32, 46, 61, 62, 65, 68, 71, 73–6, 79, 84, 96, 98, 101, 103, 107, 112–16, 138, 144, 145, 148, 150–1, 155, 160, 162–7, 171, 173, 178, 185, 193
nationalism viii, 10, 21, 47, 53, 69–70, 76–9, 88, 112, 116, 151, 157, 187, 191
national veto 42, 101, 103–4, 107–9, 140, 193
neofunctionalism *see* functionalism
Netherlands 4, 6, 32, 53–4, 86, 183
New Zealand 105, 121
Nield, Sir William 102
Nixon, Richard M. 116–18
Nobel Peace Prize 122, 135, 191
Noordwijk conference *see* European Economic Community
norms viii, 1, 44, 46, 179–80, 182, 193
North Atlantic Treaty Organisation (NATO) 53, 61, 73, 80, 95, 142
Norway 100
nuclear energy 55–6, 196
nuclear weapons 86

Oder-Neisse line 142, 170
O'Neill, Sir Con 107, 116–17
Organization for European Economic Cooperation (OEEC) 32, 73–4, 76–7, 95
Ostpolitik 96–8, 101, 105–6, 118–19, 122–3, 126, 127, 129

Pan-Europeanism 120, 121, 136
Paris 32, 53, 56, 59, 60, 64, 74, 81, 85, 86, 87, 97, 103–5, 113, 122–3, 126, 140–1, 148, 155, 186, 193
Paris summit (1972) *see* Pompidou, Georges
Parliament 43, 68, 79, 109, 184; in Britain 74, 76, 91, 102, 104–5, 108, 110, 116, 118, 138, 160, 164–5; in France 53, 56–7, 60, 65–6, 70, 84; in Germany 3, 66; parliamentary sovereignty 160
Parti Communiste Français 53, 57, 69
Partij voor de Vrijheid 180
path-dependency 7, 11, 22, 24, 26
patriotism 77, 115, 161, 173
personal diplomacy *see* diplomacy
Perussuomalaiset 180
Piedmont 195
Pinay, Antoine 55, 71, 82
Pineau, Christian 56, 58, 59, 83, 84, 85, 89

Pleven, René 53
Poland 98, 142, 180, 183, 192; and elections of 4 June 1989 136; and Oder-Neisse- line 142, 170
political capital 2, 4, 9, 33, 38, 59–61, 66, 111, 123, 137, 144, 155, 185
political will 1, 6, 55, 63, 65, 105, 107, 136, 138, 147, 192, 194, 196
Politik der kleinen Schritte *see* Brandt, Willy
Pompidou, Georges 9, 11, 19–20, 29, 94–114, 119–20, 122–3, 125, 126, 127, 129, 131, 132, 153; and Brandt 11, 19, 94–106, 109–11, 113, 119, 122–3, 126, 129, 131; and de Gaulle 20–29, 94–7, 99–101, 106, 108–9, 111–12, 123, 125, 126, 129, 153; and the Hague summit (1969) 99–101, 110; and Heath 9, 64, 95, 100–10, 114, 119–20, 122–3, 129, 131
populism viii, 6, 180, 185, 187, 191, 192
Portugal 4, 6, 140, 180
Poujadism *see* France
prestige 2, 4, 21, 33, 60–1, 65–6, 96–7, 107, 109, 137, 155, 166, 185
productivity 30, 31, 96, 178
prosperity 6, 21–2, 29–30, 46, 115, 121, 156, 161, 180, 187, 191
Prussia 195

Radford Plan 67
Rajoy, Mariano 181
rationality of actors 7, 21–7
realism (theory of international relations) 22
referendum 95, 183–4; in Britain on EU membership (Brexit) (2016) 2, 12, 183, 192; in Denmark and France on Maastricht Treaty (1992) 137, 142, 153, 171, 175, 183–4; in France and the Netherlands on the European Constitutional Treaty (2005) 138, 183; in France on British EEC membership (1972) 110–11; in Ireland 180; in the Saar (1955) 58
refugee crisis 178, 180, 183, 186, 191, 192, 196
regimes 23, 31, 191
'Rélance européenne' (1955) 4, 29, 32, 56–8, 61–2, 65, 68, 71–2, 74, 77–9
Renzi, Matteo 181, 195
revolution 64, 164; and 1989 136, 140, 145, 147, 172

Richtlinienkompetenz 65, 143
Rippon, Geoffrey 102–3
Roman Catholicism 10, 66, 68
Russia 12, 128, 142, 186, 187, 191, 192, 195, 196

Saar agreement 57–9, 67, 71, 84, 85
Sarkozy, Nicolas 9, 97, 181, 183
Schäuble, Wolfgang 158, 174
Scheel, Walter 109, 135
Schengen agreement 8, 12, 193
Schmidt, Helmut 139–40
Schuman, Robert 87, 149, 184
Schumann, Maurice 102
second *rélance* (1969) 99
Section Française de l'Internationale Ouvrière (SFIO) 58, 70, 83, 84
security 3, 7–8, 12, 21–2, 28, 66, 68–9, 75, 79, 100, 113, 115, 117, 121, 138, 142, 145, 151–3, 156, 161, 163, 166, 178, 186–7
security dilemma 142
Single European Act (SEA) (1986) 150, 159
Single Market *see* Single European Act
Soames, Christopher 102, 103, 104, 108, 126
socialism 58, 62, 66, 88, 138, 139, 149
South Africa 44
sovereignty 19, 24, 28, 29, 67, 71, 74, 77, 112, 116, 120, 137, 138, 149, 160, 161, 171, 182, 184, 185
Soviet Union 6, 21, 22, 59, 70, 79, 85, 97, 98, 99, 106, 113, 118, 120, 121, 127, 128, 136, 143; and expansionism 60, 69
Sozialdemokratische Partei Deutschlands (SPD) 54, 65, 88, 97, 127, 145, 171
Spaak, Paul-Henri 30, 42, 54–7, 61–5, 71–2, 74, 76–9, 81, 82, 83, 87, 88, 91, 120, 138, 192, 195
Spaak Report 55–7, 64, 71
Spain 2, 4, 140, 180, 181, 183
Speyer 147
'Spillover' *see* neofunctionalism
Spinelli, Altiero 149
Stability and Growth Pact *see* Economic and Monetary Union
Strasbourg 141
Strauss, Franz-Josef 55

structuralism 6, 11, 12, 20–4, 27, 29, 32–3, 37–8, 45, 61, 68, 70, 137, 160, 165, 169, 193
Stuttgart 136
Suez crisis (1956) 11, 57, 59, 61, 63, 67, 68, 70–2, 75, 85
supranationalism 19, 21, 22, 24, 26–7, 29, 32, 45, 47, 54, 55, 57, 62–4, 66, 73–4, 77, 83, 100, 106, 114, 116, 120, 126, 145, 149, 150, 173, 178, 184
symbols 46, 168
Syria 180, 186
Szydło, Beata 195

Taoiseach 195
terrorism 192; and Jihadism viii, 186, 187; and Paris attacks (2015) 186
Thatcher, Margaret 137, 141–3, 147, 148, 153, 161, 179; and Bruges speech (1988) 161
Treaties of Rome (1957) 4, 29, 55–6, 60–1, 64, 81, 82, 84, 93, 121
Treaty of Lisbon (2007) 138, 180, 182, 183, 184
Treaty of Maastricht (1992) 137, 138, 143, 146, 147, 153, 159, 160, 163, 167, 171, 175, 179, 183, 184
Treaty of Paris (1952) 53
Turkey 8, 195

Ukraine 191
unemployment viii, 43, 122, 178, 180, 185
Union of Socialist Soviet Republics (USSR) *see* Soviet Union

United Kingdom *see* Britain
United States of America 53, 56, 66–9, 71, 73–6, 78–9, 85, 93, 95, 97, 99, 100, 108, 113, 116–19, 121, 127, 134, 155, 156
Uri, Pierre 64

Val-Duchesse 64
values 10, 37, 41, 45–6, 121, 127, 142, 155, 180, 185, 192
Védrine, Hubert 148, 169
Venice conference (1956) 56
Vienna 152
Vietnam War 117
von Brentano, Heinrich 66, 81, 84
von der Groeben, Hans 64

Waigel, Theo 144
wartime state 30
welfare state 30, 31, 180, 196
Werner Plan *see* Economic and Monetary Union
Western European Union (WEU) 53, 61, 73
West Germany *see* Germany
West Indies 105
Westintegration *see* Adenauer, Konrad
Westpolitik 97, 99, 119, 129
Whitehall 72, 114, 115, 116, 118
Wilson, Harold 94, 100, 101, 124
Wolff, Michael 108
World Economic Forum 156
Wormser, Olivier 82

Yemen 186
Yugoslavia 143, 157

Zurich 117, 154